From Civil Rights to Armalites

Derry and the Birth of the Irish Troubles

Second Edition

Niall Ó Dochartaigh
Lecturer in Political Science and Sociology
National University of Ireland, Galway

First published 1997 by
Cork University Press

Second edition published 2005 by
PALGRAVE MACMILLAN
Houndmills, Basingstoke, Hampshire RG21 6XS and
175 Fifth Avenue, New York, N.Y. 10010
Companies and representatives throughout the world.

PALGRAVE MACMILLAN is the global academic imprint of the Palgrave
Macmillan division of St. Martin's Press, LLC and of Palgrave Macmillan Ltd.
Macmillan® is a registered trademark in the United States, United Kingdom
and other countries. Palgrave is a registered trademark in the European
Union and other countries.

ISBN 1–4039–4430–X hardback
ISBN 1–4039–4431–8 paperback

This book is printed on paper suitable for recycling and made from fully
managed and sustained forest sources.

A catalogue record for this book is available from the British Library.

A catalogue record for this book is available from the Library of Congress.

10 9 8 7 6 5 4 3 2 1
14 13 12 11 10 09 08 07 06 05

Printed and bound in Great Britain by
Antony Rowe Ltd, Chippenham and Eastbourne

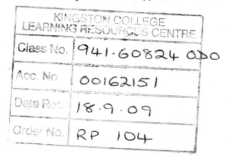

Contents

Acknowledgements

Thanks to my parents, Niamh and Eóin, and to my grandparents, Labhrás and Frances Ó Nualláin, whose support and encouragement was invaluable. Thanks are due to my supervisor, Professor Paul Bew, for his encouragement and help throughout the writing of the Ph.D thesis which formed the basis for this book. Thanks too to Gearóid Ó Tuathaigh who supervised my MA dissertation and helped me immensely when I was just starting to carry out research.

I was given generous help by staff at the libraries of Queen's University, Belfast, Magee College, Derry and Boston College, and Belfast city library, Derry city library, and Public Records Office Northern Ireland and by Robert Bell at the Linenhall Library, Belfast and Tom Horan at the American–Irish Historical Society in New York.

I am grateful to all who agreed to be interviewed by me and to others who gave me the benefit of their time and knowledge on an informal basis: among them Garbhan Downey, Eoghan McTigue, Elaine Huey, Pádraig de Paor, Danny Sokatch, Tamara Metz, Aogán Mulcahy, Alice Feldman, Eric Reginensi, Máire Lynch, Tanya Power, Robbie and Claire Dobbins, Andy and Terry Barr, Guus Meijer, John Darby, Pat Curran, Gillian Robinson and everyone at INCORE, Patrick King, Alan Finlayson, Paul O'Connor, Laura Pozo, Colin Burns, Lisa Rodgers, Eileen King and James Tierney. Thanks are due too to Zoe Watson in Belfast who typed much of the manuscript and to Frank Canavan in Galway who drew most of the maps. Thanks to Eamon Melaugh who let me pore through his photos from Derry in the early 1970s and trusted me enough to loan me the negatives. Thanks to the reviewers, who made several helpful suggestions and to my examiners, Margaret O'Callaghan and Paul Arthur, who were of great help. Some material from the book previously appeared in a different form in an article in *Irish Political Studies* and I am grateful for permission to reproduce it here.

I'm grateful for the generous help I was given by Brendan Duddy, Garbhan Downey, Eamonn McCann, Angela Hegarty, Paul O'Connor, Ivan Bailey, Colin Burns and Lisa Rodgers when I was writing the new chapter 'Bloody Sunday in Context' in 2004.

Most of all, thanks to Carol-Ann Barr, who gave me the motto 'No panic – just adventure'.

Abbreviations

(a) In Endnotes

DJ   *Derry Journal*
IP   *Irish Press*
IT   *Irish Times*
LS   *Londonderry Sentinel*

(b) In the Text

APC   Armoured Personnel Carrier
CBSI   Catholic Boy Scouts of Ireland
CCTA   Central Council of Tenants' Associations (Derry)
CESA   Catholic Ex-Servicemen's Association
CI   County Inspector (RUC)
CJNI   Committee for Justice in Northern Ireland (Boston)
CLF   Commander Land Forces
CND   Campaign for Nuclear Disarmament
CO   Commanding Officer
CSJ   Campaign for Social Justice (Dungannon)
DCAC   Derry Citizens Action Committee
DCCC   Derry Citizens Central Council
DCDA   Derry Citizens Defence Association
DHAC   Derry Housing Action Committee
DI   District Inspector (RUC)
DUA   Democratic Unionist Association
DUAC   Derry Unemployed Action Committee
DUP   Democratic Unionist Party
GAA   Gaelic Athletic Association
GOC   General Officer Commanding
IAC   Irish Action Committee (USA)
IDF   Internees' Dependants Fund (Derry)
INLA   Irish National Liberation Army
IRA   Irish Republican Army
IRSP   Irish Republican Socialist Party
JSC   Joint Security Committee
LAW   Loyalist Association of Workers

LDC	Londonderry Development Commission
MP	Military Policeman (or Member of Parliament)
NAIJ	National Association for Irish Justice (USA)
NICRA	Northern Ireland Civil Rights Association
NIHE	Northern Ireland Housing Executive
NILP	Northern Ireland Labour Party
OC	Officer Commanding
PUA	Protestant Unionist Association
PD	People's Democracy
RUC	Royal Ulster Constabulary
SDLP	Social Democratic and Labour Party
UDA	Ulster Defence Association
UDR	Ulster Defence Regiment
ULDP	Ulster Loyalist Democratic Party
UPV	Ulster Protestant Volunteers
UVF	Ulster Volunteer Force
WAC	Womens' Action Committee (Derry)
WUUC	West Ulster Unionist Council
YRA	Young Republican Association
YUHAC	Young Unionist Housing Action Committee (Derry)

A Short Historical Background to the Conflict

The conflict which broke out in Northern Ireland in October 1968 emerged out of a situation of rapid social and political change that began after the end of the Second World War in 1945. These changes disrupted a set of relationships, in particular a tradition of quiescence by the Catholic population in Northern Ireland, on which the very existence of the Northern Ireland state had been based. The political effects of these changes were focused in the city of Derry where by the late 1960s a large Catholic majority was still being ruled by a Protestant Unionist corporation dominated by local businessmen and minor gentry.

The walled city of Londonderry in the north-west of Ireland was built in the early 1600s as part of the plantation of Ulster by Protestant settlers from England and Scotland. It was built as a Protestant town and served as a refuge for Protestants during the rebellions of 1641, 1650 and 1689.[1] Only in the late 1700s did Irish Catholics begin to settle around the walled city as penal laws against Catholics were relaxed. But if Protestants thought the native Catholic population had been accommodated or 'tamed' by then, the large-scale rebellion of 1798 shattered this belief. The Catholic population of Derry grew quite rapidly from about 1800 but there was considerable sectarian tension in the town and throughout the early 1800s there were regular sectarian riots in Derry, often breaking out during nationalist or loyalist parades.[2]

By 1850, Catholics formed a majority of the population of Derry but, in an age of very limited suffrage, had no influence on the political life of the city which was ruled by a wealthy Protestant oligarchy. However, as the franchise was extended in the late 1800s, Catholics formed an ever-increasing proportion of voters. By 1920, a majority of voters in the city were Catholic, though the determinedly Protestant Unionist party continued to hold power because Catholic voters were concentrated in certain areas of the city. But then, in 1920, the British government, appalled at Sinn Féin victories throughout Ireland, introduced proportional representation in local government elections in Ireland to strengthen smaller parties. The effect in Derry was to return to power in 1920 the first Catholic mayor in the history of the city and a corporation controlled by Irish nationalists and republicans.[3]

Shortly after this, however, Ireland was partitioned and Derry became part of the Northern Ireland state set up to cater specifically for northern Irish Protestants who did not wish to be part of the independent Irish state. The border curved around Derry in a semicircle four miles from the town centre, cutting the city off from its economic hinterland of Co. Donegal. The new Unionist government of Northern Ireland abolished proportional representation. Derry once again had a Unionist corporation and as the Catholic population increased gradually in the succeeding decades, the ward boundaries were redrawn on a number of occasions with the effect of retaining control in the hands of a Unionist minority. Over the following half century Unionists retained control of Derry as the Catholic majority steadily increased.[4] Unionist control was buttressed by voting restrictions. Only ratepayers could vote in local government elections. One-third of voters in the Catholic Bogside in 1964 did not have a vote in local elections. In the neighbouring Protestant working-class area, the Fountain, one-quarter of voters could not vote in local elections.[5]

Derry stagnated economically in the 1920s and 30s and then briefly enjoyed a dramatic but temporary economic boom during the Second World War. After the war a Labour government was elected to power in Great Britain. In 1948, the new British government began to introduce radical new social legislation which the Unionist government, somewhat reluctantly, implemented in Northern Ireland. In Derry, the social changes which this legislation produced had direct political effects and would ultimately threaten not just the local power structure but the Northern Ireland state itself.[6]

One result of the new 'welfare state' which the British government began to construct was a massive expansion of the public health service, of public education and of related areas in the public sector. The welfare state created many more jobs in middle-class occupations such as teaching or medicine where service professionals in Northern Ireland generally served their own religious community. To take the most dramatic example, in 1948/9 there were 1,450 second-level (i.e. secondary) school teachers in the North. By 1968/9 there were 6,582.[7] The school system was almost completely segregated by religion and the new expanded Catholic middle class, working in this and other service professions, did not become integrated into the dominant Unionist middle class. In addition they often served working-class Catholic communities and were aware of the grievances in these communities.

In Derry, as elsewhere in the North, teachers, doctors and businesspeople from the newly expanded Catholic middle class saw nothing attractive in the stagnant politics of the Nationalist party and looked to other forms of organisation. From the mid-1960s onwards a loose group of Catholic moderates, in alliance with a few Protestants in the Liberal and Labour parties, was extremely active in Derry – in the 1965 campaign to have the North's new university located in Derry, in tenants' associations and housing groups and in local election campaigns – but without aligning themselves with any party. This loose group, involving people such as John Hume, Michael Canavan and Claude Wilton among others, provided the sort of 'respectable' but energetic leadership which had simply not existed a decade or two before. By 1968, the group had the political and organisational experience, and the range of contacts necessary, to head a civil rights campaign in the city which had been initiated by local radicals. Many of these 'moderates' would later be founder members of the SDLP.

If the development of a new expanded Catholic middle class provided a corp of leaders and organisers, it was probably the expansion of public housing in the new welfare state which created the conditions for mass political action and for the development of a relatively strong radical left-wing movement in Derry, which had long had a strong Labour tradition.[8] In 1948, virtually everyone in Derry still lived in private housing. In working-class Catholic areas like the Bogside and the Brandywell the overwhelming majority of people were the tenants of private landlords. There was no central agency with which tenants as a body could negotiate or to which they could protest and they were on their own against often unscrupulous landlords in a city with a chronic housing shortage. In 1950, the newly established Northern Ireland Housing Trust, which had been set up to make up the chronic shortfall in accommodation in Northern Ireland after the war, began work on its first estate in Derry: Creggan. In 1963, the trust began work on the redevelopment of the Bogside. For the first time tenants had a central agency to bring their grievances to and they gradually began to take advantage of this. The first tenants' association in Derry was established in Creggan in 1967. By the summer of 1968, there were several active tenants' associations, all in Catholic areas of the city. The various associations had links either with Catholic moderates, with the Nationalist party, with Republicans or with the radical wing of the local Labour party. They mobilised a number of community activists who would later play a role in the civil rights movement.

Housing discrimination by the Protestant-controlled corporation had always been bound up with the need to ensure that Catholics were not housed in areas where their votes might tip the balance against the delicate Unionist control of the city. In 1965, the Stormont government decided not to locate the North's new university in Derry. It was claimed by a Nationalist MP at Stormont that the leadership of the Unionist party in Derry had used its influence to prevent the university being sited in Derry because it would create population changes which the party could not manage. The claim was widely believed in Derry, even by many Unionists. After this, anti-Unionists in Derry began to argue that the Unionist corporation was an active hindrance to the development of the city, most importantly because of its housing policy. By 1961, Derry was 67 per cent Catholic but it was still under Protestant control. In 1967, elections to Londonderry Corporation were contested for the first time in decades as the local Labour party challenged both Nationalist and Unionist candidates. The Unionist party took 32.1 per cent of the vote but took 60 per cent of the corporation seats, retaining control of the corporation and illustrating precisely why these elections were so rarely contested.[9]

The Unionist control of the corporation, which had been maintained in earlier years by the creative adjustment of ward boundaries, was being perpetuated in the 1960s by simply not building any more houses. There were 1,400 families on the city's waiting list in 1967 but in that year the corporation built not a single house. Houses were being built by the Housing Trust but it was generally allowed by the corporation to build only in the overwhelmingly Catholic South Ward where there was virtually no building land left by 1967.[10] In this context, the aims of local housing and community groups had wider political implications as the very fact of Unionist control of the corporation was seen as the central obstacle to progress on housing issues.

It was in this context that, in early 1968, the Derry Housing Action Committee (hereafter DHAC), a small group of radicals co-operating in housing agitation in the Bogside began to mount public protests; picketing the Guildhall, occupying the corporation chamber and carrying out acts of civil disobedience. The radicals were a loose alliance of local Republicans, who had been agitating on social issues since 1964, local members of the Northern Ireland Labour Party (hereafter NILP), and a few others. By the summer of 1968, the corporation was under severe pressure from these direct-action tactics. In July 1968 the local radicals announced a plan to march into the old walled city centre, the heart of the Protestant plantation city and long a symbol of Unionist control of the city. The last time an anti-Unionist group had tried that was in 1952 when a Nationalist party march was banned and then batoned off the streets, provoking one night of rioting. The July 1968 march was banned from entering the walled city and the organisers did not attempt to challenge the ban. Then, in August 1968, the Northern Ireland Civil Rights Association (hereafter NICRA) held the first civil rights march in Northern Ireland, from Coalisland to Dungannon, Co. Tyrone where the Unionist-controlled council was accused of housing discrimination. The Derry radicals took part in the march, part of a crowd several thousand strong. On the way back from Tyrone they decided to ask NICRA to sponsor a march in Derry.[11] The local radicals in Derry now organised another march, this time under the sponsorship of NICRA, to take place on 5 October 1968 and to march into the walled city centre of Derry. This march too was banned but this time the organisers decided to defy the ban. They aimed to provoke the government and the RUC into an overreaction and thereby create wide publicity and spark off a popular response. They hoped that this would put the radical left at the forefront of anti-Unionist politics in Derry.[12]

Every indication is that the Unionist government decided that it was time to put an end to the agitation in Derry by traditional methods. The marchers were batoned off the streets by the RUC. But things had changed dramatically since the Nationalist march had been broken up in 1952. In October 1968, repression sparked off three days of rioting, followed by a massive popular civil rights campaign and then a series of events which would culminate in armed conflict and the disintegration of the Unionist state.

Notes and references

1 For the background to the Londonderry Plantation see T.W. Moody, *The Londonderry Plantation, 1609–41. The City of London and the Plantation in Ulster* (William Mullan and Sons, Belfast, 1939).
2 D. Murphy, *Derry, Donegal and Modern Ulster, 1790–1921* (Aileach Press, Derry, 1981), pp. 41, 50, 57.
3 Frank Curran, *Ireland's Fascist City* (Derry, Derry Journal, 1946), pamphlet, p. 13 and pp. 23–66.
4 See Frank Curran, *Derry. Countdown to Disaster* (Gill and Macmillan, Dublin, 1986).
5 Figures calculated by the author from the 1964 Londonderry County Borough Register of Electors. The precise figures are 34 per cent in the Bogside and 26 per cent in the Fountain.
6 For this and following paragraphs see Niall Ó Dochartaigh, *Before the Troubles: Derry in the 1960s. An Examination of the Origins of a Violent Conflict* (MA, UCG, 1989); Niall Ó Dochartaigh, 'The Politics of Housing; Social Change and Collective Action in Derry in the 1960s', in *Derry and Londonderry: History and Society* (Geography Publications, Dublin, 1997).

7 *Statistical Abstract of Ireland*, the Stationery Office, Dublin, 1958–1972; six counties (later Northern Ireland) section, Table xxxiii.
8 See Ó Dochartaigh, *Before the Troubles*, pp. 125–7.
9 Ibid., pp. 147–55.
10 See Ó Dochartaigh, 'The Politics of Housing'.
11 Interview with Eamon Melaugh, member of the Republican movement in Derry from the early 1960s until *c.*1967. Prominent in the Derry Unemployed Action Committee in the mid-1960s and the Derry Housing Action Committee in the late 1960s. Member of the DCAC and prominent civil rights activist. Later active in the Workers Party.
12 See Eamonn McCann, *War and an Irish Town* (Penguin, Harmondsworth, 1974), pp. 35–41.

Introduction

In conditions of civil disorder and conflict, the world contracts and the local situation becomes the central political concern of many more people. When a small city, village or neighbourhood becomes the site of regular killings, riots, bombings and the daily disruption of normal life, the local environment becomes ever more important as a focus for political activity. This book traces the development of violent conflict in one local environment, the city of Derry. It covers the years 1968 to 1972, the first years of the Troubles in Northern Ireland, a time when Derry was often at the centre of the conflict.

The conflict in Northern Ireland is distinguished above all by its duration. After rapidly pitching forward towards full-scale civil war in the early 1970s, the level of violence began to slowly decrease. It seemed to many that the situation was being inexorably brought under control and that violence could be reduced to an 'acceptable level'. However, despite predictions that the conflict would gradually dissipate[1] it persisted for over two decades after reaching its peak in 1972. This book describes the process by which the city of Derry, and Northern Ireland as a whole, moved from the first civil rights marches in 1968 to the virtual civil war of 1972. It seeks to explain the fundamental changes in social and political relationships that occurred during those early years. It examines how, in the course of those first years, the conditions were created for a conflict which endured for over a quarter of a century.

Conflict and the local

In a conflict situation, local politics and activism take on an unaccustomed importance and become central to the political process. This is due at least partly to the nature of violent conflict which, because of its

1

immediacy, is intimately bound up with the particular place or 'space' in which it occurs.[2] Conflict is intrinsically concerned with space and with the staking-out of territory: whether it is the insistence of state forces that they should patrol every part of the state, or attempts by insurgents to set up 'free' zones where the state does not have authority. Conflict is bound up with the defence of boundaries against the encroachment of opposing groups; whether by public protest, by diffuse personalised violence or by the building of barricades. Conflict is bound up with the securing of certain zones.

Michael Keith, writing about conflict between police and black people in Britain has suggested that 'Because conflict is realized in space it becomes "local" by definition, even when the experience of conflict is national.'[3] One indication of this in Northern Ireland is that much of the negotiation and confrontation between opposing forces has taken place at a local level. In the late 1960s and early 1970s, the British government and army found themselves negotiating and dealing with purely local 'citizens committees', 'defence associations' and even tenants' associations, as often as with centralised political parties or movements in Northern Ireland. It was often through specifically local coalitions that the Catholic community and the Protestant working class in Northern Ireland were first mobilised and entered into the political equation. It was through a local 'Protection Association' that the military structures of the Irish Republican movement were first reactivated in Derry,[4] and it was from local groups that the largest loyalist paramilitary group, the UDA, originally emerged.[5] It is at the local level that the complex interaction between the different parties to the conflict can be best understood.

In addition, the control of political power at local level was a central factor in the beginning of the Troubles. Prior to 1968, local authorities had extensive powers, including powers to allocate public housing. Sectarian discrimination at local government level was at the heart of Catholic dissatisfaction with the *status quo* in Northern Ireland and was the principal focus of the early civil rights mobilisation. Several of the largest local government districts with Catholic (and anti-Unionist) majorities were under Unionist control.[6] These local government authorities were accused of sectarian discrimination that was aimed in part at perpetuating minority Unionist political control of these districts.[7] A number of writers have examined the extent to which Northern Ireland operated as a systematically discriminatory state prior to 1968.[8] Hewitt has absolved the Unionist government of this accusation on the grounds that whatever discrimination there was confined to a number of local government districts in the west of the state. However, it is precisely because discrimination was thus localised that the civil rights campaign and the conflict began not in Belfast, which had a long history of sectarian street violence, but in Derry and in rural areas where Unionist control of local authorities was maintained partly by housing discrimination. In Derry, a shrinking Protestant minority of 33 per cent had retained control of the city corporation for half a century after Protestants had ceased to form even a voting majority in the city. It was precisely because there were such atypical places in Northern Ireland, where a local Catholic majority could be politically neutralised only by dubious practices that the state was so unstable. It was no coincidence that it was in Derry that virtually all of the early civil rights marches took place (between October and December 1968) and in Derry that most of the early rioting took place (up until August 1969). In this case the local 'exception' must be central to any understanding of how the conflict developed.

Hidden history

In the conclusion to *Interpreting Northern Ireland*, his 1990 guide through the existing research on the conflict in Northern Ireland, John Whyte noted that 'Areas only a few miles from each other can differ enormously – in religious mix, in economic circumstances, in the level of violence, in political attitudes.'[9] He made the 'tentative suggestion' that 'the next stage in the development of research in Northern Ireland will be a greater concentration on these sub-regional variations'.[10] The bulk of academic analysis deals with the conflict at regional or national level and has relied on historical narratives at these levels – histories of Northern Ireland or of Ireland. Regional or national level narratives are essential to any understanding of events. However, they can pay only minimal attention to specifically local conditions and events. They necessarily exclude a whole series of events which were important in certain areas and provided the motivation for action in these areas. By relying solely on such higher level narratives and imagining them to be in some way comprehensive, we run the danger of developing academic theories on the basis of a chronology of events that is insufficiently detailed and which obscures the specifics of place. We risk building theories on sand. Accounts written at local level cannot be comprehensive either, but they can fill in many of the gaps in our understanding. Although it often seems that we are in danger of drowning in the vast literature of the Troubles, there has been a dearth of such local studies.[11]

Rich but neglected local sources are so extensive that they amount to a 'hidden history' that has failed to filter through into academic narratives. The written records available at local level provide a wealth of information – in local newspapers, news-sheets, council minutes, the records of local organisations – which is new to the academic debate. These records, supplemented by interview evidence, provide sufficient detail to allow us to give much clearer answers to some of the key questions surrounding the development of the conflict.

When we look closely at how events were experienced in one particular place, in this case Derry, we unearth an unfamiliar story. We find a whole series of events and encounters, a local chronology of compromise, confrontation, negotiation and shifting balances of power which were under-reported or never reported outside the local press, or never placed in print at all. It is a chronology of which people beyond the city have little knowledge. People in Derry experienced the conflict not alone through national and international media; it was a personal experience, experienced through personal and family connections, at first or second-hand to those directly involved in particular events. This network of personal contacts formed part of a web of local knowledge which both drew on, and fed into, the widely read local newspapers.

The important qualification has to be made that there were two distinct, if interconnected, webs of knowledge in Derry. Catholic and Protestant communities were divided by family and personal networks and by divided allegiances to the local press which consisted of the resolutely Catholic/Nationalist newspaper, the *Derry Journal*, and the determinedly Protestant/Unionist newspaper, the *Londonderry Sentinel*.

Both papers provided extensive and detailed coverage of events in Derry and acted as the principal source of information for many people in the city. They are a key source for this book. As historical sources, the two newspapers, each reporting on the same local events from widely different perspectives, provide a useful system of 'checks and balances' for the researcher.

Both local newspapers placed different emphases on different events and fed off and fed into the radically different 'stories' which the two communities developed about what was happening. Both papers de-emphasised events of major significance to the other communities, although in this they were probably reflecting as much as determining attitudes in their own community. In this way, events which entered the calendar of one group as major landmarks, seemed far less significant to the other group and were more easily forgotten. Not only is there disagreement on the facts, more seriously, there is disagreement on which events are significant and worthy of remembering, beginning from the very moment when they occur. The result is two very different stories of 'what has happened'.

The web of local knowledge is an important part of the structure of any place. The local story of what has happened provides much of the explanation for the actions of people from both the Protestant and Catholic communities in Derry. The actions of people in Derry may seem illogical and inexplicable in the light of the select sequence of events that have been reported in national and international media, but in the light of the sequence of events, the chronology, available to people in Derry, they can seem perfectly logical. A local narrative is essential to any understanding of those actions. If we seek to develop an analysis, 'taking the definitions and beliefs of the participants seriously, attempting to connect the action with the interests, griev- ances and aspirations of everyday', then it is necessary to study events at the local level, in the local environment in which most people live their lives.[12]

One of the most valuable products of providing a new narrative based on such a hidden history is that the simple presentation of local detail can abruptly, and even casually, puncture general assumptions. It can completely disrupt the accepted chronology of events and subvert the- ories which supposedly apply to the whole. It is worth outlining here one of the clearest examples of how the narrative of events in Derry does this.

Over the past few decades, it has been repeatedly written that the first violent clashes or the first serious violent clashes between British troops and Catholic youths in the North took place in Ballymurphy in Belfast in April 1970.[13] The *Sunday Times* Insight Team described these clashes as 'the first conflict between British troops and Irish Catholic civilians for two generations'.[14] These clashes are seen as the appropriate focus for any explanation of the collapse of the 'honeymoon' between British troops and Catholics. The implication is that explaining those riots will explain how the 'honeymoon' ended. However, more than three months before the Ballymurphy riots, on New Year's Day 1969, small- scale clashes broke out between youths and soldiers after a New Year's dance in the Bogside in Derry.[15] It was the first in a series of increasingly violent clashes between Catholic youths and the British army in Derry, which preceded the magic date of April 1970 in Belfast. There was riot- ing in Derry again in late January, early February, early March and late March. During these riots in Derry, British army tactics gradually changed and the army went 'on the offensive', seeking to arrest large numbers of people during riots, well before April. A brief look at the chronology of events in Derry suggests that the rupture between Catholic youths and the army was not abrupt, as the focus on Belfast might suggest. Neither was it dependent on the 'flashpoint' of Orange marches. It suggests a much slower process, beginning earlier, of the breakdown in relations than the existing debate on the honeymoon has suggested. It also suggests, simply through the timing and location of clashes, some of the reasons for that breakdown in relations. These are discussed in more detail in chapter 4.

In this way a local narrative can interrogate the existing academic literature quite effectively by introducing a series of events which have quite simply gone unrecorded in the literature. Thus, general theories can be measured against the local narrative and we can begin to develop some useful and original 'micro-theories' about the conflict.

Micro-theories

A local narrative allows us to address a range of key questions around the conflict through an account of events which is detailed enough to actually provide some answers. It can help us to develop a range of modest micro-theories about the development and embedding of conflict in Northern Ireland. One of the underlying assumptions of this book is that the experience of conflict itself played a major role in creating the conditions for protracted conflict, that explanations must be sought in the course of events as much as in underlying social structures. We cannot understand *why* things happened unless we know in detail *what* happened. This book does not offer a single comprehensive explanation but a whole series of little explanations, addressing widely different areas of debate about the conflict.

A local study such as this cannot address the big unhelpful questions like 'Why can't they all just stop fighting and get along with each other?' (Answer: because of a long and complex series of past events and a set of intermeshing and shifting social and political relationships.) What it can do is address a series of more modest questions, questions which people have been asking since the conflict began, questions like: Why did the civil rights campaign lead to civil disorder? Why did so many Unionists reject reform? How did the 'honeymoon' between Catholics and the British army break down? Why did reform not 'solve' the conflict? How did both the Provisional and Official IRA become such significant forces? Why did large sections of the Protestant working class turn to 'extreme' loyalism? Why did Catholic 'moderates' not support the repression of Republicans? In this way, we can start to provide some better answers to the larger question: why did the conflict continue for so long?

An ethnic conflict

Underlying this book is an acceptance that the conflict in Northern Ireland can be usefully characterised as an 'ethnic conflict'. The terms 'Catholic' and 'Protestant' are used throughout not to denote religious belief but as the clearest way of identifying two ethnic groups. To describe it as an ethnic conflict is not to say that class, religious belief, political allegiance, nationality or outside forces are not important. It is only to say that comparisons with other situations around the world where the different parties to a conflict are associated with different communities identified by language, religion, race, national origin, or a combination of these, have been helpful in understanding this conflict. There is now a vast literature in this area[16] and it has generated theoretical insights which can usefully be applied to the study of conflict in Ireland.

Much ethnic conflict research has the merit of focusing on the contemporary, on present circumstances, as forming a large part of the explanation for conflict. It suggests that it is not necessary to reach into the dim and distant past to find the motivation for political action by ethnic groups in the present.[17] A key strand in the literature suggests that inter-ethnic conflict, far from being a hangover from the past, is intimately linked to modernisation and the expansion of the modern state.[18] Implicitly, much of the literature on ethnic conflict rejects the idea that inter-ethnic violence can be explained by 'an irrational animosity towards each other that [horrifies] outsiders'.[19]

In the mid-1970s some writers tentatively began to characterise the Troubles in the North as an ethnic conflict.[20] For both Nationalists and Unionists, there were disadvantages in conceding that two distinct 'ethnic' groups existed in the North and there was strong resistance to the concept of 'ethnic conflict'. The two communities in Northern Ireland spoke the same language, with roughly the same local accents, were influenced by the same mass media and had a long common experience of living in the same state. They had so much in common, it was argued, that they could hardly be characterised as two distinct ethnic groups. A former Alliance party leader, emphasising the common features of both communities, said in 1989 that the idea that the North was divided between two 'incompatible races' was a product of 'the highly inventive minds of the Ulster people'.[21] Rather, there was an emphasis for a long time, by those who didn't focus on class, on the religious differences and differing national identities of the two communities.[22]

The outbreak of conflict in Yugoslavia in the early 1990s, where largely secularised communities, speaking the same language and distinguished primarily by religious background rather than religious practice, became engaged in a ferocious conflict, made it much more widely acceptable to analyse the situation in Northern Ireland as an ethnic conflict. It had often been characterised as a throwback to the European religious wars of the seventeenth century. By the 1990s, as inter-ethnic tensions grew across Europe, Northern Ireland looked less like an anachronistic throwback to the past and more like a vision of a common European future.

Writers such as Hewitt have characterised Northern Ireland prior to 1968 as a British democracy deviating somewhat from British norms in order to cope with the fact of a disloyal Catholic minority.[23] Considered in terms of the literature on ethnic conflict and inter-ethnic competition on the other hand, the North prior to 1968 appears as a singularly exclusive ethnic regime. In only two other states in post-war western Europe (Belgium and Switzerland) did an ethnic minority, in these cases characterised by language, form such a large proportion of the population. Both of these states operated elaborate devolved structures in which minorities, because they were so large, were treated not as a minority but as one of two or three essentially equal communities, none of which could possibly be excluded from the exercise of political power without calling into question the legitimacy of the state.[24]

In Northern Ireland, where one community outnumbered the other by two to one (and by the early 1990s outnumbered it by five to four) there existed one of the most unstable population balances that can exist in a situation of ethnic competition. Horowitz describes a theoretical situation in which a state is shared by two groups, one forming 60 per cent of the population, the other 40 per cent. He describes the situation in many post-colonial states where, in the first elections after independence, majority groups 'appear to have gained power for the indefinite future'. According to Horowitz, variants of this situation, in which the prospect of minority exclusion from power appears permanent, 'were responsible for much of the instability in the post-colonial world in the first ten years of independence'.[25]

This problem of permanent exclusion of one group from power was compounded in Northern Ireland by the fact that the state itself had been designed as a solution to an ethnic problem in Ireland as a whole.

The partition of Ireland was explicitly intended to separate Catholic from Protestant in Ireland.[26] It was a solution which was weighted in favour of the generally more prosperous and loyal Protestant community. Two of the six counties included in the Northern state actually had Catholic majorities and the new state for Protestants was 33.5 per cent Catholic. The Catholic population in Northern Ireland was not merely a minority: it was an anomaly in what was intended to be a Protestant state. The way in which Unionists rendered Northern Catholics invisible when they spoke of the 'people of Ulster', emphasised this exclusion.[27] Catholics were accepted as a part of Northern Ireland only on the basis of quiescence. The sharing of political power as a way of incorporating this large minority was never considered seriously by the ruling Unionists. Neither was cultural assimilation seriously contemplated, notwithstanding 'liberal' Unionist prime minister Terence O'Neill's stated belief that 'if you give Roman Catholics a good job and a good house they will live like Protestants'.[28]

Catholics were excluded from the exercise of political power at virtually every level in Northern Ireland. No Catholic was ever included in the government based at Stormont. Virtually everyone who ever served in a Stormont government was a member of the Orange Order,[29] an exclusively and determinedly Protestant organisation. At local government level, Catholic electoral majorities had been neutralised in many areas.[30] The fact that the state's second city, Derry, had a large Catholic majority and a Protestant-controlled corporation was only the most blatant example of this. Particularly gratuitous was the gross under-representation or exclusion of Catholics from public bodies or committees. This singular policy of the almost total exclusion from political power and influence of such a large minority was inherently unstable.

The lifetime of such an arrangement, in which there is no attempt at incorporation, is limited to the duration of the quiescence of the minority community and constrained by the capabilities of the state to repress minority dissent. Unionist prime minister Terence O'Neill's minor 'liberal' innovations in the 1960s were concerned with securing continued Catholic quiescence and a definitive acceptance by Catholics of a state which excluded them. The innovations were not about incorporating Catholics. The state's capability for repression, on the other hand, was restricted by the form that dissent took in the late 1960s. The civil rights campaign was not easily repressed and, crucially, was successful in attracting outside attention and support. The central political fact of the late 1960s in Northern Ireland was that, for a variety of reasons, Catholic quiescence had come to an end. That the conflict should erupt has a great deal to do with the fact that the state founded for northern Irish Protestants in 1920 neither knew how, nor had any desire, to incorporate the Catholic community into the political process. Catholics were regarded as disloyal and untrustworthy and therefore unworthy of exercising power.[31]

The system of almost total exclusion lasted for nearly five decades. When the Catholic minority began to mobilise and make demands that would have increased Catholic political power on the state, and tried to exert political pressure for change by appealing for help from external powers (principally the British government), it was probably already too late for the state to try to incorporate Catholics. Horowitz has noted that in situations of ethnic conflict, 'there will generally not be the requisite determination to enact appropriate measures until ethnic conflict has already advanced to a dangerous level; but by that time the measures that are adopted are more likely to be deflected or ineffective'.[32] In the context of Northern Ireland, once the Catholic community had mobilised and conflict had broken out, it was already too late to resolve the situation through reforms.

It may be overly pessimistic to suggest that it was the simple fact of Catholic mobilisation which restricted the Unionist government from implementing changes because they would now appear as concessions. It is perhaps overly optimistic to suggest that a Catholic minority disloyal to the state and with a degree of loyalty to another state – the Republic of Ireland – might have been incorporated if Unionists had made changes earlier. It is probably also over-optimistic to suggest that the state, which continued to be permeated at all levels by the exclusivist Protestant ethos embodied in the Orange Order, would have ever considered implementing reform without severe pressure. Nonetheless, the fact that Unionists had never tried to implement serious reforms meant that they could only respond to Catholic demands for reform of the most blatant injustices with resistance and repression, thus beginning a cycle of conflict.

In the course of that conflict, existing social structures and relationships were severely disrupted. A new set of relationships developed, forming a new and durable political framework; a framework within which conflict could be sustained for decades.

Within a few years of the outbreak of conflict, the tiny and mostly hereditary Republican tradition had become a major political force in the Catholic community. The Unionist party which had ruled Northern Ireland for fifty years had splintered into fragments. Catholic 'moderates' who had sought to work within the state and even Catholic 'conservatives' who were concerned above all with the preservation of public order had gradually and reluctantly come to regard, not only the Unionist government but the British government too, as aggressive and hostile opponents.

It was not so much that Northern Catholics turned enthusiastically towards the ideal of a united Ireland but rather that they turned decisively away in these years from what they came to regard as a malevolent state.

The structure of this book is both chronological and thematic, progressing from October 1968 to mid-1972 (and later) in chronological order, but focusing on a different theme in each chapter. Several of the chapters focus on a single actor, be it the British army, the IRA or the Unionist party, and deal with different specialised literatures, literatures which often have very few points of contact and little common ground. Each chapter deals with a wide variety of issues surrounding the conflict.

Summary

Chapter 1, 'Civil Rights', deals with the civil rights campaign in Derry. It describes the explicitly local nature of the campaign and how it became essentially a civic campaign drawing in respected authority figures in the Catholic community. It examines the extent of Unionist resistance to the campaign's initial modest demands and describes how sectarian violence and tension developed around the early civil rights marches. It discusses the importance of the stewarding organisation for the civil rights marches and examines how the very existence of this organisation eroded the authority of the RUC.

When reforms were introduced, they failed to resolve the situation and violence escalated. Republican military structures were reactivated in the form of local defence groups as early as January 1969 when the first Free Derry was established. Chapter 1 offers an explanation for the disintegration of the civil rights movement and the imbedding of violence in the city. It looks at the importance of the civil rights campaign's achievement in attracting outside attention and outside pressure, particularly from the Republic of Ireland and the United States.

Chapter 2 discusses how opposition to Unionist prime minister Terence O'Neill's reforms was led in Derry by the leadership of a highly autonomous local Unionist party organisation. Because of its essentially local nature, the party was run by people who had a lot to lose from changes in local government control which these reforms were likely to produce and the party in Derry was urgently opposed to the very substance of even the most modest reforms.

This chapter also examines how, as the Unionist party set out in 1969 on the long road to disintegration, the Protestant community was forced to look to other forms of organisation to respond to the massive crisis in the city and in local areas. It looks at how, particularly in working-class areas, Protestants began to look to local, neighbourhood forms of organisation, and how, as the Troubles progressed, working-class community activism, previously confined to Catholic areas, developed in Protestant areas. Tenants' associations and community groups began to emerge and often took on roles connected to the conflict.

Chapter 3 describes the events which led to the creation of Free Derry after fierce clashes in August 1969. It illustrates how it was run in defiance of state authority by the Derry Citizens Defence Association, an uneasy alliance of Republicans, moderates, and Labour party and other left-wing activists. When the British army was deployed in Derry in August 1969, it initially accorded generous recognition to Free Derry as an autonomous unit. That recognition was gradually withdrawn. Chapter 3 discusses how the initial good relations with the army were in large measure due to the fact that the military had no 'policing' duties and left the policing of 'Free Derry' to local groups for several weeks. The chapter describes how even moderate Catholic forces, initially enthusiastic, rapidly lost faith in the October 1969 reform of the RUC and the B-Specials and how, in the absence of an acceptable reformed police force, the British army settled into a long-term 'policing' role in Northern Ireland, apparently with eagerness. In the process, the British army became deeply involved in local political manoeuvring. This set the stage for the growing estrangement of the British army from large sections of the Catholic community.

Chapter 4, 'The British Army: August 1969–April 1970', focuses on the deterioration in relations between the British army and sections of the Catholic community. It emphasises that this deterioration began within weeks of the army's arrival in Northern Ireland and was closely related to the operational role which the army assumed. It shows how sections of Catholic opinion that initially accepted the restrictions on movement introduced by the army gradually came to oppose them. The chapter discusses the army's extensive 'hearts and minds' campaign and its warm links with conservative Catholics who were closely associated with the Catholic church. It outlines the slow gathering of criticism of the British army's role and the dynamics of the gradual alienation of moderate Catholic forces from the British army and government.

In the absence of effective reform of the RUC the army became embedded in the life of the city and opportunities for confrontation multiplied. The 'hearts and minds' campaign of the army might well have compounded the problem. Chapter 4 describes how the army, with extensive recent experience of colonial campaigns, began to treat Catholics as the 'problematic' population. Moderate Catholic support for the army survived many upsets but was gradually eroded and attitudes to rioters began to shift. Protestant criticism of the army was a regular occurrence but open confrontations were rare and Protestant relations with the army improved as the army began to act 'firmly' against Catholics.

Chapter 5, 'Republican Revival', traces the growth and splintering of the Republican movement. In the early stages, Republicans had close connections with elements of the Irish government. It describes how the military campaigns of various Republican groups began and looks at the success of the Provisional Republicans in securing the support of the bulk of Irish Republicans in the US. As violence increased, elements of the Nationalist party and the nascent SDLP in Derry made attempts to set up short-term arrangements to reduce rioting. They set up the Derry Citizens Central Council which would operate for three years as a local political organisation, mediating body and occasional policing agency. Chapter 5 describes the lines of negotiation between Republicans and the army, how moderates acted as go-betweens, and theorises that this had an influence in limiting the conflict in Derry until July 1971.

Chapter 6 begins at the point in mid-1970 when British government policy began to concentrate on repression of unrest and move away from further reform. At the same time, the IRA began to launch a small-scale military campaign which in many ways was an outgrowth of rioting. It looks at the gradual deterioration of the situation and at the attempts by a range of forces to halt or slow this deterioration. This chapter looks in detail at the activities and role during this period of, among others, the Provisional Republicans, the Official Republicans, Labour party radicals, the SDLP and the more conservative forces for stability in the Catholic community. This chapter also looks at how the political phenomena of rioting and civil unrest were accompanied by an erosion of all forms of authority and an increase in 'ordinary' crime in Derry.

It traces the escalation of street riots, the alienation from the army of ever more sections of the Catholic population and the various responses of the Protestant community as violence escalated up to July 1971 when the conflict moved on to a new plane. Chapter 6 also takes a detailed look at a group I call 'conservative' Catholics, those for whom the preservation of public order was a priority and for whom religion was probably a good deal more important than nationality. It shows how this group, frequently focused on institutions and initiatives connected to the Catholic church, accepted the authority of the army as an essentially benevolent presence long after 'moderate' Catholics had rejected it.

Chapter 7, 'On to a New Plane', deals with the period from July 1971 onwards. In that month, the Provisional IRA began to open fire regularly at troops in Derry. In the same month, the British army shot dead two civilians in Derry, the first people killed by the army in the city. After July 1971, there was a massive escalation of the conflict, partly as a result of increased Provisional IRA activity. There was also a fundamental shift in relationships as the army ceased to negotiate with even the most moderate and conservative sections of the Catholic community. Although large numbers of Catholics, even at the height of this alienation from the state, continued to reject the IRA, the army could no longer rely on any local Catholic support, even from those elements who had been most prepared to see the state take charge of restoring 'law and order'. This was a dramatic shift from the situation of only a few months before. In May 1971, off-duty British soldiers had still been able to walk into the Bogside to visit friends; by August 1971, the only way they could enter was in groups several hundred strong, at the dead of night. This chapter outlines how such a dramatic shift took place in such a short space of time and traces events through the key experiences of internment in August 1971 and of Bloody Sunday in January 1972 up to the destruction of the final Free Derry in Operation Motorman in July 1972. Chapter 7 discusses developments since 1972 as they affected both the Catholic and Protestant communities in the city.

The final chapter deals with Bloody Sunday and brings significant new material to the public debate around the Bloody Sunday Inquiry. It places the events of the day in the context of well-established patterns of conflict and secret negotiation which had gradually developed in Derry over the previous three years.

Notes and references

1 See, for example, David Barzilay, *The British Army in Ulster*, 4 vols (Century Services, Belfast, 1973–81), vol. 3, 1978, p. 14.
2 For a discussion of theories stressing the central importance of 'space' see Edward W. Soja, *Postmodern Geographies. The Reassertion of Space in Critical Social Theory* (Verso, London and New York, 1989).

3 Michael Keith, *Race, Riots and Policing. Lore and Disorder in a Multi-Racist Society* (UCL Press, London, 1993), p. 164.

4 See chapter 1 below.

5 Steve Bruce, *The Red Hand. Protestant Paramilitaries in Northern Ireland* (Oxford University Press, 1992), pp. 49–50.

6 Christopher Hewitt, 'Catholic grievances, Catholic nationalism and violence in Northern Ireland during the Civil Rights Period: a reconsideration', *British Journal of Sociology*, vol. 32, no. 3, 1981, pp. 362–80; Denis O'Hearn, 'Catholic grievances, Catholic nationalism: a comment', *British Journal of Sociology*, vol. 34, no. 3, 1983, pp. 438–45.

7 Campaign for Social Justice in Northern Ireland, *Londonderry: One Man, No Vote*, CSJ, Dungannon, 1965; Campaign for Social Justice in Northern Ireland, *Northern Ireland: The Plain Truth* (2nd edn.), CSJ, Dungannon, 1969.

8 J.H. Whyte, 'How Much Discrimination was there under the Unionist Regime, 1921–1968?', in T. Gallagher and J. O'Connell (eds), *Contemporary Irish Studies* (Manchester University Press, 1983); Tom Wilson, *Ulster, Conflict and Consent* (Basil Blackwell, Oxford, 1989); Hewitt, 'Catholic grievances'.

9 John H. Whyte, *Interpreting Northern Ireland* (Clarendon Press, Oxford, 1991) (paperback edn.), pp. 258–9.

10 Ibid., p. 259.

11 There are of course many notable exceptions. Among those books focusing on specific local areas during the early years of the conflict are Eamonn McCann, *War and an Irish Town* (Penguin, Harmondsworth, 1974); Nell McCafferty, *Peggy Deery. A Derry Family at War* (Attic Press, Dublin, 1988); Raymond McClean, *The Road to Bloody Sunday* (Ward River Press, Dublin, 1983); Aileen McCorkell, *A Red Cross in My Pocket. Derry/Londonderry 1968–1974* (Workers Educational Association, Belfast, 1992); Shane O'Doherty, *The Volunteer. A former IRA man's true story* (Fount, London, 1993) – all on Derry; Frank Burton, *The Politics of Legitimacy: Struggles in a Belfast Community* (Routledge and Keegan Paul, London, 1978) – on 'Anro', a Belfast neighbourhood; Ciarán De Baróid, *Ballymurphy and the Irish War* (Pluto, London, 1990) – on Balllymurphy, Belfast.

12 Introduction by Charles Tilly in Charles Tilly and Louise Tilly (eds.), *Class Conflict and Collective Action* (Sage, Beverly Hills and London, 1981), p. 15.

13 See Simon Winchester, *In Holy Terror: Reporting the Ulster Troubles* (Faber, London, 1974), p. 30; Charles Allen, *The Savage Wars of Peace. Soldiers' Voices 1945–1989* (Futura, London, 1990), pp. 211–12; Des Hamill, *Pig in the Middle. The Army in Northern Ireland 1969–1985* (Methuen, London, 1986), pp. 31–2.

14 *Sunday Times* Insight Team, *Ulster* (Penguin, London, 1972), pp. 201–2.

15 DJ, 6/1/70, p. 6 and see chapter 4 below.

16 Two of the classic works in the field are Don L. Horowitz, *Ethnic Groups in Conflict* (University of California, 1985) and Walker Connnor, *Ethnonationalism: The Quest for Understanding* (Princeton University Press, 1994).

17 John McGarry and Brendan O'Leary, *Explaining Northern Ireland. Broken Images* (Blackwell, Oxford, 1995), pp. 215–17.

18 See Horowitz, *Ethnic Groups in Conflict*, pp. 99–105 for a survey of writings on ethnic conflict and modernisation.

19 Allen, *The Savage Wars of Peace*, p. 209. The putative 'outsiders' are British soldiers.

20 See, for example, John Darby, *Conflict in Northern Ireland: The Development of a Polarised Community* (Gill and Macmillan, Dublin, 1976), pp. 169–75; F.W. Boal, R.C. Murray and M.A. Poole, 'Belfast: the urban encapsulation of a national conflict', in S.E. Clarke and J.L. Obler (eds.), *Urban Ethnic Conflict: a Comparative Perspective* (Institute for Research in Social Science, University of North Carolina, Chapel Hill, 1976), pp. 77–131.

21 Oliver Napier, speaking in 1989. IT, 8/4/89.

22 McGarry and O'Leary, 1995, pp. 173–7; Whyte, *Interpreting Northern Ireland*, pp. 67–71.

23 Hewitt, 'Catholic grievances'.

24 Arend Lijphart, *Democracy in Plural Societies: A Comparative Exploration* (Yale University Press, New Haven and London, 1977). This is not to say that these states are comparable to Northern Ireland in other respects. In particular the issue of 'loyalty' to the state has not been as important in Switzerland or Belgium as it has been in Northern Ireland.

25 Horowitz, *Ethnic Groups in Conflict*, p. 629. Lijphart also noted the dangers of a situation where one group forms a permanent political majority: in Arend Lijphart, 'The Northern Ireland Problem: Cases, Theories and Solutions', *British Journal of Political Science*, vol. 5, no. 3, 1975, pp. 83–106.

26 When the boundary commission sat down shortly after partition to adjust the border 'in accordance with the wishes of the inhabitants', it was 'invited by both parties to the boundary controversy [i.e. Northern Ireland and the Irish Free State] to rely upon the census returns of 1911, showing the religious denominations to which inhabitants belong as affording an indication of the wishes of the inhabitants', *Report of the Irish Boundary Commission*, 1925 (Irish University Press, Shannon, 1969), pp. 30–1.

27 J.H. Whyte, 'Interpretations of the Northern Ireland Problem: An Appraisal', *Economic and Social Review*, vol. 9, no. 4, July 1978, p. 269.

28 *Belfast Telegraph*, 5/5/69, cited in Michael Farrell, *Northern Ireland: The Orange State* (Pluto, London, 1980), p. 256.

29 See Darby, *Conflict in Northern Ireland*, chapter 4.

30 Hewitt, 'Catholic grievances'.

31 See, for example, D.P. Barritt and C.F. Carter, *The Northern Ireland Problem: A Study in Community Relations* (Oxford University Press, London, 1962), p. 123.

32 Horowitz, *Ethnic Groups in Conflict*, p. 684.

1
Civil Rights:
October 1968–July 1969

Civil rights

For six weeks in October and November 1968, a civil rights campaign, based in and more or less confined to Derry, brought thousands of people out to demonstrate on the streets of the city. The campaign proved impossible to repress or ignore. It exerted pressure on the Unionist government of Northern Ireland, not only as a huge media spectacle, but also through sheer force of numbers on the streets. That pressure operated on the ground and also, via media coverage, through Westminster and Dublin. Perhaps the central success of the campaign was to attract outside attention and to bring outside pressure to bear on the Northern Ireland government.

But its most dramatic result was to politically mobilise huge numbers of people in Derry. Northern Ireland had continued relatively undisturbed for so long precisely because its Catholic population had never been effectively mobilised. Derry had been a particular site of apathy. Unionist minority control of the corporation had lasted so long that it was accepted with 'leaden resignation'.[1] Now that they were on the streets in confrontation with the state and in particular with the Royal Ulster Constabulary, a chain of events began which caused large sections of the Catholic community to lose confidence in the RUC as a police force. This process seriously undermined the state.

5 October 1968

When local radicals announced a civil rights march for 5 October 1968, the Nationalist party, which dominated Catholic politics in the city, and local Catholic moderates declined to get involved, not trusting the

17

organisers. Only the local Labour party and the local Republican movement backed the march, which was sponsored by the Northern Ireland Civil Rights Association in Belfast. When the government banned the march however, many prominent Nationalists and Catholic moderates turned up to take part.[2]

Even so, when the march assembled, the numbers were disappointingly small in comparison to the first NICRA march in Co. Tyrone in August 1968 in which thousands had taken part. In Derry, probably fewer than one thousand people turned out to march on 5 October. Though the number is most frequently put at 2,000, the *Derry Journal* put it at 1,000[3] while several of those who were there put it at between 400 and 600.[4] The march seems to have been top-heavy with politicians, Republican activists, tenant activists and left-wing students, and it would appear that relatively few politically uninvolved local people had turned up.

Many people were probably reluctant to march behind the local radicals, possibly into violent confrontation. Others were reluctant to cross over the River Foyle to the Waterside, a mainly Protestant area of the city, to march. Clusters of people waited in the Diamond, in the city centre, for the marchers to come over the river. The low turn-out at the march demonstrated that apathy was still a powerful political force in the city.

As the crowd and the RUC came into confrontation in Duke Street., there was a ragged but violent RUC baton charge. Placards and then stones were thrown by some marchers as the RUC 'punched, batoned and pursued civil rights demonstrators in a brutal and sickening display ... of concerted violence'.[5] Dozens of marchers had to be hospitalised and hundreds more were terrified and horrified by the police action.

Even as the RUC action continued in Duke Street, word reached the crowd in the Diamond that the RUC were 'murdering the marchers in Duke St'. Rumours began to spread too that a girl had been killed in the baton charge.[6]

When some of the marchers straggled into the Diamond and unfurled a CND banner, the RUC moved in to arrest them.[7] The crowd in the Diamond jeered and shouted at the police. The RUC then launched a baton charge against the crowd, forcing them outside the city walls, into the Bogside. The crowd responded by throwing stones at the RUC. It marked the beginning of three days of rioting as flimsy barricades were erected and crowds of up to 1,000 people armed with bricks and the occasional petrol-bomb fought running street-battles with the RUC.[8]

The organisers of the march had aimed to create a confrontation but some at least were totally unprepared for the scale of that confrontation and watched the riots in amazement. To one of the organisers, the '... effect seemed to be out of all proportion' to the issues the march had been intended to address.[9] Derry had abruptly entered a new era and from that moment the chance that repression, the short sharp shock or the swift slap, could restore order, was probably gone. The march and the chaotic riots that followed revealed that a state which had for decades seemed implacable and stern to its opponents was in reality desperately unstable and insecure.

The Derry Citizens Action Committee

The 5 October march had been attended by many prominent local moderates, people who had co-operated on a variety of issues in recent years: in the campaign to have a university sited in Derry and in local election contests. Most of them had declined formal political involvement.[10] This loose group was prominent now in devising a response to these events. The riots had been a graphic illustration of how much potential for violent conflict existed in the city, and a principal motivating factor in the organisation which emerged was the desire to prevent a repeat of the violence and 'channel all this energy in a positive direction'.[11] It was undoubtedly also a matter of concern to some that the local radicals should not remain in charge of events. Apart from all this, the events of the weekend had brought Derry massive media coverage, raising interest in London and Dublin. A historic opportunity had arisen to pressurise the Stormont government to respond to long-standing grievances and it was necessary to organise to take advantage of this opportunity.

A few days after the 5 October march the radicals announced another march over the same route for the following week. However, unknown to them, the former chairman of the University for Derry campaign, John Hume, and an associate of his were getting in touch with people around the city to organise a response to the events.[12] The result of this was that, unknown to the original organisers, the DHAC, a meeting was organised by word of mouth by local moderates to discuss the events. It was attended by 100 to 150 people, including local professionals, business people, trade unionists and clergy. The loose group of moderates was prominent among them.

The radicals, who had not been invited, got word of the meeting and turned up at it. The radicals asserted themselves and Eamonn McCann took over the chairing of the meeting. Although angry at being usurped, the original organisers agreed to the establishment of a committee to include the five organisers of the original march and eleven others to be elected from the meeting. It would be called the Derry Citizens Action Committee (hereafter DCAC). Eamonn McCann was alone among the radicals in rejecting this and walking out at the end of the meeting.[13] Many of the elected committee members, including John Hume, Michael Canavan, Paddy Doherty (who were all active in the Credit Union), Ivan Cooper and Claude Wilton, had co-operated loosely on various campaigns in recent years. Most of them would later be active in the Social Democratic and Labour Party (hereafter SDLP). There was only one Nationalist party politician, James Doherty, on the sixteen-member committee and this was probably the moment when the Nationalist party effectively lost its leadership position in the Catholic community in Derry.

The left had certainly been swamped, but if the new committee was more cautious it was also better connected than the 'original organisers'. Not only did it embrace virtually every anti-Unionist political force in Derry but its members had particularly strong and extensive contacts in the city. Through organisations such as the Credit Union, through business, professions or trade union work and through the 1965 University for Derry campaign in which several of them had been involved, committee members were widely known in the city. Thus the campaign they ran was not so much a purely political one, led by political activists, as a civic one, run in large part by prominent local business people and professionals. It was dedicated to the local and the civic: to Derry. At the beginning, it was by no means clear that this committee was launching a campaign for 'civil rights' as the term later came to be understood, particularly as its title did not include the term 'civil rights'. The DCAC campaign was mounted and run with no input from the Northern Ireland Civil Rights Association and had virtually no contact with them.[14] The committee appears to have deliberately avoided becoming part of a Northern Ireland campaign for civil rights and in these months there was just a Derry campaign supported by others throughout Northern Ireland. The DCAC, although founded after a NICRA-sponsored march, was far more the child of the 1965 university campaign and years of housing activism in Derry than a 'civil rights' organisation. This came through strongly in early meetings.

The first action of the committee was to set about taking statements from those who had been injured by the RUC during the weekend of violence after 5 October. The first demonstration, which would be held two weeks after the 5 October march, was a sit-down protest which would, of its nature, be passive. When the DCAC announced that it would be holding this protest, it provoked the resignation of Campbell Austin. Austin was a liberal Unionist who had broken with the party in Derry over the university issue.[15] For a very short time, his support had been retained by the DCAC because the committee, with its central concern for developing Derry, could claim direct descent from the university campaign. His exit from the committee, because he could not endorse civil disobedience, marks a break with that legacy. It also illustrates the limits of this particular brand of Protestant dissent. Once the campaign began to directly confront the state, it would find it hard to retain the support of the substantial number of liberal-minded Protestants in the city, whose liberalism stopped at measures which directly challenged the state, as controversial public protest did.

Before holding the sit-down, the DCAC set about building a stewards' organisation which would take charge of ensuring that no confrontations took place. The stewards, though loosely organised at times, would give the DCAC an active presence on the streets in the coming weeks. Committed to preventing violence, they became in a sense an alternative force to the RUC. Particularly during the later marches, the fact that only the presence of the stewards prevented violence and preserved public order diminished the authority of the RUC. The stewards' organisation mobilised large numbers of people in a clear practical contribution to the civil rights campaign. Stewarding was the first political involvement of many who later became active in more formal politics in Derry.[16]

The list of priorities and demands which were voiced at that first sit-down protest, while framed by some of the speakers in terms of a demand for civil rights, reflected the specifically local priorities of the committee. They certainly do not suggest the first steps in a Northern Ireland civil rights campaign. When the sit-down was announced, the DCAC declared that the themes of the meeting would be 'What is wrong with our city' and 'What can be done about it'. It emphasised that the protest meeting would be 'concerned solely with a campaign to root out the causes of discontent and disharmony in the Derry area'.[17]

At the heart of this local campaign was the central demand of all anti-Unionist groups in the city for several years past: that Unionist control of Londonderry Corporation should be ended. It should be ended, not just on the principle that it was undemocratic but because Unionist control and the efforts to maintain that control by gerrymandering and housing discrimination had hindered the development of the city.[18] The great majority of Protestants in the city, despite being disillusioned with the Unionist hierarchy over the university issue, did not want to see control of Derry pass out of Unionist hands and into those of the Catholic majority. This ensured that the DCAC campaign, unlike the university campaign, would have to rely overwhelmingly on Catholic support.

The DCAC had two prominent Protestant members, Ivan Cooper and Claude Wilton, who were active in the Labour and Liberal parties respectively. These parties, although mixed, had always relied in Derry principally on Catholic voters for support.[19] Cooper and Wilton represented a small liberal and anti-Unionist Protestant tradition which was marginal to Protestant politics in the city and was strongly connected to the Catholic community.

On 19 October in Guildhall Square a crowd of 4,000 to 5,000 gradually built up as people tentatively joined the sit-down. Although the turn out was impressive enough, it was clear that there was still a great deal of local apathy and uncertainty about the campaign. Far more people had protested publicly during the university campaign in 1965. As the meeting got underway, the members of the DCAC, one after the other, took the platform and voiced their demands and complaints.[20]

Chief among the demands was that, as John Hume put it, 'the basic fundamental evil in their society – minority rule' (in Derry) should be ended, through an extension of the city boundary and the introduction of universal adult suffrage – one person, one vote – in local elections. This would end Unionist control of Derry and thus clear the way for a crash housing programme and the attracting of outside industries to end the stagnation of the city. Although one speaker urged that the meeting should oppose the Special Powers Act which principally affected Republicans, all of the other speeches dealt with specifically local affairs tied up with the social issues of housing and unemployment which had been important in Derry in recent years. They proposed too the solution which had been popular in the city for years, an end of Unionist control of the corporation.

At the end of the meeting a suitably vague resolution was passed proclaiming that 'We, the citizens of Derry, demand equal rights, equal opportunity and deplore the fact that we are deprived of them'. A whole series of demands were beginning to come together but the fact that they were shaped into a civil rights campaign had as much to do with the catchphrase of the times as with the substance of many of the demands. The three demands which the meeting endorsed by vote hardly constituted a civil rights charter. They were a two-year crash house-building programme in Derry; 'some form of legal control in the renting of furnished accommodation'; and, more directly connected to classic civil rights demands, a fair points system for the allocation of housing.[21]

This is not to say that this was not a 'real' civil rights campaign. In the United States too the black civil rights campaign had emerged from a complex set of demands, and opposition to clear-cut racial discrimination was woven in with concern for social issues such as unemployment and housing. The campaign in Derry became a civil rights campaign, and was recognised as such by the world media, to its great benefit, in large measure because it was informed by the experience of the civil rights movement in the United States and awoke echoes of that campaign. From the US, it consciously borrowed the rhetoric of civil rights, the commitment to non-violence and the tactics, which NICRA had been reluctant to use, of civil disobedience and the deliberate breaking of 'unjust' laws.[22]

During these first months, apart from the setting-up of People's Democracy at Queen's University, Belfast, civil rights marches in Northern Ireland were confined almost exclusively to Derry, where they were organised by the DCAC and did not involve the Northern Ireland Civil Rights Association. It was a Derry campaign and, if the Stormont government had reacted with a few well-placed concessions to local grievances, it might even have been able to implement a 'Derry solution'. But, by the time of the 19 October sit-down, the Unionist government had made no hint of concession and seemed determined, despite British pressure for reform, to weather the storm. And so the DCAC intensified the pressure. The next demonstration was a symbolic march across the route of the 5 October march by the sixteen members of the Derry Citizens Action Committee and was held on 2 November, two weeks after the sit-down. The march of the committee members was watched by 3,000 to 4,000 supporters who fell in line behind them as they marched into the city centre, providing an impressive display of well-organised, peaceful protest.[23] By this time, external pressure on the Unionist government was beginning to intensify. The Irish prime minister, Jack Lynch, had already met British prime minister, Harold Wilson in London and was making noises about the failure of partition, suggesting that the violence in Derry called into question the very existence of Northern Ireland as a state. Shortly afterwards, the Unionist prime minister of Northern Ireland, Terence O'Neill, would meet Wilson to discuss events since the 5 October march.

It was crucial to the future course of events that the Unionist government during these weeks made a determined effort to resist and then to repress the civil rights campaign in Derry. From the beginning, not only the hard-line home affairs minister, William Craig, but also the supposedly liberal Terence O'Neill reacted with hostility to the campaign and to the outside pressure it had generated.

Unionist resistance

Immediately after the first civil rights march in Derry on 5 October, which had attracted world-wide publicity, the Stormont government reacted as though nothing had changed and nothing needed to be changed in Northern Ireland. William Craig defended the RUC in the strongest possible terms[24] and, in England, Terence O'Neill described the march as 'an act of pure provocation' which the police had had no alternative but to prevent.[25]

Pressure from the British government, impelled by dramatic media coverage and the presence of three British Labour MPs on the march, was exerted on Stormont almost immediately. Two days after the march Harold Wilson expressed his desire that O'Neill should suggest a date in the near future for a meeting where they could 'discuss the constitutional relationship between the two countries' (i.e., Great Britain and Northern Ireland).[26] But there seems to have been little substance to the threat implied in Wilson's reference to 'the constitutional relationship'. Simultaneously, Wilson expressed his desire that Westminster should avoid becoming 'embroiled in the communal feuds of the Irish'.[27] By the time the meeting took place a month later, the Unionist government had given no public hint of moves towards reform.

At that meeting on 4 November, attended by O'Neill, Faulkner and Craig, Wilson focused, as he had done a month earlier, on the dramatic slogan 'one man, one vote' and pressurised O'Neill to change the franchise at once. O'Neill responded with what would become a familiar argument, that a review of local government in Northern Ireland was due to report in the next two to three years and that he expected it to recommend changes in the franchise.[28] A month before, Wilson had been adamant when talking publicly that he wanted to see the franchise reformed at once.[29] After this meeting there was no announcement of reform or of any change in Unionist policy although O'Neill would later write that at that meeting they had agreed to bring in reforms.[30] O'Neill also seems to have suggested to Wilson that right-wing Unionists would not accept reform and that therefore, regardless of his own wishes, he was constrained in what he could deliver.[31] Directly after the meeting, O'Neill directed his attention to Jack Lynch who had had amicable discussions with Wilson a few days before and had suggested that an end to partition would be a 'just and inevitable' solution to the problems of the North.[32] O'Neill condemned these remarks saying, 'What we ask in Northern Ireland is to be allowed to make up our own minds about our own destiny ... Leave us in peace and there will be peace. That is all we seek. We do not intervene in the domestic affairs of the South of Ireland.'[33] It is tempting to speculate that he was also sending a coded message to Wilson about 'interference' from Westminster.

The autonomy of Stormont from the British government seems to have remained intact after this meeting and a few days later the Unionist government used that autonomy to try and suppress the civil rights campaign in Derry. On 13 November, William Craig, labouring under the delusion that the DCAC represented a further development in a secret Republican plot, (misreading the conspiratorial ambitions of the Republicans as evidence of temporal power), announced a one-month ban on all marches within Derry's walls. He announced that the police would use force if necessary to uphold the ban.[34] The DCAC had already announced a full-scale march for 16 November to enter the city walls and now decided that it would go ahead with the march and defy the ban. On the eve of that march, Terence O'Neill 'issued a blunt warning to would-be marchers that the law would be maintained'.[35] At this stage, Unionist concessions had been limited to the acceptance by Londonderry Corporation of a number of Nationalist party motions on housing policy, including a proposal to set up a corporation committee to allocate houses and to use a points system based on need.[36] Though it appears Derry Unionists had been asked to take the heat off the government by making a few local concessions, things had already gone far past the stage where the civil rights campaign in Derry would be content with so little. With the Unionist government resisting pressure for change from Westminster and the DCAC determined to march, it seemed as though 16 November was shaping up to be a massive confrontation. There were fears that there would be a repeat of the events of 5 October and the rioting which followed. The night before the march, shopkeepers shuttered their windows in the city centre, and ecumenical vigils for peace were held in the Church of Ireland and Catholic cathedrals in Derry throughout the night. The vigils were attended by thousands of people.[37]

In defying the ban, the DCAC was for the first time deliberately breaking the law and there was a fear that the government might clamp down hard. Fearing that the RUC special branch would try to arrest them and thus prevent the march taking place, the members of the DCAC each designated a substitute to fill their place in that event. The night before the march some committee members took the precaution of sleeping away from their homes in case the RUC came to arrest them.[38]

On the day of the march it was clear that there was no danger of a repeat of the RUC action in Duke Street on 5 October. A huge sea of marchers, estimated at 15,000 and upwards, including people from all over Ireland and further afield and far outnumbering any of the gatherings that had gone before it, filled Craigavon Bridge. The march was led by hundreds of stewards wearing white armbands. Ahead, enforcing the ban was a line of RUC men behind a row of police barriers. The huge crowd became impatient as the march was halted at the police barriers. Stones, pepper bombs and coins were thrown at the RUC and scuffles broke out in the crowd as stewards tried to hold the marchers back. As a Protestant crowd behind the police lines raised a Union Jack, some marchers surged forward but were restrained by the stewards.[39]

The RUC, however, had realised beforehand that they could not hope to control the march without the co-operation of the DCAC. They had secretly arranged with a member of the committee that they would permit a token breach of the police line and therefore of the ban.[40] Thus, a few members of the committee climbed over the barriers formally defying the ban. The crowd was informed of what had happened and then flooded around the cordon and into the city centre by other streets which had been left open. As marchers walked into the city centre, they came under attack from stone-throwers around the small Protestant Fountain area.[41] As the huge crowd filled up the city centre inside the walls, the RUC were overwhelmed and massively outnumbered. After a short time the RUC got into their tenders and drove back to barracks leaving the city centre to the marchers.[42] On a practical level, it had become clear that the RUC simply did not have the capacity to enforce the government ban or to suppress the civil rights campaign by the sort of tactics they had traditionally used against banned opposition marches.

The following Monday, as the Stormont cabinet met to consider the situation in Derry, the ban on marches inside the city walls was defied over and over again. It began outside the courthouse after charges were adjourned against forty-six local people for offences committed on 5 October. Hundreds of people triumphantly chaired the defendants down the street. When there were brief clashes between this group and the RUC, they sparked off a protest march by several hundred dockers chanting 'SS, RUC' and then a march by over 1,000 women shirt-factory workers and finally a march by a crowd of 100 youths who did a circuit of the city walls chanting 'We want work'. DCAC members rushed from one group to the other making brief impromptu speeches and trying to ensure that the situation did not become violent.[43]

That day, announcing its intention to take steps to deal with 'the underlying causes of the current unrest', the Stormont government announced its first concession: it would accelerate the Derry Area Plan, speeding up house-building and job-creation in Derry. The government hinted that it might set up a commission for the job but warned that there should be no more unrest in the city. It was a suitably local response to a local campaign but it was still the most minimal of concessions and it only provoked calls for further changes.[44] The following day, as more impromptu marches took place, minor clashes broke out in Derry city centre between marchers and the RUC in which eighteen people were injured.[45]

During the week that followed, the DCAC held a large public meeting in Derry city centre at which it was said that it wanted no more promises from Stormont, but action now.[46] There would be no let-up in the pressure. At the end of that week the Unionist government, under intense pressure from the British government and having lost all control of the streets in Derry, finally announced proposals for reform.[47] The Unionist party regarded these reforms as a maximum concession. Dr Conn McCluskey of the Dungannon-based civil rights group, the Campaign for Social Justice (hereafter CSJ), wrote to British prime minister Harold Wilson that 'The reforms are totally inadequate and satisfy very few here except all the members of the Unionist party. This itself condemns them.'[48] Few in the civil rights movement in Derry regarded them as adequate.

The reforms included a promise that the review of local government in two years time would deal with the issue of 'one man, one vote'. However, by then, international attention might have evaporated, and it was feared that, even if Stormont introduced universal suffrage, it would be able to negate the effects on Unionist control through a new gerrymandering of local government districts, perhaps even leaving Derry in Unionist hands.[49] It was also announced that the Special Powers Act would be abolished as soon as practically possible, but comments at the time by home affairs minister William Craig suggested that he did not consider that this would be 'practically possible' for some time to come. There seemed to be a strong possibility that if outside attention faded the Special Powers Act might well remain in force. In addition, local authorities would now be 'encouraged' to use a merit-based points system for allocating public housing, though it seems they would be able to devise the systems themselves. Again it seemed as though loopholes had been left open for a Unionist pull-back and a return to the *status quo* once things had settled down. There would also be an ombudsman appointed to deal with complaints from the public about the government. Finally, the government announced that it would appoint a development commission to replace Londonderry Corporation and speed up implementation of the area plan. This was the greatest concession to the civil rights campaign, finally ending Unionist control of Derry and removing an important grievance. But it also served to further postpone majority Catholic control of the city. The abolition of the corporation was welcomed but in a mood somewhat short of euphoria. 'For this deliverance at least thanks be', as the *Derry Journal* put it.[50]

O'Neill himself paints a picture of a relatively swift response to civil rights demands delayed only by the reluctance of his right wing to agree to a reform package.[51] But the Unionist government had stalled so determinedly, using bans, batons and threatening the use of the B-Specials, (a part-time and almost exclusively Protestant militia)[52] that by the time the reforms came through there was little trust in O'Neill's reputed liberalism. In any case, for some years past there had been little faith in O'Neill's liberalism in Derry. He was seen as responsible for the decision in 1965 not to locate a new university in Derry lest it disrupt Unionist control of the city.

After the reforms, John Hume, for the DCAC, announced that he had no great confidence in the Stormont government. On the issue of one person, one vote, Hume said that the DCAC would 'not rest until this, the simple background to normal democracy, is put into effect'.[53] After the reform promises, the DCAC pledged not to relax its vigilance, 'just in case even that promissory note should bounce' as the *Derry Journal* put it.[54]

This programme of reforms was not so much a case of 'too little, too late' as a case of 'too late, too late!' Although liberal Protestants who had retained some sympathy for the civil rights movement were 'quite happy [that] everything seems to have come to a peaceful conclusion' and 'hoped it would stay that way',[55] those in the civil rights campaign, including many moderates, were far from satisfied, although glad to have achieved something. It was also, crucially, too late for O'Neill to sell changes to the Unionist right which might conceivably at one time have been portrayed as simply organisational or technocratic. Now O'Neill had lost the initiative[56] and any reform appeared as a concession to the civil rights campaign. These reforms could easily be seen, as some nationalists saw them, as a forced confession of the illegitimacy of past Unionist behaviour[57] and called into question the legitimacy of the state itself.

When Terence O'Neill made his famous 'Crossroads' speech shortly after this, appealing for support and for time to allow the reforms to work and the situation to stabilise, the DCAC was to an extent 'wrong-footed' by O'Neill[58] and had to respond if it did not want to appear unreasonable. It responded by agreeing to suspend all marches for a month (as did NICRA). After the speech there was in the DCAC 'a feeling that they should hang back a bit'[59] and give O'Neill a chance, particularly as he was coming under pressure from his own right wing. However, opinions on the issue were divided and even some moderate members of the committee felt they should not back off now.[60] And so it was with a measure of ambiguity that the DCAC called off the campaign. It had not come to repose any great trust in the Unionist government and the DCAC certainly did not feel that it had secured its aims.

O'Neill's speech made a big impact and he received a flood of public support after it. His support was concentrated in the areas around Belfast which were overwhelmingly Protestant and relatively prosperous and where Unionist supporters had little to lose from measures which might give more powers to Catholics at local government level. In Derry at least, public messages of support for O'Neill came almost exclusively from groups and organisations associated with the Protestant community and from the Protestant-dominated business and professional associations in the city.[61] As 1968 drew to a close, civil rights radicals felt the movement had been tricked and even the 'moderates' were far from happy. One of the last DCAC statements of 1968 expressed regret that the recent queen's speech had made no mention of one person, one vote and that it appeared that the Special Powers Act was still in force in Northern Ireland.[62] However, O'Neill's speech had slowed the momentum of the campaign and DCAC statements now had little weight behind them.

Thus when the mainly Belfast-based students and left-wing activists of People's Democracy decided they would march from Belfast to Derry in the first days of 1969 to maintain the pressure for reform, the DCAC was ambivalent about it. Some leading moderates such as John Hume advised against the march because it would pass through rural areas which were overwhelmingly Protestant and they feared it would lead to sectarian clashes[63] but the only public criticism from within the DCAC came from the cautious Nationalist party.[64] Some of the left wingers in the DCAC supported the march wholeheartedly.[65] As the march moved across the country, encountering opposition along the way, it gathered emotional support, swinging popular Catholic opinion behind it. A day or two before it was due to arrive in Derry, the DCAC, in response to this gathering support for the marchers, announced that it would arrange a reception for the marchers in Derry.[66] The night before the march was due to arrive in Derry, Ian Paisley held a meeting in the Guildhall where a hostile crowd gathered outside and clashed with the RUC. The RUC escorted Paisleyites from the building by leading a baton charge accompanied by the Paisleyites. This rioting increased the anger of both Catholics and Protestants locally. The following day, the last day of the march, the marchers were attacked at Burntollet Bridge just outside Derry by local Protestants. The space for ambiguity and neutrality narrowed and the tension in Northern Ireland was racked up a notch. Events surrounding Burntollet demolished what little faith there was in Catholic areas of Derry in the RUC as a police force. It led to the establishment of the first no-go areas in Derry and for the first time the civil rights campaign began to take on the appearance of an insurrection.

Sectarianism and the civil rights campaign

Just as the Catholic population was being mobilised and politicised by the civil rights campaign, so some sections of the Protestant community were being mobilised and politicised in opposition to the campaign. The huge, overwhelmingly Catholic civil rights marches in Derry regularly went or tried to go along the edge of the working-class Protestant Fountain area. This had definite sectarian implications which, while not apparent to many outsiders, aroused popular loyalist resentment.[67] Despite this, opposition to the DCAC campaign in Derry in October and November 1968 was led, not by local Unionists, but by 'Paisleyites', led by the eccentric Major Bunting. It was loyalists from outside Derry who had taken the initiative in opposing the campaign, but their counter-demonstrations attracted the support of local Protestant youths from working-class areas of Derry such as the Fountain and Irish Street and of people from some of the strongly loyalist villages in the surrounding countryside.[68]

When Ian Paisley led a march through Derry in late November 1968 in his first political appearance in the city, the parade consisted entirely of bands and groups from outside Derry. The marchers were brought to the city in buses and a 'special' train. They were applauded by groups of local Protestants, of which the largest group was gathered at the edge of the Fountain, but none of the platform speakers came from anywhere closer than Coleraine, thirty miles away. The Reverend Charles Tyndall, the Church of Ireland Bishop of Derry and Raphoe, a noted liberal, referred to the march as an 'invasion from Belfast'.[69]

Relatively few Protestants in Derry supported the civil rights campaign and the campaign itself 'antagonised a lot of Protestants'.[70] However, there is some evidence that there was a great deal of Protestant ambiguity about the campaign and the legitimacy of its demands. Although the Protestant business community complained about how the marches were disrupting their business,[71] there was praise from the *Londonderry Sentinel* for the control which the DCAC exerted at its demonstrations[72] and references to the 'dignified behaviour' of marchers.[73]

When the Stormont government placed its one-month ban on parades inside Derry's walls in November 1968, a petition calling on O'Neill to rescind the ban was signed by leading Methodist, Church of Ireland and Catholic clergy in the city (though not by a Water-side Presbyterian Minister, the Reverend Bertie Dickinson who was later a prominent loyalist).[74] Such tentative Protestant support for the civil rights movement was short-lived. As soon as the government had made the least concession, announcing it would speed up implementation of the area plan in Derry, the *Londonderry Sentinel* asked impatiently what more the protesters wanted now.[75] As January 1969 brought the seemingly gratuitous provocation of the Belfast–Derry march, and the ominous appearance of Free Derry, such Protestant ambiguity as there had been over the civil rights campaign dissolved. After Free Derry it seemed, at the very least, as though the civil rights campaign was being exploited by the IRA.

The civil rights campaign in Derry had been avowedly non-sectarian but it was inevitably associated with the Catholic community simply by the fact of challenging the Unionist government. At every march held by the DCAC there had been the danger of sectarian clashes but they had more or less been averted. However, the campaign itself did lead directly to a renewal of sectarian violence in Derry.[76] Derry had long prided itself on being free of the bitter sectarian animosities which existed in Belfast. Prior to 1968, sectarian incidents in the city had been few and far between.[77] After the 5 October march and the riots that followed, there was relief and some satisfaction expressed that 'the affair never became a Protestant versus Catholic or a Unionist versus Nationalist quarrel'[78] and that there 'was no conflict between the people of Derry'.[79] Neither of the local papers made any mention of sectarian rioting while the *Irish Times* in its extensive coverage stated explicitly that there had *not* been sectarian riots on 5 October.[80] Despite this, a number of reports across the globe reported the events as 'religious riots in Ireland'.[81] One account of the 5 October weekend describes in vivid detail a sectarian riot taking place as Catholics attacked the Fountain area and were repelled.[82] It appears that this account has influenced other accounts since.[83] Contemporary accounts in Derry do not support this account nor its implication: that as soon as the civil rights marches began, Derry suddenly went 'back to the old days for the hell of it: Catholic versus Protestant, three hundred years of history on their backs'.[84]

Even if sectarian violence did not break out on 5 October, the civil rights campaign did lead to increasing sectarian tension and small-scale sectarian clashes in the city. Paisleyite counter-demonstrations against the civil rights marchers aroused Catholic resentment and provided an opportunity for Catholic and Protestant youths at least to curse and make obscene gestures at each other over the lines of RUC men and DCAC stewards. In early November, there was the first hint that something more serious could result from this when Catholic and Protestant youths hurled abuse at each other in the city centre after a civil rights march had ended and resisted pleas to disperse. Clashes were only narrowly averted.[85]

A short time later, the first serious sectarian clashes in Derry took place when loyalist crowds gathered at a shirt factory on the edge of the Fountain where the Protestant DCAC member Ivan Cooper worked as manager. The crowd attacked Catholic women workers as they left and two had to be treated in hospital. Although the RUC arrived on the scene it was felt they had not responded quickly enough.[86] The following night a crowd of 150 people who had been at a civil rights meeting decided they would go down to ensure the workers got out safely. Clashes broke out with a loyalist crowd outside the factory and when the RUC appeared on the scene they appear to have ended the conflict by baton-charging the Catholic crowd.[87] These events tended to further erode Catholic faith in the RUC.

In January 1969, after the Burntollet march, there was a marked increase in sectarian violence in Derry. While it would be untrue to say the civil rights movement had caused sectarianism, it had made Catholic criticism of the state visible. It had brought people on both sides out on the streets where they could be seen and identified and many of the sectarian attacks now appear to have been carried out on people who had taken part in marches or counter-demonstrations. In a little over a week in January 1969 seven teenagers, both Catholic and

Protestant, boys and girls, were slightly injured in knife attacks in different parts of Derry. Almost all of them were students at the technical college, one of the few places where the young people of marching age of both religions came in contact.[88]

There was also a growing number of sectarian assaults and beatings in different parts of the city as people were attacked near their homes and places of work.[89] Incidents began to occur in which youths were asked their religion late at night on an empty street. This was then followed by a series of other questions designed to discover if they had told the truth or had correctly guessed the religion of the inquisitors and had answered with the appropriate response to avoid a beating. One Catholic youth for example was first asked his religion, then asked to curse the pope and finally was physically searched for holy medals before being assaulted.[90] Such attacks, often carried out on a quiet street at night, were personal, almost intimate and they were utterly new to Derry. It was a variety of sectarianism which brought the underlying sectarian boundaries in the city into sharp relief. Territory became a less abstract matter and began to become for some a matter of personal safety. There was something irreversible about such a development.[91]

The civil rights movement was central to these developments. When people on both sides put themselves out on the street and allowed themselves and their politics to be seen, it disrupted aspects of a delicate communal harmony based on a sort of wilful mutual ignorance.[92] The sight of thousands of civil rights marchers on the streets shattered the Protestant delusion that the Catholic population was content with the *status quo* and had nothing to complain about. Unionists had long held that Nationalist party claims of discrimination were simply another tactic to undermine the state, thus implying that complaint itself was evidence of disloyalty.[93] As one writer has put it, 'complaints about Protestant discrimination ... [were] part of the stock in trade of nationalist politicians ... Since many nationalists believed that a separate "Six County" state could not survive if Catholics "got their rights" we can explain why they joined the civil rights movement.'[94] It is easy to move from this to the conclusion that support for civil rights demands of itself constituted support for the destruction of Northern Ireland as a state.

Now that huge numbers of Catholics were marching in support of these complaints, Protestants could conclude either that the claims were true, or that all of these marchers were actively seeking to undermine the state. It would seem that most Protestants came to the latter conclusion. The appearance of the counter-demonstrators on the other hand shattered any Catholic illusions that the Unionist system was only being maintained by a small group of well-off Unionists or that support for ultra-loyalism was confined to Belfast.

The importance of 'being seen' is illustrated by one incident which took place in April 1969. At the beginning of that month, Ivan Cooper arrived to speak at a civil rights meeting in the mainly Protestant town of Limavady. The meeting was packed out with loyalists who disrupted the meeting, throwing large old pennies at the speakers on the platform. A hostile crowd gathered outside the building and Cooper was forced to flee the building over a back wall.[95] A few days later, two Protestant youths who had played a prominent role in disrupting the meeting went to their place of work as usual. The factory was on the outskirts of Derry and Catholic workers outnumbered the few Protestants there by a huge margin. After being verbally abused at length for their role in the attack on the civil rights meeting and told to go home by fellow workers, they had to leave the factory. They later complained to a local Unionist politician about this incident.[96]

At this stage, there seems to have been a degree of naïveté on both sides, exemplified by the two workers who seemed to imagine that their public displays of ultra-loyalism would have no repercussions at their place of work. It was a decades-old naïveté and ignorance about the political beliefs of the other community which was rapidly dissipated by events surrounding the civil rights campaign. In a society where people were so fundamentally divided in their allegiances, peaceful co-existence in integrated environments had depended to an extent on avoiding even discussing politics and therefore avoiding any form of confrontation. It is often said that conflict is a result of ignorance of the other side, but in a divided society increased knowledge of the 'other side's' views could be a cause of conflict.

Because the Protestant community dominated the state, and because its political identity had official legitimacy, there was a greater range of political opinion which Protestants could freely express. This co-existence to a great extent relied principally on the Catholic population not displaying overtly their sympathies or discontents. This imbalance was expressed in the privileged position allowed by the state to the Orange Order which enjoyed almost limitless freedom of public expression through marching.[97] One of the things the civil rights movement did was to parade Catholic dissent and discontent on the street after years of relative silence.

Every sectarian attack and mini-riot in these early months also marked out territory for one side or the other, in the neighbourhoods, in the workplace, in the city centre. Although these boundaries had long existed, they took on a new importance and became more rigid. This was a process that began not with paramilitary violence or large-scale intimidation, but with the low-level personalised sectarian tension which surrounded the very first civil rights marches.

Free Derry and the Republicans

When the People's Democracy march set out from Belfast on 1 January, 1969, the DCAC was equivocal about the march. There were those, even on the left of the committee, who thought the march 'would cause nothing but f**king sectarianism'.[98] However, when the marchers were harassed by loyalists as they crossed the countryside, Catholic public opinion swung behind them. On the last day of the march the marchers, and local Catholics who had joined the march in Dungiven and Claudy, were attacked at Burntollet Bridge, a few miles from Derry. The RUC men accompanying the march for the most part stood by and watched. Some of them also attacked the marchers. The attackers were mostly local Protestants from the farmlands and villages around Burntollet. About half of them were later identified as off-duty B-Specials.[99] The B-Specials were a large armed auxiliary police force which acted essentially as a local Protestant militia. Several of the marchers were taken to hospital. Some walked on to Derry. As the marchers entered Derry, they were stoned at the Protestant Irish Street estate and at Spencer Road. When they arrived into Derry city centre battered and bleeding, 'a sight to touch any heart', as the *Irish Times* put it, a huge crowd was waiting to greet them.[100] Even civil rights activists who had opposed the march were angry.[101] If the march could be criticised as being provocative or ill-considered, the attacks on the march had been more than ill-considered: they had been calculated and brutal.

After the march and the rioting which followed, Terence O'Neill made a speech in which he reserved his strongest condemnation for the marchers rather than their attackers, and threatened to mobilise the B-Specials (many of whom had been involved in the attack) and extend the Public Order Act to restrict further public protest.[102]

That afternoon, after a civil rights meeting to greet the marchers, severe rioting broke out in Derry city centre and continued for several hours. Moderates such as John Hume alleged that the rioting was provoked by the RUC.[103] Late that night, after the rioting had died down, a group of RUC men, at least some of them drunk, conducted a revenge attack in streets on the edge of the Bogside, smashing windows and attacking people in the streets.[104] These events prompted the DCAC to withdraw the marching truce which it had declared before Christmas, and moved the group significantly further away from the Unionist government. The DCAC strongly condemned the RUC and went so far as to congratulate People's Democracy for its 'restraint'. From now on, Ivan Cooper of the DCAC said, 'it would be hard-line militancy until they got what they wanted'.[105]

The morning after the RUC's late-night sortie into the Bogside, several thousand people, men and women, gathered in the area, angry at the RUC action. Around them, hundreds of men and boys 'roamed around', armed with sticks, hurleys and iron bars.[106] A public meeting was held and members of the DCAC tried to channel people into a peaceful protest while others were more militant. Seán Keenan, the most prominent of the older Republicans in the city, declared that 'we have only two cheeks and we have turned the other for the last time'. If the police action was repeated he said 'it would be met with what they had to offer'.[107] The DCAC moderates tried to defuse the situation by organising a peaceful protest of women and children from the meeting in the Bogside to the nearby RUC station on the Strand Road. The RUC response, however, was not conciliatory and feeling remained high.[108] When the march returned to the Bogside the DCAC members, presumably under some pressure from people such as Seán Keenan, agreed with the proposition that local vigilante committees should be set up in every street to defend the area against the possibility of a further RUC attack. Events had pushed moderates such as John Hume and Ivan Cooper into the sort of situation where they were uneasy and no longer in control. It was the sort of situation where talk of defence implied the readiness to use violence against the state, which the small number of Republicans in the city felt more comfortable with than any other group did. It was not so much that people in Derry looked automatically to the Republicans as traditional defenders – after all, there were hardly enough of them to perform this role very well. Rather, as events strayed into the illegal with the establishment of vigilante committees, the Republicans were one of the few groups prepared to take charge of organising this illegal activity. That said, at this stage there were also individuals who had been active as DCAC stewards and would go on to join the SDLP, who were involved in organising these vigilante patrols.[109]

That night, barricades were built around the Bogside and vigilante groups were set up to patrol the streets. Paddy Doherty, the DCAC committee member who had generally organised the stewarding of the civil rights marches, was now involved in organising the defence of the Bogside and his house became a centre of activity.[110] The Derry

Republicans were active in putting up barricades and mounting patrols.[111] The challenge to the authority of the RUC which the stewards' organisation had represented was now expressed in the form of vigilante groups in which Republicans were heavily involved. It was a further diminution of the authority of the state. For five days, defended by barricades and served by its own pirate radio station, 'Free Derry' existed with no RUC presence. Finally, DCAC moderates 'descended on the area' and made speeches appealing successfully for the barricades to be taken down.[112] However, it was clear that the authority of the DCAC had been diminished.

During those five days, there emerged in Free Derry a 'new grassroots leadership' which was not averse to violence.[113] The veteran Republican Seán Keenan became chairman of the St Columbs Wells Protection Association in Free Derry, one of the local vigilante groups.[114] Keenan and other older Republicans had enthusiastically backed the civil rights campaign, and Keenan had spoken at a number of meetings.[115] Now, as the situation became violent and more and more people became alienated from and afraid of the RUC, he and other Republicans clearly saw the demand for some form of organised defence and the opportunity to thus advance the Republican cause. In this first Free Derry, the Republicans began to exert their influence.[116]

Since October 1968, Seán Mac Stiofáin, an IRA army council member who had been pushing for a military response to the new situation, had been visiting Derry and meeting Keenan regularly.[117] Mac Stiofáin had proposed that an auxiliary IRA unit be set up in Derry under Seán Keenan to organise for defence of Catholic areas in the event of violence, but, according to Mac Stiofáin, this was rejected by the IRA leadership in Dublin.[118] Despite this, Keenan and other local Republicans took the initiative on the ground in January 1969 and it would appear that some at least of the vigilante groups were effectively IRA auxiliary groups.[119]

One reason the leadership might have rejected Mac Stiofáin's proposal was because there was an existing IRA unit in the city which was dominated by the young, left-wing, Republicans. They had devoted their energies to housing activism rather than military activities.[120] Mac Stiofáin's proposal could well have been seen as an attempt to undermine the existing IRA structure in Derry and strengthen the position of older traditionalists such as Keenan.

It is important not to over-emphasise the Republican role at this stage. They were a small marginal group that had enthusiastically supported the civil rights campaign. But the outbreak of violence definitely made them less marginal and led them to re-assess their role and position. In Derry it was a small group of mostly young left-wing Republicans who had taken the initiative to become active on social issues in the early 1960s. This younger group regarded the IRA border campaign of the 1950s as 'a total buckin' disaster' because it had ignored social issues and had been purely militaristic.[121] They became deeply involved in trade-union activity and agitation on housing and unemployment in the mid- and late-1960s but they did not completely abandon the military aspects of the Republican tradition.

According to a former Republican activist in Derry, in 1963 these younger, left-wing Republicans established a Derry branch of the Fianna Éireann, the Republican scouting movement from which IRA recruits were traditionally drawn. They were in regular contact with the national organiser of the Fianna in Dublin, but they were not on particularly good terms with the older Republicans in Derry, people such as Neil Gillespie and Seán Keenan. The older Republicans were few in number, mostly ex-internees and their activities centred around the annual commemoration of the 1916 Easter Rising.

Around mid-1964 the left-wing Republicans revived the IRA in Derry. It had been effectively moribund since the death of an IRA man in the city during a training accident in 1960. This newly revived IRA had only a handful of members and their military activities were limited to training sessions with a few old weapons.[122] The Derry IRA was enthusiastically involved in activism on housing and unemployment. An internal Republican newspaper claimed that a majority of the members of housing committees in Derry (presumably a reference to the Derry Housing Action Committee, a coalition of Republicans and left-wing radicals) were IRA members. In 1967, the Derry Republicans had taken part in resisting an eviction in the Bogside under the name of the Young Republican Association (YRA). The same internal paper described this as an action by an army (IRA) section,[123] suggesting that certain Republican public protests in Derry in the mid and late 1960s were effectively run as IRA operations.

This was exactly the sort of direction the Dublin leadership wanted the IRA to go in, to become effectively 'an army of the working class', with training emphasising not military activity but public protest on economic and social issues.[124] It appears that the Derry IRA was regarded as a model by the Dublin leadership[125] with whom they were in close contact.[126] The Republican paper, the *United Irishman*, carried regular, enthusiastic articles about the housing agitation of the Derry Republicans. Military activity had not been ruled out and training continued but the prospect of armed revolution was a distant one. While the Belfast IRA was kept happy, as Patterson put it, by a mixture of politics and violence during the 1960s and was unenthusiastic about social protest,[127] the Derry IRA launched headlong into social activism. In Derry, where the Unionist corporation was under great pressure, it was easier to see the direct effect such agitation had on Unionist control.

In the mid-1960s there was a modest surge of younger recruits to the Republican movement in Derry, inspired by Republican participation in the 1964 Westminster election campaign and by the fiftieth anniversary of the Easter Rising, in 1966. Many of these younger recruits were extremely active in housing agitation and protest in 1967 and 1968. When the civil rights campaign began, they worked as stewards on the marches.[128] Some of them at least were members of the Fianna[129] and some would go on to become active IRA members after August 1969.[130]

Although there were precious few active Republicans in Derry when the civil rights campaign began[131] and the politics of the Catholic community were dominated by the Nationalist party, the fact that there was a scattering of active Republicans is not insignificant. They were predominantly young, energetic and active. Given the transformation about to occur in the city in which the Nationalist party would slowly dissolve and the SDLP would emerge from nowhere, it was not an insignificant base from which to expand. The fact that many of these activists were members of the largely demilitarised IRA or the Fianna was not of great significance while the civil rights campaign dominated the political scene. Once the campaign began to fall apart and issues of defence arose, military matters took on a new significance. The Republicans' military activities may have been confined to desultory weapons-training, but a military structure did exist, and by the summer of 1969 at the latest the IRA was running training camps in Co. Donegal,[132] presumably for recruits from Derry.

After Burntollet, many Republicans began to see a renewed role for the movement outside simple support for the civil rights campaign. The IRA structure which had been used almost exclusively for social activism was now used for local defence. In Derry, older Republicans felt more comfortable with this and moved back into active involvement. The two wings of the movement came together as they had not done in years.

It seems likely that Keenan and the older Republicans were not alone in Derry in believing that a historic opportunity for the Republican movement was opening up. The left-wing leadership in Dublin began to shift its emphasis, becoming more militant, describing the limited deployment of British troops in the North in the spring of 1969 for example as an action to 'consolidate ... tyranny'.[133]

In April 1969, for the first time ever, the Derry Republicans held their Easter commemoration in Derry city centre. The platform was shared by Seán Keenan, the traditionalist and Johnnie White, head of the radicals. The year 1966 was apparently the only time when both tendencies had shared the platform. Up until 1967 the traditionalists had run the annual commemoration ceremony but in 1968 the radicals had run it for the first time.[134] By this time, the civil rights campaign was in disarray and the prospects for an internal reconciliation in Northern Ireland had receded. The 5,000 strong march, respectable enough that it was attended by leading Nationalists such as Eddie McAteer, though not by local moderates[135] was notably larger than recent civil rights demonstrations in the city had been. The Republican parades traditionally drew crowds numbered in the dozens and, although many came along as they would to any march, it was a big change. There had been a distinct resurgence of basic nationalist feeling in Derry. This was illustrated in a small way when Linfield football team came to play Derry in January 1969. Linfield was a Belfast-based team with a strongly loyalist following. Elements in the Derry crowd were openly nationalist, waving the Irish flag, singing the Irish national anthem and republican songs as well as the civil rights anthem 'We shall overcome'.[136] This was in direct contrast to earlier matches between the two sides when only the Linfield supporters had been overtly political in their chants and symbols.[137] The Nationalist party which had been seen as one of the least militant supporters of the civil rights movement was not likely to be the beneficiary of such recently awakened nationalist feeling, but the Republicans might be.

At the Easter commemoration in 1969, Seán Keenan called on people to join the Republican movement and help to achieve 'a free united Ireland'.[138] Around this time, the Fianna Éireann were growing in numbers on a national level[139] and at the Derry parade the Fianna flag was carried.[140] It seems reasonable to assume that the Derry Republicans around this time were recruiting new people to their small military structure and expanding the ranks of the Fianna, however slowly. They were also asserting a distinctive identity which had been submerged in support for civil rights. At the same meeting Keenan said, 'Let no man ... say that the people of Derry are British or that we want British standards ... The enemy is still England.'[141] It appears that the left-wing Republicans were just as enthusiastic about these developments as the older Republicans. It is notable also that older Republicans such as Seán

Keenan became re-involved with the Republican movement in Derry in early 1969, unlike the older Republicans in Belfast who would not become re-involved until after August 1969. This was at least partly because there never developed in Belfast the mass popular civil rights movement that developed in Derry.

In May 1969, in the vacuum left by the ending of the DCAC campaign, the Republicans launched a small civil rights campaign of their own in Derry, concentrating on the issues of repression which affected Republicans and trying to raise the issue of a united Ireland. A branch of NICRA was now finally established in Derry, headed by Gerry 'The Bird' Doherty, a veteran Republican.[142] The Derry Unemployment Action Committee, (hereafter DUAC), originally founded by Republicans and leftists in the early 1960s was revived and the Derry Housing Action Committee (hereafter DHAC) reasserted themselves in the spring of 1969.[143] All of them, it seems, were now dominated by Republicans.

In May, the DHAC and DUAC, supported by the Derry branch of NICRA, staged a picket at a border customs post on the outskirts of Derry, and declared that 'the conquest of Ireland is still a reality'.[144] The Republicans were beginning to push their own agenda a little more and trying to place the focus on the partition of Ireland but it is notable that, even at this late stage, the Derry Republicans and presumably the IRA were still committed to the tactics of public protest (which allowed their members to be identified by the RUC) and to the rhetoric of civil rights.

Around this time the Derry Republicans established a new area executive headed by Johnnie White which stretched out to Coleraine, Limavady and into Co. Donegal.[145] It was a threadbare structure relying on a scattering of individuals in each area and its strong point was Derry. Still, it is an indication that the Republicans were developing new organisational structures and were hoping to expand.

Although still weak, the IRA in Derry was active in its own right, and not simply in support of civil rights, as early as January 1969. To suggest that the IRA suddenly emerged in August 1969 in Belfast with a few rusty weapons, utterly unprepared, is to ignore the extent to which Republicans had adapted to changing circumstances, just as other groups had, as the civil rights movement gave way to violence. In Derry, those older traditionalist Republicans, who would later establish the Provisionals, had become active again in the movement from January 1969 onwards and operated within it for several months in close co-operation with the radicals as part of a unified movement.

The evidence in Derry suggests that both radical and traditionalist Republicans began to see the turmoil in early 1969 as a chance to push forward the objective of a united Ireland.

The 1969 election and the demise of the DCAC

In February 1969, under pressure from his right wing, Terence O'Neill called an election for the Stormont parliament. Three members of the DCAC stood for election. Claude Wilton stood as a Liberal in the City of Londonderry constituency which he had come close to winning over the university issue in 1965. Ivan Cooper stood first as Northern Ireland Labour Party and then as an Independent (prompting accusations of opportunism)[146] in his home territory of Mid-Derry. John Hume stood against the leader of the Nationalist party, Eddie McAteer, in Foyle. Hume was accused by the Nationalist party of 'cashing-in' on his involvement in the civil rights campaign.[147] The decision of DCAC committee members, particularly Hume and Cooper, to stand for election caused dissension and they were accused of weakening the DCAC. One member resigned in protest.[148] John Hume saw his decision to stand as a way to 'translate all this [the civil rights campaign] into political action'[149] and make further gains through parliamentary politics at Stormont.

The election disrupted the easy cross-party unity which had ensured the DCAC of solid support from all anti-Unionist groups in the city. It also significantly weakened the DCAC by the simple fact of removing two of its most prominent members, Cooper and Hume, who both resigned shortly after the election.[150] Perhaps even more importantly, the election removed from the civil rights campaign a veritable army of people who had been involved in stewarding and marching during the civil rights demonstrations. Hundreds of people whose first experience of politics had been the civil rights campaign now became election workers for John Hume in the Foyle constituency.[151] After the election many of them became active in the Independent Organisation in Foyle, the constituency party now set up to support Hume in parliament (it would later become the Derry branch of the SDLP). The Independent Organisation began to hold regular meetings and public talks which drew crowds large enough that the meetings had to be stewarded by members.[152] Among these stewards were people who had been involved in the stewarding of the civil rights marches.

The Independent Organisation quickly set up a network of advice centres and area committees, built links with tenants' associations and began to operate as an organised political party with a mass membership and mass involvement.[153] Interest in politics was at a high pitch and meetings held by the organisation were well attended. When the Independent Organisation held party fund-raising functions the only problem encountered was that tickets sold out too quickly.[154]

The organisation absorbed the energies of people such as Michael Canavan, Raymond McClean, Willie O'Connell, Hugh Doherty and many others who had previously devoted their energies to the civil rights campaign, particularly in the area of stewarding. When the reduced DCAC launched a revived civil rights campaign in March 1969 after the election a huge swathe of people who had been involved at all levels in the earlier campaign did not get involved.

However, the Independent Organisation did not by any means absorb all those who had been mobilised and politicised by the civil rights campaign. In particular, huge numbers of teenagers who had come out to march and some of whom had been involved in stewarding found no way to channel their interest. Even if they had wanted to, they couldn't have joined the Independent Organisation which did not take any steps towards establishing a youth wing until several months later.[155] In any case, this sort of formal political activity did not hold the attraction which marching had done. Although the radicalised Labour party would try to involve younger people in political activity, this was not particularly successful.[156] The civil rights campaign had brought large numbers of young people on to the streets, educated them about Catholic grievances and got them discussing these grievances. The successes of the campaign had given them a sense of power and achievement.

By spring 1969, the civil rights campaign was petering out, having achieved some but by no means all of its demands. Moreover, a huge store of new grievances against the RUC had built up and these had not been resolved. There was massive widespread hostility to the RUC as a force, particularly among the young. In the circumstances the Derry teenagers who had taken part in the civil rights campaign were like a huge army expected to demobilise without victory, with no prospect of further political involvement and with nothing to go home to in many cases but unemployment and boredom.[157] In the circumstances, it is little surprise that many of them chose to stay on the streets.

In March 1969, the Unionist government made good on a threat Terence O'Neill had made after the Burntollet march. At the end of that month, a new Public Order bill was passed at Stormont restricting or outlawing a range of tactics used in the civil rights campaign, including sit-downs.[158] The bill in a sense delegitimised the civil rights campaign in retrospect and also ensured that political pressure could not be so easily exerted by such means again. When the bill was introduced at Stormont, it was strenuously opposed by the new MPs, Ivan Cooper and John Hume.[159] Its passage represented a failure for their parliamentary opposition. When the DCAC relaunched the civil rights campaign in Derry in March 1969, this time principally to oppose the Public Order bill (although one person, one vote had not yet been granted either), it was supported by the two MPs.

The new DCAC campaign deliberately imitated the successful campaign of the previous October and November, gradually building up from a sit-down to mass demonstrations. In late March a sit-down protest was held. The turnout, with around 1,000 people taking part in the sit-down while a thousand others watched, was not a great success.[160] The principal grievance which had inspired people to protest in Derry was Unionist control of the corporation. The end of this control had removed the sense of urgency and much of the motivation for protest in Derry. While the sit-down was taking place, a group of loyalists on the city walls threw stones and shouted at the crowd. Some of the crowd rushed up to confront them and scuffles broke out which were then broken up by stewards.[161]

Much the same potential for trouble had existed at some of the earlier demonstrations but it had been prevented by massed ranks of stewards. The same level of stewarding was not present now, largely because of the large numbers who had withdrawn from the campaign to become active in the Independent Organisation.[162] In addition, the civil rights campaign had been a tense and stressful experience for many stewards. There had been a feeling of relief when it had ended and there seems to have been no great enthusiasm amongst this pool of stewards for a revived campaign.[163]

After the sit-down, at which the RUC presence had been minimal, groups of youths headed towards the RUC station and began to stone it, resisting pleas from Hume, Cooper and chief steward Paul Grace for them to stop.[164] At the sit-down, John Hume had declared that 'the politics of the street must continue until fundamental justice has been achieved'.[165] After this meeting there were clearly doubts about the new campaign and it was obvious that not enough people had committed themselves to organising and controlling it. But it is notable that, nominally at least, this campaign enjoyed the support of all those groups from the Nationalist party to the Labour left, who had supported the earlier campaign.[166]

The following weekend the DCAC held a march retracing the 5 October route, again in protest at the Public Order bill. It was a notable success, drawing a crowd of about 5,000, indicating that large numbers of people still wanted to march. This time the RUC were not so casual and 500 policemen with riot trucks policed the march. After the march, despite the RUC presence, sectarian clashes broke out between Catholic and Protestant youths in the Diamond. This was seen as a major failure for the campaign and Ivan Cooper now said that he would 'press for an end to marches' because they were getting out of control.[167] The moderates were finally pulling out of the campaign.

There seems to have been a certain inevitability, resulting from poor stewarding and a general lack of organisation, about the events a few weeks later when a march to re-trace the route from Burntollet, organised by the North Derry CRA, was cancelled in some confusion at the last minute.[168] Teenagers who had gathered in Derry city centre to wait for the march to arrive took matters into their own hands and staged impromptu sit-downs. The RUC broke up the sit-downs and in addition large numbers of loyalists who had been opposed to the march confronted Catholic crowds in the city centre. The RUC launched baton-charges against the Catholic crowds and three days of ferocious rioting began, the worst yet seen in the city.[169] The DCAC was swept aside. 'The kids on the streets had taken control', as Paddy Doherty put it later.[170]

During the riots, a group of RUC men pursued rioters into a house in William Street in the Bogside. The rioters escaped out the back of the house and the RUC men assaulted several members of the household including the father, Sammy Devenny, a middle-aged man well known locally and known to be unaggressive.[171] News of this incident inflamed local opinion and the situation worsened.

The following morning several hundred RUC men gathered at the edge of the Bogside. Moderates, among them John Hume, played a role in evacuating a large section of the population of the Bogside area and moving the crowd of several thousand people up to Creggan estate. With the help of Protestant churchmen the moderates eventually negotiated an RUC withdrawal and people returned to the area.[172] During these riots the Republicans once again organised defence committees.[173] On one occasion during the riots an RUC man found himself cornered and fired a number of shots, though not hitting anyone. It was the first time since the civil rights campaign had begun that shots had been fired in Derry and it seemed to some as though the stakes were rising a little.[174]

After these riots the DCAC campaign was dead. Although prominent moderates had played a role once again in negotiating for an end to hostilities, the situation had shifted further towards territory in which Republicans were happier operating than the moderates were. The issue of civil rights had given way almost entirely to the issue of 'defence', and complaints about 'discrimination' to complaints about the RUC.

In response to the riots in Derry, NICRA and People's Democracy held demonstrations across the North, many of which ended in rioting which was especially severe on the Falls Road in Belfast. The riots in Derry also prompted the first organised Republican attacks in Belfast where the IRA planted incendiary devices in several sub-post offices around the city.[175]

Shortly after these events, Terence O'Neill resigned under pressure from the Unionist right wing for failing to restore order and after a series of bomb explosions which were attributed to the IRA. These explosions were actually carried out by the revived UVF, a loyalist paramilitary organisation which had been sporadically active in 1966 in Belfast. In an effort to end the chaos on the streets and reduce the backlog of grievances, the government of the new prime minister, James Chichester-Clark, finally conceded one person, one vote and declared an amnesty for all those charged or convicted in connection with civil disturbances since the previous October.[176]

The amnesty was welcomed by the DCAC who called for the government to follow it up with swift electoral reform and an impartial boundary commission to ensure Unionists did not gerrymander the new local government districts. The DCAC also called for the abolition of the Special Powers Act which was still in force.[177] The civil rights campaign was now focused on the increasingly important issues of repression and policing and on ensuring that the Unionist government did not backtrack on reform.

Chichester-Clark's initiative failed to end the trouble in Derry because the issue of RUC behaviour had now became the principal Catholic grievance and these changes did little to address this concern. Catholics had been awaiting progress on the prosecution of RUC men and B-Specials in connection with their behaviour in January and the beating of Sammy Devenny. The amnesty raised the prospect that they would not now be prosecuted. This provoked protests from the DCAC.[178] Ground-level hostility to the RUC had hardened to a degree unimaginable a few months before and had spread to moderate Catholics as well. The effect which the Devenny case had is illustrated in a small way by the actions of the Creggan tenants' association. In late March 1969, they had called on the RUC to set up a police station on the estate.[179] After the Devenny beating a few weeks later they announced that they were withdrawing all co-operation from the RUC.[180] Things had reached the point where it was unlikely that the RUC in its existing form would ever be accepted again by most Catholics in Derry, however much some Catholics might be concerned that rioting should end and order be restored. The issue of policing went to the heart of the problems of the state and was not addressed in these months. By this stage too the crisis was spreading, and the first sectarian rioting had started to break out in Belfast. Up until the summer of 1969 most of the violence in the North was confined to Derry. In July 1969 however, in the highly charged atmosphere largely created by events in Derry, violence broke out around loyalist parades in several centres across the North. In that month two elderly Catholic men died, one in Belfast and one in Dungiven (a largely Catholic town about twenty miles from Derry) after RUC baton charges against Catholic crowds. In Belfast in particular there was serious sectarian rioting.

In the spring and summer of 1969, rioting in Derry took on a new character. It was no longer provoked by confrontations at civil rights marches. Rioting broke out on the weekend of 12 July in Derry as youths attacked the RUC and resisted all the entreaties of clergymen and prominent moderates to desist. It was so clear that confrontation had been initiated and sustained by the young rioters that the DCAC praised the RUC for 'acting with commendable restraint'.[181]

A few days after this, Sammy Devenny died of a heart attack. Although the RUC would not list his death among those attributed to the 'Troubles' that year there was no doubt how his death was perceived by local Catholics. His funeral was attended by 15,000 people. According to the *Londonderry Sentinel* it was one of the largest funerals ever seen in the city[182] and was on the same scale as the largest civil rights demonstrations. The last major action of the DCAC was the organisation of this funeral. It told the RUC to stay away from it completely, that they were not wanted even on traffic duty.[183]

A few days after this funeral, the Derry Republicans set up a Derry Citizens Defence Association (hereafter DCDA) and invited the DCAC to nominate delegates to it. The Republicans had taken the initiative and began to make preparations to defend Catholic areas when the expected violence broke out at the Apprentice Boys of Derry march on 12 August. The events surrounding that march would transform the political situation in Northern Ireland and open a whole new phase of the conflict.

Outside attention

One of the most significant achievements of the civil rights campaign was to attract international attention to the grievances of the Catholic minority in Northern Ireland. From the beginning, reports of marches in Derry were carried as far afield as New Zealand, Thailand, Zambia and, of course, Britain and the United States.[184]

The most important external pressure that came to bear on the Unionist government came from the British government at Westminster but there were also significant pressures from the Republic of Ireland and, as time went on, from the United States.

The civil rights campaign produced a wave of national interest in the Republic of Ireland but as civil rights turned to violence, support from the Republic took on a new character and the issue of partition came to the fore.

The events in Derry on 5 October initially produced a restrained reaction from the Irish government, in tune with their recent lack of interest in the issue of civil rights in the North.[185] The Taoiseach, Jack Lynch, issued a statement which described the partition of Ireland as the root cause of the violence in Derry, but his remarks were brief.[186] Within days of the October violence, Eddie McAteer went to see Lynch in Dublin, thus re-establishing the Nationalist party practice of appealing to the Irish government which had tailed off after 1965 when the Irish government had urged the Nationalists to recognise the Northern state and co-operate with the Unionist government.[187] McAteer urged Lynch to call for United Nations intervention in the North.[188] At the end of October 1968, Lynch met British prime minister Harold Wilson in London, where he made more remarks about the desirability of ending partition. His remarks provoked fierce criticism from Terence O'Neill and stoked up Unionist fears of a hidden nationalist agenda behind the civil rights campaign.[189] At this early stage, talk of partition appears simply to mask the absence of any considered Irish government policy on the North. In recent years the Irish government, to the great frustration of nationalists in the North and the Irish Labour party, had deliberately avoided raising the issue of civil rights with the Northern government as part of its 'good neighbour' policy. Now that the North suddenly seemed unstable, the Irish government rapidly returned to a traditional nationalist policy for lack of any real alternative. But for all its talk of partition, the Irish government was concerned principally at this stage to pressurise Britain to exercise control over the Northern Ireland government. In short, it was ultimately trying to secure British intervention as the civil rights movement was.

At the beginning of November 1968, a member of Lynch's Fianna Fail cabinet, Neil Blaney, made a speech in Letterkenny, Co. Donegal, just over the border from Derry. Blaney directly challenged the civil rights vision of a reconciliation within Northern Ireland and condemned those who concentrated on civil rights and ignored the issue of partition. Defending Jack Lynch's remarks about partition, Blaney stated that, 'The partition of Ireland was imposed by Britain and it must be undone by Britain'.[190] There was no talk yet of the use of force and it was notable that Blaney was issuing another variation of the call for Britain to intervene, this time to undo partition. His speech did not reflect public opinion in the Republic which sympathised with the civil rights movement's aim of improving the situation of Catholics in Northern Ireland.

Blaney's speech was vehemently criticised by Stormont Republican Labour MP, Gerry Fitt. He condemned Fianna Fail for its long neglect of the civil rights issue and warned that such talk could only benefit the Unionist party by clouding the issue.[191] Eddie McAteer reacted somewhat ruefully to the remarks, saying that 'a very right thing can be said at a very wrong time'.[192] The Nationalist party had spent decades arguing that a united Ireland was the sole meaningful political goal for Northern Catholics. Having finally accepted the strategy of the civil rights movement, recognising that it had broken the political log-jam, renewed talk of a united Ireland placed them in something of a dilemma. Until its demise a few years later, the Nationalist party was to spend a lot of its energy pondering its identity and goals, torn between traditional nationalism and its support for civil rights.

The first months of the civil rights campaign, non-violent and concentrated in Derry, aroused intense interest in the Republic of Ireland. It was Telefís Éireann, the Irish national television station, which had captured the footage of police brutality on 5 October, and it was the Irish national newspapers, in Dublin, which covered the unfolding events most extensively. The Irish national media gave extensive and sympathetic coverage to the civil rights campaign, both reflecting and reinforcing public awareness in the Republic. As violence broke out, the crisis in the North was seen as a national one. As one provincial paper in the Republic put it, 'No matter what they may say, they are our fellow countrymen and we are theirs ... We are not on the outside looking on in the way the people of other countries look on. What happens there concerns our future as much as it does theirs.'[193] Britain was seen as another outside power looking in. At this stage, with Stormont still in control and Britain acting as a reluctant watchdog, this view was entirely credible. It was still believable that, in the event of catastrophe, the British would wipe their hands of the matter.

The civil rights movement in the North was in something of a quandary as it became apparent how strong their support was in the Republic; not the ideological support for civil rights which the campaign had aimed at, but an emotional support based on a sense of ethnic community. The more radical elements in the movement reacted strongly, advising people in the Republic to campaign for civil rights in their own jurisdiction.[194] However, even many of these anti-nationalist radicals began to develop cross-border campaigns and alliances. It seemed to some that one way to prove their non-sectarian progressive credentials to Northern Protestants was to campaign for changes in the Republic.[195] By early 1969 the movement in the North had inspired groups all over Ireland: in the west, for example, those such as Cearta Sibhialta na Gaeltachta (Gaeltacht Civil Rights) in Connemara[196] and the Western Civil Rights Movement, based in Galway.[197]

The Burntollet march, in January 1969, provoked strong emotional reactions south of the border. Irish national newspapers gave pages of coverage to images of battered marchers and descriptions of events. While liberal Unionists might be equivocal over the attack on the marchers and British politicians could express a detached concern at the descent into violence, there was very little of such vaguely disinterested neutrality in the Republic. Public opinion in the Republic was based on a strong sense of identification with the Catholic community in the North. Nonetheless, the violence in Derry which followed the march, and then the violence at a march in Newry shortly afterwards, were unsettling to many in the Republic and voices were raised, questioning whether the civil rights marchers might push things too far.[198] In the event of that happening, however, it was clear which 'side' most people in the Republic would be on.

The civil rights campaign in Derry received extensive coverage in the US from the beginning.[199] The fact that Derry attracted such attention is a measure of the novelty to Americans of an 'Irish' riot and a 'religious civil rights march' at a time when both riots and civil rights were associated with black Americans. Prior to October 1968 the only group in the US connected to a civil rights group in Northern Ireland was the American Congress for Irish Freedom, based in Buffalo, New York which had developed links with the Campaign for Social Justice in Dungannon, Co. Tyrone.[200] The events in Derry inspired the establishment of many new locally based American support groups. The first was established in San Francisco calling itself 'Citizens for Justice in Ireland'.[201] The Derry-born secretary of the group, Moira Ó Scannláin, visited Derry within weeks of the first civil rights march, and met with prominent activists such as John Hume and Michael Canavan.[202] This sort of international support provided an immediate boost to the morale of civil rights activists in the North.

In general though, interest was slow to take off in the US and it was not until after the Burntollet march, for example, that a group was set up in that most 'Irish' of American cities, Boston. When this group turned up with a civil rights banner and another one saying 'Ulster is Irish' at the St Patrick's Day parade in South Boston in March 1969, parade officials attempted to prevent them from marching because 'this would introduce politics into the parade'. The group persisted and joined the march despite this opposition.[203] In Philadelphia, the St Patrick's Day committee agreed to allow Clan na Gael, the American wing of the Irish Republican movement, to march in the parade only if they made it clear that they supported civil rights in Ireland and not black civil rights in the US.[204] There was a marked reluctance among Irish-Americans to support a civil rights campaign and limited interest in a topic which did not have the same emotional appeal as the 'struggle for Irish freedom'.[205]

In April 1969, the Boston group held a public meeting in the city to which 800 people turned up to hear Gerry Fitt speak. Fitt also addressed the Massachusetts House of Representatives and Senate and the Boston City Council. This was the first indication that the city and state politicians who represented the 'Irish' neighbourhoods of cities such as Boston were taking an interest in events in Northern Ireland. At national level too, certain powerful Irish-American politicians began to take an interest, prominent among them being Tip O'Neill and Ted Kennedy.[206]

Over the following months spokespersons for the Boston group addressed public meetings around Boston and appeared on local television programmes,[207] seeking to create a 'foundation of concern'[208] over events in Northern Ireland. In some of their literature they made explicit comparisons between the position of blacks in the American south and Catholics in Northern Ireland.[209] As the Irish civil rights campaign had drawn inspiration from black Americans there were those on the left in the US who hoped that Irish-American sympathy for northern Irish Catholics could be parlayed into solidarity with black Americans. This was one of the sources of conflict with more conservative Irish-Americans and one of the reasons for the limited support which the civil rights campaign in Northern Ireland received from Irish-Americans.

The Boston civil rights group contained a number of professional people and many recent Irish immigrants including a small group of Irish-born Republicans who had left Ireland during or after the IRA campaign of the 1950s. They had remained in touch in Boston since

1957 and some of them had become disillusioned with Irish Republicanism.[210] One of them who had emigrated to the US from Derry in 1965 made regular trips back to Derry and provided a direct contact with the situation in the North. However, none of the other Irish-born Republicans were from the North.[211] In New York, Irish Republicans had remained organised in Clan na Gael and were in touch with the Republican leadership in Dublin.[212] They became involved in supporting the American Congress for Irish Freedom when it set up a branch in New York.[213] These Republicans were enthusiastic about the civil rights campaign and it is a measure of their readiness to broaden their contacts that when Ivan Cooper visited the US, in March 1969, he stayed with IRA veterans such as Mike Flannery in New York and Vincent Conlan in Philadelphia who would later go on to support the Provisional Republicans.[214] This was a time when most Irish-Americans were not interested in Northern Ireland and the fact that the Republicans were involved from the very beginning put them in a very strong position when interest began to grow.

As the violence escalated in Northern Ireland, money raised in the US was regularly brought over to Ireland for dispersal to families who had suffered due to the riots.[215] It was the beginning of a financial support network which allowed some elements in the Catholic community to pull further away from the state in Northern Ireland. Distribution of this money was informal and somewhat haphazard and a great deal of the money raised at this early stage was channelled through the Catholic church, simply because it had the necessary network of transatlantic contacts.[216] Sums of money donated to the Catholic church in the US, for example, were passed on to the Catholic Bishop of Derry who then passed it on to the 'Emergency Aid Centre' in Derry which was run by moderate Catholics associated with the church.[217] The fact that many of the early Irish civil rights supporters in the US were Irish immigrants who regularly returned to Ireland helped them in building direct personal links with the civil rights movement and allowed them to appear at civil rights rallies in Ireland.[218]

Over the coming years, Republicans would come to dominate Irish-American support groups for Northern Ireland and the US would become a major source of finance and weapons for the Provisional Republicans. Irish-American support would play a major role in the growth of the Provisional IRA. The fact that Irish-American support was slow to gather in 1968 and 1969 indicates that there was nothing inevitable about widespread Irish-American interest. This would only really be generated by events following internment in August 1971.

After civil rights

If the slogan of 'British rights for British citizens', 'rang out'[219] in Derry in October 1968 it doesn't appear to have rung out very loudly.[220] In Derry the defining characteristic of the campaign was not the abandonment of traditional nationalism but the dedication to the local and the civic, to the development of Derry and the abolition of its Unionist corporation. Although campaigning for change within the state there were precious few individuals in the civil rights campaign who were actively committed to the maintenance of the state. There were fewer still when the state responded to the campaign with repression. Even some of the most 'moderate' elements in the campaign regarded the re-unification of Ireland as an ideal outcome. Many moderates such as John Hume saw the reform of Northern Ireland 'as a necessary prerequisite to the eventual and inevitable marriage of the two parts of Ireland'.[221]

When the civil rights campaign dissolved into violence in the summer of 1969 and the issue of a United Ireland began to emerge, it seemed to many Unionists as proof that the demands of the civil rights movement had been made in bad faith, that Catholics had never given up their aspirations to a united Ireland and had used the civil rights campaign to revive their quest for a united Ireland.[222] This view totally ignores the importance of the events which surrounded that campaign as the Unionist government resisted reform, and the bitterness these events aroused in the Catholic community. Already, by the spring of 1969, things had gone beyond the issue of civil rights to the question of the relationship between the RUC (and, implicitly, the state) and the Catholic community in Derry. By then, in certain areas, relations were so bad that it was unlikely that the RUC would ever be accepted again in its existing form. The experience, first of the stewards' organisation, and then of the vigilante groups in Free Derry, had pointed the way towards alternatives to the RUC. While the RUC remained unacceptable and there was no initiative to provide an alternative form of policing and government, disturbances and a creeping secession from the authority of Stormont would continue in Derry.

The emergence of the Provisional IRA after August 1969 convinced many Unionists that the civil rights campaign had been a Republican conspiracy to prepare the ground for a military campaign.[223] Nonetheless, the small numbers of Republicans in the North, however great their conspiratorial ambitions were, did not control RUC behaviour on 5 October or at Burntollet. They did not control the Unionist government which delayed reform as long as it could. They did not control the Paisleyites and the B-Specials. Left-wing Republicans had planned an entirely different conspiracy, a slow unfolding one, using essentially peaceful methods.[224] Besides, it was not these Republican 'conspirators' who set up the Provisionals: it was, for the most part, Republicans who had never had faith in the gradualist strategy. The Republicans found themselves adapting to a rapidly changing political situation in 1969, just as other groups in Northern Ireland did, and probably had far less influence on the course of events than the Stormont government.

The civil rights campaign had disrupted the balance of power in Northern Ireland by the simple fact of mobilisation of the Catholic community. It was not so much that Northern Ireland could not be reformed. By the summer of 1969, it already had been reformed to some extent. It was that it could not incorporate its Catholic minority into the political process. It could not offer Catholics the prospect of political power. Simple political exclusion was possible while the Catholic minority were quiescent but once they entered the political equation it became totally impractical. Once mobilised, it would be impossible for the Catholic community to return to the near-total political quiescence of previous decades. By mid-1969 many civil rights reforms had been enacted in Northern Ireland. It is quite conceivable that renewed Catholic quiescence would have allowed the state to implement the reforms even against Protestant opposition. However, this would require an end to all marches, protests and riots, an end to demands for further reform, for reform of the RUC or for the prosecution of RUC men. There was no possibility at all of such renewed quiescence. Since the Catholic community had never sought to actively preserve the state, the danger of its collapse did not inhibit them from maintaining pressure, particularly in Derry where the danger of mass sectarian violence did not exist on the scale it did in Belfast. By the summer of 1969, there were many people in Derry, and not only Republicans, who felt that Northern Ireland was on its last legs. Many more people were looking beyond Stormont to both the Irish and the British governments.

Notes and references

1 Conn McCluskey, *Up Off Their Knees. A Commentary on the Civil Rights Movement in Northern Ireland* (Conn McCluskey and Associates, Republic of Ireland, 1989), p. 16.
2 Ibid. and Frank Curran, *Derry. Countdown to Disaster* (Gill and Macmillan, Dublin, 1986), p. 79; also, interview with Patrick L. Doherty ('Paddy Bogside'),

head of the Inner-city Trust; formerly a member of the DCDA, DCAC and founder member of the Credit Union in Derry; interview with Ivan Cooper; member of the Young Unionist party in mid-Derry in the mid-1960s, member of the Derry Labour party in the later 1960s; former chairman of the DCAC; former Independent and, later, SDLP MP at Stormont for mid-Derry; interview with Dermie McClenaghan, former Derry Labour party activist and member of the DHAC, the DCAC and the DCDA.

3 DJ, 8/10/68, p. 5.

4 Eamonn McCann, *War and an Irish Town*, p. 47; Makowski in Margie Bernard, *Daughter of Derry. The Story of Brigid Sheils Makowski* (Pluto, London, 1989), p. 57; Proinsias Mac Aonghusa in *Comhar*, Nov. 1968, p. 3.

5 As Fergus Pyle put it in IT, 7/10/68, p. 1; see also Cameron Report, *Disturbances in Northern Ireland. Report of the Commission appointed by the Governor of Northern Ireland*, Northern Ireland Cmd. 532, HMSO, Belfast, Sept. 1969, pp. 50–4.

6 Interview with Willie O'Connell, formerly a senior member of the Independent Organisation, the DCDA and the DCCC, SDLP member of Derry City Council and former mayor of Derry; also, IT, 7/10/68, p. 13.

7 Belfast Campaign for Nuclear Disarmament (CND) at the time was a focus for co-operation between young Republicans, socialists and communists. I am indebted for this information to one of the anonymous reviewers who read the manuscript before publication.

8 Curran, *Countdown*, pp. 83–4; IT, 8/10/68, p. 1; *Fortnight*, no. 266, Oct. 1988, pp. 6–8.

9 McClenaghan, interview.

10 See Niall Ó Dochartaigh, *Before the Troubles; Derry in the 1960s. An Examination of the Origins of a Violent Conflict* (MA, UCG, 1989), pp. 119–124.

11 Interview with John Hume; MEP, MP, former Stormont MP for the Foyle constituency; former member of DCAC; former member of the DCCC; chairman of the University for Derry Committee (1965) and founder member of the Credit Union in Derry.

12 Ibid. and Paddy Doherty, interview. Paddy Doherty was one of those who was approached. For years afterwards the local radicals did not know who had organised this meeting.

13 McCann, *War*, 1974, pp. 43–5; McClenaghan, interview; Raymond McClean, *The Road to Bloody Sunday* (Ward River Press, Dublin, 1983), pp. 46–7. Also draws on interviews with Paddy Doherty and Ivan Cooper.

14 Hume, interview, and DJ, Oct–Dec. 1968, *passim*, which contain no references to any input from NICRA into the campaign.

15 Cooper, interview; interview with Claude Wilton; Ulster Liberal party candidate for City of Londonderry seat in 1965 and 1969; former chairman of the DCAC and of the SDLP; former Northern Ireland Senator for the SDLP and solicitor; Hume, interview.

16 See McClean, *Bloody Sunday*, p. 47; interview with Pat Devine, former DCAC steward; leader of the SDLP group on Derry City Council; former mayor of Derry.

17 DJ, 18/10/68, p. 1.

18 Sentiments expressed by speakers at the sit-down meeting, DJ, 23/10/68, p. 6.

19 Ó Dochartaigh, *Before the Troubles*, pp. 79–81 and pp. 147–55.

20 DJ, 22/10/68, pp. 1, 6; McClean, *Bloody Sunday*, p. 48.

21 DJ, 22/10/68.

22 On the US civil rights campaign see, for example, *Report of the National Advisory Commission on Civil Disorders* (Bantam Books, New York, March 1968), pp. 223–6 or David J. Garrow, *Bearing the Cross. Martin Luther King, Jr and the Southern Christian Leadership Conference* (Jonathan Cape Ltd, London, 1986).

23 DJ, 5/11/68, p. 1; McClean, *Bloody Sunday*, pp. 50–1.

24 IT, 7/10/68, p. 13.

25 *Times*, 8/10/68, p. 3.

26 Ibid., p. 1.

27 Ibid., p. 13.

28 *Times*, 5/11/68, p. 2.

29 *Times*, 5/10/68, p. 2; 6/10/68, p. 15.

30 Terence O'Neill, *Autobiography* (Hart-Davis, London, 1972), p. 105.

31 *Times*, 6/11/68, p. 4.

32 *Times*, 31/10/68, p. 2.

33 *Times*, 5/11/68, p. 2.

34 DJ, 15/11/68.

35 *Times*, 16/11/68, p. 1.

36 DJ, 12/11/68, p. 6.

37 *Times*, 16/11/68, p. 1.

38 Cooper, interview.

39 DJ, 19/11/68, pp. 6, 7; *Times*, 18/11/68, p. 8; Curran, *Countdown*, p. 97.

40 Cooper, interview and McCann in *Socialist Worker*, no. 51, p. 6, Oct. 1988.

41 *Times*, 18/11/68, p. 8; Cooper, interview.

42 Curran, *Countdown*, p. 98.

43 *Times*, 19/11/68, p. 2; DJ, 19/11/68, pp. 2, 3.

44 DJ, 19/11/68, p. 1; *Times*, 19/11/68, p. 2.

45 *Times*, 20/11/68, p. 1.

46 DJ, 22/11/68, p. 11.

47 See Patrick Buckland, *A History of Northern Ireland* (Gill and Macmillan, Dublin, 1981), p. 124; Michael Farrell, *Northern Ireland: The Orange State* (Pluto, London, 1980), p. 248; *Times*, 23/11/68, p. 2; DJ, 26/11/68.

48 McCluskey, *Up Off Their Knees*, p. 116.

49 A fear expressed by the *Derry Journal*, DJ, 26/11/68, p. 4.

50 DJ, 29/11/68, p. 8.

51 O'Neill, *Autobiography*, pp. 105–7. Buckland tends to accept O'Neill's view on this, noting, however, that 'His response was not entirely voluntary' (Buckland, *History*, p. 123).

52 DJ, 22/11/68, p. 1.

53 DJ, 26/11/68, p. 5.

54 DJ, 26/11/68, p. 4.

55 As Church of Ireland Bishop of Derry and Raphoe, Charles Tyndall, put it, DJ, 26/11/68, p. 5.

56 Paul Bew and Henry Patterson, *The British State and the Ulster Crisis. From Wilson to Thatcher* (Verso, London, 1985), p. 15.

57 DJ, 26/11/68, p. 4.

58 Paddy Doherty, interview.

59 Ibid. and Hume, interview.

60 Cooper, interview.

61 LS, 11/12/68, p. 1; 18/12/68, p. 14.

62 LS, 24/12/68. For a view of the moderates as more content with these reforms see McCann, *War*, p. 49.

63 Hume, interview; Paul Arthur, *The People's Democracy* (Blackstaff, Belfast, 1974) p. 38.

64 LS, 1/1/68, p. 1, quoting Eddie McAteer.

65 Paddy Doherty, interview.

66 Interview with Michael Canavan, founder member of the Derry Credit Union, formerly a senior member of the DCAC, the DCDA, the DCCC and the Independent Organisation, former SDLP assembly member; also LS, 1/1/68, p. 1.

67 Interview 1 with Gregory Campbell, leader of DUP group on Derry City Council; DUP activist since the early 1970s; member of the Young Unionists in the early 1970s.

68 Cooper, interview.

69 LS, 13/11/68, p. 19.

70 Wilton, interview.

71 LS, 6/11/68, p. 1.

72 LS, 20/11/68, p. 6.

73 LS, 6/11/68, p. 19.

74 LS, 20/11/68, p. 23.

75 Ibid., p. 6.

76 Stewart's statement that the civil rights movement took on a 'sectarian form' in 1969 can hardly be a suggestion that it became a sectarian organisation: A.T.Q Stewart, *The Narrow Ground: Aspects of Ulster, 1609–1969* (Faber and Faber, London, 1977), part 4, section 6. If he simply means that it became totally identified with the Catholic community we would suggest that this was more or less the case, unavoidably, from the beginning. This was partly because liberal Unionism in Derry often did not even extend to support for universal suffrage (See ch. 2 below).

77 See Ó Dochartaigh, *Before the Troubles*, pp. 180–8.

78 Albert Anderson, Unionist MP for City of Londonderry, in Stormont House of Commons debates, 16/10/68, p. 1027.

79 Eddie McAteer in IT, 7/10/68, p. 13.

80 IT, 7/10/68, p. 13.

81 A headline in a paper in Portugal as Inez McCormack recalled it in Michael Farrell (ed.), *Twenty Years On* (Brandon, Kerry, 1988), p. 26.

82 Max Hastings, *Ulster 1969. The Fight for Civil Rights in Northern Ireland* (Victor Gollancz, London, 1970), p. 55.

83 For example, Conor Cruise O'Brien, *States of Ireland* (Panther Books, St Albans, 1974), p. 152; Bernard, *Daughter of Derry*, p. 58.

84 Hastings, *Ulster 1969*, p. 55.

85 DJ, 5/11/68, p. 5.

86 LS, 20/11/68; 27/11/68; DJ, 22/11/68, p. 1; Cooper, interview.

87 Cooper, interview.

88 LS, 15/1/69, p. 24; 22/1/69, p. 22.

89 See LS, 8/1/69, p. 5; 15/1/69, p. 20; 22/1/69, p. 23.

90 LS, 29/1/69.

91 See Gerald Suttles, *The Social Order of the Slum. Ethnicity and Territory in the Inner City* (University of Chicago Press, 1968), on the importance of small-scale changes in ethnic 'territory' (a park bench or a basketball court, for example) in Chicago.

92 As Harris noted, in rural Ulster, while Catholics and Protestants mixed, they knew little of the politics of the other community. Rosemary Harris, *Prejudice and Tolerance in Ulster: A Study of Neighbours and 'Strangers' in a Border Community* (Manchester University Press, 1972), ch. 7.

93 Even such liberal commentators as Barritt and Carter had regarded Nationalist party objections to restrictions on Nationalist marches as 'incidental to their general campaign against the constitution, rather than evidence of a harmful degree of discrimination'. D.P. Barritt, and C.F. Carter, *The Northern Ireland Problem: A Study in Community Relations* (Oxford University Press, London, 1962) p. 127.

94 Christopher Hewitt, 'Catholic grievances, Catholic nationalism and violence in Northern Ireland during the Civil Rights Period: a reconsideration', *British Journal of Sociology*, vol. 32, no. 3, 1981, pp. 373–4.

95 Cooper, interview; LS, 2/4/69.

96 LS, 9/4/69, p. 17.

97 See, for example, Andrew Boyd, *Brian Faulkner and the Crisis of Ulster Unionism* (Anvil Books, Kerry, 1972), pp. 22–3 on the Longstone Road and Dungiven marches of the 1950s and early 1960s.

98 McClenaghan, interview.

99 See Bowes Egan and Vincent McCormack, *Burntollet* (LRS publishers, London, 1969).

100 IT, 6/1/69, p. 13.

101 McClenaghan, interview. See also Arthur, *People's Democracy*, pp. 39–43; IT, 1, 2/1/89 (reflections, twenty years later, of some of the marchers).

102 IT, 6/1/69, p. 1.

103 LS, 8/1/69 p. 15.

104 IT, 6/1/69, p. 9; LS, 8/1/69, p. 15; McCann, *War*, pp. 51–2.

105 LS, 8/1/69, pp. 16–7.

106 IT, 6/1/69, p. 9.

107 LS, 8/1/69 p. 17.

108 IT, 6/1/69, p. 9; Curran, *Countdown*, pp. 110–1; Cameron Report, ch. 9.

109 McCann, *War*, p. 54.

110 Paddy Doherty, interview.

111 Patrick Bishop and Eamon Mallie, *The Provisional IRA* (Corgi, London, 1988), p. 95.

112 McCann, *War*, p. 54.

113 Paddy Doherty, interview.

114 LS, 8/1/69 p. 1.

115 DJ, 22/11/68, pp. 8 and 11.

116 Cooper, interview.

117 Bishop and Mallie, *Provisional IRA*, p. 103.

118 Seán Mac Stiofáin, *Memoirs of a Revolutionary* (R. and R. Clarke, Edinburgh, 1975), p. 112.

119 Auxiliaries would not be members of the IRA and not necessarily committed Republicans at all, but the leadership would be IRA (as outlined in MacStiofáin, *Memoirs*, p. 145).

120 Interview with Fionnbarra Ó Dochartaigh (also known as Finbar Doherty), formerly a member of the DHAC and the DCAC; member of the Republican movement in Derry from the early 1960s; member of the Official Republican movement after the 1970 split; founder member of the IRSP.

121 Ibid. In Derry 'buckin' is a polite way of saying 'fuckin', used much as 'feckin' is in Galway.

122 Ibid.

123 Bob Purdie, *Politics in the Streets. The Origins of the Civil Rights Movement in Northern Ireland* (Blackstaff, Belfast, 1990), p. 126.

124 Ibid., p. 125, citing a document seized by Gardaí in the Republic.

125 Ibid., p. 126.

126 F. Ó Dochartaigh, interview.

127 Henry Patterson, *The Politics of Illusion. Republicanism and Socialism in Modern Ireland* (Hutchinson Radius, London, 1989), p. 97.

128 Interview with Mitchel McLaughlin, Sinn Féin member of Derry City Council; joined the Republican movement in 1966; stayed with the Officials after the split in 1970 but later joined the Provisionals.

129 Tom Collins, *The Irish Hunger Strike* (White Island, Dublin, 1986), pp. 253, 254, 257. For example, Seán Séamus O'Hara, one of these young Republicans joined the Fianna around 1965 (at age thirteen), took part in housing protest in Derry, acted as a steward on 5 October 1968 and later became a Provisional IRA member.

130 McLaughlin, interview; interview with John Carlin, member of the Republican movement in Derry from the mid-1960s and of the Provisional Republicans after the split; former Sinn Féin election agent; former internee; F. Ó Dochartaigh, interview; interview with Eamonn McCann, active in the Derry Labour party in the late 1960s and early 1970s; formerly a member of the DHAC and the DCDA; editor of the *Starry Plough*, the Official Republican paper in Derry in 1972: as McLaughlin put it, 'some of the people who'd been involved with me in the early agitational work in housing were now suddenly active service IRA volunteers'.

131 McLaughlin, interview, says there were no more than a hundred Republicans of any variety in the city.

132 Bernard, *Daughter of Derry*, p. 65.

133 *United Irishman*, May, 1969.

134 DJ, 16/4/68, p. 1.

135 DJ, 8/4/69.

136 DJ, 29/1/69 p. 18.

137 See Ó Dochartaigh, *Before the Troubles*, pp. 182–3.

138 LS, 9/4/69, p. 18.

139 *United Irishman*, June, 1969.

140 DJ, 8/4/69.

141 Curran, *Countdown*, p. 122.

142 LS, 7/5/69, p. 19.

143 LS, 19/3/69, p. 24.

144 LS, 14/5/69, p. 17.

145 *United Irishman*, May 1969.

146 *Fortnight*, 5/3/71.

147 LS, 19/2/69, p. 28.

148 LS, 12/2/69, p. 14.

149 Hume, interview.
150 LS, 19/3/69, p. 6.
151 Hume, interview; McClean, *Bloody Sunday*, pp. 64–5.
152 Independent Organisation minutes, 10/6/69.
153 Ibid., 7/3/69–12/5/70.
154 Ibid., 7/10/69.
155 Ibid., 30/9/69, 11/11/69.
156 McCann, *War*, p. 57.
157 Ibid.
158 Farrell, *Orange State*, p. 254.
159 LS, 19/3/69, p. 13.
160 LS, 26/5/69, pp. 23, 25.
161 Ibid.
162 McClean, *Bloody Sunday*, pp. 64–7. McClean, for example, seems to have taken no part in this renewed campaign.
163 McClean, *Bloody Sunday*, p. 58.
164 LS, 26/3/69, pp. 23, 25.
165 Ibid., p. 25.
166 LS, 26/3/69, p. 25.
167 LS, 2/4/69, p. 5.
168 LS, 23/4/69, p. 1.
169 Curran, *Countdown*, pp. 123–4; McClean, *Bloody Sunday*, pp. 68–9; Barry White, *John Hume, Statesman of the Troubles* (Blackstaff Press, Belfast, 1984), pp. 75–6; McCann, *War*, p. 56.
170 Paddy Doherty, interview.
171 Cooper, interview.
172 Hume, interview; White, *Statesman*, pp. 76–7.
173 Bishop and Mallie, *IRA*, p. 95.
174 McCann, *War*, p. 56.
175 Farrell, *Orange State*, p. 255; Kevin Kelley, *The Longest War. Northern Ireland and the IRA* (Brandon, Kerry, 1982), p. 114.
176 Buckland, *History*, p. 129.
177 LS, 14/5/69, pp. 6, 7.
178 LS, 21/5/69, p. 14.
179 LS, 2/4/69, p. 20.
180 LS, 7/5/69, p. 19.
181 Cameron Report, p. 34 onwards.
182 LS, 23/7/69, p. 16.
183 Paddy Doherty, interview.
184 DJ, 29/10/68, p. 4.
185 See Ó Dochartaigh, *Before the Troubles*, pp. 170–3.
186 IP, 7/10/68, p. 1.
187 See Ó Dochartaigh, *Before the Troubles*, pp. 170–3.
188 IP, 10/10/68, p. 6.
189 IP, 31/10/68.
190 DJ, 12/11/68, p. 5.
191 Ibid.
192 Ibid.
193 *Connacht Tribune*, 28/2/69.

194 Ibid., 10/1/69.
195 Arthur, *People's Democracy*, pp. 53–5.
196 *Connacht Tribune*, 21/3/69.
197 Ibid., 4/4/69.
198 Ibid., 17/3/69.
199 See, for example, *Boston Globe*, 8/10/68, p. 1; also DJ, 18/10/68, 22/10/69, describes coverage in US papers of the 5 October march.
200 *American Conference;* article in *Free Citizen* (paper of People's Democracy, Belfast) no. 7, late 1969 (undated).
201 'Paper-Hat Irish'; article in *United Irishman*, Nov. 1969.
202 DJ, 1/11/68, p. 1.
203 *The Rising of the Moon* (paper of the Committee for Justice in Northern Ireland, Boston) no. 1, 10–24 May, 1969.
204 Bernard, *Daughter of Derry*, p. 65.
205 Interview with Seán Cronin, former Washington correspondent of the *Irish Times*, former O/C of the IRA during the 1950s campaign and former officer in the Irish army.
206 Seán Cronin, *Washington's Irish Policy, 1916–1986, Independence, Partition, Neutrality* (Anvil Books, Kerry, 1987), p. 294.
207 *The Rising of the Moon*, 10–24 May, 1969.
208 Interview with Liam Deeney, former member of CJNI, Boston and spokesman for the Boston unit of Noraid, formerly an active Republican in Derry in the 1950s.
209 *The Rising of the Moon*, 10–24 May, 1969.
210 Deeney, interview.
211 Ibid.
212 Interview with Mike Flannery, founder member of the Irish Action Committee and former president of the Irish Northern Aid Committee (Noraid) in the United States.
213 Ibid.
214 Cooper, interview.
215 Deeney, interview.
216 Ibid.
217 DJ, 2/9/69, p. 1.
218 As with Brigid Makowski from Philadelphia (DJ, 8/11/68) and Donal McCaughan from Boston (LS, 2/4/69, p. 13) who spoke at rallies in Strabane and Derry in late 1968 and early 1969.
219 Jeffrey Dudgeon in *Fortnight*, no. 266, p. 10, Oct. 1988.
220 We find only one reference to 'British rights' in the local press in Derry during the early civil rights campaign, used by Stephen McGonagle, perhaps the most moderate member of the DCAC (DJ, 3/12/68, p. 7).
221 DJ, 13/3/69, p. 11.
222 Hewitt, article, op. cit., 1981.
223 William Craig in IT supplement, 3/10/88, p. 2.
224 See Des Hamill, *Pig in the Middle. The Army in Northern Ireland 1969–1985* (Methuen, London, 1986), p. 20, for Special Branch and Scotland Yard reports on the IRA and the civil rights campaign which contradict Craig's assessment of the importance of the IRA.

2
Unionist Collapse and Adaptation:
January 1969–June 1970

Unionist collapse

The civil rights campaign destabilised Northern Ireland by the simple fact of politically mobilising the state's Catholic minority which had previously been quiescent. But the state did not collapse solely because of this. Pressures had been building up for decades within the Protestant community too. Discontent was expressed in everything from Desmond Boal's desire for greater democracy within the Unionist party to Ivan Cooper's frustration with the domination of the party in Mid-Derry by an ageing local hierarchy.[1] These pressures were released by the crisis produced by the civil rights campaign. While the first reforms encouraged the further growth of Catholic political activity, and therefore put ever-increasing pressure on the state, the reforms also tore apart the ruling Unionist party in the space of a few months.

The reforms and the violence surrounding the civil rights campaign induced fear and distrust among large sections of the Protestant population, especially those most immediately threatened by reform. The resulting loss of confidence in the Unionist leadership prompted many working-class Protestants, who had left the running of the Unionist party to the gentry and the businessmen, to become politically involved. In the process, Unionist politics, as they had operated for the previous half-century, were completely transformed.

Irish republicans, nationalists and socialists had long held as an article of faith that the Northern Protestant working class were being manipulated and duped into support for the union with Britain by a wealthy Unionist ruling class whose interests were tied to those of Britain. Prior to 1968, there was ample evidence to support this view. The Unionist party was indeed led by the aristocracy in alliance with well-off businessmen and large farmers. The Unionist party had very little internal democracy and it appears its candidates in Derry were often businessmen 'invited' to stand by the local party hierarchy.[2] As often as not, Unionist representatives entered local government or parliament without the formality of actually consulting the electorate.[3] In Derry, with the exception of two by-elections, corporation elections were uncontested between 1949 and 1967. The fact that Londonderry Corporation met on weekday mornings made it difficult for people who worked a nine to five job to be on the corporation. Working-class Unionists in Derry found it virtually impossible to advance through party ranks and were grossly under-represented in the party hierarchy.[4] It was not difficult to conclude that this shell of a party maintained its hegemony by 'duping' the Protestant working class.

The expansion of public housing and free education brought in by the British Labour party government after the Second World War had transformed the Catholic community in Northern Ireland, providing the impetus for the growth of numerous community groups, action groups and local initiatives. Although there was discontent with the Unionist party, the changes did not have the same political impact in the Protestant community. In Derry, there had been no local initiatives in Protestant areas, no agitation, no protest, no organisation. There simply did not exist the room for such dissent in the Protestant community. The fact that Unionists controlled the corporation by such a narrow margin inhibited Protestants from taking action that might undermine Unionist control of the city in any way.

The political turmoil created by the civil rights campaign broke down those inhibitions. The Protestant working class, organised in the Orange Order and the Apprentice Boys, the Young Unionists, and the youth of the Protestant public-housing estates, began to challenge and question the Unionist leadership. From 1969 on, the Unionist party was rid of many of its squires and colonels and company managers. And the changes were not confined to the party. Protestants finally began to set up tenants' associations, action committees and community associations and even the traditional Protestant commitment to 'law and order' was eroded as Protestants began to take to the streets in 1968 and 1969 to stage sit-ins, pickets, demos, rallies and even to take part in rioting.

But if socialists and republicans had been correct in portraying the old Unionist leadership as unrepresentative and out of touch with the Protestant working class, they were wrong in thinking that the shattering of that Unionist party structure would open the way for working-class Protestants to embrace socialism and even Republicanism.

As the Protestant working class became active, it moved steadily to the right, becoming ever more enthusiastic about repression of the Catholic minority. And as the Protestant community began to lose its inhibitions about challenging the established authorities by way of demonstrations, it became more tolerant of other forms of action which might once have been seen to clash with Protestant respect for law and order. Protestant communities, as time went on, became more tolerant of squatting and barricade-building, of intimidation and vigilantes, and eventually of paramilitary violence.[5]

Loyalty to the Unionist party had depended on the certainty of continued Unionist control. It was loyalty to stability, to Protestant unity. Once that stability and certainty were shaken, the ties of loyalty to the party leadership were weakened. In Derry, where the reforms faced Protestants with the immediate loss of the Unionist corporation, the Protestant community had to abandon old certainties and look to new forms of organisation, to new means of protecting their interests and mediating with the authorities.

It was crucial to the fate of Northern Ireland that the civil rights campaign, rather than facing a stable, secure opponent, faced a Unionist party which was an empty shell in terms of popular participation and involvement. The ensuing conflict was as much the result of swift Unionist collapse as of the pressure exerted by the civil rights campaign. It was central to the subsequent course of events that when the Protestant working class finally emerged from many decades of quietude it was at a time of grave civil unrest. Many of the earliest local organisations and initiatives in Protestant working-class areas were prompted by the need to deal with the problems arising from this unrest. In the new uncertain situation, these groups were concerned to maintain certain things as much as to change them, and though the practice of Unionist unity had dissolved, they still adhered to its essentially conservative principles. These groups were certainly less inclined to make common cause with Catholic areas than they were to condemn those from the Catholic community who they saw as responsible for the civil unrest which had led to the collapse of their way of life.

The First Unionist split

On 11 December 1968, prime minister Terence O'Neill made his 'Ulster at the crossroads' speech. In the speech he called on Catholics to give the November reforms time to work and on Protestants to accept the reforms and for moderates on both sides to do their best to help defuse the increasingly violent political crisis in Northern Ireland.[6] The civil rights leadership responded to the speech by agreeing to suspend all marches for a month in order to avoid further confrontations and to allow time for the November reform package to work. It seemed to many that a dangerous corner had been successfully turned. Through modest reform, a peaceful solution to the crisis created by the civil rights campaign could now unfold.

The speech, which had convinced the civil rights movement to suspend its campaign, seemed also to have succeeded in damping down the simmering discontent on the right wing of the Unionist party. Messages of support for O'Neill's policies of modest reform flooded in from all over Northern Ireland. In Derry twenty-six local organisations voiced their support for O'Neill.[7] Among them were organisations representing local solicitors, doctors, dentists and Protestant schoolteachers, virtually all the Protestant professional classes in the city. Heavily represented in this chorus of support too were the business class in the city, the Chamber of Commerce, the Shirt-Manufacturers Federation, the Women's Business and Professional club, traders' associations, the Rotary Club, the Round Table and the Port and Harbour Commissioners. The messages from Derry also included many from the Unionist right-wingers who had been unhappy with O'Neill's policies, from individuals such as Gerald Glover, the most senior figure in the Unionist party in Derry, and groups such as the Londonderry Loyalist Committee (established by the local Unionist party to respond to the crisis), and its parent body, the Londonderry and Foyle Unionist Association (hereafter Londonderry UA).

It was notable, though, that the messages of support from right-wing Unionists in Derry were phrased in terms of support for O'Neill *and* for William Craig, his hardline home affairs minister. These messages also voiced support for the RUC whose behaviour had come under heavy media criticism in recent months.[8] The right wing of the party was signalling that it was prepared to accept the November reform package but that in return it expected that priority would now be given to ensuring an end to civil disorder and disruptions and that no more concessions would be made to the civil rights marchers. The governing body of the Unionist party only accepted the reforms, as Brian Faulkner put it, 'on the understanding that no further concessions to the agitations were contemplated'.[9] William Craig criticised the 'Crossroads' speech and O'Neill, buoyed by his new-found popularity, proceeded to sack him. Many right-wing Unionists now felt they had been tricked into supporting the O'Neill government.[10]

The first signs of organised rebellion within the Unionist party were prompted by the events at the beginning of 1969. These events culminated in the establishment of the first no-go area in Northern Ireland; that is to say, the first Free Derry which lasted for several days. It confirmed the worst fears of the Unionist right wing of a Republican conspiracy manipulating the civil rights campaign. Free Derry was a direct challenge to the sovereignty of the state and over the following years, Unionists would constantly demand that all such 'no-go' areas be brought fully back into the state.

Those right-wing Unionists who had never conceded the need for reform became ever more convinced by these events that demands for reform veiled a conspiracy by forces who were determined to dismantle Northern Ireland and establish a united Ireland. Central to the growth of right-wing Unionism was the adherence of senior Unionists to often outrageous conspiracy theories built around the reality of considerable Communist and Republican involvement in the civil rights movement. In the circumstances these Unionists believed that to concede further reforms would simply be to feed the conspiracy. However diverse their political philosophies, the Unionists who began to turn against O'Neill were united on one thing at least: they believed the security of the state now required a policy not of reform but of retrenchment and repression.

Within a week of the January riots, the O'Neill government, under British pressure, had agreed to the establishment of the Cameron commission, to investigate the causes of the violence and to make recommendations for the future. Among other things, the commission was to investigate allegations of RUC misconduct in Derry after the Burntollet march. The RUC, under pressure in riots and demonstrations week after week, had become a focus for Protestant loyalty and sympathy, and there was widespread Protestant outrage that those who had been on the frontline of what many saw as a struggle against rebellion and anarchy, were to face investigation. It was also feared that the commission would recommend further reforms which the Unionist party would then be obliged to enact. Mutterings of dissent grew in the local Unionist associations. The Unionist party across Northern Ireland, a party for which Protestant political unity was an article of faith, began to face into the first major split in its history. It was the beginning of a swift Unionist disintegration which would match the pace at which the state itself was being altered and disrupted.

Towards the end of January 1969, local Unionist associations in and around Derry held their customary annual meetings. Many of the local associations passed motions in support of the RUC.[11] In the same month, 3,600 people signed a public petition in Derry to affirm their confidence in the force.[12] The Apprentice Boys of Derry also called for full backing of the RUC at their quarterly meeting in January 1969 and for the re-establishment of law and order in all parts of Northern Ireland, emphasising their concern at the brief existence of Free Derry.[13] For these Unionists the principal issue now was law and order, not reform.

The Stormont MP for the City of Londonderry constituency, Albert Anderson, the most senior elected representative of Derry Unionism, turned up to speak at several local Unionist association meetings in Derry in January 1969. When he spoke in the Waterside he was accompanied on the platform by Major Gerald Glover, the man regarded as the 'real' leader of Unionism in Derry, once referred to by the Derry Labour party paper as 'the most faceless of the faceless men. Public enemy number one.'[14] Glover was a businessman, a landlord and a member of the corporation. In addition, he was the B-Special commandant for Derry's border district[15] and an Apprentice Boy. Also on the platform was Dr Russell Abernethy, the governor of the Apprentice Boys of Derry. Abernethy was also the vice-president of the Waterside Unionist Association and, up until a short time previously, had been chief medical officer with the corporation. This section of the party hierarchy in Derry was deeply connected to institutions such as the B-Specials and the Apprentice Boys which were based fundamentally on principles of Protestant solidarity. It was this section of the party in Derry, headed by Glover and Abernethy, which was instrumental in convincing Albert Anderson, MP, to join the anti-O'Neill camp shortly after these meetings in Derry.

The Burntollet march and its aftermath renewed Catholic mistrust of Unionist intentions and focused attention again on the issue of one person, one vote. For the civil rights movement it became the central unfulfilled demand while, for right-wing Unionists, opposition to 'one man, one vote' became a rallying point. When Gerald Glover asserted at the Waterside meeting that the voting system already in place was 'the best', and Albert Anderson agreed with him, they were declaring outright opposition to one person, one vote.[16] Implicit in their opposition to this reform was the hope that, once outside media attention had abated, the conditions should exist for the resumption of Unionist control of local government in Derry.

But if certain key figures in the Unionist party in Derry were lining up with the opponents of O'Neill, there were also many senior figures within the party who were preparing to support him. In the Middle Liberties, which stretched north of the city, the local Unionist Association was firmly in the hands of O'Neillite liberals by early 1969.[17] Two years previously it had been headed by the Reverend John Brown, the B-Special commandant for Derry city and a notorious right-wing Unionist and Orangeman.[18] This area included a string of upper-class suburban housing estates along the Culmore road where Unionist businessmen and professionals were heavily concentrated. It seems that, as this rural area had become suburbanised, the respectable Protestant upper middle class had taken an initiative to take over the local Unionist party organisation (see maps 2 and 3).

At their annual meeting in January 1969, the Middle Liberties Unionists called for Protestants to get away from 'the fortress mentality', and urged 'tolerance'.[19] However, it is also indicative of how conservative and traditional this O'Neillite liberalism was that the Middle Liberties Unionists would not support the principle of one person, one vote.[20] The *Londonderry Sentinel*, the local pro-Unionist paper, took a strongly pro-O'Neill stance. While it stopped short of openly endorsing universal suffrage, it described it as the last unresolved issue and believed that it would be implemented.[21]

Elsewhere in Derry the divisions in the party caused disruption at local meetings. At the meeting of the Enagh Lough Unionist Association on the north-eastern outskirts of Derry, argument reached such a pitch that Albert Anderson was moved to implore his fellow Unionists, 'do not let us get down to the level of the Lecky Road' (in the Bogside). 'Let us be the decent Protestants we are!'[22]

As discontent with O'Neill grew in January 1969, there was a series of resignations by right-wing Unionists from the Stormont government. These culminated in the formal challenge to O'Neill's leadership of the Unionist party on 3 February by a group of twelve MPs, about a third of the Unionist MPs at Stormont.

Among the twelve 'rebel MPs' who formed what was dubbed the 'Portadown parliament', was Albert Anderson. In all of his statements during the ensuing election it is clear that Anderson was a reluctant sort of rebel, constantly referring to the need for Unionist unity[23] and claiming to support policies of reform and reconciliation, but not the way O'Neill was proceeding with them. As soon as the election was over, he declared that the leadership issue was settled and that he now supported Terence O'Neill.[24] Thus in order to understand why conservative-minded Unionists such as Anderson were brought to the stage of open rebellion, we would do better to examine the local party organisation which brought pressure on Anderson to join the rebels than to look at the Stormont MP's personal politics.

During this time the importance of the local Unionist Associations as autonomous units becomes clear. Unionism had originally acted as an ethnic alliance rather than a political party and it still retained the organisational structures of that ethnic alliance.[25] Each local Unionist association was bound by its own rules, there being no central party guidelines on, for example, selecting candidates. It was also totally at their own initiative that local Unionist associations reserved places on their ruling councils for nominees of the Loyal Orders: the Orange Order and the Apprentice Boys (in Derry about one in seven of the council seats).[26]

Opposition to O'Neill's reforms was led in Derry by the leadership of a highly autonomous local party organisation which, because of its essentially local nature, was run by people who had a lot to lose from the changes in local government control which these reforms were likely to produce. The prominent Unionists in Derry who opposed O'Neill, people such as Gerald Glover, Russell Abernethy and the Reverend John Brown were virtually all tied into that long-established tight ethnic Protestant network. This network focused on the Loyal Orders, the Ulster Special Constabulary and the Protestant churches just as much as on the Unionist party. For such people, these organisations were part of what it was to be a Unionist, while the Unionist party was principally important as a vehicle for Protestant unity and the maintenance of Protestant political control and was just one focus for Protestant political loyalties. In most of the areas of the North where O'Neill got strong support,[27] Catholics formed a small minority with no propect of gaining any level of political control from the reform package. Opposition was strongest where reforms themselves threatened local Unionist control in areas where Catholics were a majority or a strong minority.

Anderson's decision to side with the rebels, against the majority of the parliamentary Unionist party, was publicly supported by the Londonderry UA, and by two of the local ward associations, the Waterside Unionist Association and the Bond's Glen Unionist Association. He was also backed by the Young Unionist Association in the city and the Middle Liberties Young Unionists, a bastion of extremism.[28] Most of the local Unionist Associations in Derry cautiously made no comment. The *Londonderry Sentinel*, however, condemned Anderson and the local associations that had backed him, for raising the possibility of a split in the Unionist vote if an election were to be held.[29] Ironically, for this pro-O'Neill newspaper, the issue of over-riding importance was Unionist (and Protestant) unity, a principle dear to the hearts of most anti-O'Neill Unionists. From this Unionist point of view it was the rebels, led by William Craig, who were out of step with Unionist tradition, damaging the party by their public display of dissent.

Following Anderson's decision to side with the rebels, a statement signed by a few hundred local Protestants, many of them prominent Unionists, declaring support for O'Neill and condemning Anderson, was printed in the *Londonderry Sentinel*.[30] This was followed up by a public petition in the city eventually signed by 4,000 city electors calling on Anderson to reverse his decision and to support O'Neill.[31]

But the home addresses of those who had signed the statement in the *Londonderry Sentinel* show that active support for O'Neill in Derry had a narrow class base. Those who signed were overwhelmingly from Derry's upper-middle-class Protestant areas along the Culmore Road, the Northland Road and the Limavady Road. Almost no-one from Protestant working-class areas such as the Fountain or Irish Street Estate was represented there. This narrow base would prove fatal for the O'Neillite cause in Derry.

When Terence O'Neill called an election in February 1969 to face down the rebels, the candidate who emerged to oppose Albert Anderson for the Unionist party nomination in Derry, Peter Campbell, was almost a caricature of what O'Neillism represented.

The election

Peter Campbell was a former Royal Navy commander who had only recently left the navy after twenty-one years of service.[32] He was strongly connected to the aristocratic Unionist tradition which Terence O'Neill exemplified. His wife's father was the Duke of Abercorn while her brother was the Marquis of Hamilton, Unionist MP for Fermanagh at Stormont.[33] The *Londonderry Sentinel*, which supported Campbell strongly at the beginning (though its support tailed off despondently towards the end), proudly told its readers that Peter Campbell's wedding in the Church of Ireland cathedral in Derry a few years previously had been attended by several members of the British royal family.[34] Peter Campbell was not reticent either about declaring who he represented. He was putting himself forward for election, he said, after being approached by 'business and professional' interests in the town.[35]

Both Anderson and Campbell competed in February 1969 for the local Unionist party nomination as candidate for the City of Londonderry seat. The candidate was selected by the 100 members of the Derry Unionist council. Only fifteen of the 100 were directly elected by members of the City of Londonderry and Foyle Unionist Association while the others held seats either by virtue of elected offices they held (the twelve Unionist members of the corporation, the nine Unionist members of the Rural District council and the local Unionist MP were all automatically members of the council), as nominees of local Unionist ward associations and the Loyal Orders or because they had been co-opted. Essentially the council was composed of local Unionist party stalwarts and members of the Loyal Orders, few of whom had faced any electoral competition or contest to attain these positions. Even the fifteen elected seats on the council seem to have been filled each year from an agreed list circulated by the leadership, without the formality of an actual election.[36] These people were likely to have a strong loyalty to their sitting MP and to the long-serving local party hierarchy, virtually unshuffled at the top for at least a decade.[37] In this selection contest, a network of longstanding personal relationships was probably every bit as important as any analysis of the recent government reforms.

The council, no doubt strongly influenced by decades of loyalty to the local party leadership and to their sitting MP, but also convinced that O'Neill's course of reform would prove disastrous, voted by 68 votes to 22 to re-nominate Anderson.[38]

While the bulk of the Unionist party hierarchy in the city backed Anderson, it is significant that a quarter of the council members backed the O'Neillite outsider. After this vote, eight members of the Derry Unionist council resigned their seats, condemning the lack of democracy in the party, particularly the fact that 'outside organisations' such as the Orange Order and the Apprentice Boys were represented on the council.[39] Among those who walked out were a former Unionist mayor, the head of the Londonderry Port and Harbour Commission, and the former presidents of two local Unionist Associations.[40] O'Neill's policy of reform was strongly supported in Derry by prominent Unionists with little reputation for liberalism and with long service in the same party structures which they were now criticising. In Derry in particular, reform was seen by such people as a necessary strategy to end the unrest which was damaging the economic life of the city. This section of the Unionist party in Derry strongly supported Peter Campbell and were heavily involved in his subsequent election campaign. When Campbell failed to get the local party nomination he was endorsed by the Unionist Central Council in Belfast. He thus contested the election as a candidate of the central party in Belfast against the party in Derry.[41] It was the high degree of autonomy enjoyed by the local Unionist associations which made such a situation possible.

The O'Neillites in Derry launched an election campaign where liberal rhetoric was freely used. Terence O'Neill came to Derry to canvass in the Catholic Triangle area in the Waterside, while Peter Campbell called for an end to segregation in schools, in housing and in jobs[42] and for a 'tolerant Ulster'. In a sense, O'Neill and his supporters had been pulled to the left, partly by the need to try to win some Catholic votes but also because they were attracting some who were genuinely interested in a liberal Unionist party. The O'Neillite campaign, in Derry at least, expressed liberal sentiments which had rarely been so clearly heard during the previous six years of O'Neill's leadership.

In contrast, Albert Anderson, who had always been fond of the rhetoric of reconciliation and cross-border co-operation and had been at the centre of highly publicised 'reconciliation' trips to Dublin and Galway, was pulled sharply to the right in the course of the election.[43]

Most of those who backed Anderson in the election were united by their fear that the civil rights campaign masked a conspiracy to destroy Northern Ireland. Although Albert Anderson's personal conspiracy theories may not have been shared by all those who backed him, they give a flavour of the confused paranoia of many right-wing Unionists at the time. Trying to make sense of the recent unrest in Derry, Anderson told his fellow Unionists in the Waterside that 'Londonderry was chosen as the flashpoint for all Ulster. Flashpoints were chosen for all other parts of the British Isles and Europe, but Derry was the place in which to make a start ... the people behind this ... are not just people with a spontaneous cause. There was a planned campaign of people who called themselves revolutionary socialists, anarchists, communists and whatever you like.'[44] Later, a colleague of his from North Derry put it more bluntly when sharing a platform with Anderson at a local Unionist Association meeting near Derry. 'This is not a question of Roman Catholic versus Protestant', he said, 'This is a Communist-controlled affair from start to finish.'[45]

Once Anderson and other Unionists began to interpret the course of events in terms of a smoothly running plot, a tightly controlled and well-planned conspiracy, they inevitably became converts to repression. The fact that such theories multiplied out of control among Unionists testifies to their lack of understanding of what was happening in the Catholic community and inevitably damaged their ability to respond to the crisis.

Even before he had been formally selected as the Unionist candidate in Derry, Anderson's election campaign was launched at a huge rally in the Apprentice Boys Memorial Hall, organised by the Derry Young Unionists. The hall was full to overflowing. Over 1,000 people were there, spilling over into the street.[46] It represented a populist revival for the Unionist party organisation in Derry.

At the rally it became clear what the driving forces behind this Unionist revival were. Some, but only a few, of the old Unionist Corporators were there. But leaders of the Apprentice Boys and the Orange Order were prominent as were the Young Unionists. Membership of the Loyal Orders, particularly among younger people, was growing steadily in response to the increasing tension.[47] The Young Unionists had been weak in Derry as recently as 1967 when the sole branch in the city was 'in a precarious condition'. Because of a Unionist party recruitment drive and then the outbreak of unrest there were six branches in Derry by 1970.[48] The Young Unionists were younger, often working-class, Protestants, whose first political experiences were the civil rights marches and the counter-demonstrations. Some would go on to join the DUP.[49] If the party hierarchy was happy to get this new support, it was hardly in control of it and while much of the leadership remained, the party in Derry had been drastically changed.

The rally was addressed by the right-wing Stormont MPs William Craig and Harry West. They both described the civil rights movement as a cover for an IRA conspiracy. Also on the platform were Russell Abernethy, Gerald Glover and former councillor Alfred Wallace, the head of the 'Londonderry Loyalist Committee', established by the Londonderry UA. The fear was of 'conspiracy'; the solution was to be swift repression.[50] The meeting seems to have been dominated by a certain sense of desperation, perhaps heightened by the fact that the corporation was to be abolished in several weeks time and there was deep uncertainty about the future.

The mood at the rally was tense and when two people at the back of the hall declined to stand when Craig walked up to speak, their chairs were pulled from under them, they were jeered and a chair was thrown at them before they were escorted from the meeting.[51] Such aggression was a novelty for Derry's staid Unionists. It marks another sharp break with the 'respectable' confident Unionist party of the past.

There were more signs of tension a few days later when the Derry Unionist council met at Unionist party headquarters in the Fountain to choose between Anderson and Campbell. Outside the building about a hundred Young Unionists stood and jeered. An egg was thrown at Campbell supporters and they were poked with an umbrella. The Young Unionists then besieged Campbell supporters inside for a couple of hours. During this mini-siege, a local press photographer had to escape from the scene by climbing on to the roof of the building and making his way across the rooftops of the little houses in the Fountain.[52]

It was a measure of Protestant frustration that the press itself now became a focus for resentment and aggression. Unionists resented the contribution which the media had made to the cause of 'civil rights' by the simple fact of reporting it. Hostility to the media was not due to the tone of media coverage alone but to the very fact of media coverage of Catholic grievances. After attacks on their members at Unionist meetings in Derry and Limavady, the Northwest Ireland branch of the National Union of Journalists threatened to cease covering events held by these local Unionist associations.[53]

The violence associated with the anti-O'Neill Unionists during this election campaign forced many middle-class and wealthy Protestants out of the party and out of politics altogether. The experience of the Campbell campaigners in the Irish Street Estate during that campaign must have been particularly disenchanting. As a group of canvassers made their way through the loyalist estate, a group of youths shouting 'Up Anderson' and 'Up Paisley' began to hurl bricks and stones at them before surrounding and kicking Lady Campbell's car and spitting through the windows at those inside.[54] The humiliation of the experience must have been a powerful incentive for these upper- and middle-class Unionists, who had been involved in the commercial and political life of the city for decades, to abandon the Unionist party once O'Neill had fallen.

However, the contest for the City of Londonderry seat was not a straight fight between two brands of Unionism. There was a third candidate, Claude Wilton, a member of the tiny Ulster Liberal party, a solicitor who had represented many people from the Bogside, and who was a Presbyterian. Most recently, he had been a prominent member of the Derry Citizens Action Committee. He had contested the seat in 1965 and had come close to unseating the sitting Unionist, winning the Catholic vote and the vote of Protestants disgruntled over the university issue.[55] Even O'Neillite Unionists were now appalled at the prospect of a split in the Unionist vote that might allow Wilton to win the seat.[56] Wilton supporters, on the other hand, were horrified that the best chance he was likely to get to unseat Anderson was being wrecked by members of the Unionist establishment in the city who were now claiming to be 'liberals' and were trying to get Catholics in the constituency to vote for them.[57]

The constituency was just under 40 per cent Catholic, and if the O'Neillites could get a respectable percentage of this vote, they could probably be assured of winning the seat. Some prominent Catholics did throw in their lot with the O'Neillites, creating yet more bitterness among supporters of Wilton.[58] When the election failed to secure O'Neill's leadership of the Unionist party, there were those Unionists who apportioned part of the blame to the failure of Catholics to support O'Neill in sufficient numbers,[59] to not dare to make the step across the historical divide and vote for liberal Unionists in the interests of progress. In the circumstances in Derry, where Catholics had the option of voting for a proven liberal like Wilton or supporting an aristocratic 'liberal' Unionist backed by much of the old Unionist hierarchy in the city, it is little surprise that Wilton, the Liberal (with a big *L*), candidate took virtually all of the crucial Catholic vote in the election. Wilton had always been associated with the Catholic vote in the area to an extent parodied in the unofficial election slogan, 'Vote for Claude, the Catholic Prod'.[60]

With the vote split three ways, Anderson won the seat, taking about 40 per cent of the vote, that is, about two-thirds of the Protestant vote. Virtually all of the Catholic vote went to Wilton, who got 35 per cent while his liberal Protestant supporters seem to have defected to the O'Neillite, Peter Campbell, who took 25 per cent of the vote, thus ensuring that Wilton could not win the seat. Campbell appears to have taken some Catholic votes as well (perhaps a few hundred) and it was probably the first time a Unionist in Derry had ever achieved this.[61]

Class

In the course of the battle for the City of Londonderry seat, Ulster Liberal Claude Wilton was moved to wonder aloud where all those local 'liberals' now supporting O'Neill and Campbell had been for the previous twenty years.[62] The fact was that, apart from anger at the Stormont decision in 1965 not to site the new university in Derry and Campbell Austin's resignation from the corporation over a zoning decision in 1966, most of them had been contented Unionists who had made little attempt to change the *status quo*. Why some Derry Unionists should support O'Neills reform strategy while others opposed it bitterly as a betrayal of Unionism had less to do with idealistic liberalism than with commercial interests and class.

For example, among the most enthusiastic campaigners for Peter Campbell were T.F. Cooke, chairman of the Londonderry Port and

Harbour Commission, a body which was elected solely by Derry's *male* business owners,[63] Gerald Black, recently elected president of the Derry Chamber of Commerce,[64] and Campbell Austin, owner of Austin's of the Diamond, the biggest department store in the city. For many Unionist businessmen in Derry, a central issue raised by the recent crisis was how to restore the conditions for peaceful and prosperous trading which had been severely disrupted by rioting. They were not as inclined as others to concern themselves with elaborate theories of Republican conspiracy.

After the first outbreak of rioting in Derry, the *Londonderry Sentinel* had remarked of the civil rights marchers who were baton-charged by the RUC in Duke Street that, 'those demonstrators did not resort to attacking property; for that they must be given credit', but the paper was less tolerant of the 'immature' rioters in the Bogside who 'indiscriminately lobbed stones and missiles at shop windows'.[65] This displays a set of priorities probably shared by many of the shop-owners of Derry city centre. These shop-owners, whose property was damaged during riots and whose trade was suffering because people were reluctant to shop in the city centre, were exposed to the immediate consequences of the civil unrest. In addition, in a town such as Derry, many Protestant businessmen in the city centre relied to a great extent on Catholic custom and would be wary of a strategy of total repression which might alienate the Catholic community in the city.

They were thus more prepared than other Unionists to support a strategy which, though it might endanger Unionist hegemony in local government, could end the unrest and restore the conditions for prosperous trading. In their outlook, which was to an extent cosmopolitan and which sought to make the Unionist party more like the British Conservative party, they came close to the 'moderate', 'British' Unionism which both Aughey[66] and Todd[67] describe from different angles. It is worth noting that most of these 'British' Unionists, while roused by the university issue, had operated with minimal complaint in the local party for decades.

The shop-owners and businessmen of the city centre had formed an important and prominent section of the Unionist party in Derry for decades, dominating the corporation. During this election a large group of them actively supported the pro-O'Neill candidate while only a few supported Anderson. After the election they were left in a political limbo, alienated from the local party hierarchy. Some of them made bitter statements claiming that they had been the financial backbone of the party. When the local party was comprehensively taken over by the right-wingers two years later and the last old O'Neillites withdrew, they claimed that the Unionist party in Derry would now get into financial difficulty.[68] After the 1969 Stormont election, many of the most prosperous upper- and middle-class sponsors of the Unionist party in Derry simply dropped out of the party, after having dominated it for half a century. Those who their loyalist opponents referred to dismissively as the 'fur-coat brigade' withdrew from involvement in politics – for good, as it turned out.[69]

This process did not, however, transform the Unionist party into a working-class movement. The leadership were still well-to-do businessmen or professionals but the abandonment of the party by most of the city fathers forced those who remained in control of the party to look to the Protestant working class in a variety of ways and to forge links with the Paisleyites. This process moved the Unionist party in Derry decisively to the right, towards the conspiracy theorists and the advocates of repression, away from those who sought pragmatic compromises. As Unionist political power and influence in Derry became ever weaker, it was increasingly dominated by elements whose central concern was for more repression.

But if support for the pro-O'Neill candidate was concentrated among the relatively small aristocracy and the Protestant middle class in the city, Albert Anderson was not exactly a working-class candidate either. Like his pro-O'Neill opponent, Anderson had served as an officer in the British armed forces, and he too had family connections in the Unionist party. His father before him had served as both mayor and Stormont MP for Derry.[70] What distinguished Anderson's well-off supporters was that they had more of a stake in the maintenance of direct Unionist control of local government in Derry and relied more on the continuance of local Unionist party patronage than their O'Neillite opponents did. In this respect, it is probably worth noting that both Anderson and Glover had been publicly accused of using their membership of the corporation to further their own business interests.[71]

As important as this close interest in the maintenance of Unionist control of local government was the fact that the right-wing Unionist leadership in Derry was prominently involved in the Apprentice Boys and the Orange Order in the city. This involvement with the Loyal Orders, which had a much heavier working-class representation than the Unionist party itself,[72] no doubt made them more aware of the fears of the Protestant loyalist working class and less distanced from the fears of conspiracy and collapse which were gaining ground in this community. Working-class Protestants certainly stood to lose out in real terms if the Unionist party lost control of local government in Derry. The fact that they would no longer have a corporation sympathetic to them as a group, no longer a corporation controlled by a party intimately linked to the Loyal Orders and thus directly to them, had a special impact on that section of the Protestant community which relied most on public housing and the prospects of public employment. Also important were the close links between the Unionist right wing and the B-Specials. The Ulster Special Constabulary was an even more strongly working-class institution than the Orders, and it was explicitly devoted to combating the IRA. The O'Neill supporters in Derry were far less involved with these determinedly Protestant, heavily working-class organisations.[73]

This network of contacts in the Loyal Orders and the B-Specials gave the right-wing Unionists a far wider range of contacts and a much broader base for political support than the O'Neill supporters could muster. Given the infrequency of electoral contests, there was no section of the party with a great deal of experience of democratic mobilisation and electioneering but because of their connections, the right-wingers were probably the section of the party in Derry best able to adapt to the demands of contesting elections and canvassing popular support. They were able to use these networks to mobilise support and organise rallies.

In addition, the Anderson campaign, as an anti-O'Neill campaign, benefited from the gradually growing political support for Ian Paisley in the city, particularly in working-class estates. When Stormont MP John Taylor spoke at a Unionist party meeting in Derry shortly after the election and condemned Paisley as well as O'Neill, it provoked shouts of 'Up Paisley' from the floor, indicating that the right-wing Unionists were enjoying the tactical support of many who clearly saw Ian Paisley as the real saviour of Unionism.[74]

While the 1969 Stormont election produced a victory for Anderson in Derry, it hardly represents an emphatic rejection of reform by Derry Protestants, particularly as Anderson himself had proclaimed himself a supporter of the November reforms and of 'reconciliation'. What it does show is the importance of local party hierarchies to the anti-O'Neill campaign. In their campaign against O'Neill, the Londonderry UA acted not as the local branch of a political party but as the political wing of a local Protestant ethnic alliance just as it was designed to be decades before. The battle for the Unionist party in Derry was waged as much within the Apprentice Boys and the Orange Order as it was in the Unionist party.

While hardly a working-class phenomenon, the anti-O'Neill campaign in February 1969 did represent a sentiment that was stronger among the Protestant working class than among the middle class, that enough ground had been conceded to the civil rights campaign, that peace would not be achieved through further reform but that it could, and should, be achieved through repression as had been the case in the 1920s, the 1940s and the 1950s.

Social activism: adapting to the new order

As the Unionist party lurched from one internal split to another and rioting in the Bogside became a regular event in the spring and summer of 1969, new forms of organisation developed in the Protestant community in Derry. With the dissolution of the Unionist corporation in April 1969, Derry Protestants, particularly in working-class areas, found themselves in need of political intermediaries with the new power in the city, the Londonderry Development Commission which had replaced the corporation. This need was made ever more urgent by the spread of rioting and civil unrest which created a range of new problems for the Protestant community and raised fears of sectarian attacks on exposed Protestant areas. The Unionist party in Derry had been a party of power and, when it lost power, many of its bewildered and elderly councillors simply dropped out of politics. The abandonment of the party by much of its old hierarchy left Protestants feeling leaderless and vulnerable.[75]

Some Unionists turned to the sort of clientelist constituency work characteristic of local electoral politics elsewhere. In Derry, where Unionist councillors had seldom faced the electorate, and had rarely had to mobilise popular support, this was a distinctly novel development. As various new forms of political action emerged in the Protestant community, the class divisions in Unionism which had emerged during the recent election were reinforced and Unionist activism at ground level became ever more 'proletarianised'.

In the course of the 1960s, a variety of community organisations had been set up in Catholic areas in Derry to take local action on a range of pressing social issues such as housing, public transport or the need for play areas. Many of those who had been involved in these initiatives went on to provide leadership for the civil rights campaign.[76] But it was only after the fall of the Unionist corporation that these sort of autonomous local groups began to be established in Protestant areas of Derry for the first time. For example, although several tenants' associations existed in Catholic areas of Derry by 1968, it took the fall of the Unionist corporation to create the space for the first tenants' association in a Protestant area of Derry. However, the tenants' associations which were now being set up in Protestant areas were not inspired by the motives which had inspired those in the Creggan and Bogside. Their development illustrates how the Protestant working class moved to the right even as it emerged as a political force for the first time in decades.

The first tenants' association to be set up in a Protestant area of Derry was the Lisnagelvin tenants' association, established in the staunchly loyalist Irish Street Estate in the spring of 1969, shortly after the abolition of the corporation. It was established by a former Unionist councillor, Leonard Hutchinson (who lived in a middle-class area some distance away) and by James Wallace, a prominent member of the Apprentice Boys[77] and later of the Unionist party,[78] who lived on the estate. The first public act of the association was to call for an end to a recent spate of graffiti-writing on the estate.[79] Rioting and the breakdown of social order in other parts of the city, and also the loosening of loyalty to the old monolithic Unionist hierarchy, had had an effect on Protestant youths in such areas. The opposition to civil rights demonstrations and then the election campaign had given these youths their first opportunity to become involved in Unionist politics, on the streets. The tenants' association was impelled at least partly by the desire to fill the political vacuum in the Protestant community left by the abolition of the corporation and to ensure that there was not a breakdown in social control.

The first public meeting of the association was directly related to the civil unrest. On 14 July 1969, Derry experienced its first large-scale sectarian clashes when several hundred people gathered on each side of Bishop Street where the Protestant Fountain met the Catholic Long Tower.[80] Many of the crowd on both sides had come from other areas and many of those in the Fountain had journeyed over from the Irish Street Estate in the Waterside. Prominent Unionists and Apprentice Boys had tried to prevent trouble at the interface on previous nights and it was these groups, along with representatives of the Lisnagelvin tenants' association, who organised a public meeting in Irish Street on the night of 14 July. There they appealed for local Protestant youths not to go over to the Fountain to take part in rioting.[81] At a further meeting a few days later, the tenants' association praised the RUC for their action during recent riots, blamed the violence in the city on 'vandals fanning out from the Bogside' (implicitly absolving Protestant youths of blame), but also urged local parents to keep their children from going to troublespots such as the Fountain to take part in sectarian rioting.[82] In the coming months, prominent Unionists were active in the estate trying to stop local youths stoning passing buses full of Catholics[83] and it seems clear that many Unionists were deeply concerned at the breakdown in respect for law and order in some Protestant working-class areas. To some extent at least the tenants' association was a product of this concern.

While the central concerns of the Lisnagelvin Tenants' Association were a far cry from the usual concerns of a tenants' association, it was exactly the sort of ground-level organisation which Protestants in Derry looked to in the new uncertain situation. The fact that it was led by authority figures from longstanding institutions such as the Apprentice Boys and the Unionist party rather than by the sort of local community activists who had emerged in Catholic areas over the previous decade ensured that, while it addressed issues of importance to the Protestant working class in a way which the Unionist party had not done, it would remain an essentially conservative body.

The Derry Young Unionists who had been so prominent in the anti-O'Neill election campaign were the first group in the Protestant community to imitate the radical 'action' groups which had been so important in Catholic areas of the city. The Londonderry Young Unionist Housing Action Committee (hereafter YUHAC, named with deliberate irony after the Derry Housing Action Committee, the organisers of the first civil rights march in the city), was in existence by June 1969. Since the Development Commission had taken over from the corporation in April, groups from the Catholic community had sent delegations to the commission and presented their grievances and their concerns. The YUHAC now became the very first Protestant group to send a delegation to the Development Commission.[84] At that meeting they asked for information about specific housing allocations in Derry, and it seems likely they were concerned that Catholics were now being allocated houses in mainly Protestant estates on the West Bank. Their public demand of a few weeks previously for a fair points system in the city can probably best be understood in the light of these concerns.[85] But the Young Unionists went a little beyond this sort of sectarian rearguard action with their announcement that they aimed to get landlords in the city to reduce rents in poor housing and to improve the upkeep of properties.[86] This statement was probably intended to emphasise that Catholics were not the only ones in poor housing conditions in Derry and, therefore, that claims of discrimination were unsustainable. However, such proposals had disruptive implications for a local Unionist party which was top heavy with landlords, chief among them Gerald Glover.

When the committee called on the Derry Unionist Association, headed by Gerald Glover, to speak out about the poor housing conditions which many Protestants had to suffer in Derry, the Middle Liberties Young Unionists, who had very strong links to William Craig and the leadership of the party in Derry, pulled out of the committee,[87] probably because of the implied criticism of the local leadership.

When sectarian rioting broke out in mid-July 1969, the Young Unionists took their first direct action, helping six Protestant families to squat in houses in the Fountain, saying they had moved the families for 'both protection and better accommodation'. While three of the families had moved from Catholic areas of Derry where they had experienced some form of sectarian intimidation, the other three families had simply been living in poor or expensive housing in Protestant areas and had not been affected by the civil unrest. The Young Unionists promised to resist attempts to evict these families and began collecting rent from the families to cover the cost of back rent and possible fines.[88] These tactics had been used by radical groups in Catholic areas of the city, often with great success. The Young Unionists, however, were not to be so successful. They could hardly expect support from the local Unionist party organisation whose leaders may well have owned some of the squatted houses. And they were isolated in a community where respect for the rule of law and for private property was still strong. For many Protestants such action was still seen as being disreputable by its very nature. In the summer of 1969, there was little local reaction in the Fountain as the squatters were visited by the owners of the houses and, despite the fact that some of them were 'refugees' from 'rebellion', were taken to court, found guilty and fined.[89]

When trouble broke out again in August 1969, some Protestant residents of the predominantly Catholic Long Tower area represented their own case for rehousing to the Londonderry Development Commission.[90] This was a further erosion of Protestant reluctance to deal with the Development Commission, to organise for collective action.

The toppling of the corporation had given Protestants the freedom to demand things from their local authority, but it was a freedom they were unaccustomed to and they were slow to take advantage of it. But certain inhibitions about complaining or criticising did break down. In early 1970, for example, the *Londonderry Sentinel* criticised poor housing conditions in a corporation-built estate and, a week later, supported calls for the demolition of houses in another area of the city.[91] The paper which had devoted years to defending the housing situation in the city now finally found it acceptable to criticise it. In the summer of 1970, the Unionist Association in Derry finally recognised the importance of this social issue by establishing a party 'Housing Committee'.[92]

But if public housing was a working-class issue it was also a sectarian issue and as Protestants organised to get concessions from housing authorities they also organised to maintain the 'Protestant' make-up of their estates.[93] In Derry, systematic integration would theoretically leave Protestants in a minority in every estate. Such a development would, at the very least, have a devastating effect on popular loyalist culture in the city. The Unionist corporation had maintained housing segregation for years but with its demise, segregation would have to be maintained by other means. Only gradually would statutory bodies accept that segregated estates should be preserved.[94] The Unionist party and the new local organisations became implicated in this process. The first reports that Catholics were being intimidated out of the Irish Street Estate appeared directly after the 'Battle of the Bogside', in August 1969, but were denied by the Lisnagelvin tenants' association.[95] In November 1969, a Catholic family did leave the estate after attacks on their house and car,[96] while in the Fountain a local Protestant was jailed for sectarian intimidation.[97]

When a mixed-marriage couple with one child (and expecting another) were allocated a house in Irish Street Estate by the Development Commission in June 1970, a crowd of about fifty people gathered outside the house in the night and smashed the windows.[98] Locals complained that the couple should not have been entitled to the house, having only one child, but the sectarian implications are obvious. It is most unlikely that a Protestant family would have been attacked in the same way. The commission said the family were entitled to the house because their previous accommodation had been so poor.[99]

The reaction of the housing committee of the Londonderry Unionist Association was to call on the Stormont development minister, Brian Faulkner, to set up an official inquiry, no less, into how the decision had been made to allocate the house to this family. They mentioned the violence, not to condemn it, but only to say that this allocation decision 'had led to ill-feeling and a deterioration in good community relations in the estate'.[100] The head of the Lisnagelvin tenants' association attacked the Development Commission for what he called an 'unimaginative' allocation, claiming that local anger was due to the small size of the family, not to their religion.[101] Clearly the Unionist party in Derry were beginning to treat acts of sectarian violence as 'understandable' responses to fears of Catholic encroachment. A tenants' association which had first been established to combat graffiti-writing now viewed window-smashing with relative equanimity.

In addition to their concern with the maintenance of Protestant 'turf', the Lisnagelvin Tenants' Association and those which emulated it in other Protestant areas of the city, were set apart from their counterparts in the Bogside and Creggan by a cautious conservatism and a certain reluctance to challenge or make excessive demands on the state. Although the Lisnagelvin Tenants' Association did develop links with tenants' associations in Catholic areas, there was considerable friction[102] and their different attitudes to the state and the proper limits of protest set a limit to joint action. For example, when the other tenants' associations in Derry decided to call a rent strike over the issue of repairs in January 1970, the Lisnagelvin Tenants' Association only reluctantly joined and then called off its strike before the others did.[103] Protestants were caught between the need to make demands on the state over public resources (such as housing) and the danger of in any way destabilising the state. While activists in the Catholic community were content to push out the boundaries of protest, unconcerned, to say the least, with the effect on the security of Northern Ireland as a state, Protestants were inhibited in their protests by the danger of the state collapsing.

Paisleyism

Although Ian Paisley and his supporters had led the initial opposition to the civil rights movement in Derry in 1968 and gathered a measure of local support, there was only sporadic activity by Paisleyites in Derry through most of 1969 while the small Paisleyite organisation in Derry tinkered with a variety of different names. During the summer of 1969, it was people associated with the Unionist party and the Loyal Orders who were most involved in street-level activism in Derry.

In the months following the 'Battle of the Bogside' in August 1969, however, there was an increase in Paisleyite activity in the city by the Ulster Protestant Volunteers (hereafter UPV). This activity was headed by a local graduate of Queen's University, Belfast,[104] Gordon Hegarty, and not by outsiders as the early demonstrations had been. Although Ian Paisley had addressed social issues in his election campaign in Bannside in 1969, the UPV was not greatly concerned with such issues at this stage.[105]

In February 1970, the Derry UPV held their first locally led public rally. At the rally, Gordon Hegarty demanded first and foremost that normal policing be restored in the Bogside and Creggan. Rejecting claims of discrimination against Catholics, he said that high Catholic unemployment was simply a product of Catholic attempts to 'out-breed' Protestants. Calling Northern Ireland 'the Protestant quarter of Ireland', he suggested that the Irish government build a 'Craigavon': a new town in Co. Donegal to house Derry Catholics.[106]

The Paisleyite cause received a major boost in April 1970 when Ian Paisley and a colleague were elected to Stormont at by-elections. This hailed Ian Paisley's entry into parliamentary politics and it illustrated that Northern Protestants were deeply unhappy about the uncertain situation in Northern Ireland and were losing confidence in the Unionist party. It was seen by most outside opinion as a disaster.

Although the UPV continued to operate after these elections, there was a move towards a more formal political organisation with the establishment of the Protestant Unionist Association (hereafter PUA), the forerunner of the DUP. In Derry both groups were run by more or less the same small group of people and, as the Westminster elections of June 1970 approached, those people began to flex their political muscles in Derry for the first time. The PUA in Derry was still a small, marginal organisation, centred on a few individuals and one particular family which had converted to Free Presbyterianism.[107] Its successor, the DUP, would remain a marginal force in the city into the mid-1970s.[108] Where they did gain importance now was from their potential to split the Protestant vote, allowing anti-Unionist candidates to win and thus depriving the Unionist party of parliamentary seats.

The Westminster seat which covered Derry city and county had a modest Unionist majority and was held by Robin Chichester-Clark, a right-winger who had tried to walk the fine line between pro- and anti-O'Neill factions in 1969. His campaign was being run mostly by Derry city Unionists who had taken the anti-O'Neill side in 1969. Among them were prominent members of the Loyal Orders and one of his nomination papers represented the Apprentice Boys of Derry.[109]

In June 1970, shortly before the election, the PUA in Derry announced that they were considering nominating for election, the Reverend Wylie of Coleraine, a Free Presbyterian minister prominent in the early Paisleyite demonstrations in Derry city.[110] If Wylie had stood, it might well have cost Clark the seat. It was fortunate for the Unionists that the PUA did not stand a candidate but instead announced their support for Robin Chichester-Clark. Suspicion was rife that the Unionist party across the North had made a deal with the Paisleyites,[111] something which at that stage the party still felt obliged to deny. In Northern Ireland as a whole, only two Unionist candidates took it upon themselves to criticise Paisleyism during the campaign while the ongoing reform programme was mentioned by none of them.[112] It was widely believed at the time that Unionist party strategy depended on, and was simply waiting for, the election to power of a Conservative government in Britain which would give the Unionists a free hand to clamp down on the no-go areas and resurgent Republicanism, thus ending divisions in the party.

Ian Paisley himself issued a statement claiming that the Unionist party had made a deal with the PUA in Derry.[113] His statement claimed that the PUA had negotiated with Gerald Glover, Russell Abernethy, Jim Guy and others associated with the anti-O'Neill section and with the Loyal Orders. Paisley said these Unionists had negotiated not only with Gordon Hegarty but also with members of the Hay family who had moved from the Unionist party to the UPV and PUA. Months later Guy and Glover claimed that they had never negotiated with the PUA but only with the UPV.[114] The difference is academic as the two organisations were headed by the same individuals; there can be little doubt that a deal was made with the Paisleyites.

Events during this Westminster election went a long way towards convincing Catholics that the Unionist party government, and therefore the British government which was backing them, could not be trusted. It was hard for the Unionist party to pretend to any sort of 'neutral' liberalism when Unionist candidates either avoided criticism of Paisley or actively co-operated with Paisleyites to win seats. Still, at this stage, the taboo against weakening Unionist unity and continued Protestant inhibitions about the sort of tactics the Paisleyites were prepared to use, such as their poorly supported sit-ins,[115] ensured that the PUA would remain at the political margins in Derry for some time to come. The social activism which would later win the DUP working-class support was as yet little in evidence in Derry.

The Alliance party

The Alliance party of Northern Ireland was established at the beginning of 1970 as an anti-sectarian, liberal, pro-union party, embodying the liberal ideals of what Todd has called 'British Unionism'[116] which many had associated with Terence O'Neill. In the event, those prominent Derry Unionists who had backed O'Neill in early 1969 declined to become involved in the Alliance party and the party in Derry was not a direct successor to moderate Unionism although it may have been elsewhere.

After the bitter 1969 election, those many prominent Derry Unionists who had supported O'Neill withdrew from the party. They did not, however, withdraw from politics altogether. They met regularly and were, as they put it, 'active behind the scenes', meeting with church leaders and with the Development Commission over housing allocations, for example.[117] They established the Londonderry Parliamentary Association (claiming at one stage 200 members) to formalise this activity. At the first meeting of the association, the defeated O'Neillite candidate, Peter Campbell, called for the Unionist party to become part of the British Conservative party and to break its links with the Orange Order. Condemning the lack of democracy within the party, he expressed support for the new Unionist prime minister, James Chichester-Clark. This first meeting thus had a decidedly 'Unionist' atmosphere, with attendance dominated by Unionist businessmen. There was even an Independent Unionist MP to lend credence to the prevailing conspiracy theories by saying 'we are in the grip of highly-trained professional agitators'.[118] However, it is also clear that the establishment of this group meant that these O'Neillites had left behind all hope of a reconciliation with the local Unionist party leadership. Instead it seems likely they harboured the hope of eventually supplanting it.

Although the association was established by Unionists, it drew in a substantial number of Catholic professionals and businessmen in the city[119] who saw in the association a form of Unionism they could support. The association in Derry gradually developed links with the New Ulster Movement, which contained the seeds of the Alliance party and when a branch of the Alliance party was set up in Derry in May 1970 it was welcomed by the association.[120] Virtually all of the Catholics who had joined the association now joined the Alliance party but barely a single O'Neillite Unionist joined the party that was seen by many as the successor to O'Neillism.[121] Protestant support for the Alliance party in Derry was concentrated, not among former O'Neillites, but rather among liberal-minded Protestant professionals who had been largely uninvolved in local politics prior to this.[122] The Alliance party in Derry was born not out of the O'Neillite legacy but out of the new involvement of those middle-class people, Catholic and Protestant, who had never seen a role for themselves in the tight confrontational politics of the city before this.

The O'Neillite Unionists may have declined to join the Alliance party simply because they couldn't bring themselves to join a party which would be critical of the Chichester-Clark Unionist government or of the Unionist legacy in the city. They still could not bring themselves to oppose the Unionist party. In addition, as evidenced by their interest in the Conservative party, these O'Neillites were not particularly 'Liberal' and may have been uncomfortable in a liberal-minded party.

Various O'Neillite Unionists continued to make political statements into 1971, suggesting at one stage that they might set up a local branch of the British Conservative party.[123] But eventually these Unionists withdrew from the political life of the city, some to the extent of physically leaving the city, while some became involved in unelected tiers of local government such as the newly established area boards. By then, Unionist politics had become almost a disreputable pursuit for the Protestant middle class.[124]

In the end the Alliance party in Derry came to be identified primarily with the Catholic middle class. It is ironic that two of the senior members of the Alliance party in Derry, Dr Jim Cosgrove and Ivor Canavan, were the brothers of two senior SDLP figures in the city, Dr Joe Cosgrove and Michael Canavan. This, added to the fact that the party was virtually devoid of former Unionists, may have added to the impression of the party in Derry as a Catholic-dominated group.[125] If it was seen as an unsuitable vehicle even for O'Neillite Unionists, then the party, particularly in a time of great Protestant fear, would find it hard to get Protestant votes. Much as was the case with the Northern Ireland Labour Party, the Alliance party gathered most of its support in Belfast from Protestants and in Derry from Catholics, from the more secure community which could afford a little flexibility in its political preferences.

When it came to Catholic votes, the Alliance party was in competition with the SDLP and while the party was distinguished from Unionism by its anti-sectarianism and liberalism, it was distinguished from the SDLP principally in its commitment to the maintenance of the Union. While a great many Catholics may not have been bothered by 'the Union', at the same time it had never been a big vote-getter in Catholic areas. Ultimately, the Alliance party lost out to the SDLP in Catholic areas while in Protestant areas its make-up did not look sufficiently 'Unionist' to warrant the leap of trust required to switch from the Unionist party.

The Alliance party also suffered greatly from a lack of ground-level organisation in working-class areas and attention to clientelist politics[126] which the SDLP and even the Unionist party were now concerning themselves with. By the time the Alliance party did become involved in tenants' associations and clientelism in 1973,[127] most community groups had built up strong links with other political parties.

The Londonderry Development Commission

When it was announced in the very first wave of reforms in November 1968 that the Derry Corporation and Rural District Council were to be abolished and replaced by a Londonderry Development Commission (hereafter LDC) made up of government appointees, Derry Unionists mourned the end of the corporation and predicted that 'the new heart will never beat as loyally as the old heart'.[128]

Although initially resistant, after a while Unionists began to see the benefits of the commission, not least in the fact that it had prevented an immediate switch to Catholic control of the city. And so the Unionists began to assimilate the LDC, according it retrospective legitimacy. In a remarkably disingenuous editorial, the *Londonderry Sentinel* treated the establishment of the LDC as a victory for Derry Unionism, claiming that it was in effect the 'New Town Commission' to speed up local development, which had been recommended in the report of a corporation steering committee a few years previously.[129] Thus, Unionists could accept the abolition of the corporation while still not acknowledging that there had been any validity to Catholic claims of gerrymandering and discrimination.

There were some Unionist complaints of course: complaints that none of the old corporation members, with all their experience, had been chosen for the commission[130] and that some of the local Protestant businessmen appointed to the commission had previously 'refused to serve on the corporation';[131] that is, they had turned down Unionist party invitations to take a seat on the corporation. There were still many Unionists who refused to accord legitimacy to the commission, and while groups from Catholic areas made regular appeals to the commission from its first week in office, Protestants only reluctantly and gradually began to make demands on the commission.[132] As the commission came to be accepted, local Unionist attention was directed towards pondering the future after the commission. There was a genuine Protestant fear that if Catholics took control of local government they would 'sock it to us as they think we've been socking it to them'.[133] It was that specific deeply rooted fear that John Hume had been addressing during the civil rights campaign when he said, 'when we get our civil rights there will be no revenge'.[134]

In any case, Unionists in Derry began to come up with a series of proposals to ensure that the temptation to 'revenge' would never be placed in front of Derry Catholics. While there was an element of pure fantasy in the ideas for the future which surfaced in Unionist circles in Derry, these ideas were also a measure of the possibilities for restoring Unionist control, even of Derry, which local Unionists felt were still open to them in 1970 and 1971. It also emphasises that, right up until the abolition of Stormont in March 1972, many Unionists were trying to roll back the gains made by the civil rights movement.

A month before the Development Commission took over from the corporation in 1969, the *Londonderry Sentinel* expressed the opinion that all local government in the North should be abolished and that all of Northern Ireland should be ruled directly from Stormont.[135] A week later, the *Londonderry Sentinel* mentioned in passing that an old corporation area plan had suggested that any New Town Commission for Derry should extend twenty miles into the countryside, to Strabane and Limavady.[136] Such an area, if its boundaries were delineated creatively, could well have secured Unionist control of the city. If the new Derry area was restricted to the old corporation and rural district areas covered by the commission, it would certainly be Catholic-controlled.

Those who feared that Unionists might try to implement a new gerrymander once the media attention generated by the civil rights campaign had died down had some justification for their fears.[137] Virtually all of the civil rights demands, from an end to discrimination to the call for 'one person, one vote', were connected to Unionist control of local government. If Unionists could re-organise local government to their own satisfaction, the effects of the civil rights campaign on Unionist control of local government could be obviated.

The *Londonderry Sentinel* reiterated its call for the complete abolition of all local government structures and in, June 1969, called on the government to 'wipe out the councils', ostensibly because it was an 'age of amalgamation'.[138] Of course these schemes had the attraction for Unionists in western Ulster and in Derry in particular that never again would any part of Northern Ireland be controlled by Catholics at any level.

A month later, in July 1969, the Stormont government published its proposals for the re-organisation of local government, the Macrory Report, and it was clear that there was little chance for the *Londonderry Sentinel*'s dream plan. The Macrory Report would have handed Derry over to Catholic control but it minimised the area thus controlled, limiting it to the area covered by the Development Commission. Thus, while Derry city council was to cover 20 per cent of Co. Derry, Protestant-controlled Coleraine Council, centred around the modestly sized and mainly Protestant market town of Coleraine, would cover the other 80 per cent, and parts of other counties too.[139] If Derry Catholics were outraged at the plans, Derry city Unionists must have felt as though they had been thrown to the wolves.

Thus both Unionist and Catholic political groups in Derry complained that the proposed Derry Council area was too small. Gerald Glover, head of the Unionist association in the city, said that the number of councils should be reduced from the seventeen suggested by Macrory to between three and six,[140] a course which would have allowed Unionists to regain control of Derry. The *Londonderry Sentinel* agreed.[141] It had become clear, however, that the Unionist leadership in Belfast was not prepared to stick its neck out for the Derry Unionists who, on realising this, began to fix their hopes for the future on the Development Commission. If Derry was to be controlled by Catholics it should be delayed as long as possible, the area it covered should be as small as possible and the new council in Catholic hands should have as few powers as possible.

In early 1970, the Stormont government stripped local authorities of many of their powers, a process which had been ongoing but which was convenient for Unionists in Derry. While the move brought strong opposition from some Unionist quarters in Northern Ireland (from the Orange Order in particular)[142] the *Londonderry Sentinel* welcomed the move.[143] Catholics would never control the life of the city as the Unionists had done. Above all, they would not control housing.

But while certain powers were being centralised, others were being diffused to area boards with powers over areas such as education and health. The *Londonderry Sentinel* opposed the creation of these boards, which would have placed Derry under jurisdictions with a Catholic majority. They called for the county councils to take over these powers, indeed for the county councils to be used as the new structure for local government.[144] This would of course, once again, have left Derry in Unionist hands.

As 1971 wore on and rumours spread that elections for a new city council might be held the following year, the *Londonderry Sentinel* took a firm stand suggesting the Development Commission run the city at least until the early 1980s.[145] In this desire to postpone local democracy, the *Londonderry Sentinel* was supported by Gerald Black, the president of the Chamber of Commerce, formerly a prominent O'Neillite who exclaimed 'abolish the Commission? It would be absolute crackers!' though he was prepared to accept an elected council operating alongside the commission.[146] The Alliance party too were keen to retain the commission[147] as, at one stage, was the Derry Trades Council.[148] Only the Derry Labour party[149] and the Official Republicans made strong demands for the restoration of local democracy. It may have been that, as violence escalated through 1971 and 1972, it suited most of the political groups in the city that there should be no local political forum or assembly which would have to respond to the traumatic events on the streets or which would have to reach a *modus vivendi* with the no-go areas of 'Free Derry'.

When the new city council was elected in 1973 the powers left to it to wield were minimal and, with the Development Commission having made huge inroads into the housing problems in the city, the greatest changes were perhaps symbolic.

Unionism without power

Apart from the last fantastic hope that Unionist control of Derry could be re-established through the re-organisation of local government, the political programme of Unionism in Derry was reduced in the early 1970s to the demand for ever-increasing repression. Unionist statements were dominated by calls to the British army to 'take off the gloves', to smash the no-go areas, to end the crisis by force.

The Unionist party, and to a great extent the Protestant community, became marginal to the political life of the city. Political organisations on the Catholic side, from the SDLP to the two IRAs, had limited dealings or negotiations with Unionists after the fall of the corporation.[150] They were talking, not to local Unionists, but to the Development Commission, to the British army and directly with the Stormont and British governments.

Reform and riot shattered the Unionist party and with the party, the state. As the Unionist party set out in 1969 on the long road to disintegration, the Protestant community was forced to look to other forms of organisation to respond to the massive crisis in the city and in its local areas. Particularly in working-class areas, Protestants began to look to local, neighbourhood, forms of organisation. The story of Protestant politics in these years is one of collapse but also of adaptation. But as Protestants moved from a confident sense of belonging to, and controlling the city, to a sense of fear and isolation, they looked away from the Catholic community. This led ultimately to the circumstances in which loyalist paramilitaries could flourish. The Protestant working class had finally 'awoken', but it had awoken to the sounds of rioting and gunfire.

Notes and references

1 Ed Moloney and Andy Pollak, *Paisley* (Poolbeg, Swords, Co. Dublin, 1986), p. 268; interview with Ivan Cooper; Member of the Young Unionist party in Mid-Derry in the mid-1960s. Member of the Derry Labour party in the later 1960s. Former chairman of the DCAC. Former Independent and, later, SDLP MP at Stormont for Mid-Derry; see Sarah Nelson, *Ulster's Uncertain Defenders. Protestant Political, Paramilitary and Community Groups and the Northern Ireland*

Conflict (Appletree, Belfast, 1984), especially pp. 17–19, for a discussion of Protestant working-class discontent with Unionist party hierarchies.

2 LS, 2/4/69. This is implied by the local Unionist MPs' critical reference to local businessmen who had 'refused' to serve on the corporation.

3 See Sydney Elliot, *Northern Ireland Parliamentary Election Results, 1921–1972* (Political reference publications, Chichester, 1973), for the catalogue of unopposed Stormont MPs.

4 Cooper, interview; interview with Jim Guy, Independent Unionist councillor, former mayor of Derry; former Ulster Unionist party councillor; former secretary and Lieutenant-Governor of the Apprentice Boys of Derry; former secretary and Grand Master of the City of Derry Grand Orange Lodge; former honorary secretary of Londonderry and Foyle Unionist Association; interview with William Hay; DUP member of Derry City Council; former Mayor of Derry. DUP activist since the early 1970s; active member of the Young Unionists in the late 1960s. Claude Wilton interview; Ulster Liberal party candidate for City of Londonderry seat in 1965 and 1969. Former Chairman of the DCAC and of the SDLP, former Northern Ireland Senator for the SDLP and solicitor.

5 See Nelson, *Ulster's Uncertain Defenders*, p. 14 on Protestant attitudes to law and order.

6 Terence O'Neill, *Autobiography* (Hart-Davis, London, 1972), pp. 145–9.

7 LS, 11/12/68, p. 1, p. 6, p. 36; 18/12/68, p. 14, p. 21.

8 Ibid.

9 Brian Faulkner (ed. John Houston), *Memoirs of a Statesman* (Weidenfeld and Nicolson, London, 1978), p. 49.

10 LS, 18/1/68, p. 23. A reader's letter bitterly expresses this belief.

11 LS, 29/1/69, p. 16.

12 LS, 22/1/69, p. 1.

13 LS, 29/1/69, p. 11.

14 *Ramparts*, vol. 1, no. 3, c. 1969. Also Frank Curran, *Derry. Countdown to Disaster* (Gill and Macmillan, Dublin, 1986), p. 114; Guy, interview; Cooper, interview.

15 Northern Ireland Constabulary list and directory, 1969, p. 93.

16 LS, 29/1/69.

17 LS, 29/1/69, p. 15.

18 He was one of only three people to be censured by the Cameron commission for refusing to give evidence to them; Cameron report, *Disturbances in Northern Ireland. Report of the Commission appointed by the Governor of Northern Ireland*, Northern Ireland Cmd. 532 (HMSO, Belfast, Sept. 1969), p. 100.

19 LS, 29/1/69.

20 Ibid.

21 LS, 1/1/69.

22 LS, 5/2/69, p. 15.

23 LS, 5/2/69, p. 7.

24 LS, 12/3/69.

25 See John F. Harbinson, *The Ulster Unionist Party, 1882–1972* (Blackstaff, Belfast, 1973), ch. 7, esp. pp. 74–7.

26 Guy, interview.

27 See F.W. Boal and R.H. Buchanan, 'The 1969 Northern Ireland Election', *Irish Geography*, vol. 6, no. 1, 1969, pp. 22–9.

28 LS, 5/2/69, p. 6, p. 13, p. 15; 12/2/69, p. 16.

29 LS, 5/2/69, p. 6.

30 Ibid., p. 5.

31 LS, 12/2/69. It seems likely that this petition, set up outside the Guildhall, would have attracted the signatures of many Catholics who nonetheless would be unlikely to vote for any sort of Unionist at election time. Thus it probably overestimates the extent of *real* support for O'Neill in Derry.

32 LS, 12/2/69, p. 1.

33 LS, 12/2/69, p. 5.

34 LS, 5/2/69, p. 15.

35 DJ, 11/2/69, p. 4.

36 See LS, 10/3/71, p. 1 and 31/3/71, p. 18 where complaints by the residual O'Neillites in the party give some insight into how the party operated.

37 Ulster Unionist Council yearbooks, 1960–1970.

38 LS, 12/2/69, p. 16.

39 LS, 5/3/69, p. 16.

40 Ibid.

41 LS, 12/2/69, p. 1.

42 LS, 12/2/69.

43 Niall Ó Dochartaigh, *Before the Troubles: Derry in the 1960s. An examination of the origins of a violent conflict* (MA, UCG, 1989), pp. 91–3.

44 LS, 19/2/69, p. 1; 5/2/69, p. 7.

45 LS, 18/2/70, p. 27.

46 LS, 12/2/69, p. 10.

47 Guy, interview.

48 Harbinson, *Unionist Party*, p. 65.

49 Hay, interview; interview 2 with Gregory Campbell, leader of DUP group on Derry city council, DUP activist since the early 1970s, member of the Young Unionists in the early 1970s.

50 LS, 12/2/69, p. 10.

51 Ibid.

52 Ibid., p. 16.

53 LS, 19/2/69, p. 28.

54 LS, 26/2/69, p. 6.

55 See Ó Dochartaigh, *Before the Troubles*, pp. 80–1.

56 LS, 5/2/69, p. 6.

57 Curran, *Countdown*, p. 118.

58 Curran, *Countdown*, p. 118; interview with Berna McIvor, chairperson of the Foyle Constituency branch of the SDLP; former SDLP election agent; member of WELB; member of WHSSB and of the probation board for Northern Ireland.

59 Faulkner, *Memoirs*, p. 53; Tom Wilson, *Ulster, Conflict and Consent* (Basil Blackwell, Oxford, 1989), p. 157.

60 Interview with Teresa Barr, long-time resident of Derry; McClenaghan interview who attributes it to Jeremiah Mallet, a local left-wing activist.

61 Elliot, *Parliamentary Election Results*, p. 77.

62 LS, 26/2/69, p. 24.

63 LS, 5/3/69, p. 16. Women business-owners did not have a vote.
64 LS, 26/2/69, p. 6.
65 LS, 9/10/68.
66 Arthur Aughey, *Under Siege. Ulster Unionism and the Anglo-Irish Agreement* (Blackstaff, Belfast, 1989), ch. 1.
67 Jennifer Todd, 'Two Traditions in Unionist Political Culture', *Irish Political Studies*, vol. 2, 1987.
68 LS, 10/3/71, p. 1.
69 Guy, interview; interview with Tony Crowe, chairman of the Diamond Trust for the regeneration of the Fountain area.
70 Harbinson, *Unionist Party*, p. 201.
71 LS, 6/4/66; *Ramparts* undated c. 1968; also, interview 2 with Eamonn McCann.
72 Guy, interview. For example it was not unusual for those considered not good enough in class terms to be selected as a Unionist councillor to nonetheless hold high office within the Loyal Orders.
73 Crowe, interview.
74 LS, 2/4/69, p. 5.
75 Crowe, interview.
76 John Hume, Eamonn McCann and Paddy Doherty, just to name a few, had been active on housing issues prior to the civil rights campaign.
77 Apprentice Boys of Derry, *Members Ticket*, 1971.
78 LS, 10/3/71, p. 1.
79 LS, 18/6/69, p. 22.
80 Scarman Report, *Report of Tribunal of Inquiry into Violence and Civil Disturbances in Northern Ireland*, 1969, vols. 1 and 2, Cmd. 566 (HMSO, Belfast, 1972), p. 34.
81 Scarman tribunal transcripts, Day 5, evidence of Rev. R. Dickinson, pp. 41 onwards.
82 LS, 23/7/69, p. 19.
83 DJ, 28/10/69, p. 4.
84 Londonderry Development Commission, Municipal Functions minutes, 6 June 1969, p. 14.
85 LS, 24/2/71, p. 1. The Derry Protestant Unionist Association in February 1971 claimed that when Protestants moved out of public housing on the West Bank of Derry the houses were usually allocated to Catholics.
86 LS, 14/5/69, p. 7.
87 LS, 25/6/69, p. 19.
88 LS, 23/7/69, p. 3.
89 LS, 30/7/69; 19/12/69, p. 1.
90 LDC minutes, 19/8/69.
91 LS, 18/2/70, p. 1; LS, 25/2/70, p. 24.
92 DJ, 12/6/70.
93 Not necessarily exclusively Protestant, but overwhelmingly Protestant.
94 Interview with Peter Simpson, former secretary of the Wapping Lane Community Association (which included the Fountain estate) and head of its security sub-committee in the early 1970s.
95 DJ, 9/9/69, p. 4.
96 DJ, 25/11/69, p. 4.

97 DJ, 18/11/69, p. 1.
98 DJ, 12/6/70.
99 LS, 26/6/70.
100 DJ, 16/6/70.
101 DJ, 16/6/70.
102 Interview with Mary Nelis, founder member and former chairperson, secretary, PRO of Foyle Hill Tenants' Association (Creggan); former SDLP candidate for Derry City Council; currently a Sinn Féin member of Derry City Council.
103 LS, 14/1/70, p. 17; 4/2/70.
104 Hay, interview.
105 Campbell, interview 2.
106 LS, 11/2/70, p. 24.
107 Hay, interview; Campbell, interview 2.
108 Campbell, interview 2.
109 LS, 10/6/70, p. 15.
110 LS, 3/6/70.
111 DJ, 9/6/70, p. 1.
112 DJ, 19/6/70, p. 8.
113 DJ, 16/6/70; also see Moloney and Pollock, *Paisley*, pp. 205–6.
114 LS, 10/2/71, p. 19.
115 DJ, 13/10/70, for example.
116 Todd, 'Two Traditions'.
117 LS, 18/6/69, p. 22.
118 LS, 25/2/70, p. 3.
119 Interview with Bertie Faulkner, former Alliance party member of Derry City Council; worked closely with tenants' associations on the Waterside.
120 DJ, 26/5/70, p. 1.
121 LS, 3/6/70.
122 Faulkner, interview.
123 LS, 10/3/71, p. 1.
124 Crowe, interview; Cooper, interview; Guy, interview.
125 Faulkner, interview.
126 Simpson, interview; Faulkner, interview.
127 Faulkner, interview.
128 DJ, 26/11/68, p. 1.
129 LS, 5/2/69, p. 6.
130 LS, 5/2/69, p. 11.
131 LS, 2/4/69, p. 5.
132 LDC minutes, 1968/69.
133 Simpson, interview.
134 DJ, 22/11/68, p. 11.
135 LS, 5/3/69.
136 LS, 12/3/69, p. 6.
137 John Hume in DJ, 23/9/69, p. 1; Ivan Cooper in DJ. 10/10/69, p. 1.
138 LS, 18/6/69, p. 6.
139 M.A. Busteed and Hugh Mason, 'Local Government Reform in Northern Ireland', *Irish Geography*, vol. 6, no. 3, 1971.
140 LS, 9/7/69, p. 14.

141 Ibid., p. 6.
142 LS, 9/6/71, p. 13.
143 LS, 18/2/70, p. 6.
144 LS, 7/4/71; 5/5/71.
145 LS, 12/5/71, p. 1.
146 Ibid.
147 LS, 26/5/71, p. 23.
148 LS, 9/6/71, p. 7.
149 LS, 9/6/71, p. 24.
150 Canavan interview, founder member of the Derry Credit Union, formerly a
     senior member of the DCAC, the DCDA, the DCCC and the Independent
     Organisation, former SDLP assembly member; interview with Terry Robson,
     chairman of Derry Labour Party Young Socialists in the early 1970s
     and member of the NILP executive; member of the Official Republican
     movement from late 1971.

3
Free Derry:
August–October 1969

The approach to 12 August 1969

By July 1969, the crisis in Northern Ireland had deepened. It had already gone beyond the possibility of resolution through the granting of the original civil rights demands. In Derry, the authority of the DCAC had crumbled and the initiative had passed to local youths. Marches, which were sometimes followed by riots, had given way to regular and often unprovoked rioting on the streets. Hostility to the RUC had deepened after the beating of Sammy Devenny in April and had spread to the moderates who had been instrumental in preventing rioting on previous occasions. The death of Sammy Devenny in mid-July eroded even further the commitment of moderates to actively preventing attacks on the RUC.

In this context, it seemed certain that violence, perhaps on an unprecedented scale, would break out in Derry on 12 August when 15,000 Apprentice Boys from all over Northern Ireland and beyond would march along the edge of the Bogside escorted by the RUC. Moderates no longer had sufficient authority to prevent violence. Local youths would probably stone the RUC and a clash which might bring thousands of loyalists streaming into the Bogside behind an RUC baton charge would ensue.

As 12 August approached, the Derry Republicans set up a Defence Association (hereafter DCDA) which succeeded in drawing in some moderates and which displaced the authority of the DCAC. At this stage, it still appeared that the British government would be reluctant to intervene if violence broke out on 12 August. A few days before the Apprentice Boys march, Jim Callaghan, the British home secretary, was asked by Labour MPs to visit the North to assess the situation. He declined, and instead 'urged how desirable it was that the problems of Northern Ireland should be solved within Northern Ireland without any outside intervention'.[1]

Partly because of apparent British lack of interest, but also because members of the Defence Association were disinclined to look to London, they now looked to Dublin. Since the civil rights campaign had begun, it had received strong emotional and financial support from people in the Republic and political links had developed. The fact that the DCDA looked to Dublin was an important shift in emphasis. For a brief period after 12 August 1969 it seemed to many in Derry that the disintegration of Northern Ireland and the 'liberation' of Derry by Irish troops was imminent. By the time British troops arrived in Derry, many people in the Bogside had rejected the authority of Stormont and the RUC so thoroughly that it would be difficult to restore acceptance of the state's right to rule in the Bogside.

In an attempt to restore acceptance of the state's right to rule, the Stormont government, impelled by Britain, introduced a series of reforms to deal with grievances about the RUC and the B-Specials which had emerged in the course of the civil rights campaign. This process of reform began hopefully but ultimately failed. This chapter will address the question of how even Catholic moderates became alienated from the state and how these reforms failed to restore the position of only a year previously, when they accepted the state and agreed with the desirability of internal reform.

The Derry Citizens Defence Association

On 17 July, the DCAC met. The previous weekend severe rioting had broken out in the city and the DCAC had been powerless to stop it. Now the DCAC considered the prospect that violence might break out on 12 August. However, on the day of this meeting, Sammy Devenny died and the DCAC became involved in making arrangements for his funeral.[2] It failed to agree on any plan of action for 12 August.[3]

On 19 July, Sammy Devenny was buried. His death increased Catholic hostility to the RUC in Derry.[4] The day after the funeral, the Derry Republicans set up the Derry Citizens Defence Association. The DCDA was a purely Republican initiative and it involved both the younger radicals and even more of the older Republicans who had been involved in the 1950s and earlier.[5] The Defence Association made their existence public a week later and on 30 July they held a public meeting. Their purpose was to prepare for the defence of the Bogside in the event of an attack on 12 August. The Republicans invited other groups, including the DCAC, to nominate representatives to the Defence Association.

The actions of the DCDA were regarded by some as an attempt by the Republicans to 'take over the civil rights movement',[6] to take on the mantle of the DCAC, of united mass action but in the cause now of 'defence' against the RUC and loyalists. The local Labour party radicals were apparently annoyed that the left-wing Republicans they had been working with had acted unilaterally in setting up the DCDA, without consulting them.[7] It appears the younger Republicans were now co-operating ever more closely with traditionalist Republicans.

The Derry Republicans had been involved in organising 'defence' groups since January 1969, an activity approved by the Dublin leadership as an alternative to a military campaign.[8] Now, however, they seemed to be attempting to usurp the position of the DCAC by establishing the DCDA which was clearly more than a local street committee. However, although established by the Republicans, the DCDA began to draw representatives from other groups.

The consequent involvement in the DCDA of some prominent local people who had been involved in the DCAC legitimised the defence organisation for many people. However this was not a one-way process of assimilation of moderates to a Republican perspective. The entry of non-Republicans into the DCDA also served to dilute its Republican character.

The response of John Hume's constituency party, the Independent Organisation, provides an illustration of how Catholic moderates came to be involved with the DCDA. The Independent Organisation sent an observer to the first public meeting of the DCDA on 30 July.[9] The observer, Independent Organisation secretary Willie O'Connell, reported back to the organisation which was fearful about the prospect of violence on 12 August. At that party meeting, one member said he had 'no confidence in the power of the RUC' to prevent an attack on the Bogside by loyalists but also had no faith in the ability of the DCDA to 'control its members.'[10] The only alternative suggestion he could come up with was that they in the Independent Organisation should set up its own 'police force.' This would, however, have been just as much a challenge to state authority as the DCDA was and the moderates were simply not prepared to present such a challenge.

In the event they decided to send O'Connell to 'put their viewpoint' at DCDA meetings. This gave them some influence over the DCDA, and O'Connell and a number of other Independent Organisation activists became members of the Defence Association. However, if the

Republican-inspired DCDA gained legitimacy from the involvement of moderates, it gained popular support because of the genuine sense of fear in the Bogside as 12 August approached.[11]

On 10 August, the DCDA convened a public meeting in Celtic Park, the GAA ground in the Bogside. Seán Keenan presided. At the meeting both left-wing and traditional Republicans spoke, but also present were Eddie McAteer, Nationalist party chairman James Doherty, John Hume and Eamonn McCann for the Labour left. Keenan said they would be trying to prevent sectarian strife but, if that failed, they would 'defend our people' and put up barricades if necessary. Eddie McAteer's remarks attracted the most outside attention. If the Bogside was attacked, he said 'I pray to God that our watching brethren will not stand aside any longer.' It was a clear call for Irish government intervention and, while it was consistent with Nationalist party traditions it was a break with the party's recent cautious attitude.[12]

The Nationalist party had lost a lot of support because it had not been very prominent or militant in the civil rights campaign. Now it seemed to be trying to regain some support through a return to first principles, as it were, by displaying its fundamental hostility to the Northern state. The meeting demonstrated that there had been an increase in militancy across the political spectrum within the Catholic community, taking in even those on the cautious fringes.

The basic fear in the Bogside was that on 12 August loyalists would attempt to enter the area and that the RUC would either fail to hold them back or would join in with the attack. In the event, this fear was realised only to a slight extent and Catholic youths in the Bogside played a major role in initiating violence.[13]

From a Unionist point of view, the fact that a huge attack by the parade marchers on the Bogside did not occur demonstrated that no attack on the Bogside had been planned, that if Catholic youths had not started rioting there would have been no violence and that therefore the plans of the DCDA for 'defence' were, in reality, plans to set up another Free Derry. When the Irish government became involved, it seemed to point to a grand conspiracy, originating with the DCDA, to destroy Northern Ireland.

Unionists had a point. Although there were fears of a loyalist 'invasion' the DCDA did not only fear or prepare for an unprovoked loyalist attack. They had to assume an outbreak of rioting on the Catholic side by local youths and had to plan accordingly. Over the previous months, no force in the city had been able to control the regular outbreaks of rioting by Catholic youths. Much more likely than an unprovoked loyalist invasion was conflict between Catholic youths and the RUC men guarding the parade. To prevent this might have been possible but it would have required a heroic effort, uniting all those groups, from the Republicans to the Catholic moderates, who had stewarded the early civil rights marches.

By this time, the Republicans, Labour radicals and even many Catholic moderates were not interested in making such a strenuous effort. Without such an effort there would certainly be riots, RUC reaction and the consequent necessity to keep the RUC and any accompanying loyalists out of the Bogside.

The distinction between the DCDA not being committed to preventing the riot which would make defence necessary, and actually seeking a confrontation with the state is a fine one. However, it is clear from the minimal arrangements made for stewarding by Republicans in the DCDA[14] that their commitment to preventing that initial violence was minimal. Although it was said that the DCDA had asked the DCAC to provide stewards, very few stewards turned up on the day.[15] The stewarding system did not operate effectively and stewards made only a 'token effort' to prevent violence.[16] Thus, the Republicans at the very least were failing to make strenuous efforts to stop conflict beginning. It does not seem unreasonable to suggest that they saw 12 August as an opportunity to bring the very existence of Northern Ireland into question.

As 12 August approached, other individuals became involved with the DCDA. Paddy Doherty had been selected as one of the DCAC representatives to the DCDA.[17] In the DCAC he had been in charge of stewarding and it is another mark of the Defence Association's lack of commitment to stewarding that he was not in charge of the stewards on 12 August. Doherty was not a Republican but was strongly nationalist in his outlook. He and Seán Keenan became the senior figures in the DCDA and neither of them looked to London in the way in which the early civil rights campaigners had done. The DCDA was embarking on a confrontation with the government of Northern Ireland and to look to Britain or the British army did not, in the circumstances, seem a natural course of action. Once the DCDA had accepted the inevitability of the confrontation and made plans to barricade the area, the question arose of where things would go from there. The DCDA needed to be sure that, in the event that the Stormont government made a determined effort to smash the barricades by, for example, bringing in the B-Specials, they would have a fallback position.

Shortly before 12 August Seán Keenan and Paddy Doherty set off for Dublin to request aid from both the Irish government and the IRA leadership. Keenan had suggested that the IRA would take charge of the defence of the Bogside and would provide men and weapons to do this. Paddy Doherty regarded the IRA as a 'myth' and did not believe it had any such capacity. He looked to the Irish government as the only force which could effectively come to their aid in that situation.[18]

In Dublin Keenan and Doherty met with the Secretary to the Taoiseach and then with two civil servants from the Irish department of Foreign Affairs. According to Doherty, the civil servants, when pressed on the Irish government's response to an attack on the Bogside or to people being killed, assured them that 'We'll not let you down' and that 'the government will act to protect our people in Northern Ireland.'[19] Doherty had been hoping for stronger assurances. They then met with Cathal Goulding, chief of staff of the IRA. Keenan asked him to use IRA resources to defend the Bogside. According to Doherty, Goulding replied that he 'couldn't defend the Bogside. I haven't the men nor the guns to do it.'[20] This effectively put an end to the dreams of those Derry Republicans who had seen this as an opportunity for a revival of the IRA.

After their failure to get IRA help, the DCDA decided that they would not use guns nor permit the use of guns in their defence of the area. In the event of their being shot at, however, the whole scenario would change.

The Derry IRA, which was dominated by the younger Republicans, also decided that they would not use weapons unless the RUC used them first.[21] The decisions of both the DCDA and the Derry IRA in a way made a virtue out of necessity. Of the few guns the Derry IRA had access to, it is said that half were useless. Some of the older Republicans who had recently become re-involved in the movement in Derry had complained bitterly at the 'de-militarisation' of the Derry IRA under the younger radicals.[22] The IRA, neither at national nor local level, had the capacity to defend the Bogside militarily. The DCDA were relying now on 'sticks, stones and the good old petrol bomb'[23] and, in a doomsday scenario, on the intervention of the Irish army. In early August 1969, that did not seem at all an unlikely prospect to some in the DCDA.

On 10 August, a meeting was held between senior figures in the Apprentice Boys of Derry and members of the DCDA, including senior Republicans. Apprentice Boys at the meeting would later regret they had not found out who all the DCDA members present were.[24] The DCDA asked the Apprentice Boys to call off the march but, according to Paddy Doherty, the Apprentice Boys said it had 'been going on so long we can't stop it.[25] A few days before, the governor of the Apprentice Boys, Russell Abernethy, had been more forthright in rejecting cancellation or changing of the parade route when he said, 'It would be acknowledging insurrection if any change were to be made.'[26] However, at this meeting, the Apprentice Boys gave some 'acknowledgement of insurrection' and made three minor changes to the route which would ensure that the parade would pass a little further from the edge of the Bogside than usual at two points.[27]

The meeting seems to have been a serious attempt on both sides to ensure at least that a large-scale sectarian confrontation did not break out. Both sides agreed to provide stewards at the interface between the Long Tower and the Fountain the night before the parade and they were successful in preventing sectarian violence that night. The DCDA promised to provide stewards on the day of the march and the Apprentice Boys said they would provide one steward for every ten marchers. The DCDA also made a point of assuring the Apprentice Boys that they had no firearms. According to an Apprentice Boy present, the DCDA claimed the Irish army was massing at the border and, if it became necessary, would answer their calls for help.[28]

If this is so, it gives a far less conspiratorial tinge to the arrangements between the DCDA and the Irish government. The DCDA were not being secretive about their fallback position and there seems to have been an element of bluff in such a claim, as it does not appear that the Irish army had yet moved up near the border and the DCDA were uncertain about the assurances they had received from the Irish government.

This meeting provided a fleeting glimpse of hope that violence could be averted but, in reality, the DCDA did not have sufficient commitment to maintaining peace. In the days before the march, tens of thousands of empty milk bottles went missing in the Bogside in preparation for making petrol bombs, and the first barricades in the Bogside went up the night before the parade. Preparations for the defence of the Bogside were therefore well under way before the Apprentice Boys parade began.[29]

The battle of the Bogside

On 12 August, as the thousands of marchers in the Apprentice Boys parade passed through Waterloo Place, a large crowd was gathered at the mouth of William Street, on the edge of the Bogside. They were separated from the parade by lines of RUC men and a thin line of DCAC stewards. Among the stewards were prominent moderate politicians, John Hume and Ivan Cooper and the Nationalist leader Eddie McAteer.[30] However, there were not enough stewards, they were not well enough organised and they could not restrain the crowd. Seán Keenan later suggested that so few stewards turned up that day 'because of the abuse they had got from the police on previous occasions',[31] but he was being disingenuous.

There was also a certain ambiguity about the commitment to the maintenance of the peace by the DCDA peace corps who were present. Among them in William Street were those with stones in their pockets waiting for the inevitable riot to break out.[32] However, most of the marchers had passed through Waterloo Place before the first stones were thrown, aimed at the RUC rather than at the marchers (see map 4).

Although the main focus of attention was William Street, where the RUC delayed taking action against the stone throwers for two hours in the hope that the DCAC could control the situation,[33] the first serious clashes took place around the corner in Little James Street. This violence is variously described as beginning with an attack by youths from the Bogside on the RUC[34] or as an outbreak of fighting between crowds of Protestants and Catholics.[35]

In any event, sectarian clashes broke out in Little James Street between Protestants, who had been following the parade, and Catholic youths. For a while the RUC stood by. Then the RUC charged forward, throwing stones and forcing the Catholic youths into William Street. The Protestant crowd moved forward with the RUC and with the encouragement of some RUC men.[36] Moderates such as Dr Raymond McClean, chairman of the Independent Organisation, saw this as a realisation of their fears of attack by loyalist mobs and the RUC.[37]

As clashes took place in Little James Street, the RUC held the line around the corner at Waterloo Place until finally the DCAC stewards gave up their efforts and the RUC decided to take action against the crowd. By this stage the Apprentice Boys' march was over. Apprentice Boy stewards had tried to ensure that groups of marchers did not remain in Waterloo Place and that groups from outside Derry left the city after the parade.[38]

After the DCAC stewards withdrew, the RUC launched a charge down William Street, throwing stones as they went. They swept down to the barricade across the mouth of Rossville Street which blocked access any further into the Bogside.[39] It was the first barricade they had come up against. At the same time, the RUC men around the corner in Little James Street moved down to the barricade followed by a large crowd of loyalists. It was said that most of these loyalists were outsiders, but in the Bogside it was claimed there was at least one prominent local Young Unionist among them.[40] Certainly, that night, local Protestant youths were out on the streets behind police lines.[41] According to one account, two RUC officers argued over whether to try and breach the barricade and the more junior officer, who had headed the RUC in Little James Street, won the argument.[42] It seems likely that the Protestant crowds milling around the RUC would have been demanding such action and this would have influenced the RUC decision to do so. Shortly after 7 p.m., 100 RUC men, beating their batons on their shields, supported by Land Rovers and followed by between 50 and 200 Protestant civilians, breached the barricade. The RUC charged down Rossville Street throwing stones and batoning people. The Protestant civilians behind them smashed windows along the street.[43]

The RUC and the loyalists were well down Rossville Street when the crowd, about 1,000 strong, turned and pushed them back up Rossville Street. There were those Unionists who felt later that rioting might have been ended if the RUC had acted more forcefully, arresting people, not being content to hold the line but pushing into the area.[44] This charge into Rossville Street, and subsequent retreat, demonstrated that they did not have the numbers to do this unless they used firearms or called up the B-Specials in support. Either of these courses of action would have altered the situation dramatically and provoked outside intervention.

Before this RUC advance, the DCDA had had the support of some moderates but its plans were still regarded with suspicion by most. The charge seemed to confirm that, if the RUC managed to get into the area again, loyalists would too. It had now become genuinely a matter of 'defence'. It was this RUC baton charge which changed the views of many more respectable Catholics. Now, those who had been to the forefront of preventing violence a few months before abandoned all attempts to do so.

Father Anthony Mulvey, a Catholic priest who had been prominent in stopping riots in recent months, said that after that point he believed there was no longer simply a riot in progress: there was a 'community in revolt'.[45] This was the point, for example, at which Raymond McClean volunteered his services at a first-aid post in the Bogside.[46] Now that many more moderates and 'respectable' citizens became involved in the cause of defence, the mantle of the DCAC came to rest securely on the shoulders of the DCDA.

For Northern Ireland as a state, this was a disastrous development. One RUC officer later claimed that many Catholics would be glad to see them back patrolling the Bogside and that resentment against them had been 'engineered'.[47] There was a grain of truth in that. Many Catholics with a traditional respect for authority, property and law and order were undoubtedly appalled by the riots. However, after 12 August, even they found it hard to see restoration of RUC control as a reasonable solution to these problems. By then, according to Nationalist party chairman James Doherty, 'the vast majority of the Catholic people were hostile to the police in Derry'.[48]

After the charge into Rossville Street and subsequent retreat by the RUC, stalemate ensued. As pressure built up on the RUC, they received permission from Stormont to use a new weapon – CS gas. It had never been used in Ireland before. Before authorising its use, Robert Porter, Unionist minister of home affairs, tried a test dose on himself and decided it was acceptable to use it.[49] Starting that night, the RUC began firing CS gas into the Bogside, an average of one canister every two minutes: 1,147 units over the next two days.[50] Given their lack of other riot control weapons it appears the RUC also used the gas canisters as 'bullets', firing them at rioters.[51] The gas was designed to disperse unruly crowds but was used by the RUC, who had virtually no training in its use, as a 'defensive' weapon, preventing rioters from getting near RUC lines. Huge amounts were used and the Bogside became blanketed with gas. As Scarman put it, 'By dawn the area had become enveloped in a pall of gas, covering the streets and penetrating the houses.'[52] CS acted as a sort of mass alienation device. Even those who had wanted nothing to do with the 'trouble', who had stayed in their homes and kept their children off the streets, found gas seeping into their houses. That evening 500 women and children were evacuated from the Bogside and crossed the border to take refuge in Co. Donegal.[53]

When the morning of the 13 August came, the RUC were holding a line across the top of Rossville Street but they had no prospect of advancing. By now, resistance was massive. First-aid stations, run by the Order of Malta, treated casualties; in the back streets women and children were making petrol bombs. Children were tearing up paving-stones for ammunition and bringing them to the 'front line' in wheelbarrows.[54] A group of teenagers had occupied the roof of the high flats on Rossville Street and were supplied with petrol bombs, ensuring that the RUC could not advance up the street. Two academic observers noted that

> the feeling of being surrounded and under attack had produced a strong sense of cohesion and something like perfect consensus politics were working ... The organisation of the fighting seemed to be largely spontaneous and ad hoc ... Better known figures moved from place to place and gave instructions and advice, but there appeared to be no centrally co-ordinated body. The idea of leadership was expressed in the phrase 'people'll listen to so and so'.[55]

Two separate newsletters began to circulate in the area, one produced by the DCDA which was now based in Paddy Doherty's house in the Bogside. The other, produced by Derry Labour party members, represented the views of the radicals in the area, who had become involved with the DCDA but who saw Free Derry as an opportunity for the left rather than for Irish nationalism.

These newsletters appeared daily, reporting on 'the battlefronts' and the fight against 'the enemy', proclaiming, 'Derry is in a state of war'. They gave instructions for the storage and use of petrol bombs ('they should not be stored in crates which are easy to remove if captured ... Try to throw the petrol bombs high in the air unless at very close range. This causes more panic as well as doing more harm.')[56] As one prominent moderate put it, 'an entire community [was] at war with what was supposed to have been their own police force, a community determined and united, a community used to economic depression, emigration and hopelessness–now on its feet and with a spring in its step.'[57] In spirit, the Bogside had already seceded from Northern Ireland.

By 13 August, it seemed possible to many that the crisis would end with the disintegration of Northern Ireland rather than with the restoration of RUC control over the Bogside. That evening, after a further day of intense fighting, the DCDA held a press conference at which Paddy Doherty and Dr Donal McDermott spoke. The press conference was later described by Lord Scarman as a 'call to arms'.[58] The DCDA appealed for 'every able-bodied man in Ireland' to come to Derry to help in the fighting.[59] After the press conference, the DCDA turned on the radio to listen to a broadcast by the Irish prime minister, Jack Lynch. Lynch announced that he was asking the British government to apply for a UN peace-keeping force in the North and called for negotiations on the 'constitutional position' of Northern Ireland. He said that Irish army field-hospitals would be set up near the border, just a few miles from the fighting in the Bogside and casualties from the Bogside would be treated there. In a sense, the Irish government was now acting in support of the DCDA. Lynch also declared that the Irish government could 'no longer stand by and see innocent people injured and perhaps worse'.[60]

In Derry the belief was now widespread that the Irish army was about to enter the city and 'relieve' the Bogside.[61] This belief was not confined to Catholics. After Lynch's announcement, many Protestants believed 'Dublin was about to invade'. There were even rumours that 'the Dublin troops were in the Bogside and had established camps in the Bogside'.[62] After the broadcast, the Bogsiders redoubled their efforts but also several hundred Protestants from Derry and the surrounding villages responded to the broadcast by coming into the city and gathering behind RUC lines in Great James Street at the edge of the Bogside. Some wore crash-helmets and were armed with sticks. The RUC 'were brushed aside' as the loyalist crowd confronted the Bogsiders.[63] Then the RUC began to advance up Great James Street mixed in with or leading the Protestant crowd.[64] Rumours spread that the loyalists intended to burn down St Eugene's, the Catholic cathedral at the top of the street.

People in Creggan Estate had felt somewhat removed from events in the Bogside over the previous year[65] and had been reluctant to join in the rioting during these days, but now the DCDA tried to get their support. Responses were slow in the estate until a youth started shouting in the street, 'The church has been attacked and Father Mulvey has been burnt to death.'[66] Believing the church was in danger, ever more conservative Catholics came out on the street and as the RUC advanced, prominent moderates such as Michael Canavan and respected figures such as Eddie McAteer and Father Mulvey were among the crowd behind the barricade.[67]

As the RUC advanced, an RUC man or men opened fire and two or three people were wounded, being quickly carried away to a nearby first-aid post.[68] News of the shootings spread rapidly. The DCDA had decided not to use guns but implicit in this was the assumption that the RUC would not use guns either. Now an angry group of young men cornered Seán Keenan and there was an impromptu meeting on the Lone Moor Road behind the 'frontlines'. Some of the men were from the Waterside and it would hardly be surprising if a few were younger Republicans. They demanded that guns now be supplied and used to stop the RUC advance. Essentially they were demanding that the IRA now conduct an armed defence of the area. Keenan rejected these demands and argued that they should not use guns.[69] That night, a man from outside the city approached the DCDA and, according to Paddy Doherty, offered them 200 rifles and 100,000 rounds of ammunition. The offer was refused. Doherty saw this as 'maybe a personal tactic' on his part.[70]

There were those, Republicans among them, who had expected that armed IRA men would appear on the streets at some stage during the fighting[71] but this never materialised. However, the IRA was not entirely inactive. Republicans were active in the rioting and it can be assumed that they played an important role simply because they were a relatively coherent and organised group. There are hints that Republicans tended to be involved in key activities: for example, the presence of at least one Fianna Éireann member on the roof of the high flats,[72] or the presence of another young Republican leading a group carrying petrol bombs and cans of petrol to skirt RUC lines and attack the RUC from the rear in Great James Street.[73] However, the militancy of local youths had reached such a pitch that the young Republicans stood out only in terms of planning rather than in their hostility to the RUC. In any case, when people looked to the IRA for defence, they were thinking of stronger measures than these.

At one stage in the fighting, Derry IRA members did decide to take action distinct from rioting but it is notable that before doing so they consulted the Defence Association. Mickey Montgomery who had been involved in the 1950s campaign in Derry (and who was later associated with the Official IRA) told Paddy Doherty that he had an IRA unit ready to act. They had been planning to burn down the house of a prominent local Unionist but wanted to consult the DCDA first. Doherty suggested they abandon this plan. He named two targets deep behind 'enemy lines' and suggested that if they wanted to help, this would make a significant contribution. In the event, neither target appears to have been attacked and this was the extent of IRA 'guerilla' activity in Derry during these early days.[74] This was in direct contrast with the situation in Belfast where, in response to the news of events in Derry, large-scale rioting broke out and a small number of IRA members conducted an armed defence of the Catholic Lower Falls area. In the space of two days in Belfast, seven people were shot dead, four by the RUC, two by the IRA and one, a sixteen-year-old member of the Fianna Éireann, by loyalists.[75]

Republicans had founded the Derry Citizens Defence Association but any dreams of using it to start a renewed IRA campaign had dissolved because of the lack of IRA military capacity. As time went on, the Defence Association became ever less dominated by Republicans to the extent that it seemed to some Republicans that Seán Keenan ended up as a 'token Republican' on the DCDA.[76]

On the night of the 13 August, the RUC eventually convinced the Protestant crowd in Great James Street to withdraw by telling them they would carry out a 'pincer action' to get round the barricade.[77] Some of the Protestant crowd headed towards the city centre where they attempted to set fire to the City Hotel (where the international media were based) and a Catholic hall.[78] Strengthened by reinforcements, the RUC pushed further on around the cathedral (which no-one attempted to burn), and forced the crowd back into the Lone Moor Road where the situation ended in stalemate. By now the RUC was certain it would need the assistance of the British army.[79]

The conduct of the RUC during these days of fighting was later the subject of protracted discussion. In its defence, the RUC represented its actions as 'doing their best to keep two opposing groups apart'.[80] Any apparent partiality towards the Protestant crowds was explained in operational terms – 'the police could not afford a fight on two fronts'.[81] RUC officers could afford to turn their backs to a Protestant crowd without being attacked, therefore it made policing sense to concentrate on the Catholic crowd. To Catholics, this was manifested as an RUC charge supported by a Protestant crowd. The RUC explained the failure to disperse Protestant crowds in operational terms too: 'It was better to keep them in the street and keep an eye on them than to disperse them and not know what they might do.'[82] Thus, what appeared to the observer as sectarian partisanship was represented as a tactical decision dictated by the exigencies of the situation. However, even the terms in which the RUC asserted its neutrality reveals how utterly different its relationships were with the Protestant and the Catholic communities. One RUC officer told the Scarman Tribunal about a police log book entry which mentioned that during sectarian rioting in July, Protestants complained to the RUC that 'Protestants were being held back'. He regarded this as proof that the RUC was playing a neutral role.[83]

It was not that the RUC consciously acted as a sectarian vanguard for Protestant rioters but they had a relationship with them which could easily move from tolerance to impromptu co-operation as when RUC men stood aside and Protestant crowds replaced them in holding the line against Bogside rioters.[84] In addition, the RUC tended to respond to some extent to the urgings of Protestant crowds to advance,[85] if only on the grounds of getting them to then disperse and go home. Apart from all this, Scarman had no doubt that there were some RUC men who had encouraged the loyalist crowds and welcomed their help.[86] As one British journalist wrote, 'It wasn't the RUC's stoning or rare petrol-bombing that shocked; it was their hate that really stunned, matching that of the Catholics. The obscenities, the threats, the religious tauntings – and all coming from a peace-keeping force.'[87]

In the circumstances, people in the Bogside on 12 August could easily interpret the RUC advance as a sectarian attack in league with extreme loyalists. Moderates who had long tried to stop the rioting now accepted the need for 'defence'. It was a major shift in the political balance within the Catholic community in Derry.

A remarkable feature of the fighting in the Bogside was the presence and participation of young teenagers and even children. In one sense it was only natural. Children rioted for much the same reasons as they had gone to the early civil rights marches and to meetings. It took place on the street and it was a dramatic spectacle which children could appreciate. Particularly in the Bogside where there were few play spaces, and particularly during the school holidays in summer, the streets belonged to children and youths. Civil rights marches and then rioting brought the adult world of 'politics' on to these streets where children operated. It was a unique development which brought political speeches, drama and conflict within earshot of children. Photographs show small children, and particularly young teenagers, as a ubiquitous presence at sit-downs and political meetings and when the DCDA put its first barricades up there were children there too.[88]

When massive rioting broke out on 12 August, the streets of the Bogside became an ever more exciting environment for many children. As the fighting led to stalemate and took on a ritual form, children became more involved now that there was less immediate danger. It was youths of thirteen, fourteen or fifteen years of age and even children who looked as young as five[89] who were making and throwing petrol bombs from the roof of the Rossville flats.

This phenomenon, of child-rioting, has most commonly been discussed in terms of social breakdown, loss of parental control[90] or in terms of manipulation.[91] However, the fact that even children had lost any respect for law and order, and any fear of authority was regarded by many in the Bogside not as a sign of social breakdown but of the total rejection of the RUC by the Bogsiders.

Within the Bogside, child involvement was regarded, even by moderate 'respectable' elements, as more heroic than reprehensible. The *Derry Emigrant Bulletin*, associated with moderate Catholics and the church, reported that the 'boys' on the high flats were being 'acclaimed as heroes',[92] although there were girls there too, making the petrol bombs. It also said of the defence of the area, 'Do not think it was only the men and the boys who displayed such courage. The women and children played their parts too.' Dr Raymond McClean also acclaimed the youth on the high flats as heroes.[93] Given that there was a degree of acceptance within the area of the role of children, it would be wrong to treat this as a 'social problem', isolated from its political context. The civil rights campaign and then rioting had brought politics to the young. Rioting provided a means by which youths participated in the sphere of politics. It provided the comprehensible issue of opposition to the RUC and a means of contributing to that struggle which was equally comprehensible. Involvement in such conflict had a politicising effect in its own right and drew the young further into the world of politics.[94] For the young, with their interest aroused and their hostility to the state increased through confrontation, the politics of nationality and a struggle for freedom would be far more attractive and comprehensible than the politics of advice centres, lobbying and fund-raising. The process by which young rioters become armed militants cannot adequately be explained in terms of breakdown. It is a political process developing out of street confrontations which is not unique to Northern Ireland but appears to be a common feature of conflict situations.[95]

While there are also elements of 'breakdown' and of manipulation in these developments, it would be wrong to cite these as the basic 'causes' of youth involvement. The involvement of youth had profound implications for the political balance of forces within the Catholic community. In Derry, teenagers moved from rioting to IRA activity over the following months and strengthened the hitherto weak Republican organisation. In the process, the character of the Republican movement was totally changed.

On the morning of 14 August, Derry woke to a third day of rioting. The RUC would not be able to hold out much longer on their own. Already some B-Specials had been mobilised in the Fountain the night before. When sectarian rioting broke out on a large scale in Bishop Street on the 14th, there were B-Specials among the Protestant crowd, restraining them but also joining in the riot on the Protestant side.[96]

Around 4 p.m. a call went out for the general mobilisation of the B-Specials and, in the Fountain, B-Specials went rushing up to the interface at Bishop Street 'in loose formation'.[97] In addition, sixty B-Specials, carrying batons, marched to RUC lines in Waterloo Place. When the B-Specials appeared on the city walls and at the edge of the Fountain, it looked in the Bogside as though another attack was about to begin, one which might bring the Protestant crowds on Bishop Street streaming in behind the RUC and the B-Specials.[98] In William Street, on the other hand, the RUC were pulling back under pressure and the crowds were advancing up towards Waterloo Place.[99]

Just then, British troops marched into Waterloo Place and replaced the RUC at the mouth of William Street. The RUC were relieved. The Bogsiders were relieved though uncertain. They did not attack the army and the army did not attempt to advance into the Bogside. Rioting began to die out. Less than twenty-four hours before, Bogsiders had been expecting the Irish army to arrive and even now some who heard that the army had arrived thought it was the Irish army which was on the streets.[100] Just how close the Irish army had come to 'liberating' Derry was illustrated by the fact that both the Irish and British commanders concerned had instructions that, if they were to go into Derry, they should stop if they came up against the opposing army and in effect, set up a cease-fire line.[101] In retrospect, however, Jack Lynch's speech can probably be best understood as an attempt to force Britain to intervene in some way, though not necessarily by sending the British army in. It is likely the Irish government was extremely reluctant to actually breach UK sovereignty and come directly into conflict not just with Stormont but with the British government too.

It was true, as James Callaghan said, that 'Both sides asked for the troops'[102] but this disguises important distinctions. On the Catholic side, individuals such as Gerry Fitt had called for the troops to be sent in. However, the DCDA had made no such call, not at any stage, and when the troops came in their reaction was less one of delight that the troops were in than one of satisfaction that Stormont and the RUC were no longer in control.[103] Even two weeks after the arrival of British troops, some DCDA members were expecting the Irish army would still come in.[104] In addition, as one rioter later put it, 'the people who'd done all the rioting were not the ones who welcomed the Brits'.[105] On the Catholic side, calls for British troops in Derry did not represent a concerted policy. On the other hand, the RUC and the Stormont government definitely wanted the troops in. They could no longer contain the disorder on their own.[106] To suggest the army was sent in as a sort of neutral arbiter is to obscure their principal function, of helping to restore order which ultimately meant restoring the authority of the Stormont government.

When hostility to the troops developed, Unionists saw it as yet further proof that Catholic protestations about 'defence' masked a Republican plot. But, though the troops were generally welcomed by people behind the barricades,[107] the attitude to them was marked by a certain equivocation from the beginning.

Free Derry and the British army

Officially, the British army had come in to Derry 'in aid of the civil power', the RUC, but the aid they gave was limited. It did not extend to restoring Stormont authority in the Bogside and Creggan by force. Even though British troops were now on the streets, the British government was still trying to minimise its involvement. When the DCDA approached the army shortly after they arrived in the city and offered to bring an end to rioting if the RUC were pulled back and if the army stayed out of Free Derry, the British officer in charge agreed cheerfully, apparently without consulting a higher authority.[108] It seems that the army in Derry had been politically instructed to, above all, avoid becoming involved in a confrontation. Thus, British recognition of the 'no-go' area and their willingness to deal with a 'rebellious' group like the DCDA, can be attributed principally to a political decision to minimise British involvement, to hold the line but do nothing more than that.

This British army decision in Derry apparently represented an official recognition of the DCDA and of its authority. For the following month Free Derry, surrounded by barricades and policed by the DCDA peace corps, was administered by the DCDA in constant negotiation with the local British army commanders. In the process, the DCDA displaced the political authority of the local MP, John Hume, and of all the local political parties. Brian Faulkner later complained that it had been a major mistake for the army to 'tacitly accept the right of various Republicans and known IRA men to rule and speak for these areas'.[109] However, at this stage local moderates and non-Republicans became more prominent in the DCDA and it would be quite inaccurate to say that the area was under Republican rule. The initial deal with the army, for example, was negotiated by Michael Canavan and Paddy Doherty in the company of a British Labour party MP.[110] Canavan and Doherty had political backgrounds which stretched back through the DCAC to the Credit Union movement and, although both were now co-operating with Republicans, they by no means had the same interests as the Republicans. Unionists refused to acknowledge that hostility to the RUC and the government had become so widespread and continued to view the DCDA as part of a Republican conspiracy.[111] The following day, Doherty and Canavan met the army again, refused a request to let British troops in to the area,[112] and made a series of demands, which included the abolition of Stormont, thus making clear how totally they rejected the Unionist government. During the following weeks, the barricades remained up as political bargaining tools for demands including the abolition of Stormont, the abolition of the B-Specials, the abolition of the Special Powers Act and the disarming of the RUC,[113] and not primarily for 'defence'. Thus, with the British army a little reluctantly staying outside the area, a curious interregnum began.

During these first weeks, the army appears to have operated under only 'hesitant direction'[114] from the British government. Local commanders acted with a great deal of autonomy and the army became immersed in the local political scene, to the extent of trying to attend meetings of the local political parties.[115] In the absence of decisive political direction from above, the army became a political force, developing its own priorities and analyses and at times acting almost as a local administrative body. In the first few days after the arrival of the troops, relations between the army and the DCDA were extremely cordial. The Unionist government was in a state of shock and there was now a British acceptance that Catholic fears had been genuine and their responses understandable. The army presence was widely welcomed and if Republicans in Derry were 'disgusted' at this[116] they did not make it public. Seán Keenan, the most prominent of the older Republicans, was one of those who was now involved in regular contacts with the army and British politicians.

Good relations were possible not only because the army accepted the authority of the DCDA but also because there was little opportunity for friction to develop on the ground. The 500 members of the 1st Battalion of the Queen's Own Regiment who were posted to the city a few days after 14 August to replace the Prince of Wales Own Regiment[117] took up positions in sandbagged posts around the edge of the Bogside, thus maintaining the interface with the commercial city centre which the RUC had been so concerned to hold during the rioting. However, these troops did not stop or search or question people. They just sat there, outside the barricades. In these early weeks, army 'policing' duties were limited to manning a checkpoint on the Craigavon bridge[118] and checkpoints on the border roads out of Derry. The almost total absence of 'policing' by the army was crucial to the maintenance of friendly relations. If anything, people in the Bogside and Creggan seem to have been more annoyed at being stopped and questioned by DCDA peace corps members in their own area[119] who were often local youths, identified only by the white armbands they wore.[120] However, if the peace corps checkpoints annoyed people, army checkpoints might do so too.

An incident in the first few days after the arrival of the troops illustrated how far the army was prepared to go to maintain good relations in this initial period. During the 'Battle of the Bogside', a brand new bus had been hijacked. It had ended up as the centrepiece of a formidable barricade in Rosemount where it provided resting quarters for peace corps members on duty at the barricade.[121] The bus company was concerned to get the bus back and approached the army. A compromise was worked out through the army whereby the bus company would provide an older bus in exchange for the return of the new model being used in the barricade. Lt Col Millman, commander of the 1st Battalion, Queen's Own Regiment, said that if this arrangement did not suit the DCDA the army would provide alternative materials for the barricade and, if necessary, the army would rebuild the barricade themselves. In the event, that wasn't necessary and the DCDA handed back the new bus in return for an older replacement.[122] A key figure in these negotiations was Colin Wallace, an assistant from the army's public relations unit, based at headquarters in Lisburn. He had accompanied the first troops into Derry on behalf of the army's PR unit. A few years later, he would be at the centre of a major controversy over the role of British intelligence and public relations operations in Northern Ireland.[123]

In these early days, the army gave generous recognition to the DCDA. A 'hot-line' was set up to deal with any problems and the army acted as a go-between with outside agencies such as the post office.[124] When Derry City Football Club enquired about security arrangements for an upcoming match at their grounds in Free Derry, the army told them to contact the DCDA. The DCDA offered to steward the match but this was turned down.[125] When a small British military convoy entered the Bogside, apparently by mistake, Seán Keenan and Paddy Doherty caught up with it, complained about the incursion and later received an apology and an assurance that such an incident would not be repeated.[126] Behind the barricades, the DCDA met virtually every night and carried out a range of functions.[127] Policing was under the charge of the DCDA and barricades were manned by peace corps members from 8 p.m. to 8 a.m.[128] As one RUC county inspector sourly put it, the DCDA were 'the *de facto* government of the area.'[129]

During these first weeks in Free Derry, the DCDA expanded rapidly. It came to represent a wide range of opinion in the area but the radical left (both Labour and Republican) and the older Republicans were probably over-represented on it. The DCDA eventually had forty-four members of whom about fifteen were on the left.[130] It also included at least nine of the older Republicans, people like Seán Keenan, Tom Mellon, Barney McFadden, Tom Carlin and Liam McDaid, who would become prominent Provisionals, and others such as Gerry Doherty who would stay with the Officials. At least three of them would be interned in August 1971. It also included at least five active members of the Independent Organisation and representatives from tenants' associations who also tended to have other political affiliations, either 'moderate', Nationalist or Republican.[131] Thus, although the DCDA spanned the political spectrum, Republicans and the left tended to be over-represented partly because they were more enthusiastic about the DCDA than moderates. Although Independent Organisation members had become involved with the DCDA at an early stage, there was by no means contentment with this among all members of the party. At an Independent Organisation meeting where a report on the DCDA was given, details about the composition and terms of reference of the DCDA were sought.

When the information wasn't forthcoming, there was a 'heated discussion' and eventually the meeting decided to obtain a list of DCDA members before backing the committee.[132]

The first few weeks of Free Derry were a time of great excitement, and radical students and foreign journalists flooded into Derry. During this time, Free Derry press passes were issued to journalists from around seventy-four different countries.[133] All around the area posters went up saying 'barricades are nice'.[134] The Bogside police were commanded by an American journalist who, rumour had it, was a CIA agent; the pubs stayed open all night long and 'Radio Bogside' called for people to send in 'entertaining stories about the present troubles'.[135] There was a Free Derry *Fleadh Ceoil* (music festival), the first of its kind in Northern Ireland, which drew musicians such as the Dubliners, Tommy Makem and Shay Healy.[136]

Some of the radicals saw the barricades as a way to maintain pressure for the disarming of state forces, their disbandment and the eventual dismantling of the state.[137] The Republican and Labour radicals within the DCDA acted as an organised group more resistant to removing the barricades than the rest of the DCDA were. Eventually, the more Utopian ambitions were abandoned and the radicals accepted it was 'impossible to build a socialist society in one ghetto'[138] although some would still suggest the barricades remain in place until 'social justice is attained'.[139] However, they did try to promote a socialist agenda within the area. At one stage, the radicals put forward a programme calling on the DCDA to use its authority in the area to, among other things, control rents, ensure that overtime and minimum wage rates were paid, demand equal pay for women and provide free travel on the two bus routes in the area for students, the unemployed and pensioners.[140] The programme was proposed by the Labour Party Young Socialists who were a focus for radical Labour/Republican co-operation.

The moderates could make common cause with traditionalist Republicans in resisting such plans for social transformation behind the barricades. Both groups simply wanted to use the barricades to extract short-term political concessions and were not interested in building an alternative society behind them. Maintaining the barricades, as one of the older Republicans put it, would 'make partition more confounded'.[141]

Pressure on the British army to remove the barricades, by force if necessary, was exerted by the Unionist government at an early stage. For Unionists, army negotiations with Defence Committees in Derry and Belfast amounted to an 'acknowledgement of insurrection'. The DCDA responded to early Unionist statements calling for the removal of the barricades by holding a meeting at which they decided to keep the barricades up.[142] At this stage, pressure from moderates to remove the barricades was minimal and John Hume condemned calls for their removal.[143]

This decision by the DCDA obviously distressed the army who requested a meeting with them and said they now wanted to see a return to 'normality' and were prepared to offer certain guarantees in return for the removal of the barricades.[144] The meeting took place but did not result in any agreement. However, it is notable that army statements were now being issued through an army public relations officer rather than directly from a local commanding officer.[145] The army, which had begun almost naïvely,[146] was becoming just a little more calculating. Shortly after this, Chichester-Clark spoke at a meeting of the Middle Liberties Young Unionist Association, a stronghold of the 'Craigite' right in Derry, and promised them that the barricades would be removed.[147] This put more pressure on the army.

It was into this situation of slightly increased tension that James Callaghan, the British home secretary, arrived in Derry and was escorted into the Bogside by peace corps members to meet four members of the DCDA, including Seán Keenan.[148] His visit gave recognition to the DCDA but it seems clear it was intended to hasten the removal of the barricades through this gesture of British interest and goodwill. By now the Hunt Commission on the future of the RUC, a major concession to Catholic opinion, had begun its work and when the DCDA made demands which included the abolition of Stormont, Callaghan rejected them as unreasonable.[149] However, during the meeting DCDA members also complained about the fact that twenty-six Republicans had been interned since mid-August under the Special Powers Act.[150] Shortly after the meeting these internees were released.

With the Hunt Commission and the Scarman Tribunal to enquire into the events leading up to August 1969 under way and the symbolic victory represented by Callaghan's visit to the Bogside, the moderates became more inclined to take the barricades down.[151] The *Derry Journal*, associated with the Nationalist party and conservative Catholics, considered that the reforms were now well under way and a conservative columnist in the paper called for the barricades to be removed. The only concession the DCDA made, however, was to modify the barricades to let vehicles through and they announced that the barricades would remain until there was 'concrete evidence' of the reforms.[152]

This mounting pressure on the DCDA to remove the barricades eased when it was announced that RUC men, investigated over events at

Burntollet and in Derry in January 1969, were to face only internal disciplinary action. Suspicions grew of British government intentions and the extent to which Stormont was still in control. John Hume accused Callaghan of 'seeking the middle road between the suspension of Stormont and doing nothing'. The *Derry Journal* now wondered if Stormont could be trusted to implement the proposed reforms while Eamonn McCann said the decision had 'shattered confidence' in the reform process.[153] It gave a new lease of life to the barricades in Derry.

On 7 September, about a week after Callaghan's visit, 2,000 people turned up at an open-air public meeting held by the DCDA. The meeting agreed to maintain the barricades but to breach the main barricade in Rossville Street. The left opposed this decision and claimed that people had been bullied at the meeting.[154] The left were not the only ones unhappy with the DCDA. Independent Organisation members criticised the conduct of the meeting and complained that a written proposal passed to the platform had not been put to the meeting.[155] They were unhappy with the situation in Free Derry, with the 'undesirables behind the barricades' (presumably a reference to the many radical students in the area) and they felt 'that this element would have to go'.[156] They were also unhappy that the pubs were staying open 'til all hours.[157] Although John Hume argued that they needed 'to maintain some form of symbolic barricade', moderates were becoming less tolerant of Free Derry and of the political role the DCDA was playing even though it had no electoral mandate. The DCDA was usurping the role of John Hume and of political parties such as the Independent Organisation.[158]

It was in these circumstances that the army began to seek to undermine the authority of the DCDA and to deal with other forces in the community. The army invited a wide range of local groups, everybody up to and including the local Legion of Mary, (as one person who was there put it), to a meeting in a local hotel to discuss the barricades.[159] The meeting also included the DCDA and groups such as the tenants' associations. Although the DCDA had carried out a number of functions in Free Derry, the tenants' associations had also seen an expansion of their responsibilities and workload as they were drawn into dealing with housing, cleaning and transport problems behind the barricades. This was 'a very difficult period' for the tenants' associations as they received 'endless complaints'.[160]

The tenants' associations were not happy with the situation created by the barricades. In addition, they had strong political connections to the moderates and they undoubtedly had considerable local influence. It seemed that they could be an alternative focus of power within the area. Sidestepping the DCDA which had rejected army proposals for a compromise policing solution for the area,[161] the army put their policing proposals to the Central Council of Tenants' Associations (hereafter CCTA) in Derry. The army proposals caused a serious split in the tenants' associations[162], but this attempt by the army to deal with an alternative focus of power failed. It was a demonstration of the continued strength of the DCDA that the tenants' associations consulted the DCDA and decided they could not take a stand on an issue of such a 'political' nature.[163] It is notable, however, that army officers were becoming involved in dealing with, and trying to manipulate, local political forces at this very low level, away from the politicians.

Stymied in negotiations with the DCDA and pressurised by Unionists, the army became more assertive. Claiming that DCDA 'vigilantes' were operating in William Street where they had 'no right' to be, the army threatened to put troops there to prevent this. The army also said that they knew there were those in the Bogside who would welcome their policing plan. It was around this time that a small army convoy made an incursion into the Bogside and, though it was said it was accidental and the army made an apology, it seemed more like an attempt to test the waters or give a warning.[164]

On 14 September, after much internal argument,[165] the DCDA finally gave way to the pressure from within the area and from the British army and agreed to allow military police, 'Redcaps', into the area. However, they could only be called in for specific purposes by the DCDA.[166] The DCDA also took down half the barricades and as negotiations speeded up, the barricades were replaced completely by a white line, a symbolic border suggested by Michael Canavan and supported by John Hume and Paddy Doherty, one of the key figures in the DCDA.[167]

This agreement was backed by moderates, Nationalist conservatives and even by the Republican veteran, Neil Gillespie who would later be a prominent Provisional.[168] (However, Gillespie also had personal reasons for this as the first investigation carried out by the 'Redcaps' was into the accidental death of his son.)[169] Pressure from the Catholic church had been instrumental in having the barricades in Belfast taken down[170] but the church does not seem to have played such a key role in Derry. This was partly because moderates closely connected to the church were already prominent in the DCDA and thus there was little need for the church to intervene directly. In addition, alienation from the RUC and the government had been more comprehensive in Derry, developing over the previous year. Many priests did not feel the need to strongly oppose the barricades but it is alleged that the extent of the alienation of others was reflected in the presence in August 1969, of certain younger priests among the rioters, masked and throwing petrol bombs.[171]

Within a week all the barricades had come down but although 'Redcaps' could be called on for individual cases the area was still being policed by the DCDA peace corps. The Independent Organisation was now very much 'dissatisfied with the tactics' of the DCDA and wanted a swift return to normality.[172] They became so disillusioned with the DCDA that they tried unsuccessfully to restore the authority of the moribund DCAC.[173]

It appears to have been at this point that Lt Gen Sir Ian Freeland, British army GOC in Northern Ireland, informed the DCDA that 'Redcaps' and regular British troops would begin to patrol the area regardless of the views of the DCDA[174] and the DCDA appear to have realised that, with local criticism increasing, there was no way they could oppose the army.

Thus, as the last barricades came down, the British army issued a peremptory statement denying that they had struck a deal with the DCDA on the removal of the barricades: 'Redcaps' would now patrol the area in whatever way the army decided.[175]

After several weeks of negotiation, the army was now refusing to recognise the authority of the DCDA and was in no uncertain terms asserting its right to police the Bogside. This marked the end of a brief period when the British government and army had accepted the right of these Defence Associations to negotiate political concessions from a position of strength. In these weeks, relations between the army and the DCDA had changed dramatically, because the army had come under political pressure to restore normality as quickly as possible. Once that pressure was applied there was never any question as to the attitude the army would take. There was no contest between generalised sympathy with 'the Catholics' and the political priority of restoring the authority of the Stormont government.

However, if the political question was not now resolved and the Bogside tried a repeat of August 1969 it would be the British army they would face. Free Derry had rejected the state and its police force. To reconcile Free Derry to this state would require a transformation. It was no longer a question of adapting Northern Ireland slightly in order to abate Catholic hostility to the state: it had to be changed significantly. The reforms which the British government now imposed on the Stormont government were absolutely crucial. They got off to an auspicious start, for Catholics, with the publication of the Hunt Report which recommended the disbandment of the B-Specials and the disarming of the RUC. As the radical People's Democracy paper, *Free Citizen*, put it, the report 'struck at the very heart of the traditional Unionist machine'.[176] It seemed as if the transformation of the way the state was run, demanded loudly by all sections of the Catholic community, was now under way.

The failure of reform

On 10 October 1969, the Hunt Report was published and it was announced that the inspector general of the RUC was to be replaced by an English policeman, Sir Arthur Young. At the same time, the British government also announced that control of housing was to be taken away from local government and centralised and that the proposed new local government boundaries which had aroused Catholic complaint would be changed. The following day, riots in protest against Hunt's recommendations broke out on the Shankill Road in Belfast. During these riots, Protestants shot dead an RUC man, the first RUC member to be killed in the conflict, and the British army shot dead two Protestants, the first people killed by the army since their arrival. The army repressed the riots in the Shankill brutally and arrested no fewer than 300 people.[177] However, if the riots convinced Catholics that the British were serious about reform, the riots also shocked the British government and contemporary sources suggested that it now diluted its reforms substantially in order to hold on to Protestant opinion.[178] The day after the publication of the Hunt Report, British military police, accompanied by regular soldiers, began to patrol the Bogside and Creggan, the first patrols of any kind in two months. Three days after that, the 'Redcaps' were patrolling in the company of unarmed RUC men. From the point of view of the British government and army it may have seemed as if there was only one small step left to take to achieve 'normal' policing, that is, for the 'Redcaps' to leave.

After the publication of the Hunt Report, the DCDA decided that their responsibilities were over and they stood down immediately. Seán Keenan declared that he now had no problem with the RUC coming into the area. The British army commander in Derry, Brigadier Peter Leng, proudly declared that 'the vigilantes' powers have now ceased' and that any local problems would be tackled through the tenants' associations. British troops set up a base in a girls' school between Creggan and the Bogside, taking over six classrooms and announced their intention to set up a permanent RUC station in the area as soon as possible.[179]

Military policemen and soldiers began to carry out joint patrols of the area in Land Rovers. When James Callaghan arrived back in Derry for a second visit, this time with Sir Arthur Young, the new head of the RUC, it became clear that the authority of those running the DCDA had been massively diminished. This time Callaghan met not only Paddy Doherty and Seán Keenan, formerly of the DCDA, but also John Hume and people from the Independent Organisation, the Labour party, tenants' associations and, significantly, local priests who had previously kept a low political profile.[180] All this showed that a large swathe of 'respectable' Catholic opinion was putting its weight behind these new arrangements, and was glad the DCDA and the barricades were gone.

Catholic political reaction to the Hunt Report was enthusiastic. The Independent Organisation said that when the Hunt Report and other proposed reforms were '... fully implemented, the civil rights movement in this country can be considered to have drawn to a hitherto unbelievably successful conclusion'.[181] They also called publicly for Catholics to join the RUC. Eddie McAteer called on Catholics to support the RUC, 'even if the uniform does bring back dark memories', a back-handed reference to the fact that not all of Hunt's suggestions had been adopted. The *Derry Journal* too called on Catholics to accept the RUC. The Derry Young Unionists on the other hand denounced the reforms as a 'sell out'.[182] While Republicans and radicals did not voice unrestrained enthusiasm, the reforms had succeeded in winning back large sections of Catholic political opinion which had been alienated and had ended up in an uneasy and uncomfortable alliance which had included the radical left and militant Republicans.

That is not to say that all was well. The first signs of tension between the troops and Catholic civilians had already appeared and when the first unarmed RUC men appeared in the Bogside they were jeered. Local people complained that it was the same old faces who were in the 'new' RUC.[183]

Although the reform of the RUC was greeted enthusiastically by many Catholics, there were a number of reasons why the force did not become fully accepted. In the first place, as hecklers in the Bogside pointed out, the RUC still contained the same personnel and therefore the men who had been at Burntollet and who had beaten Sammy Devenney but had never been prosecuted. Although personnel could be expected to change, and indeed there appears to have been an extensive 'purge' of the RUC officers in Derry,[184] this was not going to happen immediately. There was also the symbolic question of the change in uniform colour suggested by Hunt. Callaghan later said that the failure to bring this in was due to a low-level error which didn't seem worth rectifying.[185] On the other hand, a contemporary source suggested that the Shankill riots had provoked a decision to dilute the proposed changes including the proposal to change the uniform.[186] This sounds entirely plausible. The uniform was more important than Callaghan suggested and it was not at all insignificant to Catholics that the RUC were 'still proudly wearing their hated black uniform'.[187] Even after the arrival of the troops, Catholic youths had regularly thrown stones at RUC cars at the edge of the Bogside.[188] They were not about to stop now, and while moderates welcomed the changes in the RUC they still had too many misgivings about the force to become outraged by attacks on them. In the circumstances 'normal' policing could not be resumed.

Catholics had also warmly welcomed Hunt's proposal to disband the B-Specials, but they were less certain about his proposal to replace them with a unit under direct British military control. After the army had arrived, the B-Specials had remained on duty in certain areas, most notably on the roads to the border around Derry. Their conduct was a matter for complaint[189] and they were accused of firing shots on a number of occasions. The announcement that they were to be disbanded delighted Catholics as much as it outraged Protestants. How it came about that even this concession appeared to dissipate is a large part of the explanation of the failure of these major reforms.

In November 1969, the Stormont government began to recruit for the new British army regiment to be known as the Ulster Defence Regiment (hereafter UDR). From the beginning, Catholic politicians questioned the need for the regiment, asking from what it was intended to 'defend Ulster'. The inclusion of 'Ulster' in the title, a term for Northern Ireland favoured by Unionists, caused annoyance too, but the main problem was that the recruitment campaign for the UDR was run by the Stormont government and not by the British government or army. Already John Hume had complained that Stormont was playing up the oath of allegiance which had to be taken before joining the RUC.[190] Ivan Cooper attacked the UDR recruiting campaign saying 'TV and newspaper advertising has been geared to making this force unpalatable to the minority in Northern Ireland'. Cooper even went so far as to suggest the civil rights movement might have to go back on the streets. John Hume complained that UDR recruitment forms had been sent to many serving B-Specials and Cooper said 'the creation of a defence force largely composed of B-Specials will not quench our thirst for justice'.[191]

A few weeks before this, the Independent Organisation had considered the question of encouraging Catholics to join the UDR. Despite objections within the party to this 'it was generally agreed that', if they didn't, they 'would be back to square one'.[192] Now the Independent Organisation, claiming that the Unionist government at Stormont was trying 'to take over' the UDR, made a number of calls for changes to the proposed regiment. Most of the demands were simply calls to fully implement the Hunt Report's original recommendations. Among other things they wanted the name changed, the force reduced to the size Hunt had recommended, and that former B-Special county commanders should not be transferred into the force as the UDR battalion commanders.[193]

When the UDR became operational in April 1970, all of the UDR battalion commanders were former B-Specials, and of the 300 Co. Derry UDR men, half were former B-Specials.[194] The Co. Derry battalion was 20 per cent Catholic. (The UDR as a whole was initially 18 per cent Catholic.) Given that Catholics formed around half the population of Co. Derry, while Northern Ireland as a whole was about 35 per cent Catholic, this suggests an even lower representation of Catholics in the Derry battalion than in other areas of the North. This was not, contrary to what Callaghan said, 'sufficient to show that the UDR was not just the B-Specials under another name'.[195] In many respects, as Independent Organisation members had feared, it was now 'back to square one'. In addition, the IRA campaign which was now beginning played a major role in forcing many Catholics out of the regiment. Within a month of the establishment of the regiment, Catholic UDR men had been fired at in villages in West Tyrone near the Donegal border.[196]

However, as with the new-look RUC, even Catholic moderates never felt happy with the UDR, believing it represented a reform gone wrong, twisted out of shape by the Stormont government. Given the well of hostility to the state which had grown, the reforms were not a sufficient response. It is, of course, debatable whether they ever could have been, but the way they were implemented leached away much of the trust which Catholic moderates had reposed in the benevolent intentions of the British government. Ultimately the reforms were diluted and rendered ineffective because of British government concern to 'calm the fears of the Catholic community without awakening those of the Protestants'.[197] As Callaghan put it, 'in winning back the Catholics we could not afford to lose the Protestants'.[198]

Eventually the British government would, to an extent, 'lose the Protestants' anyway, but in this crucial period they signally failed to 'win back' the Catholics. This was because the British government seems to have failed to understand how much Catholics had rejected Stormont.

In the context of continued Catholic distrust and alienation as the reforms were diluted, British calls for integrated education and Catholic co-operation with the Stormont government in order to improve 'community relations'[199] were little more than platitudes. In August 1969, Derry Catholics had believed themselves within a whisker of a united Ireland and were fighting the RUC as a dangerous enemy. It would take a lot to restore any relationship between them and the state which was non-confrontational. The groundwork for such a relationship was not laid by these half-hearted, diluted reforms.

The limits of British pressure and of the capacity for change of the state are illustrated by Callaghan's account of asking Chichester-Clark, after the August riots, if he could broaden his government, presumably by bringing in Catholics. Callaghan seems to have reacted with equanimity to Clark's response that there was 'absolutely no possibility' of this.[200]

Now that the Catholic minority in Northern Ireland was politically active there was 'absolutely no possibility' that the state could stabilise without trying to include this third of the population politically. The Catholic minority was now active and organised as it had never been before in the history of the state. The minority, across the ideological spectrum, was now hostile to, or at least mistrustful of, the state. The British government was playing a balancing act which, by its concern not to destabilise the Unionist government, precluded any major changes to the way Northern Ireland functioned. There appeared to be no prospect of changes which would end the exclusion of the minority from the exercise of political power. The attempts to gain Catholic acceptance of the security forces were faltering and failing. In the circumstances, confrontation on the streets was likely to continue. Now, however, the British army was maintaining order on the streets and it began to become an increasingly important factor in the political equation in Northern Ireland.

Notes and references

1 As the Labour MPs put it. DJ, 1/8/69, p. 6.
2 Interview with Patrick L. Doherty ('Paddy Bogside'), head of the Inner-city Trust, formerly a member of the DCDA, DCAC and founder member of the Credit Union in Derry.
3 Patrick Bishop and Eamon Mallie, *The Provisional IRA* (Corgi, London, 1988), p. 97.

4 Interview with Ivan Cooper, member of the Young Unionist party in Mid-Derry in the mid-1960s. Member of the Derry Labour party in the later 1960s, former chairman of the DCAC, former Independent and, later, SDLP MP at Stormont for Mid-Derry.

5 Scarman Report, *Report of Tribunal of Inquiry into Violence and Civil Disturbances in Northern Ireland*, 1969. Vols. 1 and 2, Cmd. 566 (HMSO, Belfast, 1972), p. 65; interview with Willie O'Connell, formerly a senior member of the Independent Organisation, the DCDA and the DCCC, SDLP member of Derry City Council and former Mayor of Derry. Interview with Michael Canavan, founder member of the Derry Credit Union, formerly a senior member of the DCAC, the DCDA, the DCCC and the Independent Organisation. Former SDLP assembly member.

6 Paddy Doherty in W.H Van Voris, *Violence in Ulster. An Oral Documentary* (University of Massachusetts, 1975), p. 130.

7 Eamonn McCann, *War and an Irish Town* (Penguin, Harmondsworth, 1974), p. 58.

8 Bishop and Mallie, *IRA*, pp. 93–4.

9 O'Connell, interview.

10 Independent Organisation, minutes, 1/8/69.

11 O'Connell, interview.

12 DJ, 12/8/69, pp. 1, 5.

13 Scarman Report, pp. 68–70.

14 Paddy Doherty, interview. They did not use the DCAC stewarding organisation, did not use an experienced steward organiser to take charge of the stewarding and seem to have been quite unperturbed by the fact that far too few stewards turned up on the day; also Keenan, evidence given to Scarman Tribunal in DJ, 28/10/69, p. 1.

15 Keenan, evidence given to Scarman Tribunal in DJ, 28/10/69, p. 1.

16 McCann, *War*, p. 59.

17 Paddy Doherty, interview.

18 Ibid.

19 Ibid., and Paddy Doherty, *Paddy Bogside* (Mercier, Cork, 2001), pp. 118–27.

20 Ibid.

21 Interview with Anon. B, former member of the Republican movement in Derry.

22 Ibid.

23 Seán Keenan, cited in Bishop and Mallie, *IRA*, p. 98.

24 Interview with Jim Guy, Independent Unionist councillor, former Mayor of Derry, former Ulster Unionist party councillor, former Secretary and Lieutenant-Governor of the Apprentice Boys of Derry, former Secretary and Grand Master of the City of Derry Grand Orange Lodge, former Honorary Secretary of Londonderry and Foyle Unionist Association.

25 Paddy Doherty in Van Voris, *Violence in Ulster*, p. 130.

26 DJ, 8/8/69, p. 1.

27 The Reverend R. Dickinson, evidence to Scarman Tribunal, Day 5 (24/9/69) p. 41.

28 Ibid.

29 Scarman Report, p. 66; McCann, *War*, p. 59.

30 Scarman Report, p. 68.

31 DJ, 28/10/69, p. 1.

32 Interview 1 with Eamonn McCann.
33 Evidence of CI Gerald Mahon to Scarman Tribunal, in DJ, 3/10/69, p. 6.
34 *Nusight*, September 1969, p. 49; Raymond McClean, *The Road to Bloody Sunday* (Ward River Press, Dublin, 1983), p. 75.
35 Scarman Report, p. 70.
36 Ibid.
37 McClean, evidence to Scarman Tribunal, in DJ, 9/12/69, p. 1.
38 Guy, interview; evidence of the Reverend R. Dickinson to Scarman Tribunal, Day 5. (24/9/69) p. 48.
39 *Nusight*, September 1969, p. 50; Scarman Report, p. 72.
40 *Barricade Bulletin*, No. 9, 23/8/69.
41 Gregory Campbell in DJ, supplement, 14/8/89.
42 *Nusight*, September 1969, p. 50.
43 Scarman Report, p. 72 and *Nusight*, September 1969, p. 50.
44 Guy, interview.
45 Scarman Report, p. 72.
46 McClean, *Bloody Sunday*, p. 75.
47 CI Corbett evidence to Scarman Tribunal in DJ, 3/10/69, p. 6.
48 DJ, 3/10/69.
49 *Ulster, the facts*, Belfast, Ulster Unionist Council, September, 1969.
50 Evidence of DI Shillington to Scarman Tribunal, DJ, 3/10/69, p. 1.
51 McClean, *Bloody Sunday*, p. 76. He had treated a man hit in the face by a gas canister.
52 Scarman Report, p. 76.
53 DJ, 19/8/69.
54 Scarman Report, p. 77.
55 John Bayley and Peter Loizos, 'Bogside Off its Knees', *New Society*, 21/8/69.
56 *Barricade Bulletin*, No. 1, 14/8/69.
57 McClean, *Bloody Sunday*, pp. 80–1.
58 Scarman Report, p. 79.
59 McCann, *War*, p. 60.
60 Patrick Buckland, *A History of Northern Ireland* (Gill and Macmillan, Dublin, 1981), p. 133.
61 McCann, *War*, p. 60; White, *Statesman*, p. 84.
62 Interview 1 with Gregory Campbell, leader of DUP group on Derry City Council, DUP activist since the early 1970s, member of the Young Unionists in the early 1970s. Interview with Glen Barr, senior member of LAW and the UDA in the early 1970s.
63 Scarman Report, pp. 80–2.
64 Ibid.; evidence of John Porter to Scarman Tribunal in DJ, 28/11/69, p. 6.
65 Interview with Mary Nelis, founder member and former chairperson, secretary, PRO of Foyle Hill Tenants' Association (Creggan), former SDLP candidate for Derry City Council, currently a Sinn Féin member of Derry City Council.
66 Paddy Doherty in Van Voris, *Violence in Ulster*, p. 132.
67 Scarman Report, p. 80.
68 McClean, *Bloody Sunday*, p. 77; Scarman Report, p. 82.
69 Interview with Pat Devine, former DCAC steward, leader of the SDLP group on Derry City Council, former mayor of Derry.

70 Paddy Doherty in Van Voris, *Violence in Ulster*, p. 130; evidence to the Scarman Tribunal in DJ, 2/12/69, p. 6.

71 Margie Bernard, *Daughter of Derry. The story of Brigid Sheils Makowski* (Pluto, London, 1989), p. 69.

72 Sean Séamus O'Hara in Tom Collins, *The Irish Hunger Strike* (White Island, Dublin, 1986), p. 267.

73 Interview with Mitchel McLaughlin; Sinn Féin member of Derry City Council; joined the Republican movement in 1966; stayed with the Officials after the split in 1970 but later joined the Provisionals.

74 Paddy Doherty, interview.

75 See Michael Farrell, *Northern Ireland: The Orange State* (Pluto, London, 1980), pp. 262–3; Bishop and Mallie, *IRA*, pp. 105–17.

76 McLaughlin, interview.

77 Scarman Report, p. 82.

78 RUC District Inspector in evidence to Scarman Tribunal in DJ, 9/12/70, p. 5.

79 Scarman Report, p. 82.

80 Shillington in Ryder, 1989, p. 11.

81 DI McAtamney, evidence at Scarman Tribunal, DJ, 9/12/69, p. 5.

82 Ibid.

83 CI David Corbett, evidence at Scarman Tribunal, DJ, 3/10/69, p. 6.

84 Scarman Report, p. 80.

85 Scarman Report, p. 82.

86 Scarman Report, p. 68.

87 Clive Limpkin, *The Battle of Bogside* (Penguin, Harmondsworth, 1972), p. 19.

88 Frank Curran, *Derry. Countdown to Disaster* (Gill and Macmillan, Dublin, 1986), p. 74, photographs; Limpkin, *Battle of Bogside*, pp. 4–5, pp. 16–17, photographs. See also Shane O'Doherty, *The Volunteer. A former IRA man's true story* (Fount, London, 1993), pp. 47, 53. O'Doherty took part in a civil rights march at thirteen, in rioting at fourteen and joined the IRA at the age of fifteen.

89 Paddy Doherty in Van Voris, *Violence in Ulster*, p. 132; Limpkin, *Battle of Bogside*, p. 47; *Times* report cited in Des Hamill, *Pig in the Middle. The Army in Northern Ireland 1969–1985* (Methuen, London, 1986), p. 5; Aileen McCorkell, *A Red Cross in My Pocket. Derry/Londonderry 1968–1974* (Workers Educational Association, Belfast, 1992), pp. 28, 30.

90 Limpkin, *Battle of Bogside*, p. 123.

91 Morris Fraser, *Children in Conflict* (Secker and Warburg, London, 1975), pp. 7–9, p. 119; for a survey of the academic debate on political activism by children see Ed Cairns, *Children and Political Violence* (Blackwell, Oxford, 1996), pp. 107–37.

92 *Derry Emigrant Bulletin*, c. August 1969 (undated).

93 McClean, *Bloody Sunday*, p. 81.

94 See Cairns, *Children*, pp. 109–10 for a discussion on whether violence 'politicises' children.

95 See, for example, *Independent on Sunday*, 5/9/93, p. 10 on teenage militants in Gaza, and Cairns, *Children*, p. 133, citing research on South Africa.

96 Scarman Report, p. 84.

97 Evidence of Dickinson at Scarman Tribunal, Day 5 (24/9/69), pp. 66 ff.

98 DJ, 15/8/69, p. 1.

99　Limpkin, *Battle of Bogside*, pp. 26–9; McCann, *War*, p. 61; Scarman Report, pp. 83–4.
100　Bishop Edward Daly in DJ, supplement, c. 14/8/89.
101　White, *Statesman*, p. 88.
102　James Callaghan, in IT supplement, 14/8/89.
103　McCann, *War*, p. 62.
104　Conor Cruise O'Brien, *States of Ireland* (Panther Books, St Albans, 1974), p. 180.
105　Interview with Anon. D, former member of the Republican movement in Derry.
106　Hamill, *Pig in the Middle*, pp. 4–7.
107　Cooper, interview.
108　Canavan, interview; White, *Statesman*, p. 89.
109　Hamill, *Pig in the Middle*, p. 23.
110　Scarman Report, p. 84.
111　See *Ulster, the facts*, September, 1969.
112　Scarman Report, p. 85.
113　*DCDA Newsletter*, no. 12, 28/8/69.
114　Hamill, *Pig in the Middle*, p. 26.
115　McCann, interview 2; British officers asked to attend meetings of the Derry Labour party but the request was refused.
116　See Bishop and Mallie, *IRA*, p. 101.
117　DJ, 19/8/69, p. 1.
118　DJ, 19/8/69, p. 5.
119　*DCDA Newsletter*, no. 6, 22/8/69.
120　DJ, 19/8/69, p. 1.
121　Canavan, interview.
122　DJ, 22/8/69, p. 1; Canavan, interview.
123　Paul Foot, *Who framed Colin Wallace?* (Pan Books, 1990), pp. 9–10.
124　DJ, 22/8/69, p. 1.
125　DJ, 26/8/69, p. 2.
126　DJ, 12/9/69, p. 1.
127　Canavan, interview.
128　DJ, 19/8/69, p. 1.
129　DJ, 29/8/69, p. 6.
130　McCann, *War*, p. 65.
131　Canavan, interview; Paddy Doherty, interview; O'Connell, interview; Nelis, interview; photograph 'the faithful' of last meeting of the DCDA with list of twenty-nine names.
132　Independent Organisation, minutes, 9/9/69.
133　Interview with Dermie McClenaghan, former Derry Labour party activist and member of the DHAC, the DCAC and (unbeknownst to him) the DCDA, former Youth Worker with Queen St. Youth Project 1971–72.
134　Ibid.
135　*DCDA, newsletter*, 9/9/69, no. 16; McCann, interview; White 1985, p. 89; O'Connell, interview.
136　DJ, 29/8/69, p. 13.
137　Interview with Terry Robson, chairman of Derry Labour Party Young Socialists in the early 1970s and member of the NILP executive. Member of the Official Republican movement from late 1971.

138 *Barricade Bulletin*, 10/9/69.
139 Finbar O'Doherty in DJ, 16/9/69, p. 1.
140 *Barricade Bulletin*, 10/9/69.
141 Neil Gillespie in DJ, 16/9/69, p. 7.
142 *DCDA newsletter*, 25/8/69, no. 9.
143 DJ, 19/8/69, p. 5.
144 DJ, 26/8/69, p. 1.
145 DJ, 26/8/69, p. 2.
146 McCann, *War*, p. 64.
147 DJ, 26/8/69, p. 2.
148 McCann, *War*, p. 69; DJ, 29/8/69, p. 1.
149 Ibid., p. 61.
150 DJ, 29/8/69, p. 1.
151 McCann, *War*, p. 70.
152 DJ, 2/9/69, p. 4.
153 DJ, 5/9/69, pp. 1, 4, 8.
154 DJ, 9/9/69, pp. 1, 5.
155 Independent Organisation, minutes 9/9/69.
156 Ibid.
157 O'Connell, interview.
158 Independent Organisation, minutes, 11/9/69.
159 Nelis, interview.
160 Ibid.
161 DJ, 9/9/69, p. 1.
162 Nelis, interview.
163 DJ, 12/9/69, p. 6; Nelis, interview.
164 DJ, 12/9/69, p. 1.
165 Canavan, interview.
166 DJ, 16/9/69, p. 1.
167 DJ, 19/9/69, p. 1; Canavan, interview.
168 DJ, 16/9/69, pp. 4, 7.
169 DJ, 10/10/69, p. 1.
170 Farrell, *Orange State*, p. 267.
171 McLaughlin, interview.
172 Independent Organisation, minutes, 30/9/69.
173 Ibid., 23/9/69 and 30/9/69.
174 White, *Statesman*, p. 93.
175 DJ, 23/9/69, p. 6.
176 *Free Citizen*, No. 2, Oct 1969 [undated].
177 *Nusight*, November 1969, pp. 9, 10.
178 Ibid.
179 DJ, 14/10/69, pp. 1, 5.
180 Ibid., p. 5.
181 *Indfo*, November 1969.
182 DJ, 14/10/69, p. 6; 17/10/69, pp. 1, 8.
183 DJ, 21/10/69, p. 5.
184 N.I. Constabulary list and directory, 1969 and 1972. Of the thirteen senior
     RUC men in Derry in 1969, only two were still there in 1972.
185 James Callaghan, *A House Divided* (Collins, London, 1973), p. 114.

186 *Nusight*, Nov. 1969, pp. 9–10.
187 *Free Citizen*, No. 5, late 1969, undated.
188 DJ, 23/9/69, pp. 4, 5, 6.
189 DJ, 19/8/69, p. 1.
190 DJ, 14/11/69, p. 7.
191 DJ, 18/11/69, p. 1.
192 Independent Organisation, minutes 28/10/69.
193 DJ, 18/11/69, p. 1.
194 DJ, 7/4/70, p. 4, 14/4/70, p. 8.
195 Callaghan, *House Divided*, p. 134.
196 DJ, 22/5/69, p. 1; 10/7/69, p. 1.
197 Callaghan, *House Divided*, p. 70.
198 Ibid., pp. 78–9.
199 Ibid., p. 107.
200 Ibid., p. 61.

The British Army:
August 1969–April 1970

Honeymoon

British troops had been on the streets of Derry for only four days when the army GOC in Northern Ireland, Lt Gen Sir Ian Freeland, said that he suspected that the 'honeymoon' period would be short-lived, that it had probably already reached its peak and that the army could soon become an object of both Protestant and Catholic hostility.[1]

In Derry, some in the Catholic community had opposed welcoming the army from the outset. A few days after they arrived, the army searched two Catholic farms near Derry in a joint operation with the RUC under the Special Powers Act. Derry Labour party radicals stated that 'No further proof is needed that the troops, whatever they are here for, are certainly not here to protect us from the excesses of unionism'.[2] In addition, both radical and traditionalist Republicans began to prepare for an armed campaign immediately after the arrival of the troops. They naturally were opposed to the army presence.

However, the Labour left and both brands of Republicanism were still on the margins of political opinion in the Catholic community. A broad swathe of Catholic opinion, from the Catholic church and the Nationalist party through to the Independent Organisation, accepted the presence of the army. They saw it as necessary, as much for the restoration of law and order and some form of 'policing', as for the 'defence' of Catholic areas in Derry. Initially, there was a great deal of goodwill towards the army and there was what one Republican later described as a 'pathetic love relationship' between the army and people in the Bogside.[3] Apprehension in the Catholic community was centred, not on how the army's role would develop but on 'what will happen when they are withdrawn'.[4] Even a Labour radical such as

Eamonn McCann could argue at one point, that the Free Derry barricades should remain because otherwise the troops might leave and Catholics would be left again at the mercy of Stormont.[5]

The troops were seen as a temporary measure, not as a permanent fixture. Over the following months, this goodwill towards the army gradually dissipated. Most analysis of the end of the 'honeymoon' focuses on rioting in Belfast in the spring of 1970, and two distinct factors are seen as crucial: the role of the army in escorting controversial Orange marches past Catholic areas[6] and a Provisional Republican 'policy of alienating Catholics from the army by forcing soldiers to react vigorously in Catholic areas'.[7]

However, in Derry, relations between the army and sections of the Catholic community began to break down within weeks of the army's arrival. This was principally because of the new operational role which the army adopted after the barricades around Free Derry came down. This breakdown was facilitated by a number of other factors: by the continued prosecution of people arrested for rioting before the army arrived, by the lack of concerted liaison between the army and the Catholic community after the dissolution of the DCDA,[8] and by the growth of Irish nationalist sentiment and Republican sympathies among Catholic youths. However, probably the most important factor was the way in which the army became embedded in the life of the city and became involved in policing and controlling the Catholic population at a time when there was no sense of political resolution, no sense of an end to the confrontation with the Unionist government.

While they were negotiating the removal of the barricades, the army had recognised forces within the Catholic community as an alternative focus of power. Afterwards, they seem to have been reluctant to go back to such a situation of dual authority in any form. They began to police Derry on their own authority, in co-operation only with the RUC and without reference to forces in the Catholic community.

On 23 September 1969, the DCDA removed the last of the barricades around the Bogside. The following day, by a grim coincidence, the first serious rioting since the arrival of the troops took place. It began when a fight broke out between a few Catholic and Protestant teenagers leaving the technical college on the Strand Road. The college had been a focus for sectarian tension in recent months as one of the few places where young Catholics and Protestants mixed. The fight developed into a running battle and as the youths ran into the city centre, groups of Protestants came out of the Fountain to help the Protestant youths. Groups of Catholic youths began to move into the city centre and before long several hundred people were confronting each other around the Diamond.[9] At this point, troops appeared on the scene and separated the crowds by clearing Ferryquay Street and sealing either end of it with barbed wire. However, the army had a poor grasp of local sectarian geography and, as they cleared this street, part of the Protestant crowd were pushed up or rushed up a side street which led on to Bishop Street, where Catholic crowds were still gathered. Clashes broke out and by the time the troops intervened, William King, a middle-aged Protestant from the Fountain, was dead. He had suffered a heart attack while being beaten.[10] His death had much the same effect on Derry Protestants as the death of Sammy Devenny had had on Catholics, and increased their sense of fear. His funeral too was understood in political terms, and prominent local Unionists were among the 2,000 people who walked in the funeral procession along streets lined with people.[11]

The death of William King brought to a head local Protestant anger over the army's 'softly-softly' approach to Free Derry. Protestants had expected the army to crush Free Derry, not to negotiate with it.[12] Now it appeared that, on top of the failure to do that, the army was allowing free rein to 'the brutality of the Roman Catholic mob', as the Waterside Young Unionists put it. They called now for the army to 'rule with an iron fist'.[13] The army responded to the riot in which William King died, and to the fact that Catholic youths had taken to casually stoning RUC men and cars where the edge of the Bogside met the city centre, by erecting a peace line in the city. It shortly became what the army described as a 'peace-ring'.[14]

The peace-ring in Derry was utterly different from the 'peace-lines' which had been erected by the army to separate Catholic and Protestant areas in Belfast after the severe sectarian rioting of August 1969. The Derry peace-ring, made up of army barriers and checkpoints, virtually encircled the Bogside and Creggan, cutting them off not just from the Protestant Fountain area but from the city centre and the rest of Derry.

The army now imposed what was described as a 'near-curfew' on the area. From 8 p.m. until 6 a.m. each night, every road but one into the Bogside was closed to vehicle traffic.[15] The one road which was left open was in the far south of the area, where Free Derry met the countryside, far from the city centre. Even emergency vehicles had to abide by the restrictions, and ambulances now experienced significant delays in answering emergency calls in the area.[16] In addition, most roads into or out of the Bogside were also closed to pedestrians during these hours, in particular the roads into the city centre. According to one source, people going from the Bogside into the city centre had to pass through army tents where some at least had to write down their name, address and destination when they left the area.[17] To a great extent this cut Bogsiders off from the city centre after dark and, as a result, a Catholic hall in the city centre cancelled all public functions until further notice.[18] St Eugene's Catholic Cathedral, on the edge of Free Derry was obliged to alter the times of its evening masses as people could no longer pass through the necessary checkpoints after 8 p.m.[19]

The peace-ring was a dramatic and characteristically military response to the recent rioting in the city centre. The army suddenly did not appear in a benevolent light. The army had wanted the Free Derry barricades removed in order that normality should be restored. The army's peace-ring created a situation which was anything but normal. It maintained the isolation and separation of Free Derry, without any of the benefits of its limited autonomy.

The 'honeymoon' had been possible because the troops had not been involved in 'controlling' the Catholic population. Now the army were treating Catholics as a problematic population. As the army took on these new functions, it changed the way it interacted with people on the street, particularly with young males, and created conditions for tension and confrontation.

These restrictions were apparently imposed without consultation with any forces in the Catholic community, least of all the DCDA. However, the fact that the Catholic church and Catholic conservative voices were raised in defence of these measures hint that perhaps the army had in fact consulted the church as it was doing in Belfast. The restrictions may also in part have been intended to pressurise the DCDA into agreeing to allow the army to patrol the Bogside without restriction as it began to do, in any case, shortly after this. It is a mark of the faith which many still had in the intentions of the British government and army that, despite the lack of consultation, there was little initial objection to the restrictions. The Catholic Bishop of Derry, Neil Farren, made a public call for people to accept the restrictions as did 'Onlooker', the conservative columnist in the *Derry Journal*, on the grounds that they 'prevented violence'.[20]

However, nobody could prevent the inevitable friction when young British soldiers refused to allow young Derry people to walk home along a certain street after 8 p.m. In the first week after the restrictions were introduced, six men were charged with disorderly behaviour at different checkpoints around the Bogside. All had objected to being denied passage through a checkpoint, or to having their car searched. None had used violence and the strongest action most of them were accused of was 'using fairly strong language' or 'speaking in an aggressive manner'.[21] All of them were convicted. While the army might not be 'ruling with an iron fist', it was certainly using a heavy hand.

The severity of the restrictions fluctuated over the following weeks and months and criticism of them gradually grew to include those conservative Catholics who had originally urged acceptance[22] and also the Nationalist party[23] and the Independent Organisation.[24] The restrictions also annoyed William Street traders who had seen a disastrous fall-off in trade. They sent a letter of protest to Jim Callaghan calling the restrictions 'petty and unnecessary'.[25] Even those groups who had been most accepting of the army presence, were of the opinion that the army now seemed to be encircling the Bogside and Creggan rather than protecting them. If this was disquieting to the most cautious elements in the Catholic community, reaction on the street, among local teenagers, was likely to be far stronger.

It has been said that a 'military security' approach to policing tends to be 'more cavalier' than the police approach.[26] However, initial army responses to civil unrest in Derry seem to draw, not on a slightly different military approach to 'policing', but on the army's recent experiences of dealing with civil unrest. This had been gained almost exclusively in colonial situations in the course of 'counter-insurgency' campaigns. These campaigns had often focused on the control and monitoring of suspect populations rather than on dealing with specific incidents.[27] Many of the British officers posted to Northern Ireland had experienced dealing with civil unrest and conflict only in such colonial campaigns. Brigadier Peter Leng, for example, the commander of the British troops in Derry, had been a battalion CO in Aden from 1964 to 1966,[28] when the British withdrew. It is hardly surprising that such officers should draw on their colonial experiences, in Aden, Malaya, Kenya, Cyprus or Oman, when dealing with the situation in Derry. While it was a matter of dispute whether Northern Ireland was more accurately characterised as a region of the UK or as a British colony, the British army which came to Northern Ireland in August 1969 was very much a colonial army, experienced in colonial campaigns. It was therefore inclined to treat the situation as a colonial one.

As an IRA campaign began in 1970, the army would begin a counter-insurgency campaign which it quite openly regarded as the latest in a long series of colonial campaigns.[29] However, even before that, the influence of their colonial experience was evident in the focus, not on responding to specific incidents but on controlling the movement of people from one community. The restrictions which they put on movement into and out of the Free Derry area demonstrated that it was the Catholic community which the army saw as the 'problematic' population. Such crude measures were ultimately alienating and tended to unite 'extremists' and 'moderates' in resentful complaint. In the absence of a political resolution, such an approach might easily degenerate into the permanent control and repression of the dissident population.

To a great extent, the erection of the peace-ring and the imposition of such restrictions ended the 'honeymoon' in Derry. It would continue, in some form, for another eighteen months but already in October 1969, the sort of innocent welcome the soldiers had initially received as symbols of Stormont's demise had begun to unravel.

In early October 1969, British military police and troops established a base between Bogside and Creggan and began to patrol the area in Jeeps.[30] In theory, the RUC was to take over such policing duties after the Hunt reforms made the force 'acceptable' in these areas. That did not happen and even in late 1969 it must have seemed quite clear it was not going to happen in the near future. The army was clearly not suited for such duties (as the *Derry Journal* noted at an early stage)[31] but it was undertaking them in quite a high-profile way. It seems plausible that the army, which had seen its responsibilities contract dramatically over the previous two decades as the British Empire shrank rapidly, welcomed this new role which increased the army's importance, raised its profile and gave it a sense of purpose. Over the following months, army commanders in Northern Ireland would become important figures in their own right and the army itself would influence the political direction of events.

The army was taking on 'policing' duties it was plainly not suited for. This deferred the need for the sort of drastic changes to Northern Ireland's security services which Catholics had demanded. It also kept the army on the streets where it would inevitably become involved in the conflict. It is not that there was no alternative to this. The alternative was to make dramatic changes to the way Northern Ireland was run and the way Catholic areas were policed. Whether it was possible to make such changes and keep the state intact is another matter. Certainly the British government, which was very concerned not to alienate Protestants by making changes which were too drastic, was not about to take this chance.

At the end of October 1969, after the publication of the Hunt Report and at a time when army restrictions in Derry had become more relaxed, a small group of Protestants, mostly women and teenagers, staged a sit-down protest on Craigavon Bridge. It was the second such protest they had staged against the Hunt Report and, on this occasion, a group of about forty Catholic youths responded by staging a sit-down of their own, nearby on Foyle Road. The RUC tended to be tolerant of loyalist sit-downs and did not attempt to move the protestors.[32] The RUC then decided to move the Catholic youths. When both groups of protesters began to disperse, stone-throwing broke out between them and clashes spread towards the Diamond as crowds gathered. Troops were called out and separated the two groups by pushing a chanting Catholic crowd back towards Waterloo Place on the edge of the Bogside.[33]

Some of the crowd gathered outside the RUC station on the Strand Road to protest at the RUC actions in dispersing the sit-down by Catholic youths. They resisted calls by Seán Keenan to move on. As the crowds pushed a bus into another bus, soldiers drew batons and charged the crowd, forcing them back into the Bogside. It is notable that at this stage the RUC, and not the army, was still the object of the crowd's hostility, but it was the first time the army had come into direct confrontation with a Catholic crowd, as opposed to simply separating Catholics and Protestants. In the course of the trouble, soldiers arrested three youths, one of them a nineteen-year-old called Martin McGuinness. Accused of shouting abuse at soldiers, he was later bound over to keep the peace for two years.[34] This was also the first occasion on which people were convicted on the basis of long-distance identifications by British troops; in this case, by a soldier watching through binoculars from a rooftop post on the Embassy Ballroom above the scene of the riot.[35]

A few days later, there was further trouble in Waterloo Place as crowds came out of a cinema. Once again, armed soldiers were called in, this time to break up relatively minor fighting which did not appear to have sectarian undertones.[36] The army were becoming deeply involved in the day-to-day maintenance of order in the city.

Protestant reactions

In the wake of the Hunt Report, Protestant hostility to the army reached a peak but even though, on at least one occasion, a Protestant crowd in Derry stoned troops,[37] the relationship between Protestants and the army was fundamentally different to that between Catholics and the army. Protestants were far more likely to complain about the 'softly-softly' approach of the army towards the Catholics than about the army's treatment of Protestants. Protestants consistently called for more troops, and more military activity, not less.[38] They held out the constant hope that the army would come to realise that the 'real' threat came from the Catholics and the IRA. As the months went by and this hope was realised somewhat, Protestant relations with the army became warmer.

Derry Protestants had experienced the events of August 1969 in a totally different way than Catholics had. They did not experience it as a time of excitement and change as many in Creggan and the Bogside did. While Catholics were hurling petrol bombs at the RUC on the edge of the Bogside, Protestants were bringing them tea and sandwiches.[39] While the Bogside peace-corps was building and defending barricades, members of the Apprentice Boys of Derry were patrolling as vigilantes within Derry city walls, watching out for attacks on the buildings associated with the Protestant community and the state.[40]

While Free Derry was seen as a 'liberated' area by many Catholics, Unionists claimed that Protestants behind the barricades were being intimidated and forced out of their homes.[41] There were some cases of intimidation in the area. Threatening phone calls were made to a Protestant family;[42] petrol was sprayed on a street where Protestants lived;[43] and, just before the barricades were erected, sectarian graffiti was written on the doors of a few Protestant houses.[44] However, there was no sudden mass exodus of Protestants from the area.

In August 1969, Protestants put up barricades at the edge of the Fountain, in protest at the continued existence of the Free Derry barricades.[45] They put up barricades again, for defence after the death of William King.[46] Large-scale sectarian rioting in July and August 1969 had aroused Protestant fears and when the army came in they did not seem to have the same commitment to defending Protestant areas that the B-Specials and the RUC had. There was a fear, which remained constant over the following few years, that a sectarian riot in Bishop Street could easily turn into an invasion of the Fountain by Catholic rioters.[47]

However, unlike the barricades in Catholic areas, such Protestant defiance of the law was almost always designed solely to force the army to take tougher measures against Catholics. It was not intended to challenge the state or the army, but to pressurise them. Although one barricade looked much like the other, they served entirely different purposes for the two communities. Sectarian clashes in Derry in late 1969 led to a contraction of Protestant territory in the city as parts of the city centre began to be seen as unsafe. The Protestant character of public housing estates on the mostly Catholic West Bank, such as the Glen and Northland, became diluted as the sectarian housing allocation policy of the corporation ended and Catholics began to be housed in these estates.[48] These estates were too isolated to maintain their Protestant character in an organised way and, although they had strong Unionist and loyalist traditions they did not become a focus for sectarian violence[49] or, later, a focus for loyalist paramilitaries.[50]

It is constantly stressed that sectarian bigotry has not been strong in Derry. However, in late 1969, sectarian violence was endemic in the city and Protestants could easily feel that the outbreaks of fighting in the city centre, and on the edge of the Fountain, represented a major sectarian threat to them. Parts of the city centre began to seem unsafe for some Protestant youths and an alienation of Protestants from the city began. Sectarian conflict in Derry, which had first appeared on a small scale in late 1968, faded in significance in early 1970 but only because it was displaced by the conflict between the army and Catholic youths. Sectarianism was an integral part of the conflict in Derry, and the crowds of Catholic youths who rioted on the edge of the Fountain, who charged at army lines shouting 'up Celtic', in support of a Glasgow soccer team identified with Irish Catholics[51], or who stoned visiting Protestant soccer supporters from Portadown with little provocation,[52] were seen as sectarian mobs by many Protestants.

After 1970, the conflict in Derry became very much a confrontation between two forces, the army and the Catholic community. The Protestant community became marginalised and, in many respects, detached from the conflict. This was due in large part to the sidelining of the RUC, through whom information about rioting in Catholic areas had filtered back to Protestants. Now, as the role of the army expanded, Protestants had less and less contact with, and knowledge of, the conflict in the city. While this ensured that the conflict did not have such a strong sectarian component, it also served to distance the Protestant community further from the experience of the Catholic community.

Hearts and minds

By late 1969, relations between the army and the Catholic community were deteriorating and, in November, the army in Derry launched a 'hearts and minds' campaign by which it 'hoped to restore confidence in its impartiality and good intentions'.[53] However, at the same time as this campaign was being launched, one issue in particular was reuniting Catholic opinion in Derry against Stormont and its law and order policies.

The Unionist government had decided to prosecute Bernadette Devlin for her role in the Battle of the Bogside.[54] If she could be prosecuted, there were many more prominent people and thousands of others who could also face jail terms for actions which even Catholic moderates had applauded. Around the same time, the courts were hearing cases connected with the July 1969 riots and gradually more cases from August 1969. There was a perception among Catholics that the courts were quick to convict simply on the word of an RUC man.

As the prosecutions continued, Paddy Doherty and Seán Keenan who had headed the DCDA, called for a unified approach to the issue on the Catholic side.[55] It was felt that moderates who had tacitly supported or accepted Free Derry were standing back now as Stormont punished some of those involved.[56] The Derry Nationalist party spoke of a 'growing disquiet about the attitude of the police and the judiciary in Derry'[57] and met Sir Arthur Young to voice this concern. The Independent Organisation also met Young and questioned him over the summonsing of people for offences committed in August 1969.[58] Such prosecutions served to renew tension. They were also the clearest demonstration that, despite British intervention, Stormont was still in control. It was not a big step from that to the realisation that the British army was maintaining the conditions for that continued control.

The 'hearts and minds' campaign was in part a response to this growing distrust and disquiet over the reassertion of Stormont's authority. However, it was also a move which served to imbed the army in the life of the city, something the army seemed to want but which did not necessarily reduce tension. If the 'peace-ring' had displayed a military mindset, drawing on recent responses to colonial situations, the phrase 'hearts and minds' was straight out of the lexicon of colonial counterinsurgency campaigns, and awoke unfortunate echoes of American efforts in Vietnam. Once again, army commanders appeared to be deepening their local involvement without strict governmental direction or control and apparently on the initiative of military and not political leaders. For military tacticians, a counter-insurgency campaign required the co-ordination of effort by the civil and military wings of the state. This was based on the proposition that guerilla war is a total war and that a government must counter it in the same terms[59] and, as Evelegh suggests, 'manage the efforts of the whole of society as a co-ordinated campaign against insurgency'.[60] However, given the army's constant complaints about political direction from above,[61] what seems to be meant by this is that the civil administration should operate in line with army requirements, that in a conflict situation, civil authority should defer to the military. Looked at from a non-military perspective, this appears like a proposal that the army should be free to make essentially political decisions on the basis of operational requirements.

In Derry, it appears it was the army itself which was largely deciding what role it should take, and these decisions affected and changed the shape of the conflict. 'Hearts and minds', for example, was good for army morale and built some ties with the community but it probably caused more harm than good. Anything which embedded the military in the life of the city made the quick introduction of civil policing less likely. It also increased the possibilities for army–civilian contact which, for a variety of reasons, social and political, could too easily turn into conflict.

'Hearts and minds' was designed to get young Catholic males off the streets in Derry, where they might cause trouble and to build up personal links between them and British soldiers. It also seems to have been designed to improve the morale of the troops by providing an outlet for their energies and by bringing them into contact with local young women. It was a measure of the continued widespread acceptance of the army and the weakness of the Republicans that there was no public opposition to 'hearts and minds' and that soldiers were able to make friendly contact with several hundred local youths and build connections with a wide range of local youth clubs and schools.[62]

The army set up two boys' clubs, although there were already a number of well-attended boys' clubs in the city. One of the army's boys' clubs, based at an army barracks in the Waterside, an area where Protestants were in a majority, was attended weekly by up to 250 boys. The other, at the military police base between Bogside and Creggan, had a notably smaller attendance of about eighty boys, twice a week, even though there was a far larger youth population in this area. The RUC was involved in running these clubs.[63] The army also co-operated with local youth clubs, boys' clubs and schools, bringing children hiking and canoeing, and running 'keep-fit' sessions for them.[64]

While younger children were involved in these activities, the teenagers who had been out fighting the RUC and had already experienced their first confrontations with the soldiers, were not really involved. The fact that the campaign also involved activities such as an indoor soccer match between soldiers and a girls' team from the Bogside,[65] or local girls giving Christmas gifts to soldiers from the back of a lorry,[66] or even the free New Year's dance for 500 soldiers serving in the city,[67] only increased tension between soldiers and local youths. Such 'competition' between young males was inevitably a cause of tension, whether in Derry or in any garrison town in England.

The army also took other steps to improve their image, like landing a soldier dressed as Santa Claus on to the roof of a city centre department store from an army helicopter,[68] helping with Meals on Wheels and visiting patients in the local mental hospital.[69] Before leaving Derry in December 1969, Lt Col Millmann, CO of the 1st Battalion of the Queen's Own Regiment, announced that every soldier in the battalion was donating a day's special allowance to local churches for charity. He also thanked the Derry people for their kindness.[70] Local women in the Rossville flats gave the troops a gift of 1,000 cigarettes and a Christmas card before they left.[71]

The 'hearts and minds' campaign reached a sort of pinnacle in New Year 1970 as the first wedding of a soldier to a local girl took place. The bride came from a village near Derry but across the international border, in Co. Donegal. The wedding took place in Co. Donegal with the groom in full uniform. As if to emphasise how much the troops had integrated into the local Catholic community, the soldier converted to Catholicism before the marriage.[72]

However, for all of the imagery, 'hearts and minds' does not appear to have kindled widespread enthusiasm among Catholics. On two occasions the Independent Organisation discussed it at meetings and there was 'protracted discussion' on the subject[73], a phrase which does not suggest total ease with the army's programme. The low attendance at the army's Creggan/Bogside Boys' Club suggests less enthusiasm there than in the Waterside. The campaign was also, in part, directed towards improving relationships with the Protestant community. To the cynical eye it might have seemed noteworthy that, at the same time as the army was teaching Bogside children how to keep fit and to canoe, it was giving weapons and radio instruction to the schoolboy cadet force in Foyle College, a local Protestant school.[74]

When the Queen's Own Regiment troops had arrived in Derry in August 1969, the warm response they received had determined their attitudes to the Catholic community. The 1st battalion the Gloucestershire Regiment, the 'Glosters' who replaced them and began a four-month tour in December 1969, had no such link. No troops after the Queen's Own would feel such a link with the local Catholic community, and even the Queen's Own had become involved in confrontation and clashes.

A new regiment

The Commanding Officer of the Glosters, Lt Col Streather, MBE, never developed a public profile as his predecessor, Lt Col Millman, had done.

Brigadier Peter Leng, who remained in overall command in Derry, also now adopted a much lower profile.

Derry had been peaceful for some weeks before Christmas and restrictions on movement had been eased a great deal. However, in the first days of January 1970 the Glosters were involved in their first clashes. When a fight broke out after a New Year's dance in the Bogside, military police came to break it up. Some of the crowd turned on the military police and troops were called in to break up the crowd. As the troops pushed the crowd back, stones and bottles were thrown, two army vehicles were badly damaged and the fighting didn't die out until 5 a.m.[75] The troops made no arrests and there were no claims of army brutality. The army had lost its 'charmed status', its associations with the 'relief' of the Bogside now that a new regiment had arrived. It seems likely that the change of personnel helped to loosen inhibitions about attacking the army, although one Republican at least believed that troops were rotated out after four months lest they develop too much sympathy with Catholic grievances.[76] It is notable that the crowd felt free to fight the army as they had fought the RUC. It was also the first time that the troops had been involved in clashes with Catholic youths without the prelude of sectarian clashes.

The army now had to worry not just about sectarian trouble but also about dealing with Catholic crowds late at night. The army announced that late night movie showings would not be allowed in the city centre for at least three months, after which it would review the situation.[77] It was an attempt to prevent crowds gathering, but again it was a classically military response, a broad sweeping measure which altered an aspect of life for large numbers in the city and which was probably counterproductive. While the army was setting up clubs for young children, older teenagers whose access to the city centre had been restricted, who had been cut off from the busy late night cafés in William Street when the army sealed the street, who could now no longer go to a late-night movie at a time when cinema was still a major form of entertainment, experienced the army's presence as a limiting of possibilities. At the end of January 1970, there were major day-time riots in Derry city centre which it appears some Republicans helped to provoke. In early 1970, Derry Republicans, selling the *United Irishman* in defiance of a continuing ban under the Special Powers Act, complained that British soldiers were taking photographs of the paper sellers on behalf of the RUC.[78] The Republicans declared they would publicly defy the ban on the last Saturday in January. Word then spread that there was to be a sit-down protest against this ban, in the city centre. When 200 teenagers gathered, expecting to take part in a sit-down, there was no-one present to organise it. A confrontation developed between this crowd and a Protestant crowd on the edge of the Fountain. The army, this time interspersed with RUC men, separated the crowds.[79] As an army helicopter circled overhead, the Catholic crowd, singing the Irish national anthem and republican songs such as 'Seán South', were pushed back towards the Bogside. Stones and insults were hurled at the army and the RUC, and the army made three arrests. Trouble did not develop further and even now there was a certain measure of restraint in the crowd's attitude to the army.

A local NICRA leader, Eamon Melaugh, tried to get the crowd to disperse. He had long been a Republican and still co-operated closely with Republicans and Labour radicals. After the riots, he said that a number of 'irresponsible' local Republicans had asked NICRA to announce the sit-down protest, unknown to most local Republicans.[80] The Republicans denied organising a sit-down, but it is clear that some Republicans were glad to see the army become unpopular. The Derry Republicans said the rioting was a 'reflection of anger that the British army now seems to have filled the boots of the RUC in implementing repressive legislation'.[81] This was overstating the importance of the Special Powers Act but the soldiers had certainly replaced the RUC as agents of control.

The *Derry Journal* however, continued to regard the army as an essentially benevolent force and condemned the rioting and the taunting of soldiers. But moderate opinion was now more critical of the role of the army and both John Hume and Ivan Cooper condemned the re-introduction of restrictions on movement in and out of the Bogside, after this riot, as an over reaction. Ivan Cooper warned that Derry was now facing the danger of 'an Englishman versus Irishman kind of confrontation'.[82]

Moderate support for the army was waning, principally because Stormont was still seen to be in control. As clashes began to intensify, the army did not have the support even in the Catholic establishment to allow them to take severe measures. Nonetheless, there was widespread bemusement among Derry Catholics that local youths had begun to treat the army as an enemy. This shift cannot simply be attributed to the actions of the army and it would be wrong to deal with the crowds of Catholic youths as a purely reactive force, turning against the army only because of 'army brutality'. Deference to any form of authority had been eroded among Derry youths over the past year of conflict with the RUC, and these youths were not happy to recognise the authority of the army. Also, more youths were being drawn to republicanism and nationalism and were hostile to the army on these grounds. In addition, the wider political climate in 1970 did not produce sufficient pressure on them to refrain from rioting.

In early 1970, Catholic moderates believed Stormont was stalling and backpedalling on reforms as right-wing Unionists gained in strength. When charges were dropped, in January 1970, against sixteen RUC men in connection with offences dating from January 1969, John Hume condemned it as 'scandalous'.[83] 'The announcement stinks of appeasement' (of the Unionist right wing) Ivan Cooper declared, while on the other hand, William Craig proclaimed himself delighted.[84] The right-wing Londonderry Unionist Association issued a rare statement praising the government.[85] Around the same time, Chichester-Clark brought a noted right-winger into his cabinet and re-introduced the Public Order Bill.[86] The British government appeared to be letting political control slip back to Stormont and the *Derry Journal* which had been the voice in Catholic Derry most consistently accepting of British government intentions was now scornful of the idea that a transformation of Northern Ireland through reform was taking place.[87]

In this atmosphere a small-scale civil-rights campaign was re-launched in Northern Ireland by left-wing groups including People's Democracy which now, for the first time, established a branch in Derry and held a protest meeting attended by 300 people, mostly teenagers.[88] This new campaign, coming at a time when many street gatherings ended in disorder was organised solely by the left who began to be condemned in increasingly strident terms by conservative Catholics in Derry as rioting continued. However, there was no trouble at this meeting.

Right-wing Unionism was on the rise in early 1970 and when Ian Paisley came to address a meeting in the Guildhall on Friday evening, 6 February, a group of about 100 Catholic youths gathered outside, faced by an army cordon. The youths resisted appeals to disperse from Eamonn McCann and Eamon Melaugh. As a youth in the crowd waved an Irish flag, troops moved forward and arrested him. Rioting then broke out during which, according to Eamon Melaugh, three soldiers in particular 'went berserk and beat young people for no apparent reason'. According to Eamonn McCann, there would have been no riot but for 'the offensive attitude and behaviour of the troops'.[89] A Derry source, writing in *Voice of the North*, claimed many of the soldiers showed 'obvious hostility' to the youths even at 'the early stages of the incident.'[90]

The riot produced the first accusations of brutal behaviour by troops in Derry and marked yet another shift in relations. The army was beginning to collect more and more baggage, building up a bad reputation, and was becoming very much part of the conflict.

The army developed the delusion that it was a neutral force on the basis that neither side was happy with it.[91] However, Protestants were generally unhappy because the army was not firm enough with the Catholic community,[92] while Catholics were unhappy because the army was being too firm with them. The army was in the middle perhaps, but not exactly in a classically neutral position. After this riot, the conduct of the Glosters was raised at a meeting of the Independent Organisation for the first time.[93]

The riot culminated in baton charges, and an 'invasion of the Bogside' by troops, carrying out what was by now a standard strategy of pushing all riots back into William Street away from the city centre shops.[94] The army had also now decided to make arrests during each 'military operation', which necessarily involved 'invading the Bogside'.[95] It was also a source of complaint that arrests were carried out, not in the course of clashes but by 'snatch-squads', which rushed into the Bogside, batons drawn, to lift people out of the crowd and take them away.[96] This time there were nine arrests. Among the four who were later sent to jail was twenty-year-old Seán Keenan, a son of the veteran Republican. He was not alleged to have used violence but only to have refused to move on, saying 'no bastardin' British troops will move me'.[97]

This gives a glimpse into Republican connections with these early riots. Although there were only a few dozen of the young Republicans and the Labour radicals who co-operated with them, that was a significant number at any demonstration which was only 100 or even 300 strong. It is not to suggest that they fomented riot or organised it, but they were active and the presence of these young activists gave a certain character to such gatherings at which now a tricolour was invariably produced.

By early March 1970, clashes between troops and Catholic youths had become endemic. Older people, although dissatisfied with progress on the political front, were prepared to reluctantly accept army restrictions. Younger people were not. The Bogside was not in danger of attack now that the RUC were disarmed and the B-Specials disbanded. Younger people said there was 'no need for all these stupid patrols and barricades. All this strutting about in bullet-proof vests and steel helmets with batons [which] impresses only school weans'.[98] Entrance to the city centre from the Bogside was still restricted, and as a Republican paper put it, 'We shall overcome' had been replaced as an anthem by 'Don't fence me in'.[99]

There were further riots in late March and it was said that at least one incident erupted over the recent victory of Dana, a Derry singer, representing the Republic of Ireland in the Eurovision song contest. Soldiers taunted youths that it was really a win for Britain, since she was from Derry, which was in Britain.[100] These riots were extensive, did not originate with any march or demonstration and seemed particularly meaningless and gratuitous to Catholic conservatives and moderates. For the first time in recent months, 'Independent Organisation' members went out on the streets to try and prevent rioting. There was a long-delayed backlash against the rioters in the Catholic community. The *Derry Journal* said it was 'time for plain speaking' and condemned the rioting as 'sheer rowdyism and vandalism'. It was also condemned by the 'Independent Organisation' and by Eddie McAteer, who described it as 'mindless violence'.[101] Up to now, the memory of the August 1969 riots had inhibited such critics, but now they came out strongly against the rioters. None of this implied a contentment with the role of the army, however, and the tide could easily turn again.

As the Republican Easter parades approached in April, the only certainty appeared to be that there would be continued rioting.

Easter 1970

In early 1970, the Republican movement in Ireland split into two separate factions. That Easter two separate Republican parades were held in Derry and, while the Provisionals confined theirs to the 'Free Derry' area, the Officials marched into the city centre.

A crowd of a few thousand, less than had marched the previous year, took part in the Official Republican parade, but only a few hundred of them made it to see Tomás MacGiolla speaking from the platform outside the Guildhall. From the RUC station on the Strand Road, a Union Jack was flying. The last time it had been flown, it was said, was on St Patrick's Day.[102] The RUC later said the flag had been flown because it was a public holiday. By contrast, the Development Commission, which flew the Union Jack from the top of the Guildhall every day, did not fly it on this day. John Hume later said the flying of the flag had been 'particularly insensitive and even provocative'. The Derry Nationalists said it had caused a wave of resentment. As the parade passed by the RUC barracks, members of the crowd threw stones at the barracks and when a man from the crowd climbed up to try and remove the flag, people inside the station, presumably RUC men, fired stones at him and, allegedly, out at the crowd.[103] This led to an increase in the tension.

The fact that conflict began over the British flag emphasises both the increase in popular nationalist feeling in Derry, increased resentment at the symbols of British rule, and the fact that the reformed RUC was still happy to identify itself as actively opposed to Irish nationalism. The incident which began with the flying of the flag also illustrates how the British army, which could hardly be expected to stop the flying of the Union Jack could not remain neutral between two communities, one 'loyal' to Britain, the other 'disloyal'.

Troops were called out to try and clear the crowd away from the RUC barracks. The troops pushed the crowds back into the Bogside as was their usual practice. They then sent in snatch squads to grab people from the crowd. There were incidents of alleged brutality and Eamon Melaugh, who had been prominent in trying to halt recent riots, asked an officer for the name of a soldier who he said had just assaulted a march steward. When the officer refused, Melaugh attempted to photograph the soldier. At that point Melaugh was arrested by troops.[104]

Among the early arrests were those of two teenage sisters who were brought, or 'dragged',[105] down Waterloo Street 'crying and protesting' by soldiers.[106] Local youths also claimed that soldiers who had charged into the Bogside had terrorised local residents. When Father Anthony Mulvey appealed to youths later that evening to disperse, they told him (as Mulvey put it) that 'the army were as bad today as the police were in August and they will get the same treatment from us as the police did then'.[107] By now the army had definitely brought an end to any 'softly-softly' approach. It was looking to make arrests (arresting seventeen people that day) and was taking a much more organised approach to riot duty. That evening, for example, with William Street in darkness because all the street lights were smashed, the army brought in Jeeps with searchlights mounted on them to light up the street.[108] In one sense, these riots were certainly not organised. Barricades were not erected, there were no stores of petrol bombs and it seems few petrol bombs were thrown. From the point of view of Catholic youths, there had been no preparation for riot and when a little stone-throwing had broken out, the army had responded punitively. The sending in of the 'snatch-squads' to rush at crowds, wielding long batons was seen as retributive, not designed in any way to end a riot but simply to take large numbers of people into custody. In the coming months, the snatch-squads would become ever more arbitrary as the young learned to evade them and they would arrest more and more middle-aged men, teenage girls and bystanders, most of whom the compliant courts would convict and jail.[109] Their actions were also seen as an invasion of the Bogside.

These riots, with their large number of arrests and an ever more obvious army policy of using harsh tactics, demolished finally any inhibitions young rioters had about treating the army as a target as they had done the RUC. In future riots, they would attack the army from the outset with alacrity and without inhibition[110] as the local representatives of the Stormont government.

But, if many more young rioters had finally turned completely against the army, these riots provoked more and more conservative Catholics to condemn the youthful rioters in the strongest terms. Letter-writers from the Bogside condemned the youths as 'trash' and 'thugs',[111] were 'disgusted' at their foul language and asked 'why did the elders not knock hell out of the young brats.' John Hume said of the rioters 'unless it is stopped now, they will destroy the whole city and everything we have stood for'.[112]

This backlash was prompted partly by the fact that the rioting was disrupting life for residents of the Bogside who saw no sense in it. But although there were those in the Bogside who still saw the army as a force which had 'saved us from massacre by police and Paisleyites' and worthy of medals,[113] most others, while harshly critical of the rioters, did not feel warmth towards the army. Opposition to the rioters by no means implied a willingness to support army action, particularly as the army were held partly responsible for this imposition on Bogside residents. The army always pushed crowds into the Bogside and although the crowds were not 'outsiders' in Derry city centre, they were 'outsiders' in the Bogside. For example, of the seventeen people who appeared in court in connection with these riots, only four came from the Bogside, with seven from other areas within Free Derry, such as Creggan and six from other parts of the city and surrounding countryside, including one Traveller woman. Bogsiders saw no logic in such a crowd being always pushed towards them. This tactic provoked complaints from John Hume.[114]

The violence was condemned as 'a sorry sight' by the *Derry Journal* and as 'senseless' by John Hume, but both Hume and Eddie McAteer noted the flag incident and placed some blame on the RUC while McAteer suggested that the British army was beginning to look like the RUC in August 1969. Hume suggested the riots would delight only right-wing Unionists and 'the hooligan element in the RUC'.[115]

Pressure from the Catholic community on the rioters was impelled principally by the desire to lead a quiet life. It did not imply acceptance of 'snatch-squads' or baton charges and certainly not of army measures such as the use of CS gas and the treatment of the Bogside as a giant 'holding pen' for rioters, which only increased disruption. It was notable that those Bogside residents who made a public appeal for parents to keep their children in to prevent them rioting, did not accept that the return of the RUC could provide a solution.[116] It was obvious that the army, with its military tactics, could not do so either.

At this stage too, it had recently been announced that Scotland Yard detectives would take over the investigation into the death of Sammy Devenny. This, to a small extent, renewed the faith of some Catholic moderates in British intentions.[117]

The harsh local criticism of the rioting youth opened up a gap in the Catholic community in attitudes to the army; a gap, as McCann[118] described it, which had as much to do with age as with politics. Conservative Catholics, the Nationalists and moderates were all condemning the young rioters who were now being characterised, especially by the army, as 'hooligans'. The Labour left condemned 'reckless trouble makers'.[119] However, they also defended the youth, and argued that they had been left leaderless by the people who had brought them onto the streets eighteen months previously and who had praised their rioting skills only six months before.[120]

A few days after these riots, the Derry Labour party set up what it called a 'Young Hooligans Association' and began a concerted effort to politicise the youth away from rioting and into left-wing politics.[121] They were joined in this by the Official Republicans. Their aim was not just to stop the riots but to divert the energy of the rioters politically into a socialist struggle. One of their favourite points was that rioting simply allowed 'fascist pigs' to put young Derry people in jail.[122] Young people were not only most affected by restrictions on movement but were also more likely to be stopped by soldiers because of their age and because they spent more time on the streets than older people. They were being stopped by boys their own age and contact between young British soldiers and local young men, whether it be in an English garrison town like Colchester, in a German city such as Berlin or in an Irish town like Derry, was always a likely source of tension. In England, fights regularly broke out in pubs between groups of soldiers from different regiments.[123] Soldiers in the early 1970s could 'regard casual brutality as simply part and parcel of army life at the time.'[124] There was clearly great potential for conflict with local youths wherever soldiers were posted. In a situation like the one in Derry, where British soldiers restricted movement and patrolled the streets, the possibilities for conflict were limitless, on the basis of social tensions alone. It was heightened by the fact that there was, in Derry, a strong Irish nationalist tradition which looked on such soldiers as a foreign army of occupation. Relations were not improved by the fact that the British soldiers had to endure substandard living conditions[125] and the relationship between soldiers and local girls was a perennial source of tension, especially when they took to arresting some of these girls.

Discussion of the end of the army's 'honeymoon' has focused on riots in Ballymurphy, in West Belfast at the beginning of April 1970, at around the same time as the Easter riots took place in Derry. The rioting in Belfast has been seen as inspired or organised by the Provisional IRA in a deliberate attempt to disrupt relations between the army and civilians. At its most blunt it is said that the Provisionals 'engineered' a confrontation,[126] that they deliberately 'provoked a weekend of trouble luring the army into tough action that caused their "brutality" to be criticised'.[127]

An examination of events in Derry shows that by April 1970 there had been a long series of confrontations with the army. In Derry at least, it would be foolish to see riots around this time in isolation, as being deliberately provoked by the Provisionals as they gathered strength and prepared for an armed campaign. Ryder suggests that 'tough' army behaviour was deliberately provoked by the Provisionals in April 1970 when, in fact, in Derry the army had deliberately adopted 'tougher' tactics some time before this, probably as early as January 1970.

In Derry, rioting in Easter 1970 broke out at a parade by the Official Republicans. At this time the Derry Provisionals were newly formed and led by middle-aged and elderly men. There were certainly some younger people who were inclined towards the Provisionals but it was the Officials and their Labour party allies who had the strongest contacts with the young rioters and they generally opposed the rioting.

This is not to say that Republicans were not a part of these events but it attributes power to the Provisionals which, certainly in Derry, they did not have at that time. Furthermore, it absolves the British army from responsibility for the descent into chaos. The view which sees all British army tactics, from movement restriction to 'snatch-squads' and threats to shoot petrol bombers, as essentially a 'defensive' or 'peace-keeping' reaction to riots robs the army of motive and sees it as an essentially apolitical force taking decisions simply on the basis of operational requirements. In fact, the army began to see the Catholic community as the 'problematic population' at a very early stage and operated in accordance with this highly political view of the situation.

There were clearly some Republicans who wanted to riot and there is a question mark over the attitude to rioting of the Official Republicans who now worked with Labour to stop youth riots but had not tried to stop them during previous months. However, to attribute riots to Republican organisations is to diminish the importance of the process by which hundreds of youths had become hostile, firstly to the RUC and now to the army over the previous eighteen months. Republicans had little need to organise them for riots. The evidence in Derry suggests that a Provisional or indeed any Republican plan to end the 'honeymoon' was not in any meaningful sense the 'cause' of these riots. This is not to say there was no truth in claims such as that by the Waterside Young Unionists who said 'we believe that these young people are being organised by Republican youth movements and put on the streets with the specific purpose of causing disruption to the state.'[128] The Independent Organisation also believed that some group was manipulating the rioters,[129] although they were probably more likely to join conservative Catholics in pointing the finger to the alliance of Labour and Republican radicals than at the Provisionals, who had a far more 'respectable' leadership.

The evidence of the occasional conviction of young Republicans, of the ubiquitous presence of the Irish flag and the singing of Republican songs, suggests that young Republicans and radicals were usually present in demonstrations which turned to violence. When rioting broke out, young Republicans would riot 'as a team' and as one former activist put it, 'we were actually dedicated rioters'.[130] They were prominent among those who were willing to confront the army, by staging pickets, sit-downs or by marching. At the same time, both Republican wings were rapidly expanding their youth sections, the Fianna Éireann, and if the organisations were drawing new recruits from among young rioters then, *ipso facto*, Fianna members were taking part in the riots and in a more organised way than the bulk of rioters. The Officials, like the Provisionals, were now expanding their military structures in Derry, both IRA and Fianna, and were preparing for a military campaign.[131] While not encouraging riots they could easily see political contact with and education of the young rioters as an opportunity to win their support and thus gain recruits for the Republican cause and ultimately for the Official IRA. According to a former member, the Official IRA at least 'occasionally … gave out Molotov cocktails' during riots in late 1970.[132]

If there was some ambivalence in the attitudes of the Official Republicans to the riots, the Provisionals took an unequivocal attitude to those youths who were condemned as 'hooligans' by so many Derry Catholics. 'We believe', the elderly Provisional Republican Neil Gillespie said, 'that very many of the young lads give vent to a deep sense of frustration because Ireland is still denied nationhood and unity'.[133]

The Provisionals probably did not have the numbers or the influence to organise rioting, but their younger members were among the most active and organised rioters and, by such statements, they were opening their ranks to those many youths who had developed a deep hostility to the army through confrontation. The Provisionals would provide a welcome and a spiritual home for many of the young rioters, and an ideology which assimilated their hostility to the army in terms of a long struggle for Irish political independence.

By spring 1970, the British army had adopted a 'get tough' policy and when Lt Gen Sir Ian Freeland stated on television that the army might shoot live rounds at petrol bombers, it once again raised the stakes as far as young rioters were concerned.[134] Once again, the army was responding as an army, an organisation designed to fight wars, promising measures which were crude and ultimately impractical. The British government publicly backed Freeland's statement[135] and now began to act as though a political solution had been reached, that any further disruption was illegitimate, not a matter for negotiation but for repression. In many respects, the initiative passed to the army. By mid-1970 the British army had decided it would need to stay in Northern Ireland for at least another three years.[136] It was a recognition that 'normal' policing could not be restored for some years. In the meantime, however, how was the army proposing to operate? It seems that, as Republicans re-organised in 1970, the army was preparing to wage a long-term counter-insurgency campaign against the Provisional and Official IRAs and was not thinking at all about how normal policing might be restored in Catholic areas.

The Falls Road curfew in Belfast, in July 1970, when the army placed the area under curfew for thirty-six hours after a bout of rioting, conducted a house-to-house search and shot dead three civilians, demonstrated that the army was no longer inclined to deal with unrest and political dissatisfaction in the Catholic community through negotiation. The army was no longer behaving as a temporary police force. In Belfast it was openly waging a counter-insurgency campaign and was busily burning the bridges to the Catholic community in Derry and Belfast that had been built through negotiation in the first weeks after their arrival.

The end of the honeymoon

Discussion of the end of the 'honeymoon' has focused heavily on the Ballymurphy riots in Belfast in spring 1970, which have been described as the first clashes between Catholics and the army.[137] However, in Derry at least, the ending of the 'honeymoon' was a cumulative process, beginning within a few weeks of the arrival of the troops. The honeymoon ended as the army became involved in policing Catholic areas in a military way and became involved in clashes in which it responded with what Ryder calls 'tough action' and others called 'brutality'.

The central fact of the army's presence was that, as the reform programme was diluted and the authority of Stormont was restored, ' ... it would only be a matter of time before the Catholics had their worst fears confirmed: that it was not themselves who were being protected, but the Unionist government'.[138] The fact that the army tended to adopt drastic military solutions which 'denormalised' life in the city served to increase tension and created a sense of permanent confrontation.

For Catholics, the reforms had not been successful and there was no sense of political resolution. They would continue to protest against and be hostile to the state. In protecting the state, the army could not expect the wholehearted support of dissatisfied and alienated Catholic moderates and the levels of repression they used were unacceptable to moderates.

Other factors also played a major role in the end of the 'honeymoon': the growing sense of Irish nationalism, the growth of the two wings of the Republican movement, (largely a product of confrontation with the RUC and the state), the social tensions created by the presence of the army, the reduced respect for any form of authority among Catholic youths and the army's decision in early 1970 to 'get tough' with rioters.

In the absence of any acceptable policing force, the army took over responsibility for policing Catholic areas in Derry after abolishing the authority of the DCDA. Given that there was no sense of a political resolution and there was continued active Catholic hostility to the Unionist government, the army would become essentially an agent for the control of the Catholic population. As one former British CO in West Belfast put it, 'Ultimately these Catholic areas could only be governed by the British by the methods, however mollified, that all occupying nations use to hold down all occupied territories.'[139] This would only gradually become clear.

Notes and references

1 DJ, 19/8/69, p.1.
2 *Barricade Bulletin*, no. 8, 22/8/69.
3 Johnnie White in *Magill*, Aug. 1989, p. 14.
4 *Derry Emigrant Bulletin, c.* Aug. 1969 (undated), p. 2.
5 DJ, 26/8/69, p. 4.
6 Michael Farrell, *Northern Ireland: The Orange State* (Pluto, London, 1980), p. 272.

7 Des Hamill, *Pig in the Middle. The Army in Northern Ireland 1969–1985*, (Methuen, London, 1986), p. 32. See also Patrick Buckland, *A History of Northern Ireland* (Gill and Macmillan, Dublin, 1981), p. 146.

8 Interview with Michael Canavan, founder member of the Derry Credit Union, formerly a senior member of the DCAC, the DCDA, the DCCC and the Independent Organisation. Former SDLP assembly member.

9 DJ, 26/9/69, pp. 1, 6.

10 Ibid.

11 DJ, 30/9/69, p. 4.

12 *New Society*, 21/8/69, p. 278.

13 DJ, 26/9/69, p. 6.

14 DJ, 26/9/69, p. 1.

15 DJ, 30/9/69, p. 4.

16 DJ, 3/10/69, p. 8.

17 Shane O'Doherty, *The Volunteer. A Former IRA Man's True Story* (Fount, London, 1993), pp. 56–7.

18 DJ, 3/10/69, p. 3.

19 DJ, 30/9/69, p. 4.

20 DJ, 30/9/69, p. 4.

21 DJ, 30/9/69; 7/10/69.

22 DJ, 18/11/69, p. 4.

23 DJ, 5/12/69, p. 1.

24 Independent Organisation, minutes, 11/11/69.

25 DJ, 21/10/69, p. 1.

26 Buckland, *History*, p. 142.

27 Richard Clutterbuck, *The Long, Long, War*, cited in Robin Evelegh, *Peace Keeping in a Democratic Society. The Lessons of Northern Ireland* (C. Hurst and Co., London, 1978), pp. 128–9.

28 Michael Barthorp, *Crater to the Creggan. The History of the Royal Anglian Regiment. 1964–1974* (Leo Cooper, London, 1976), appendix II.

29 Hamill, *Pig in the Middle*, p. 33.

30 DJ, 14/10/69, p. 1.

31 DJ, 26/9/69, p. 8.

32 DJ, 21/10/69, p. 1.

33 DJ, 28/10/69, p. 6.

34 Ibid. By the time those two years were over he was a senior member of the Derry Provisional IRA.

35 Ibid.

36 DJ, 4/11/69, p. 1.

37 DJ, 31/11/69, p. l.

38 See, for example, LS, 21/1/70, p. 17; DJ, 30/6/70, p. 1.

39 Interview with Jim Guy, Independent Unionist councillor, former mayor of Derry, former Ulster Unionist party councillor, former secretary and Lieutenant-Governor of the Apprentice Boys of Derry, former secretary and grand master of the City of Derry Grand Orange Lodge, former honorary secretary of Londonderry and Foyle Unionist Association.

40 Guy, interview; Rev. R. Dickinson, evidence to Scarman Tribunal, Day 5, 24/9/69, p. 48.

41 Albert Anderson cited in *DCDA newsletter*, no. 6, 22/8/69, which denied his claim.

42 *Barricade Bulletin*, No. 4, 18/8/69 which appealed for such calls to cease.
43 White, 1985, p. 81.
44 DJ, 12/8/69, p. 5; McCann, interview.
45 DJ, 23/8/69.
46 DJ, 14/10/69, p. 5.
47 Interview with Peter Simpson, former Secretary of the Wapping Lane Community Association (which included the Fountain estate) and head of its security sub-committee in the early 1970s.
48 LS, 24/2/71, p. 1.
49 Though there were a few incidents, e.g. DJ, 7/8/70, p. 1.
50 Simpson, interview.
51 DJ, 3/4/70, p. 5.
52 DJ, 20/1/70, p. 4.
53 Richard Deutsch and Vivien Magowan, *Northern Ireland: Chronology of Events* (3 volumes), (Blackstaff, Belfast, 1973–75), vol. 1, 1973, p. 52.
54 DJ, 23/9/69, p. 5.
55 DJ, 7/11/69.
56 *Free Citizen*, No. 17, 30/1/70 accused John Hume of neglecting Derry prisoners.
57 DJ, 14/11/69, p. 1.
58 *Indfo*, Dec. 1969, p. 7.
59 Evelegh, *Peace Keeping*, p. 52.
60 Ibid p. 48. See also Frank Kitson, *Low Intensity Operations: Subversion, Insurgency and Peacekeeping* (Faber and Faber, London, 1971).
61 Hamill, *Pig in the Middle*, p. 34.
62 DJ, 11/11/69, p. 3.
63 DJ, 25/11/69, p. 9.
64 DJ, 11/11/69, p. 3.
65 DJ, 14/11/69, p. 7.
66 DJ, 23/12/69, p. 1.
67 DJ, 13/1/70, p. 3.
68 DJ, 14/11/69, p. 1.
69 DJ, 2/12/69, p. 1.
70 DJ, 9/12/69, pp. 3, 5.
71 DJ, 16/12/69, p. 7.
72 DJ, 6/1/70, p. 4.
73 Independent Organisation, minutes, 2/12/69, 15/12/69.
74 DJ, 18/11/69, p. 7.
75 DJ, 6/1/70, p. 6.
76 Johnnie White in *Magill*, Aug. 1981, p. 14.
77 DJ, 6/1/70, p. 1.
78 DJ, 23/1/70, p. 13.
79 DJ, 27/1/70.
80 Ibid.
81 Ibid.
82 DJ, 27/1/70, pp. 1, 4.
83 DJ, 30/1/70, p. 7.
84 Deutsch and Magowan, *Chronology*, vol. 1, 28/1/70.
85 DJ, 30/1/70, p. 7.
86 Farrell, *Orange State*, p. 271.

87 DJ, 30/1/70, p. 6.
88 DJ, 3/2/70, p. 5.
89 DJ, 10/2/70, p. 5.
90 *Voice of the North*, 22/2/70, p. 8.
91 Buckland, *History*, p. 139.
92 DJ, 13/1/70, p. 3; 10/2/70, p. 4.
93 Independent Organisation minutes, 10/3/70.
94 Report by an army CO, cited in Hamill, *Pig in the Middle*, p. 72.
95 Ibid., as this army CO put it.
96 *Voice of the North*, 22/2/70, p. 8.
97 DJ, 13/2/70, p. 1 In court he was alleged to have said 'no bastard in the British troops ... ', but the above version is more likely and was perhaps misheard.
98 Letter in DJ, 24/3/70, p. 3.
99 *Voice of the North*, 8/2/70, p. 1.
100 DJ, 24/3/70, 29/3/70, p. 3.
101 DJ, 27/3/70, p. 8.
102 *Voice of the North*, 12/4/70, p. 3.
103 DJ, 31/3/70, pp. 1, 5.
104 DJ, 31/3/70, p. 5.
105 DJ, 3/4/70, p. 5 letter.
106 DJ, 31/3/70, p. 5.
107 DJ, 31/3/70, p. 5.
108 Ibid.
109 See for example DJ, 30/8/70, p. 1.
110 DJ, 30/6/70, p. 6.
111 DJ, 31/3/70, p. 7.
112 DJ, 3/4/70, pp. 1, 5, 9.
113 DJ, 31/3/70, p. 7, letter.
114 DJ, 31/3/70, p. 1.
115 DJ, 31/3/70, p. 1.
116 DJ, 3/4/70, p. 1.
117 *Indfo*, April, 1970.
118 Eamonn McCann, *War and an Irish Town*, op. cit., p. 83.
119 DJ, 3/4/70, p. 1.
120 DJ, 31/3/70, pp. 1, 3; McCann, *War*, p. 73.
121 DJ, 3/4/70, p. 1; 7/4/70, p. 4.
122 McCann in DJ, 3/4/70, p. 1.
123 Trevor Royle, *Anatomy of a Regiment. Ceremony and Soldiering in the Welsh Guards* (Michael Joseph, London, 1990), p. 124.
124 Ibid., p. 112, Royle citing a 'senior NCO'.
125 Hamill, *Pig in the Middle*, p. 25; *United Irishman*, Dec. 1969.
126 Charles Allen, *The Savage Wars of Peace. Soldiers' Voices 1945–1989* (Futura, London, 1990), pp. 211–12.
127 Chris Ryder, *The RUC. A Force Under Fire* (Methuen, London, 1989), p. 118. Ryder seems to be suggesting that the army's action is correctly characterised as 'tough' and that 'brutal' is simply an incorrect characterisation.
128 DJ, 7/4/70, p. 2.
129 *Indfo*, April, 1970.

130 Interview with Anon. D, former member of the Republican movement in Derry.
131 See ch. 5 below.
132 Kevin Toolis, *Rebel Hearts: Journeys Within the IRA's Soul* (Picador, London, 1995), p. 303.
133 DJ, 10/4/70.
134 Deutsch and Magowan, *Chronology*, vol. 1, 3/4/70.
135 Ibid., 7/4/70.
136 James Callaghan, *A House Divided* (Collins, London, 1973), p. 134.
137 See for example, Simon Winchester, *In Holy Terror: Reporting the Ulster Troubles* (Faber, London, 1974), p. 30.
138 Hamill, *Pig in the Middle*, p. 31.
139 Evelegh, *Peace Keeping*, p. 61.

5
Republican Revival:
August 1969–August 1970

Republican revival

The events of August 1969 which brought Republicans to prominence in Defence Committees in Derry and Belfast convinced many of these Republicans that the IRA should be re-armed and re-activated. In Belfast, where Catholic areas had been attacked by loyalist crowds, there was a perceived need for defence against future attacks. In Derry, where there had been a mass communal rebellion against the state, August was seen as opening a window of opportunity. Now that there was mass hostility to the state, there seemed to be an historic opportunity to topple the state and re-unite Ireland, relatively quickly. For both of these reasons, many Republicans now began to look for arms and the money to buy arms. They also became concerned to train people in their use and to recruit from the large section of the Catholic community which had been radicalised by the events. Many of these Republicans were dissatisfied with the response of the Dublin leadership to the crisis, particularly with its failure to provide weapons or to seize the opportunity to act as 'defenders' of the Catholic areas. They began to look for arms independently of the national leadership.

The Dublin leadership responded to the events of August 1969 by increasing IRA military training activity, but with the stated aim only of providing defence in the event of future attacks on Catholic areas. Thus, in the autumn of 1969, there was a ferment of Republican activity in Ireland with many Republicans believing that the arrival of British troops heralded the end of Northern Ireland as a state. From the outset, many of the leading Republicans who had by now begun to act in defiance of the national leadership, while stressing the need for defence, wanted to re-arm and revive the IRA principally in order to begin an armed campaign to achieve a united Ireland. They embarked on this campaign because they believed the opportunity for swift success was there. This explains the sense of urgency in the Republican search for arms after August 1969. For Republicans like Seán Keenan, who 'lived for the opportunity to lead a rebellion against the British'[1] the civil rights campaign had presented an historic opportunity to re-unite Ireland and the Dublin leadership was letting it slip by.

As Keenan himself put it in April 1970, 'They had reached a decisive moment in their history. That moment must and would be used, and the aspirations of centuries would be fulfilled.'[2] According to Seán Mac Stiofáin, while the Provisionals would initially prioritise defence they always intended to launch an 'all out offensive' against British troops as soon as it was possible.[3] Thus, those Republicans who were now looking for weapons independently of the national leadership were keen not just to provide defence but also to prepare for an offensive. They had unrealistic expectations of how easily their goal might be attained.

Most of these Republicans were veterans of the 1950s IRA campaign and they appear to have believed that the conditions now existed in which the sort of military campaign which had failed in the 1950s could be successful. Crucial to this would be the general militancy of the Catholic community and the consequent availability of new recruits. In order to rebuild the IRA's military capacity they would look to a source to which Republicans in Derry had turned before the 'Battle of the Bogside', when the IRA leadership had declared their lack of resources: the Irish government.

The first recorded contacts between the Irish government and Derry city Republicans took place when DCDA members travelled to Dublin shortly before 12 August 1969 to appeal for aid from the Irish government. Then, the night before the Apprentice Boys' march in Derry, an Irish army intelligence officer (on leave) arrived in the city with a man from Belfast.[4] The officer, Captain James Kelly, met with DCDA leaders including Paddy Doherty[5] and, undoubtedly, Seán Keenan.[6] The initial connection had been made, but even after the arrival of British troops in Derry a few days later this connection between Seán Keenan and other Republicans and the Irish government, as represented by Captain Kelly, developed further.

Captain Kelly had initially dealt with Keenan in Keenan's capacity as a senior DCDA member. Technically, over the following months the Irish government dealt with the local Defence Associations in the North rather than with the IRA. However, despite the fact that these Defence Associations were broadly based, Captain Kelly dealt primarily with Republican members of these committees.

The Irish government was at this time deeply divided on the issue of the North. It was said that Jack Lynch had made his strong speech on 13 August only under pressure from other members of the cabinet, including Neil Blaney and Charles Haughey,[7] who were said to have urged an invasion of the North.[8] It was a sub-committee on the North, including Haughey and Blaney, which apparently authorised and was in charge of these contacts with Northern Republicans. According to Captain Kelly, the Irish Minister of Defence had also authorised them.[9] In any case, one section of the Irish government was working to an extent in opposition to the other. Some of these members of the government seem to have shared the wildly optimistic view of the older Republicans that the re-unification of Ireland was within easy reach and that to achieve it simply required an act of will.

Although Seán Keenan and others became deeply involved in these contacts, these dealings was not the sole reason for the split in the Republican movement. Captain Kelly also dealt with and passed money to Republicans loyal to the Dublin leadership[10] and the leadership were clearly aware of these events. These dealings did not split the movement, but they did increase the mutual distrust between the two factions.

The Irish government appears to have built particularly strong links with the older Derry Republicans, a process facilitated by the proximity of Derry to the border and to the Donegal constituency of Neil Blaney. Shortly after the arrival of British troops in Derry, while barricades still surrounded 'Free Derry' and the DCDA policed and administered the area, the Irish Department of Defence arranged for a group of nine men from Derry to receive a few weeks intensive weapons training at Dunree Fort, an Irish army base in Co. Donegal.[11] When this group finished their training on 3 October, a further twenty men from Derry were to replace them and also receive weapons-training. However, before the second group arrived, reports of the scheme were leaked to the press and the scheme was abandoned.[12]

We must assume that these men were selected for training by the DCDA leaders who were dealing with the Irish government. If so, some, if not all, were undoubtedly IRA members. This indicates that at least some of the younger Republicans in Derry were now following Seán Keenan's lead. The twenty-nine men to be trained can hardly all have been middle-aged veterans of the 1950s campaign.

It seems probable that these men were being trained on the basis of the plans that still existed after the arrival of British troops for the Irish army to seize Derry in the near future.[13] In that event, these men would be on the ground in the North to assist the advancing Irish troops. Despite these dealings with the Irish government, Seán Keenan remained an active member of the Republican movement in Derry for some months after August 1969, taking part in a picket alongside those who would stay loyal to Dublin, as late as early December 1969.[14]

Despite the fact that there was a great deal of intrigue at national level, culminating in the 'arms trial' of Irish government ministers in April 1970, it might be illuminating to look at the actions of Keenan and those supporting him in Derry, not in terms of a dissident faction preparing to split, but as a section of the local Republican movement, eager to go on the offensive, to take the opportunity provided by contacts with the Dublin government to get arms and training and to pull the organisation as a whole towards a campaign, rather than to split the movement. This helps to explain how both factions in the movement in Derry could continue to operate together and why, even when the formal split took place in January 1970, many Republicans in Derry were only vaguely aware of it and tried to ignore it.[15] The fact that Keenan's approach attracted at this early stage some of the young Republicans who had been active in housing agitation[16] emphasises also that it was not simply a split between old conservatives and young radicals, but a split between those eager to begin an armed campaign and those who were willing to accept the restraining authority of the leadership.

On 3 October 1969, as the training of men from Derry at Dunree Fort in Co. Donegal came to a premature end and just after the barricades had come down in Derry and Belfast, a meeting was held in Cavan between Captain Kelly and representatives of Defence Committees in the North. Among those present were Seán Keenan but also IRA leaders, such as Jim Sullivan, who were loyal to Cathal Goulding and the Dublin leadership. After the meeting, Kelly reported back to the Irish government that the Defence Committees needed money for weapons and training and a government fund for this purpose was established.[17] By 10 October, the DCDA in Derry had dissolved itself but even though there was no longer a defence committee in the city dealings between Seán Keenan and Captain Kelly continued.

Some of the money supplied by the Irish government after 3 October was used to set up a newspaper based in Monaghan, the *Voice of the North*, of which Seán Keenan became a director.[18] This level of involvement with Irish government initiatives was definitely not approved by the Republican leadership which refused to believe or acknowledge that Keenan was involved with the *Voice of the North*, denying such claims as late as December 1969.[19] They were obviously concerned to keep senior Republicans, such as Keenan who had become active again long before the split, within the Republican movement.

However, in early December, Seán Keenan embarked on a journey which severely undermined the authority of the Republican leadership. In December 1969, he boarded a plane for the United States and spent the next few weeks travelling through the east coast of America[20] looking for guns and money, telling US-based Republicans that the Dublin leadership had refused to supply Republicans in the North with either.[21]

Around this time or a little later, there were a number of other dissident Republicans in the US looking for arms, including people such as Jack McCabe, who was one of a group of ex-IRA men living in Dublin who were now sending guns to Republican dissidents in Belfast.[22] During this visit to Philadelphia, Seán Keenan was in the company of Joe Cahill, one of the Belfast dissident Republicans.[23] According to another account he was with John Kelly, the Belfast IRA man most closely connected to Irish government initiatives, while he was in New York.[24]

Seán Keenan was still closely connected with Irish government initiatives and one source suggests that his Irish government contacts were aware of this search for arms in the US. It is alleged that Keenan arranged an arms shipment from the US during this visit but, on his return to Ireland, Captain Kelly told him to cancel the shipment as it would take too long and that an alternative shipment from the European continent had been arranged.[25] This latter was the shipment which was seized in Dublin in April 1970 and led to the arms crisis in the Republic.

The network of contacts which Keenan was now utilising in the US was linked directly to the Republican movement in Ireland. Clan na Gael was the long-standing American support group for the Irish Republican movement. However, it had a great degree of autonomy and in the recent past Clan na Gael, or at least certain chapters of it, had supported Republican splinter groups in Ireland, based often on the willingness of such groups to begin an armed campaign.[26] Clan na Gael members were generally Irish-born Republicans, veterans of campaigns in the 1920s or 1950s and many still had direct personal links to Ireland, returning frequently. When Seán Keenan looked for support in Boston, Philadelphia and New York, he began by contacting Irish Republicans whom he knew personally.

In Philadelphia, for example, Seán Keenan and Joe Cahill contacted members of the local Clan na Gael chapter. These included Bridget Makowski, a member of a prominent Republican family in the city.

She had close links with the younger radicals in Derry, had joined the Republican Club in Derry and knew Keenan.[27] In Philadelphia, many of the Clan na Gael members (though not Makowski) backed Keenan, and Bishop and Mallie say the first major arms shipment which reached the Provisional IRA (in August 1970) began to be organised by Republican sympathisers in Philadelphia around this time.[28]

In Boston, Keenan phoned a Derry Republican, Liam Deeney, who had been active in the 1950s and had left Derry in 1965. Keenan asked him to organise support. Although Deeney, like Makowski, was reluctant to become personally involved a group of a dozen or so Irish-born Republicans living in Boston met Keenan and arranged to help him.[29] In New York, Keenan contacted Liam Kelly who had been dismissed from the IRA in 1951 and had then set up a Republican splinter group called Saor Uladh. He had also had contacts with the Derry IRA in the 1950s when Keenan had been active.[30] In recent months, Kelly had been working with people such as Mike Flannery in civil rights groups in New York and with the Republicans in the New York chapter of Clan na Gael. Keenan now met Clan na Gael members in New York.[31] According to *Magill*, Keenan arranged an arms shipment through Kelly and associates of his, presumably Clan na Gael members in New York, to be smuggled to Ireland in the New Year with the help of the Longshoremen's Union.[32] Ironically, Kelly later became the head of the Official Republicans in the US.[33]

In the months prior to August 1969, many Clan na Gael members in New York had, for their own reasons, become disillusioned with the left-wing Republican leadership in Dublin. Mike Flannery for example had urged Cathal Goulding, chief of staff of the IRA, to break with Sinn Féin and its increasingly left-wing leadership, but to no avail. New York members of Clan na Gael became involved *en masse* in a civil rights support group in New York in late 1968. After this organisation was riven by a split, Clan na Gael members set up their own organisation, the Irish Action Committee (hereafter IAC) in early 1969.[34]

Shortly after this, in the spring of 1969, NICRA in Belfast endorsed a newly formed American umbrella group, the National Association for Irish Justice (hereafter NAIJ) as their sole representative in the US.[35] The NAIJ was also supported by the left-wing Republican leadership in Dublin[36] and tried to forge links with radical groups in America and build alliances on the left. The IAC opposed this group and competed bitterly with it in New York in the summer of 1969.[37] Thus, before there was ever a split between the two wings of the Republican movement in Ireland there had been a bitter split in the US and Clan na Gael members in New York were acting in opposition to the left-wing leadership in Dublin.

Accordingly, when Seán Keenan and other dissident Republicans came to the US in late 1969, circumventing the Dublin leadership and appealing directly to Republicans in the US for aid, they were well-received. It was to be one of the most significant achievements of the Republican dissidents that they would obtain the support of the bulk of active Republicans, Clan na Gael members, in the US.

In the course of this trip to the US, Seán Keenan was expelled from the Republican movement for undertaking this trip[38] and for his association with *Voice of the North*.[39] Cathal Goulding went to the US to tell a Clan na Gael convention that Keenan was being used by the Fianna Fáil government to split the movement.[40] However, despite Goulding's efforts, most of the Republicans in Clan na Gael sided with the dissidents. When Seán Keenan returned to the US the following March, it would be to formalise links between the new Provisional Republican movement in Ireland and their supporters in Clan na Gael.

While Seán Keenan was forging links across the border and across the Atlantic, there was ferment in Republican circles in Derry and hints of military preparations, as shots were heard in Rosemount[41] and ammunition was found in the Waterside.[42] Just across the border in Co. Donegal, a variety of Republican groups from Derry were holding regular training sessions. In early January 1970, shortly before the Republican movement formally split in Dublin, Gardaí walked into a house in Donegal not far from the border with Derry. Inside they found seven men from Derry and a machine gun lying on a settee. The men included Phil O'Donnell, a former British paratrooper[43] and Neil O'Donnell, a young Republican who had been involved in housing agitation with the radical Republicans before the civil rights movement. The house was owned by relatives of another young Derry Republican.[44] All three would later be prominent Provisional Republicans.[45] Although the Provisionals had not yet officially come into existence, this was effectively a Provisional IRA unit training in Donegal.[46]

If this indicated that the Provisional Republicans were involved in military preparations in their own right even before the split, the subsequent court case demonstrated the continuing links between the Provisional Republicans and elements in the Fianna Fáil government.

Voice of the North, the newspaper financed by Irish government funds, complained that the arrested men were being used as scapegoats by the Lynch government[47] which had been concerned at the profusion of armed groups training in Donegal and wanted to clamp down on them.[48] If these men were now to refuse to recognise the court, as IRA members would be obliged to do, they would be in contempt of court at the very least. According to a senior Irish government official, Fianna Fáil minister Charles Haughey, said to be involved with Captain Kelly's actions, '... said that he would ensure that there would be no contempt'.[49] The fact that Jack Lynch had wanted a clampdown and that he now believed there had been political intervention in the case, illustrates the depth of the divisions within the Fianna Fáil government on these issues.[50] If Irish government money dried up after the arms scandal in April 1970, the *Voice of the North*, however it was financed, continued to publish, printing regular reports about the behaviour of British troops in Belfast and Derry, until December 1970.[51] We must assume that a connection between the Provisionals and some sections of Fianna Fáil remained strong at least until then, months after the Provisionals had launched a bombing campaign. Seán Keenan reacted angrily to the arms trial in April 1970, accusing Jack Lynch of ensuring that Northern Catholics would be unarmed and defenceless.[52]

The case also illustrates the generalised sympathy in the Republic with those who were seen to be arming and training to 'defend' Northern Catholics or to achieve a united Ireland. Given that none of the men had any previous convictions and that, as the judge put it, 'the Gardaí were of the opinion that they seemed to be decent men', they were placed on probation. Furthermore, the court, accepting that it might endanger them in the North if their addresses were made public, agreed that their addresses should be withheld from the public.[53]

Curran asserts that the Provisional IRA did not 'surface' in Derry until the middle of 1970[54] and that, initially, it consisted only of Seán Keenan and other older veterans of earlier campaigns.[55] On the other hand, Mac Stiofáin says that recruits flocked to the IRA after August 1969 and that arms were sent North,[56] processes which presumably operated in Derry too. The fact that the group involved in military training in Donegal was associated with the Provisional tendency suggests that the Provisional IRA was taking shape in 1969. The Provisionals also attracted some of the younger Republicans who had joined the movement in the mid-1960s, and by early 1970 at least four of the younger Derry Republicans, some of whom were associated with Seán Keenan's son Seámus, were becoming involved with the Provisionals.[57] As Michael Farrell has noted, the Provisionals attracted some younger Republicans who had been involved in housing agitation, despite rather than because of their more conservative political approach.[58] The Provisionals split from the Republican leadership on a variety of issues which included their desire to maintain abstentionism. Even so they brought in younger Republicans who, like the Officials, wanted to see the end of abstentionism[59] but who also wanted to see an armed campaign begin.

There were also many who believed that the time had come to take military action who nonetheless remained with the Official Republicans, either for ideological reasons or, particularly in the case of older Republicans, because they would not join a splinter group. Thus there was pressure within the Official IRA too for armed action. Even before August 1969, the Republican leadership had begun to put more stress on military activities, in particular endorsing IRA involvement in local Defence Committees. After August, the leadership returned to an extent to the rhetoric of military struggle and an IRA training officer from Cork was dispatched to Free Derry to give weapons instructions behind the barricades. He gave training not only to the radical Derry Republicans, but also to some of the Labour party members who had been co-operating with them and they went out on training sessions in Donegal, all in preparation for an expected imminent revolution. When it became clear that Northern Ireland was not about to collapse and that Free Derry would not be a launching pad for a revolution, enthusiasm waned and the training petered out,[60] although, for Official IRA members, it may have continued.

In the months before the formal split, 'opinions hardened' in the two sections of the Republican movement in Derry[61] and a substantial number of Republicans followed Seán Keenan's lead. The Official Republicans had also benefited from the events of August 1969. They were expanding in numbers[62] and most of the young Republicans stayed with them.[63] As 1970 began, both sides of the Republican movement in Derry were expanding both their political and military wings. Both were preparing to take military action, the Officials in the name of defence only, the Provisionals in the name of defence and in the name of an armed campaign for a united Ireland. What united Official and Provisional Republicans and many other political groups in nationalist Ireland after the arrival of British troops in August 1969 was a sense of possibility, of an historic opportunity for re-unification or revolution. During these months, Republican 'horizons were rising all the time'.[64] It was an opportunity which seemed to demand swift action to recruit those radicalised through riots, to organise and to arm. This sense of possibility was based on an often wilful underestimation of the extent of Northern Protestant hostility to a united Ireland and of the British government's intention to maintain Northern Ireland intact.

In August 1969, those who would go on to establish the Provisional IRA began to arm and prepare for a campaign which they expected would be completed in a few years. As 1969 gave way to 1970 there is no indication that any body of opinion in Northern Ireland, not least those Republicans now preparing an armed campaign, imagined that the coming conflict would last for more than a few years.

Officials and Provisionals

In January 1970, the Irish Republican movement formally split in two. The dissidents who were aggrieved at the leftward swing of the movement, the failure to send arms North in August, and the end of the principle of abstention, walked out of the Sinn Féin Árd Fheis in Dublin and established the Provisional Republican movement.

The first steps the new Provisional Republican movement made to set up an organisation in Derry were taken a month later, in mid-February 1970. A meeting was held at a hotel in Donegal town at which Ruairí Ó Brádaigh and Dave O'Connell, two of the three principal figures in the new movement,[65] were present. At the meeting Seán Keenan spoke and the meeting set up a 'North-West executive' to cover the north-west of Ireland. The fact that it had responsibility for such a large area, three of the six Northern counties (Derry, Tyrone and Fermanagh) plus Donegal and North Leitrim in the Republic, indicates Provisional weakness and emphasises the importance of the Provisional organisation in Derry. Seán Keenan was elected as chairman of the north-west executive and another older Derry Republican, Neil Gillespie, was elected publicity officer.[66] Derry would be the principal focus for the Provisionals outside Belfast and one with which the new Provisional leadership would have strong contacts, particularly as Dave O'Connell lived in Donegal and was in a position to maintain frequent direct personal contact with people in Derry. In these early stages, the Provisional national leadership appear to have been in much closer contact with the Derry Provisionals than they were with those in Belfast.[67]

A few days after this meeting, the Derry Provisionals established the Patrick Pearse Republican Club in the city in opposition to the existing James Connolly Republican Club of the Officials. The Club officers were Keenan, Gillespie and two other older Republicans, Tommy McCool, a veteran of the 1950s' IRA campaign, and Liam McDaid, who had been on the DCDA. All were middle-aged or older.[68] Tommy McCool was an active Provisional IRA member.[69]

The Derry Provisionals now publicly criticised the 'ultra-left' politics of the Officials but at the same time said they did not exclude socialism. They avoided the ideological issues in large part by saying that before deciding on any form of government for Ireland they should re-unite the country.[70]

Around this time, strongly right-wing nationalist ideas were dominant in the Provisional organisation, and were frequently expressed in the Belfast-based *Republican News*.[71] The Derry Provisionals tended to be less stridently right wing in their rhetoric. While Keenan would accuse some Official Republicans of being agents for 'the Communist party', he would also condemn 'Communism' in terms which would be unfamiliar to traditional Irish nationalists and reflected his enthusiasm for the achievements of the civil rights campaign. Keenan wrote that 'Communism as a revolutionary force has been a spent force for the past thirty years. How true this is can be seen from a study of the hostility of the Communist party to the student movements in France and to the people's uprisings in Derry and Belfast last year.'[72] This is not to say that Keenan was by any stretch of the imagination part of the 'new left' but only that he did not criticise the Officials simply in terms of conservative Catholic nationalism.

For their part, the Derry Officials criticised the Provisionals primarily for having split the movement rather than on the basis of their ideology.[73] They made a number of appeals for the Derry Provisionals to 'rejoin the Republican movement for in unity lies our strength'.[74] As Bernadette Devlin noted in Tyrone, many Republicans were reluctant to acknowledge the split at all and attended parades by both groups.[75] In Derry, the Provisionals and Officials did not split in total animosity, and three months after the split they could still hold a joint picket of the court where rioters arrested during the Official Republican Easter parade were being tried.[76] Many of the Provisional Republicans, particularly in Derry, had been enthused by the civil rights campaign and would continue to advocate and organise public protest. The Provisional Republicans also felt it necessary to frame their struggle in terms of the original civil rights campaign and legitimise it in those terms, as a struggle for the 'right' of Irish self-determination or, as Seán Keenan put it, for a united Ireland as the only 'permanent guarantee of civil rights in Ireland'.[77]

Shortly after the Patrick Pearse Republican Club was established in Derry, Seán Keenan once again set off for the United States, this time as a fully-fledged representative of the Provisional Republican movement. This time he went on a public fund-raising trip not only to raise money 'to help the homeless and distressed' in Northern Ireland but also, according to Bishop and Mallie, to arrange the first arms shipment for the Provisional IRA from the US.[78] Keenan travelled extensively, speaking and raising funds at meetings from Boston to California.[79] At the end of March 1970, he spoke in New York at the annual Easter breakfast of Sean Óglaigh na hÉireann (the Old IRA of the 1920s). The breakfast raised $2,400, much of it donated by branches of the IAC,[80] the group established by Clan na Gael members with whom Keenan had made contact in December. In the days following that breakfast, the IAC arranged to formalise its connections to the Provisional Republicans. Dave O'Connell, Seán Keenan and Belfast Republican Joe Cahill were closely involved in arranging this.[81] Dave O'Connell had strong connections in New York through his uncle, a 1920s IRA veteran who headed a trade union in New York. These contacts helped now in forging relationships with people prominent in Irish-American circles in New York.[82]

In formalising this allegiance, it was decided to officially dissolve the IAC, partly to make a clean break with the past and partly because Mike Flannery, head of the IAC, had been advised that the word 'action' in the title would draw the attention of the FBI.[83] They would set up a new organisation with a new name. Seán Keenan was one of those present when they decided it would be called the Irish Northern Aid Committee, Noraid for short.[84]

Seán Keenan and Joe Cahill were appointed as the two trustees of Noraid, and Mike Flannery, Jack McCarthy and John MacGowan were appointed as the New York representatives of the organisation.[85] All three were Irish-born IRA veterans of the 1920s. Over the coming years, Noraid would expand and attract the support of large swathes of Irish-American opinion. It would remain however under the direction and control of the American-based Republicans in Clan na Gael who had established it.

In its list of aims, Noraid said the money it raised would go to alleviate hardship in Northern Ireland and to prisoners' dependants. It would also go to citizens defence committees but in Derry, at least, there was no longer any such committee. Noraid also said it would 'provide funds for defensive measures, including first aid services'.[86] The reference to first aid is disingenuous. At this stage the Provisionals were stressing the need to arm for the purposes of 'defence'. Thus, Noraid implicitly endorsed the raising of funds to arm the Provisional IRA.

Noraid, as an organisation, channelled money to Ireland solely through An Cumann Cabhrach, an agency helping the families of Provisional Republican prisoners. However, New York Irish Republicans also set up secret committees, separate from Noraid, to channel money and guns to the Provisional IRA. Many of these people were also active in Noraid.[87]

The question of whether Noraid as an organisation supplied weapons to the IRA is somewhat academic. In its aims, it implicitly endorsed such action, while Clan na Gael, the moving force behind Noraid, had long been explicitly devoted to supporting armed campaigns against British rule in Northern Ireland. At the same time, it is clear that many of those active in Noraid were involved only in raising money for the families of prisoners.

Over the coming years Noraid would gather mass support in Irish-America partly because the group was 'the only show in town'.[88] Northern Irish moderates did not have the same network of ideological and close personal ties across the Atlantic as Republicans did and could not compete with them. However, the Official Republicans did and, as Noraid was being established, the Officials were also strengthening their organisation in the US. In Boston, for example, they set up an Irish Republican Action Committee in early 1970, headed by a man recently arrived from Belfast, which organised pickets.[89] They also set up a Friends of Irish Freedom as the 'political wing' of the Action Committee and this organisation brought Official Republican speakers over to address public meetings in Boston in March 1970.[90] They also printed a paper which featured articles by two Derry Official Republicans.[91]

Thus, from the beginning the Official Republicans were organised in the US and they retained the allegiance of at least some Clan na Gael members.[92] Their support would increase as the situation deteriorated in Northern Ireland but ultimately they could not compete with Noraid for the support of the mass of conservative-minded working-class ethnic Irish-Americans. The Official Republicans were allied with marginal left-wing groups in a country where left-wing groups were especially marginal. They quickly ran into financial trouble[93] and by early 1971 the Provisional Republicans enjoyed a virtual monopoly on Irish-American support. Noraid was associated with institutions which were a central part of ethnic Irish-American identity such as the trade unions, and the US military, marching in veterans' parades and attracting many former, and also some serving, US soldiers into their ranks.[94] This American support was significant for the Provisionals because it meant that, unlike the Officials, they would be able to provide arms and explosives to those who sought to join them and they could thus recruit more easily and launch a major offensive relatively quickly.

In line with the desires of the Dublin leadership, the Derry Official Republicans had co-operated closely with groups on the left.

The Dublin leadership looked to the East European model of socialism and was strongly influenced by the Communist parties of Ireland and of Northern Ireland;[95] the Derry Official Republicans, on the other hand, were co-operating with and being heavily influenced by Trotskyists such as Eamonn McCann and by 'workerist' groups.[96] The fact that the Derry Officials remained within the movement after August 1969 did not mean that they totally agreed with the Dublin leadership. Over the following two years, the Derry Official Republicans followed a path to a military campaign about which the Dublin leadership was unenthusiastic and did not provide whole-hearted support.[97] This was another factor which weakened the Derry Official IRA and ensured that the Derry Provisionals would rise in prominence. When the Irish Republican Socialist Party was established by disgruntled Official Republicans in 1974, the Derry Officials were central to its founding and the leadership and most of the rank and file defected to the IRSP and its military wing, the INLA.[98] Thus, it would be misleading to analyse the actions of the Derry Official IRA from 1970 to 1972 in terms of a strategy decided by the leadership in Dublin.

Although the Dublin leadership had approved Official IRA involvement in defence associations they were also concerned, as Official Sinn Féin leader Tomás MacGiolla put it in Derry in 1970, to prevent any 'premature and promiscuous use of violence'.[99] At the same time, it was their status as the 'Official' Republican movement which gave them most of their legitimacy and, as the IRA was an integral part of the movement, they needed to show that the Official IRA was still a force. Thus, in February 1970 the Derry city command of the IRA made their first public statement in many years. They announced that there had been no resignations from the Derry IRA and that they supported the James Connolly Republican Club (Official) and its forthcoming Easter commemoration.[100]

There was an indication that the Derry Official IRA was also reviving its military functions at about the same time when Finbar O'Doherty told a meeting that 'the [Republican] movement will defend the lives and property of our fellow countrymen and women if an attack took place from any native or foreign force'.[101] The Derry Officials had publicly announced the existence of the IRA and were hinting that they were prepared to take military action, although, it was stressed publicly, only in defence.

The Derry Officials had long concentrated on building a broad alliance on the left and directly after August 1969 this had even extended to including Labour radicals in weapons-training sessions.[102] Now, in the spring of 1970, the Derry Officials were trying to get their Labour party allies to accept the importance of working towards a united

Ireland. Some of the Labour radicals were unwilling to accept this and in February and March 1970 the Derry Officials publicly attacked their former allies, in particular Eamonn McCann, for continuing to work within the Northern Ireland Labour Party.[103] Some of the Derry Officials wanted to involve the Labour left in preparations for a military campaign, that is, to commit themselves to the Republican ideal of a united Ireland and to the need for armed force to achieve it.

An internal discussion document written by one of the Derry Official Republicans in February 1970 and entitled 'co-operation on what and for what', questioned the grounds on which the Derry Republicans should co-operate with the radicals in the Derry Labour party and the Young Socialists. The document criticised the Labour left in Derry for 'turning their back' on the ideal of a united Ireland. It also criticised the Labour left on other grounds: 'They talk of revolution yet they make no provision for revolution ... It is vital that we only co-operate if it advances the revolution.' It continued, 'If they want revolution then they must help in preparing the workers for an armed conflict as only armed force can bring an end to the institutions created by capitalist forces.' The document also seems to suggest that the Derry Officials wanted now to obtain more weaponry, saying 'We, on our part, if we demand these things must be able to supply the services for such.'[104]

It is clear that some of the Derry Officials shared with the Provisionals the belief that an historic opportunity had arisen and that the time for the IRA to take military action had now come. Many of the new recruits to the movement were also keen to take action. As Eamonn McCann put it, 'At every meeting [of the youth organisations run by Labour and Republican radicals in mid-1970] someone would ask sooner or later when the guns were going to be handed out'.[105] It seems that the pressure within the Officials for an IRA campaign was resisted for some time and teenage recruits disillusioned with the lack of military organisation moved on to join the Provisionals.[106] However, at least by early 1971, the Official IRA in Derry had embarked on a limited campaign which was defensive to the same extent as the Provisional campaign was; that is, it was primarily an offensive campaign.

When British soldiers first arrived, the Official Republicans had been hostile to them. In Derry, Johnnie White, a prominent radical Republican, said 'British troops in Ireland have never brought peace to Ireland and only when British troops leave this country for ever will there be lasting peace and prosperity'.[107] Cathal Goulding, chief of staff of the IRA, had warned British soldiers shortly after they arrived, 'You are in a very perilous situation for this is not your country'.[108] However, when the British army began its 'hearts and minds' campaign in Derry in late 1969, it seems the Republicans did nothing to hinder it. Off-duty British soldiers could apparently walk freely anywhere in the city. It was not until after the rioting in Easter 1970 that the Official Republicans in Derry directed their hostility openly at the British army. After the riots, the Derry city command of the IRA (Official) announced that, in retaliation for the severe sentences recently imposed on rioters, 'action will be taken against collaborators with the British occupation forces in the Bogside'.[109] The first step would be to daub slogans on the doors of suspected 'collaborators'. If the warning was not heeded, unspecified further action would be taken. It was the first time that Derry Republicans had declared that local people should shun British troops and it was the Officials not the Provisionals who had issued the warning.

Although the Derry Official IRA had not begun an armed campaign, people associated with them were taking action in the spring of 1970. In May 1970, four men, at least two of them armed, robbed a bank in Strabane, about thirteen miles from Derry. The raiders were members of Saor Éire[110] and they escaped over the nearby border into Co. Donegal with about £15,000.[111] Saor Éire was a left-wing Republican group which had split from the movement during the 1960s, before this current crisis.[112] It was based around a few individuals in Dublin but they had made some contacts in Derry in August 1969 (see ch. 3 above) and around this time, apparently, a Saor Éire unit, consisting of half a dozen members, was formed in Derry. The unit operated 'hand in hand' with the Derry Official IRA[113] and at least one of its members, Hugo Meenan, an ex-British paratrooper,[114] later went on to join the Official IRA.[115] After the Official IRA called a cease-fire in May 1972, at least one prominent Derry Official was involved in trying to provide arms to the Derry Official IRA with the help of Saor Éire. When this was discovered, he was expelled from the Official Republican movement.[116]

During the following months in mid-1970 there were a number of other robberies in and around Derry[117] and money now began to become available to the Republican groups in the city. This period, before any Republican group in Derry had embarked on an armed campaign, was a time of great confusion in Republican circles and there was confusion as to who had carried out which robbery and indeed in some cases, where the money had gone to.[118]

Thus, by the spring of 1970, three different armed Republican groups and other small groups of people loosely connected to them[119] were organising in Derry. In addition, within each faction there could be different groups of activists with little awareness of what other groups, sometimes divided from them by age, were doing.[120] What was clear was that all of these groups were growing and had benefited from the radicalisation through rioting of young Catholics in Derry.

In April 1970, the Provisional Republicans held their own Easter parade in Derry separately from the Official Republicans.[121] A colour party marched in the parade carrying hurley sticks as did the stewards, the sticks serving as symbolic weapons. They also wore berets and a paramilitary-style uniform. The parade also included about eighty members of Fianna Éireann, both boys and girls. As they marched some of the youths shouted 'Out' as they passed British military policemen along the route. One of the speakers, Sheila Duffy, called on people to join the Fianna which she said, had 140 members in Derry, with branches for both boys and girls. Around this time the Provisionals were claiming that half of the Derry IRA had joined them and that they had access to Stirling sub-machine guns and small arms.[122]

The number of young people who marched in the parade and the number of adults who marched in paramilitary uniform reinforce the point that the Provisionals and the Republican movement as a whole had recruited heavily in the months before the split. Certainly the Derry Provisionals had not gathered this support only in the two months since the setting-up of the Patrick Pearse Republican Club. The participation of so many young people also emphasises how the Republicans, of both factions, were able to politically involve the young teenage rioters in a way which conventional political groups could not. In the coming years, both wings of the Republican movement in Derry were remarkable for the extreme youth of many of their members. They were in large part composed of, and reliant on, teenagers who were not even old enough to vote.

By June 1970, the Derry Provisional IRA was preparing to begin a bombing campaign. It was around this time that the first small Provisional IRA bombs went off in Belfast. At the end of June 1970, Tommy McCool and Thomas Carlin, both prominent members of the Patrick Pearse Republican Club, and Joseph Coyle were in the kitchen of McCool's house in Creggan with chemicals and materials used in bomb-making. There was an explosion: all three men were killed as were two of Tommy McCool's young daughters, aged nine and three. All three men were middle-aged and McCool was a veteran of the 1950s campaign. The IRA would later say that the three men had died 'on active service'.[123] The explosion must have demoralised the Provisionals considerably, re-awakening memories of the last time a Derry IRA man had been killed, in a training accident almost exactly ten years before.

It changed things too. Now that the Provisionals had already lost members, they would be less likely to abandon any plans for a campaign.

By this time, after the deaths in the McCool house, the core of the Provisional IRA in Derry consisted of a small group of about ten people, most of them between seventeen and twenty years of age. Some of them had been in the Fianna Éireann prior to the outbreak of conflict in October 1968; some had started out as rioters and then moved into the Patrick Pearse Republican Club and then the IRA. Some of the rioters now joining up with the Provisionals were as young as fourteen.[124] It was this small group, several of them related by birth or marriage to the older Republicans or to each other, which formed the core of the Derry Provisional IRA right up until July 1971 when membership began to expand significantly. As they prepared a campaign in mid- and late 1970, they had very few weapons available. According to one former IRA member, they had a few revolvers, some Thompson sub-machine guns smuggled into Ireland with the Cork football team in 1921 and a number of pre-World War I rifles, including a UVF Martini Henri 303, which were unsafe. 'You would've been better off with a catapult', as this member put it. They also had, as the same activist put it, 'no organised strategy or plan'. They were training with the fifty-year-old Thompsons, and weapons expertise was in such short supply that one fifteen or sixteen year old member of the group found himself quickly moved up the ranks to the position of training officer.[125]

The deaths in the McCool household also illuminate the relationship between the Provisionals and other forces in the Catholic community. Even though they were embarking on an offensive campaign, the Provisionals were not likely to find themselves quickly isolated or ostracised. They simply had too many connections through a network of ties to people of all political persuasions in the community. Joseph Coyle, for example, was the brother of a well-known steward in the civil rights campaign who was now a prominent member of the Independent Organisation (later to become the Derry branch of the SDLP).[126] Tom Carlin had been a member of the DCDA and had worked in it with Independent Organisation members and Labour party members.

The IRA tradition in the city was popularly seen, among Catholics, as respectable, even at times heroic, and was associated with the Irish War of Independence in the 1920s and the series of minor attacks during the 1950s' campaign. The Republicans who set up the Provisionals had been public figures in the DCDA and had supported the early civil rights campaign and were far from isolated from the Catholic community. Thus, when Tommy McCool and his two daughters were buried with a guard of honour of eleven Derry IRA men, over 1,000 people walked in the funeral and among them were John Hume, Eamonn McCann and Eddie McAteer.[127] When an appeal for funds was set up for the families of Coyle and McCool, it was endorsed by several prominent figures in the city, including Ivan Cooper, John Hume, Michael Canavan and Eddie McAteer.[128]

While other groups in the Catholic community in Derry may have regarded the Provisionals as misguided, they did not see them as external or alien in the way in which some now began to see the Officials. Throughout 1970, Catholic conservatives in Derry concentrated their criticism of Republicans on the Officials. This was facilitated by the fact that at this time neither wing of the Republican movement was admitting that it was preparing for or engaging in military activity and the pretence could be maintained that only the Officials had an interest in promoting violence.

The Provisionals were led by figures, including Seán Keenan, who were well known and whose political views did not conflict too much with mainstream nationalist politics. The fact that Hugh McAteer, brother of Eddie McAteer, was also involved in establishing the Provisionals[129] provided further 'respectability'. The left-wing ideology of the Officials was anathema to the Nationalists and to conservative Catholics. When rioting broke out after the Official Republican Easter march in Derry in 1970, the *Derry Journal*, in a clear reference to the Officials, said that some people were using the name 'Republican' as 'a cover for a class war and alien cult'.[130] When the Derry Nationalist party said that they 'condemned the hidden manipulators of these boys [rioters] for their own evil ends'[131] and a conservative columnist in the *Journal* condemned the 'hidden hands' and the 'wirepullers'[132] it seems likely it was the Officials rather than the Provisionals they were referring to.

It was undoubtedly of great benefit to the Provisionals that during 1970 and much of 1971 they were not identified as a malevolent or 'sinister' force by mainstream Catholic political opinion in Derry and that the Officials were seen as far more threatening and destabilising to public order.

Public order and the courts

As rioting against the British troops became more frequent in the spring of 1970, there was a barrage of criticism of the rioters from Catholic moderates, Catholic conservatives and the Nationalist party. It has been noted that this did not imply an endorsement of tougher army responses but it did serve to isolate the young rioters politically. However, as army tactics got tougher and a number of controversial court cases took place, a level of sympathy for the rioters was restored. Within several months certain forces within the Catholic community that had harshly condemned the rioters came to focus their criticism on the army and the courts and the rioters ceased to be so isolated. This was a further major erosion of the commitment of moderate Catholics to the restoration of order by the British army. It reduced the level of army violence which they considered acceptable and justified. The fact also that army violence in dealing with rioters became steadily 'tougher' over these months led some, in particular the Nationalist party, to view the British army as an essentially malevolent force. It made it more and more difficult for the state to restore its authority as general Catholic acceptance of the army and of the army's right to enforce 'law and order' steadily decreased.

After the riots of Easter 1970, there was a long period of relative calm in Derry. For almost three months there was no reported incident more serious than the stoning of soldiers after a dance one night.[133] During these months, the British army, perhaps realising that their presence on the streets was not now seen as 'neutral', lowered their profile and tried to let the RUC take over some of their duties. RUC cars and joint RUC/army foot patrols began to police the Bogside and Creggan. There were occasional stoning attacks on these patrols[134] but the local police chief, Frank Lagan, a Catholic who later became the target of severe criticism from local Unionists, felt that things were going well, that 'people were beginning to accept us'.[135] However, a series of incidents and a procession of court cases demonstrated that there were continuing problems, persisting tension and increased Catholic distrust of the courts and of the army (rather than the RUC) even during this period of relative calm. As was so often the case, court cases served to maintain a sense of grievance after riots had ended.

In early April 1970, an eighteen-year-old Catholic youth appeared in court. According to him the events which had led to the court case had begun when a soldier on patrol verbally abused him and then warned him not to complain about the incident. This was denied in court but the following sequence of events was not. The youth went into an RUC station the following day to lodge a complaint. The RUC directed him to the army base in Brooke Park. There he was told to go to an army base at the old bus depot in the city. From there he was directed to the Sailor's Rest, a former pub which was now an army post. While he was lodging his complaint in the Sailor's Rest, an army officer told the youth that some of his soldiers were now identifying him as having taken part in a riot the previous day. The youth was arrested and in court he was sentenced to four months imprisonment on the testimony of a single soldier. No other army personnel were present in the court.[136] This case raised the suspicion that the youth had been arrested principally because he had complained, a suspicion strengthened by the fact that he had freely visited so many RUC and army bases before finally being arrested.

A few days later, another eighteen-year-old youth who had been cleared of rioting a week before appeared in court for a second time. On the first occasion, he had been found not guilty but was re-arrested by the RUC immediately after the verdict was announced because two soldiers present in the court claimed that they had seen him rioting the night after the offence he had just been cleared of. This was four days after that riot. Although the soldiers could not say at what time they had seen him in the crowd and said he had never been closer to them than thirty yards, and this was at night-time, the court sentenced the youth to six months in jail on his second appearance.[137] This raised the suspicion that, having failed to convict him on one charge, the soldiers had simply accused him of the same offence on another date.

That same day in court a seventeen-year-old youth was charged with rioting. He had been arrested while walking through the city centre five days after the alleged offence. Soldiers claimed that they had recognised him because they had spotted him from the city walls through binoculars in a riotous crowd between 6 p.m. and 7 p.m. five days previously. They said they recognised him because of his distinctive hairstyle.[138] He was sentenced to four months in jail. These youths were among dozens of Derry teenagers with no previous convictions who were now being brought to court and were often ending up serving prison terms in Crumlin Road jail in Belfast.

The Derry Labour party condemned these proceedings and its recently formed Derry Youth Movement, whose initial meeting had attracted 150 to 200 youths, picketed outside the court house. They claimed that soldiers were taking photographs of people with telescopic lenses from the city walls and that youths were afraid of going into the city centre for fear of being arrested under this practice of 'retrospective identification'.[139] Eamonn McCann called for an end to 'indiscriminate arrests and heavy sentences on very flimsy evidence'. He called on the army to 'stop pushing people about' and suggested that the reason there was so much criticism of the youths in the Catholic Community was because 'older people may not know about the way the army authorities treat young people and the insulting way they address them'.[140] Eddie McAteer, one of those who had been most critical of the rioters, now expressed his 'disquiet' at recent court cases and at the 'telescopic-eyed soldiers' giving evidence.[141]

In the midst of this, in response to continuing street violence in Belfast, the army adopted new security measures which the Nationalist party in Derry said were tantamount to martial law.[142] All of this served to awaken a certain amount of sympathy for those youths who had previously been dismissed as 'hooligans'.

The Derry Citizens Central Council: moderates on the streets

In the spring of 1970, despite the relative calm on the streets of Derry, things were not going well for the Catholic moderates who had entered the political arena. The reform of the RUC had not been effective, the army was appearing less conciliatory to Catholics, and the Unionist party was continuing to try and stall or block the reforms which had been agreed. (The Unionist party conference, for example, voted against the proposal to set up a central housing authority for the North which had been designed to prevent discrimination at local government level.)[143]

Since the end of Free Derry in October 1969, the moderates had concentrated on parliamentary action and on building up the Independent Organisation as a political party. John Hume had also been deeply involved in negotiations for the formation of a new united anti-Unionist party. These formal political efforts did not appear to have met with notable success while on the ground the situation was steadily deteriorating. As a result of the stalling of political progress there was a fall-off in attendance at meetings of the Independent Organisation in Derry.[144]

Events at the end of June 1970, when the calm of three months finally broke in Derry, galvanised the moderates to take action on the streets again. On 26 June, Bernadette Devlin was arrested by the RUC to begin serving a six-month sentence for her part in rioting during the Battle of the Bogside.[145] The jail sentence which had been imposed on her was seen as an assertion by the Unionist government that the thousands of people in Derry who had rioted in August 1969 were all criminals and that the defence of the Bogside had not been justified. But this defence was accepted as legitimate virtually across the Catholic community in

Derry and Devlin's conviction was resented, even by moderates and conservatives.[146]

The RUC had agreed that they would not arrest her until after she had addressed a meeting in Derry. A large crowd gathered in the Bogside to wait for her. The RUC, however, arrested her just outside the city on the way to the meeting.[147] There had been rioting and shooting in Belfast over previous weeks which had left a number of people dead, but Derry had remained remarkably quiet. Now, however, word reached the meeting of Devlin's arrest. As the meeting ended, youths walked over to the nearest army post on the edge of the Bogside and began to throw stones and bottles at it. The young rioters, as McCann put it, 'for the first time since August [1969], had some sort of mandate for riot, and they were joined by some who had not flung a stone in anger for almost eleven months'.[148]

Thus began three days of relentless and chaotic rioting as barricades were erected for the first time since August 1969. Crowds of youths, several hundred strong, fought the soldiers as they had fought the RUC in August. The army responded, after issuing a warning that they would fire CS gas unless the crowd dispersed, by firing CS gas for the first time since their arrival. Troops charged into the Bogside and as they pursued rioters up side-streets they were 'ambushed' by youths throwing petrol bombs, stones and bottles. Once again the Bogside was 'saturated with gas' and numerous buildings were burnt to the ground. In the course of the riots, army 'snatch-squads' made eighty-nine arrests.[149] At the same time, large-scale sectarian rioting and gun battles broke out in Belfast and eight people were shot dead in the space of a few days. Violence in Belfast was on a completely different scale from that in Derry.

This outbreak demonstrated that rioting in Derry was not going to die out naturally. It prompted concerted action by Catholic moderates to try and restore peace on the ground. On Sunday 28 June, the third day of rioting, a meeting of prominent local figures from across the political spectrum in the Catholic community was called by Michael Canavan. Canavan was a close associate of John Hume's and was active in the Independent Organisation. He had been prominent in the DCAC and had acted as the DCDA liaison with the British army during Free Derry. He now tried to rebuild the coalition which had operated to run Free Derry to try now to stop the riots. The meeting brought together Nationalists, moderates, Republicans and Labour activists. Canavan suggested they send a joint deputation to the army to negotiate an end to the riots.[150] However, the coalition of August 1969 no longer existed. Seán Keenan was present for the Provisional Republicans and he refused to become involved in the proposed deputation. He said that instead of sending a delegation to the army they should be preparing to defend themselves against the army.[151]

As early as April 1970 the Provisionals had defended the actions of rioters[152] and now Keenan was stating clearly that the Provisionals would not be involved in attempts to stop them, or to deal with the army through negotiation. However, although the young Republicans in Derry were most probably involved in these riots, the general level of hostility to the troops by now meant they had little need to provoke, incite or 'organise' the rioting. Certainly though, the Provisionals were less disturbed by rioting than any other group in the city, including the Officials.

Despite Keenan's lack of interest and the disgruntlement of the radical left with the hostile attitude of the moderates to rioters in recent months, a deputation to the army was organised. John Hume and Michael Canavan with Eamonn McCann and Nationalist party chairman James Doherty went to meet the local army commander and the local RUC chief Frank Lagan. Such an approach to the army had not been made in several months and apparently the group came to an agreement with the army. According to McCann, it was agreed that if they could halt rioting there would be no RUC patrols in the Free Derry area for an initial period of two weeks.[153] According to Hume, the agreement also provided that the British army would not enter the area either, apart from military police, and that the RUC would enter only to investigate serious crimes.[154]

To announce the agreement, a peace meeting was held in the Bogside at which John Hume said that the rioting would lead to disaster and that the area now needed organisation and discipline. However, even as he was speaking, youths were attacking the army nearby.[155] Some of the group at the peace meeting, including Canavan, Hume and Eamon Melaugh, convened a meeting in a nearby building and appealed for people to act as stewards to try and put an end to the rioting by placing themselves between the army and the rioters. They found it difficult to recruit people to act as stewards,[156] a measure of the lack of hope that something worthwhile could be achieved. Eventually, later that night, this group approached the army and although the army initially refused to take them seriously they eventually agreed to pull back and allow the group of sixty or seventy stewards to attempt to stop the rioting.[157]

However, just before the stewards' group had arrived, the army had charged into the Bogside with sixty troops and two armoured troop carriers. Among those arrested during the charge were nine teenage girls who were apparently standing to one side watching. The troops had arrested them, grabbing some by the hair and taken them behind army lines with some of the girls 'in hysterics'. It was thus at an inopportune moment that the 'peace group' rounded the corner to try and appeal to the youths to stop rioting. As they advanced there were shouts of 'Lundies' (traitors) and stones were thrown at them. Two stewards were hit on the head and John Hume was hit on the leg. The stewards withdrew and John Hume and Eamon Melaugh then approached the youths and asked them to draw up a list of demands and send a delegation to the army. The youths accepted it as a good idea but none of them was prepared to meet the army. Rioting continued for a short time after this but petered out when it began to rain.[158] It was a constant source of amazement to British troops that the crowds of youths who withstood baton charges, CS gas and rubber bullets would invariably disperse peacefully whenever it began to rain.

Although they had failed to stop the rioting, that night a coalition drawn from the Independent Organisation and the Nationalist party established a new organisation, in some ways a more moderate successor to the DCAC and the DCDA. The Derry Citizens Central Council (hereafter DCCC) would remain active for the following three years until local government elections were held in Derry.[159] It would act at different times as a political group, a policing agency and an occasional liaison or mediator between the army and Republicans.[160] The DCCC was set up to administer the agreement with the army made at that initial meeting by maintaining order in the Bogside and Creggan in return for a reduced army presence. The council had twenty-two members, a large number of them active members of the Independent Organisation or the Nationalist party, among them John Hume. In particular, it included many of the moderates who had been members of the DCDA and thus had experience of working with the Republicans. Of the twenty-two, at least seven had been members of the DCDA.[161] The DCCC was chaired by Michael Canavan and of the four office holders, two were Nationalists and two were Independent Organisation members.[162] The DCCC set up a twenty-four hour a day headquarters and organised area committees in Catholic areas around the city, not just in Creggan and Bogside. It organised patrols to operate every night from 8 p.m. to 6 a.m. and announced that it was now responsible for the control of Creggan and the Bogside with the assistance only of unarmed British military policemen.[163]

Clearly a major political initiative had been taken in the city. For the first time since the days of Free Derry the army was acknowledging the authority of a group within the Catholic community as an alternative to the forces of the state. To an extent, a new Free Derry had come into existence through negotiation with the army. Local Unionists recognised this when they complained that the army had gone back to 'bargaining with lawbreakers'.[164]

Shortly after the street meeting at which John Hume announced the deal with the army, the Joint Security Committee (JSC) in Belfast denied that any deal had been made; John Hume retorted that the JSC was lying.[165] The JSC included the army GOC in Northern Ireland, the chief constable of the RUC and the Unionist prime minister and cabinet ministers. Once a week it met in Belfast, chaired by the Stormont PM, to make political decisions on the security situation and once a week in Lisburn where the GOC, with input from the RUC chief constable, made the operational decisions.[166]

There were clearly tensions in the JSC between the operational decisions of the British army GOC and the political considerations of the Stormont government whose control he was formally under.[167] Whatever the internal JSC politics in this particular case, an agreement between the army and the DCCC had been reached and operated for the following two weeks. However, after two weeks, during which there were no incidents, the agreement was ended by the army. According to the *Derry Journal*, when an army spokesman at Lisburn was asked why the army had ended the arrangement, he replied, 'the army is subordinate to the Stormont government. We will fall in with their plans.'[168]

In June, a Conservative government had been elected to power in Britain and it seems it was reluctant to permit such a situation of dual authority. This government was seen by Catholics as more supportive of the Unionists than its Labour predecessor and a series of measures in July 1970, introduced by the conservatives, moved Catholic moderates further away from the state.

The decision by the army to cease co-operating with the DCCC was one action which served to alienate moderates. While Unionists saw it as co-operation with 'law-breakers', for Catholic moderates it represented an attempt to maintain peace through providing an 'acceptable' policing agency in certain Catholic areas. By rejecting this arrangement and insisting that the army and the RUC retain a monopoly on security even if it led to further violence, the army seemed to be deciding that repression was a preferable solution to the negotiation of an arrangement with the most moderate elements in the Catholic community.

The 'Falls curfew' in early July 1970 followed an army search for arms in the Lower Falls in Belfast, which provoked rioting. A two-day total curfew, confining everyone to their houses was imposed, with the army conducting door-to-door searches (arresting 300 men) and shooting dead three civilians.[169] This put the army in a new light. It was a classic, indiscriminate military operation that alienated an entire population, including those who desired the restoration of law and order. James Doherty, chairman of the Derry Nationalist party and member of the DCCC was asked by the Irish government to help arrange a visit to the Falls by the Irish foreign minister, Patrick Hillery, after the curfew[170] and this visit represented the first serious criticism of the British army's role by the Irish government. John Hume said that the new Conservative government 'had decided to act ... only in the interests of their Unionist friends' and when Stormont opposition MPs met the new Conservative home affairs minister, Reginald Maudling, he gave them what Hume called 'a contemptuous 25 minutes'.[171]

The Falls curfew, the tougher approach of the army, the new mandatory six-month jail sentences for rioters, the 'shepherding' of Orange marches past Catholic areas of Belfast by troops in July 1970, all drained away much of what remained of moderate faith in British intentions. In Derry, the court cases which followed the June riots caused further animosity towards the army. The trial of the nine girls arrested by troops on 28 June mobilised shirt factory workers and all Catholic political groups in their defence. After the trial, Ivan Cooper warned that there was a danger that 'people will lose all respect for justice in the courts in Derry'.[172] The nine girls were arrested by troops who claimed that a girl had thrown a stone at them as the troops ran past them during the riot on 28 June. After this, as an RUC man put it, 'every girl in the vicinity was arrested'.[173] When the girls were brought back behind army lines, a British officer 'ordered' his men to hand them over to the RUC.[174] An RUC man testified that all of the girls had clean hands, suggesting that they had not been throwing stones. One soldier claimed in court that, while he had not seen the girls throwing stones themselves, the girls had been passing stones to boys to throw. When pressed on the matter, he said he wasn't sure how many stones had been passed and agreed it might have been as few as one stone, that is, that one girl had passed one stone to a boy. Three of the girls were released when soldiers identified the wrong people in the court.[175]

Tension in the court reached a pitch as a soldier came up to testify against one of the girls. When asked by the defence if he had ever bought her a coffee in a local café, he denied it. When asked if he had asked to walk her home and that she had refused, he denied that also. When the judge found the girl guilty on the evidence of this soldier and sentenced her to three months in prison, there was uproar in the court as women and girls shouted that the soldier was a liar. This suggests that there was an element of personalised sexual tension between some of the soldiers and the teenage girls they had arrested: that the soldiers might well have arrested the girls for their own personal reasons. That the court was prepared to jail some of these girls despite this and despite strong evidence in their defence from, among others, an RUC man, can hardly have increased the faith of local Catholics in the legal system. The judge also jailed two of the other girls, both aged seventeen.[176] It would not be unreasonable to suggest that this case went a long way towards ending the 'honeymoon' between local young women and British troops serving in the city.

There were also other cases arising from the June riots which aroused widespread concern and anger. One was the case of a youth who was able to produce his time card from a local factory to show he had been at work at the time he was accused of being in a riot. He was then charged with taking part in a riot the night *after* the original charge. Even 'Onlooker' of the *Derry Journal*, who had constantly claimed that rioters were directed by a 'hidden hand' was 'disturbed' by this case and said the practice of retrospective identification 'could easily result in a serious miscarriage of justice'.[177] There were many in Derry who now believed that there had already been several miscarriages of justice.[178] There was also a tendency, as young males learnt to evade the snatch-squads, for troops to arrest those who were not so fleet of foot and those arrested in June included several men in their late forties and fifties, among them an ex-British soldier on a disability pension.[179]

Some writers have identified the introduction of a new mandatory six-month sentence for disorderly behaviour in the summer of 1970 as a major factor in increasing a Catholic sense of grievance.[180] This increased tension but it was only one of the factors that heightened the perception of the army as a hostile force; others were retrospective identification, the acceptance by the courts of dubious uncorroborated evidence from British soldiers and especially the attitude of certain judges who said that bystanders at the scene of a riot could also be convicted of disorderly behaviour.[181] Effectively, as most riots took place on the edge of the Bogside, this last factor further restricted the freedom of movement of people who lived there, as even being in the vicinity of a riot near their homes could now result in a jail sentence. Even if the law had not been altered, the way in which the existing laws were being applied would have created high levels of alienation. In the light of such cases, moderates found themselves more and more involved in criticism of the army, the courts and the government.

After its agreement with the army on the policing of Free Derry had ended, the DCCC continued to operate, to make political statements and to expand. It tried now to expand outside Catholic areas and to include Derry Protestants on the basis that they were seeking above all to preserve peace in the city. A Waterside area committee was established which included Leonard Hutchinson, the former Unionist councillor who had set up the Lisnagelvin Tenants' Association (the first of its kind in a Protestant area of Derry), a Methodist minister and Snoo Sinclair, a Protestant who later became prominent in the Alliance party in Derry. This was a major development and seemed to promise a new ground-level cross-community, co-operation in the interests of maintaining order, involving people with strong connections in both Free Derry and in loyalist housing estates.[182] However, the limits of such co-operation became evident within days. The Apprentice Boys parade on 12 August was approaching and the DCCC, like most groups in the Catholic community in Derry, called for a ban on the parade in the interests of maintaining peace. In protest at this statement, Leonard Hutchinson and the Methodist minister resigned at once from the DCCC. This 'cross-community' initiative had survived only for a matter of days.[183] Catholic moderates and Nationalists feared that, if the parade went ahead, proceeding along the edge of the Bogside behind a cordon of troops, there would be a repeat of August 1969, except that perhaps now the IRA would step in to fill the role the DCDA had filled then.

Then, in late July 1970, the Northern Ireland Joint Security Committee announced a six-month ban on processions, effectively banning the Apprentice Boys parade in Derry.[184] Local Unionists were dismayed although the MP, Albert Anderson, supported the ban, a decision which led to his de-selection by the Derry Unionist Association a few months later. Simultaneously, the JSC announced the resumption of RUC patrolling in Free Derry and the establishment of an RUC station in the Bogside, as promised almost a year previously.[185]

It was a classic balancing act between the two communities and it produced the most enthusiastic response from the Catholic community since the Hunt Report, albeit a response which was a great deal more restrained. John Hume said they would support the RUC if it acted impartially in the Bogside. Eddie McAteer said the RUC should be welcomed according to its behaviour and the *Derry Journal* asked people to give the RUC a chance.[186] A few days later, 'Onlooker' in the *Derry Journal* called for people to co-operate fully with the RUC in stopping vandalism.[187]

This showed how willing these forces in the Catholic community were to see a restoration of law and order and a normal form of policing which would allow them to make progress in the political arena without the constant fear of civil unrest.

However, despite this ban, most of the conditions for continued unrest still existed and the ban also served to prohibit all protest by the Catholic community for the next six months, creating more potential opportunities for confrontation. The moderates were over-optimistic in thinking that the RUC could now provide a solution to the problem of law and order in the Bogside and Creggan as it was still rejected by many people in these areas. However, since the establishment of the DCCC, its chairman, Michael Canavan had been in regular consultation with the British army commander in Derry.[188] Although the RUC was now patrolling, the British were still governing partly by arrangement with Catholic moderates. Clearly the moderates were doing everything to maintain that peace. Even though they would not be successful they would retain a position as intermediaries between the British army and other forces in the Catholic community, in trying to restrict, manage or limit the level of conflict. By now, though, the moderates had to contend not just with rioters but with a deliberate Republican campaign. In the space between the banning in late July of the Apprentice Boys march and the march itself on 12 August, despite the concession which the ban represented and the efforts of the DCCC, there was another outbreak of rioting in Derry. It lasted for four days and nights, marked the beginning of several months of regular, large-scale rioting, and saw the first armed IRA action in Derry.

Republicans and moderates

In the course of 1970, a variety of Republican groups in Derry began to organise for a military campaign. This was an important new element in the situation in Derry and meant that now there were groups who, at the very least, were uninterested in preventing rioting. Certainly, the growing number of younger Republicans were active and enthusiastic rioters. This Republican build-up cannot be characterised solely or even primarily in terms of a desire for defence of Catholic areas or as a response to British army actions. It began in August 1969, before serious complaints about the army had surfaced. However, against a background of a lack of political progress British army actions helped to alienate people from the army as they had previously been alienated from the RUC. Republicans benefited from this development, and sustained mass agitation provided the conditions under which they could launch an armed campaign.

To explain this in terms of a conspiracy fuelled by atavistic nationalism, a crisis 'brought on ... by quite small numbers of fanaticized pace-makers'[189] is to ignore the fact that a much broader radicalisation within the Catholic community provided the essential conditions in which the Republicans, of all varieties, could thrive. It was not the Republicans on their own who created these conditions and to identify them as the sole crucial force in this escalation is to absolve the other parties to the conflict of any responsibility for the situation.

The Provisional IRA in Derry was established by the very people involved in the failed campaign of the 1950s. In 1970, they planned a campaign in Derry which essentially was a repeat of that campaign. Now, however, they could gain recruits and operate in a generally sympathetic climate. There was also a newly politicised and mobilised Catholic population, particularly the young, who saw Catholic politicians failing to make progress while, on the streets, the relationship between troops and Catholic youths became ever more one of mutual hostility. However, this is not to say the rise of both Republican wings was inevitable. The moderates could obviously still exert pressure on the Republicans and, if certain issues, particularly that of policing, had been resolved, the Republicans would have found the political basis for their campaign eroding.

Rioting forced moderates to go back on the streets to attempt to halt the street violence which was undermining their attempts to progress politically and to maintain the pressure on Stormont for reform via the British government. As violence increased, the British tended to become more sympathetic to Stormont and more concerned to protect it and preserve its authority and less inclined to pressure it into making concessions. This seemed logical to the British government but it meant it now dealt with Catholic unrest as though Catholic demands had been met and a political resolution achieved.

When the DCCC temporarily took over policing of the Bogside and Creggan in early July 1970, it undermined both the Republicans and the authority of the Stormont government. The end of the British army agreement with the DCCC showed the limits of the British government's ability or willingness to make concessions to the most moderate sections of the Catholic community that might have restored hope in the political process. There would be no diminution of the authority of the state and its right to police any area of Northern Ireland. The Northern Irish and British governments would deal with civil disorder as though a political solution had been achieved and as though policing was now an operational issue and not a political one.

This policy, in conjunction with a mass of other factors, including harsh army tactics, court attitudes and stalled reforms, resulted in the sections of the Catholic community most concerned with the restoration of law and order coming to reject the army's authority. The extent to which they had accepted the army and vilified those who attacked them is perhaps underestimated and therefore the scale of this change in moderate Catholic attitudes in 1970 has also been underestimated.

Once these moderates were lost (and they would not be entirely lost until August 1971), the Catholic community in Derry would be policed and controlled totally without its consent, a situation which amounted to a military occupation. Once this was the case, it opened the way for mass radicalisation, and a drastic alienation of Catholics in Derry from the state which by now was as much the British state as the Northern Irish state. From such a situation there would develop a framework of repression, control and continued widespread alienation which facilitated continued conflict.

Notes and references

1 As Paddy Doherty put it. Interview with Patrick L. Doherty ('Paddy Bogside'), Head of the Inner-city Trust, formerly a member of the DCDA, DCAC and founder member of the Credit Union in Derry.
2 DJ, 10/4/70, p. 1; Seán Keenan speaking in New York.
3 Seán Mac Stiofáin, *Memoirs of a Revolutionary* (R. and R. Clarke, Edinburgh, 1975), p. 146.
4 James Kelly, *Orders for the Captain* (James Kelly, Dublin, 1971), p. 1.
5 *Magill*, May 1980, p. 39.
6 According to Paddy Doherty, Doherty interview, Keenan had stronger contacts with Captain Kelly than he himself did.
7 T. Ryle Dwyer, *Charlie. The Political Biography of Charles J. Haughey* (Gill and Macmillan, Dublin, 1987), ch. 6.
8 Michael Farrell, *Northern Ireland: The Orange State* (Pluto, London, 1980), p. 260.
9 Kelly, *Orders for the Captain*, p. 20 and *passim*
10 Patrick Bishop and Eamon Mallie, *The Provisional IRA* (Corgi, London, 1988), pp. 127–8.
11 Kelly, *Orders for the Captain*, ch. 2; Magill, May 1980, p. 47. According to Magill there were 15 men.
12 Kelly, *Orders for the Captain*, ch. 2.
13 Bishop and Mallie, *IRA*, p. 129.
14 DJ, 5/12/69, p. 1.
15 Interview with Mitchel McLaughlin, Sinn Féin member of Derry City Council, joined the Republican movement in 1966, stayed with the Officials after the split in 1970 but later joined the Provisionals.

16 See below, pp. 192, 194, 234.
17 Kelly, *Orders for the Captain*, ch. 2; Bishop and Mallie, *IRA*, p. 128. They give the date as 6 October.
18 Henry Patterson, *The Politics of Illusion. Republicanism and Socialism in Modern Ireland* (Hutchinson Radius, London, 1989), p. 133.
19 *United Irishman*, Dec. 1969.
20 Bishop and Mallie, *IRA*, pp. 294–5. They state that Keenan made the trip in November but he took part in a picket in Derry in early December. DJ, 5/12/69, p. 1.
21 Margie Bernard, *Daughter of Derry. The story of Brigid Sheils Makowski* (Pluto, London, 1989), p. 74.
22 Interview with Seán Cronin, former Washington correspondent of the *Irish Times*, former O/C of the IRA during the 1950s campaign and former officer in the Irish army; J. Bowyer Bell, *The Irish Troubles. A Generation of Violence, 1967–1992* (Gill and Macmillan, Dublin, 1993), pp. 147–9.
23 Bernard, *Daughter of Derry*, p. 74.
24 *Magill*, May 1980, p. 45.
25 *Magill*, May 1980, p. 45.
26 Cronin, interview; J. Bowyer Bell, *The Secret Army. A History of the IRA* (MIT Press, Cambridge, MA, 1974), pp. 254–6.
27 Bernard, *Daughter of Derry*, pp. 65, 74.
28 Bishop and Mallie, *IRA*, p. 295.
29 Interview with Liam Deeney, former member of CJNI, Boston and spokesman for the Boston unit of Noraid, formerly an active Republican in Derry in the 1950s.
30 Bell, *Secret Army*, p. 255.
31 Interview with Mike Flannery, founder member of the Irish Action Committee and former president of the Irish Northern Aid Committee (Noraid) in the United States.
32 *Magill*, May 1980, p. 45.
33 Farrell, *Orange State*, p. 343.
34 Flannery, interview.
35 Dr Conn McCluskey, *Up Off Their Knees. A commentary on the civil rights movement in Northern Ireland* (Conn McCluskey and Associates, Republic of Ireland, 1989), pp. 133–5.
36 'Paper-hat Irish', article in *United Irishman*, Nov. 1969.
37 Flannery, interview.
38 *An Phoblacht*, vol. 1, no. 1, Feb. 1970.
39 Bishop and Mallie, *IRA*, p. 143.
40 Bernard, *Daughter of Derry*, p. 74.
41 DJ, 9/9/69.
42 DJ, 28/10/69, p. 1.
43 Bishop and Mallie, *IRA*, p. 156.
44 Interview with John Carlin, member of the Republican movement in Derry from the mid-1960s and of the Provisional Republicans after the split, former Sinn Féin election agent, former internee.
45 DJ, 9/1/70, p. 1.
46 Carlin, interview.
47 *Voice of the North*, vol. 1, no. 12, 10/1/70.

48 *Magill*, June 1980, p. 73, states that the men were arrested in September 1969, which was not the case.
49 Ryle Dwyer, *Haughey*, p. 81, citing Peter Berry, secretary to the Department of Justice.
50 *This Week*, 15/5/70, p. 5.
51 *Voice of the North*, May–Dec. 1970.
52 DJ, 12/5/70, p. 6.
53 DJ, 9/1/70, p. 1.
54 Frank Curran, *Derry. Countdown to Disaster* (Gill and Macmillan, Dublin, 1986), p. 123, – after the Falls curfew in July 1970, according to Curran (although he says 1971).
55 Bell, *Troubles*, p. 113.
56 Mac Stiofáin, *Memoirs*, p. 124.
57 Tom Collins, *The Irish Hunger Strike* (White Island, Dublin, 1986), p. 268. Carlin, interview; interview with Fionnbarra Ó Dochartaigh (also known as Finbar Doherty), member of the Republican movement in Derry from the early 1960s, formerly a member of the DHAC and the DCAC, member of the Official Republican movement after the 1970 split. Founder member of the IRSP.
58 Farrell, *Orange State*, p. 269.
59 Carlin, interview.
60 Eamonn McCann, *War and an Irish Town* (Penguin, Harmondsworth, 1974), pp. 72–3.
61 Ibid.
62 *United Irishman*, Dec. 1969, claimed numbers in Derry were growing constantly.
63 McLaughlin, interview.
64 McLaughlin, interview.
65 The third being Seán Mac Stiofáin, chief of staff of the Provisional IRA.
66 DJ, 20/2/70, p. 5.
67 Conor Cruise O'Brien, *States of Ireland* (Panther Books, St Albans, 1974), p. 229.
68 DJ, 24/2/70, p. 2.
69 Bishop and Mallie, *IRA*, p. 156.
70 DJ, 13/3/70, p. 11.
71 *Republican News*, June 1970–Dec. 1970.
72 Letter in DJ, 10/3/70, p. 1.
73 DJ, 28/4/70, p. 5.
74 Letter from Liam Ó Comain, in DJ, 31/3/70, p. 7.
75 Bernadette Devlin in W.H. Van Voris, *Violence in Ulster. An Oral Documentary* (University of Massachusetts, MA, 1975), p. 191.
76 DJ, 3/4/70, p. 1.
77 DJ, 10/4/70, p. 1.
78 Bishop and Mallie, *IRA*, p. 295. (The shipment arranged in late 1969 would not arrive until August 1970.)
79 DJ, 10/4/70.
80 *Irish World*, 11/4/70.
81 See Jack Holland, *The American Connection. US Guns, Money and Influence in Northern Ireland* (Poolbeg, Swords, Co. Dublin, 1989), pp. 30–1.

82   Cronin, interview.
83   Flannery, interview.
84   Flannery, interview; interview with John Hurley, president of the Boston unit of the Friends of Irish Freedom, formerly president of the Boston unit of Noraid.
85   Holland, *American Connection*, pp. 30–1.
86   *Irish World*, 2/5/70.
87   Flannery, interview.
88   Deeney, interview.
89   *Boston Globe* [evening edn.] 17/3/70.
90   *The Irish Rebel*, vol. 2, no. 1, spring 1970. Speakers included Brigid Bond from Derry and Malachy McGurran who was originally from Lurgan.
91   Ibid.
92   Bernard, *Daughter of Derry*, p. 74.
93   *The Irish Rebel*, vol. 2, no. 1, spring 1970 contains an urgent appeal for funds.
94   Hurley, interview; Cronin, interview; Deeney, interview.
95   I am indebted for this information to one of the anonymous reviewers who read the manuscript before publication.
96   Gerry Foley, *Problems of the Irish Revolution: Can the IRA Meet the Challenge?* (New York, August 1972) (pamphlet).
97   Bell, *Troubles*, p. 282.
98   Derek Dunne, 'MacGiolla's Guerillas', *In Dublin*, 1/10/87, p. 20.
99   DJ, 3/4/70, p. 4.
100   DJ, 24/3/70, p. 4.
101   DJ, 24/2/70, p. 2.
102   McCann, *War*, pp. 72–3.
103   DJ, 10/3/70, p. 6.
104   Derry Official Republicans, internal discussion document, 1970.
105   McCann, *War*, p. 84.
106   Shane O'Doherty, *The Volunteer. A Former IRA Man's True Story* (Fount, London, 1993), p. 59.
107   DJ, 28/10/69, p. 2.
108   Cited in *Ulster, the Facts* (pamphlet), 1/9/69.
109   DJ, 3/4/70, p. 1.
110   Bishop and Mallie, *IRA*, p. 170.
111   DJ, 8/5/70, p. 1.
112   *This Week*, 9/4/70.
113   Interview 2 with Eamonn McCann.
114   *Fortnight*, no. 262, May 1988.
115   *In Dublin*, 29/10/89, p. 14.
116   Interview with Anon. B, former member of the Republican movement in Derry.
117   DJ, 28/8/70, p. 1; 2/10/69, p. 9.
118   McCann, interview 2.
119   McCann, interview 2; *This Week*, 29/5/70, p. 5, for example, refers to a 'maverick' group connected to the Derry Provisionals.
120   Carlin, interview.
121   DJ, 28/4/70, p. 5.
122   *This Week*, 29/5/70, p. 5.

123 Seán Keenan in DJ, 30/6/70, p. 1; National Graves Association pamphlet, 1976. Initially the explosion was reported in the local press as an 'accidental fire'.
124 Interview with Anon. D, former member of the Republican movement in Derry.
125 Ibid.
126 DJ, 30/6/70, p. 1.
127 DJ, 30/6/70, pp. 1, 9.
128 DJ, 3/7/70, p. 4.
129 Farrell, *Orange State*, p. 344.
130 DJ, 31/3/70, p. 3.
131 DJ, 20/10/70, p. 2.
132 DJ, 20/10/70, p. 4.
133 DJ, 28/4/70, p. 1. The RUC claimed that one particular teenager was a ringleader in this incident, DJ, 14/4/70. Eighteen months later this teenager would be charged with possession of explosives, aged nineteen, DJ, 5/11/71, p. 18.
134 DJ, 21/4/70, p. 5; 12/5/70, p. 1; 26/5/70, p. 1.
135 McCann, *War*, p. 76.
136 DJ, 10/4/70, p. 11.
137 DJ, 14/4/70, p. 1.
138 DJ, 14/4/70, p. 1.
139 DJ, 17/4/70.
140 DJ, 7/4/70, p. 7.
141 DJ, 21/4/70, p. 3.
142 DJ, 26/5/70, p. 4.
143 Farrell, *Orange State*, p. 272, and DJ, 19/5/70.
144 Independent Organisation minutes, 24/2/70.
145 McCann, *War*, p. 75.
146 DJ, 30/6/70, pp. 4, 9.
147 McCann, *War*, p. 75; DJ, 31/6/70, p. 6.
148 McCann, *War*, p. 75.
149 DJ, 31/6/70, p. 6.
150 McCann, *War*, p. 76; DJ, 30/6/70, p. 1.
151 McCann, *War*, p. 76.
152 DJ, 10/4/70.
153 McCann, *War*, p. 76.
154 DJ, 30/6/70, p. 1. Eamonn McCann was reported as saying that no agreement had been made at that meeting.
155 DJ, 30/6/70, p. 9.
156 Interview with Willie O'Connell, formerly a senior member of the Independent Organisation, the DCDA and the DCCC. SDLP member of Derry City Council and former mayor of Derry.
157 O'Connell, interview.
158 DJ, 30/6/70, p. 6.
159 Interview with Michael Canavan, founder member of the Derry Credit Union, formerly a senior member of the DCAC, the DCDA, the DCCC and the Independent Organisation. Former SDLP assembly member.
160 As in the incident described in Raymond McClean, *The Road to Bloody Sunday* (Ward River Press, Dublin, 1983), pp. 88–9.

161 DJ, 10/7/70, p. 15; photograph, 'the faithful', of DCDA meeting.
162 DJ, 10/7/70, p. 15.
163 DJ, 10/7/70, p. 15.
164 Waterside Young Unionist Association in DJ, 30/6/70, p. 1.
165 DJ, 30/6/70, p. 1.
166 Des Hamill, *Pig in the Middle. The Army in Northern Ireland 1969–1985* (Methuen, London, 1986), p. 46.
167 Ibid.
168 DJ, 14/7/70, p. 1.
169 Simon Winchester, *In Holy Terror: Reporting the Ulster Troubles* (Faber, London, 1974), pp. 69–72.
170 Michael McKeown, *The Greening of a Nationalist* (Murlough Press, Dublin, 1986), p. 88.
171 DJ, 7/7/70, p. 1.
172 DJ, 10/7/70, p. 1.
173 DJ, 10/7/70, p. 15.
174 DJ, 30/6/70.
175 DJ, 10/7/70, p. 15.
176 DJ, 10/7/70, p. 1.
177 DJ, 7/7/70, p. 4.
178 McCann in DJ, 7/4/70, p. 7.
179 DJ, 3/7/70, p. 1.
180 See, for example, Winchester, *In Holy Terror*, ch. 4.
181 DJ, 3/11/70, p. 1.
182 DJ, 17/7/70, p. 1.
183 DJ, 21/7/70.
184 DJ, 24/7/70, p. 1.
185 DJ, 31/7/70, p. 1.
186 DJ, 24/7/70, pp. 1, 6.
187 DJ, 28/7/70, p. 4.
188 DJ, 28/7/70.
189 Conor Cruise O'Brien, *Passion and Cunning and Other Essays* (Paladin Grafton, London, 1990), p. 270.

6
Reform and Repression:
August 1970–July 1971

From reform to repression

By the autumn of 1970 it was clear that large-scale regular rioting in Derry was not likely to fade away of its own accord. The constant cycle of riot, arrests, dubious convictions and alienation presented the prospect of a perpetual self-sustaining conflict between the British army and large numbers of Derry youths. It was a conflict that could only escalate. While Catholic moderates identified the continued reliance on military policing against a background of unresolved grievances as a principal cause of the disorder, the British government was beginning to view the disorder itself as the principal problem in Northern Ireland. Unionists had argued from the beginning that the emphasis should be placed not on resolving Catholic grievances but on preventing Catholic disruption of the state and on reaching a solution through repression rather than reform. The British government had now moved much closer to this view.

The impression that Catholic grievances had already been, or were in the process of being, redressed was widespread in Britain and further afield and was reflected in the editorial columns of papers such as the *New York Times*.[1] Apart altogether from Catholic concerns that reforms on everything from housing to local government boundaries were being diluted or stalled by the Unionist government,[2] a principal 'civil rights' issue since January 1969 had been that of policing. Violence continued precisely because this issue had never been resolved, and Derry was 'policed' by ever-increasing numbers of heavily-armed soldiers.

When an IRA bombing campaign began in the summer of 1970, the state appeared to be under a serious threat. Reform, to the extent that it weakened the authority of the Unionist government at Stormont and eroded its support among the 'loyal' Protestant majority, came to be seen as dangerous and destabilising, although it would be early 1971 before the British home secretary, Reginald Maulding, suggested in the House of Commons that it was the very success of reforms that encouraged Catholic 'extremists'.[3] The Unionist argument that Catholics ultimately sought to destroy the state, that reform would not satisfy them, that reform itself was irrelevant and even dangerous, and that the Catholics could only be governed against their will, gained ground. Thus, priority was switched from reforming the state to simply maintaining it. As Buckland puts it, with a different emphasis, violence ruined the chances for the reform programme, such as it was.[4]

The effect of this was to diminish the importance and perceived effectiveness of the new anti-Unionist politicians, such as John Hume and Ivan Cooper. The Nationalist party had faded away because it had never been seen to achieve anything. The political disadvantages for the Catholic community of being in a permanent political minority, and of never being able to achieve anything through parliamentary methods, had been reduced by the outside forces that responded to the civil rights movement, not least the British government. As the British government in mid-1970 decided that its priority was to maintain the existing government in Northern Ireland, anti-Unionist politicians were placed in the position that the Nationalist party had been in for decades, with no means of exerting political influence. This diminished their authority within the Catholic community. Continued Catholic discontent benefited the two wings of the Republican movement, thus further destabilising the state. The effect of this British government decision on those Catholic moderates who had decided to work to change the state rather than to abolish it, who had enthusiastically welcomed the reforms to the RUC recommended by the Hunt Report and who had condemned rioters for attacking the British army, was equally as detrimental to the future of the state as the revival of the Republican movement. Between August 1970 and August 1971 Catholic moderates were further alienated from the Northern state and the British government.

Crucial to the rise of the IRA was not simply the supply of weapons or recruits – though these were important – but the development of the political conditions for an offensive campaign. Related to this was the changing relationship between moderates and the state. The state could repress an IRA campaign only with the tacit consent of Catholic moderates. Without such consent, repression would have to be imposed, in places like Derry or West Belfast, on the entire Catholic community. Ultimately, it would prove impossible to end the IRA campaign on this basis. Central to this switch in British policy from reform to repression was the beginning of an undeclared IRA campaign in the summer and autumn of 1970.

An IRA offensive begins

The first recorded armed IRA action in Derry took place during fierce rioting in August 1970. Over the following year, attacks were carried out in Derry with increasing frequency by various Republican groups, chief among them the Provisional IRA. There is confusion as to which group was responsible for which attack during these months, mainly because none of them would publicly admit their actions until after August 1971. However, it is clear that by late 1970, after several months of rioting in the city, the Provisional IRA, at least, had launched an armed campaign.

In late July 1970, the British government had briefly restored the confidence of Catholic moderates in its intentions by effectively banning the Apprentice Boys of Derry march on 12 August 1970. When riots broke out in the Bogside in the first days of August, after this concession had been made and before the parade itself, it showed once again the way in which apparently hopeful political developments could be overtaken by events on the streets. This time, there were widespread suspicions, not just confined now to Catholic conservatives, that the riots had been provoked by an organised group, although there was no agreement as to which group that might be. 'Onlooker', the *Derry Journal* columnist who had long maintained that rioters were being manipulated, opined that there was 'some sinister influence or agent' behind the riots.[5] Although 'Onlooker' offered no theories as to who that might be, it seems likely that he had the local Labour and Republican radicals in mind. One of those Labour radicals, Eamonn McCann, shared with 'Onlooker' the belief that the riots were not entirely spontaneous; he blamed 'cynical manipulators' who were trying to force intervention from the Republic of Ireland.[6] This is probably a reference to those DCDA members, among them Seán Keenan, who had built links with Fianna Fáil ministers after August 1969, and had hoped for an Irish army 'invasion' of the North. It is the first statement in Derry suggesting that the Provisionals, rather than the Officials, were manipulating riots.

The riots in August showed a greater amount of organisation than had been the case in earlier riots, and also the increased importance of small tight groups of rioting youths who it seems likely were connected with the Republican movement. This does not necessarily imply that the Republican leadership was directing the riots but Republican youths were playing a key role. The level of organisation and the different character of these riots demonstrate a determination to confront the British army by coherent groups of youths rather than by large crowds. However, it also shows that to start a riot was not a simple matter and that however much people may have sought to 'manipulate' them, street riots were 'unusual, irregular, complex and ... unpredictable social processes which were not easily directed by anyone'.[7]

The immediate cause of the August 1970 riots in Derry was the shooting dead in Belfast of Daniel O'Hagan, a Catholic teenager, by the British army. O'Hagan was described famously by the *Times* as an 'assistant petrol-bomber', and in shooting him and then justifying it, the army seemed to be asserting that it was legitimate to deliberately shoot dead unarmed rioters. In Derry, where thousands of people had been involved in one riot or another in the previous two years, this had a particular significance. It is worth noting that at this stage not a single recorded shot had yet been fired at the British army in Derry since their arrival in the city a year before. After the shooting, black flags were flown from some houses in the Bogside and graffiti appeared in Derry referring to the killing.[8]

There was an announcement by the 'James Connolly Society' of a meeting at 'Free Derry' corner on the Sunday after the killing. At the appointed time, a few dozen youths turned up for the meeting but there were no speakers or organisers there. The James Connolly Republican Club (the Officials) denied any involvement in this meeting. It seems possible that, as had apparently happened several months before, some Republicans had announced a meeting in the hope that a riot would break out. Nonetheless, although a few of the youths present stoned passing army jeeps, the youths soon dispersed and there was no riot.[9] If someone had tried to provoke a riot it had been a signal failure. It demonstrates that it required a lot more than clever 'manipulation' or devious planning to provoke a mass riot. Beginning later that night, over a period of several hours, there were ten separate incidents, the last at 5 a.m., in different parts of Creggan, the Bogside and the Brandywell in which stones and petrol bombs were thrown at army jeeps and army/RUC patrols by small groups of youths, but no serious rioting developed. It is highly likely that these attacks were carried out by groups of young Republicans and that they were effectively IRA attacks. While attacks of this kind had taken place sporadically in previous months, there had never been so many on one night, in this case, a night that followed a day of relative calm. It seems to mark a shift to more organised rioting by Republicans.

The following day, Daniel O'Hagan was buried in Belfast. There was a controlled calm in Derry but locals claimed that troops made jibes and offensive gestures at people in the streets and patrolled the Bogside continuously. It was after midnight when a group of youths hijacked five cars from a city garage and five from the street outside and built a barricade. Such hijacking, a deliberate move by a small group when there was no rioting in progress, was a new development. Any time army vehicles came near the barricade, they were stoned but the army was obviously seeking to avoid a confrontation which might erode the goodwill of the DCCC and Catholic moderates that had been gained after the ban on the 12 August parade. The army waited until 5 a.m. before removing the barricade when, according to an army spokesman, they made no arrests and sustained no injuries.[10]

There had now been two nights of minor but apparently organised attacks on, or challenges to, the army and still there had been no significant rioting. However, the army would clearly not be content to play such a restrained role for much longer.

At 11 p.m. the following night, some distance from the usual rioting grounds at William Street, a crowd of about 150 youths commandeered two buses and built a barricade at the edge of the Brandywell. Once again the army resisted responding. It was only when the gathering crowd set fire to the buses an hour and a half later that the army responded. If there had been some sort of agreement between the army and the DCCC it was suspended now. After an interval the troops began firing CS gas at a crowd several hundred strong, which, according to the *Derry Journal*, was composed mostly of 'anxious lookers-on, fearful for the safety of their families and property'. Rioting then broke out in the William Street area some distance away and the troops arrested a dozen people there. In the course of these riots, six shots were fired at troops in Bishop Street, though there were no injuries. The bullets were of three different calibres, suggesting the use of three different guns.[11]

Serious rioting continued the following night and three shots were fired at an army observation post in the Long Tower area, off Bishop Street. These two shooting incidents demonstrated that some Republicans in Derry were now prepared to use the few guns available to them. However, on that second night, two of those arrested for stone throwing were prominent young Provisional Republicans, one of them a son of Seán Keenan's. This showed not just that Republicans were active in rioting but also the low level of the campaign when long-standing active members were out throwing stones and getting caught and jailed for it.[12]

The significance of these shooting incidents in Derry in August 1970 was that, apart from two isolated incidents in spring 1971, there were no other reported shooting incidents in Derry for another eleven months, despite the fact that firearms were obviously available. Shane O'Doherty, a sixteen-year-old Provisional IRA member at the time, describes a number of pistol attacks on army patrols apparently before July 1971,[13] but these would appear to be sporadic attacks by younger IRA members and the infrequency of shooting incidents suggests that there might have been a deliberate policy by both IRAs in Derry to severely restrict the use of firearms until July 1971. On the other hand, one former activist says that the Derry Provisionals still only had five or six serviceable weapons by late 1970 and that it was primarily the lack of weapons which restricted IRA activity in Derry.[14] In late 1970, Republicans in Derry were probably not in a position to withstand the British army response to shootings, but it is also likely that other considerations were involved. For example, if the IRA regularly opened fire during riots, the army was likely to fire at rioters. There was clearly local political pressure on the IRA from Catholic moderates, in particular the DCCC, not to escalate the conflict like this. In any such negotiation, one must assume that the DCCC would have played an important role.

Although there were no more shooting incidents after the first two nights, rioting continued into a second week while local priests, residents and DCCC stewards made strenuous efforts on the streets to stop the rioting. They claimed on one occasion that 'they were successful for a time but a militant group appeared intent on causing trouble'.[15] Many youths, some of them now in the Republican movement, were intent on attacking the army and would not be dissuaded by anyone.

In Belfast, the Provisional IRA had begun to systematically shoot at troops in early 1971. However, although there seems to have been a measure of restraint in Derry, one incident at the same time as these riots showed that at least one Provisional Republican from Derry was using firearms in a planned attack on British troops about twenty miles from Derry. At 3 a.m. on 4 August 1970, as riots raged in Derry, Gardaí in Co. Donegal staked out a parked car near Castlefinn, on the border with Co. Tyrone. They saw three or four figures cross into Donegal from the North in the darkness and they apprehended one of the men who, although he had a rifle and a revolver, did not resist arrest. The man was

Roddy Carlin, one of the young Derry Provisionals and a former member of the James Connolly Republican Club. He had served a month in jail in the summer of 1968 for taking part in a sit-down protest in Derry over housing conditions[16] and was one of the younger Republicans who had then gravitated towards the Provisionals.[17]

In a Donegal court he said in his defence that 'the guns were to be used against the forces of occupation in the six occupied counties of Ireland. In no circumstances whatsoever were they to be used in the twenty-six counties or to endanger civilian life.' Outside the court the Provisionals picketed with signs referring to 'our Northern defender'. Carlin said his group had crossed the border to try and attack a British army patrol near Clady on the border. (It demonstrates how elastic the Provisional definition of 'defence' had become that this could be seen as a 'defensive' act.) In the end, the Derry Republican was found guilty on a lesser charge of not having a firearms licence. He was fined £30 and he asked the court if he could have his guns back.[18] The court did not oblige, but the case revealed the importance of border areas in the Republic in the very early stages of the IRA campaign as a lightly policed area for training and for launching attacks on targets near the border.

The arrest of this Derry-city Republican in the Donegal countryside shows that the Provisionals, or at the very least 'independent' units closely associated with them, were armed and taking the offensive by August 1970. It was around this time too that the Provisionals were said to have received their first, 'huge', shipment of arms from the US.[19] Given Seán Keenan's involvement in these arms-dealings it is almost certain that some of these weapons would have been available to the Provisionals in Derry. Thus it seems likely that the Provisional IRA campaign, which now began in Derry, was restrained not solely by lack of resources but by a political decision to restrict their use of firearms. On the other hand, one former activist stresses that 'all the way up to [Operation] Motorman [in July 1972] there was a chronic shortage of weapons' and that it was only then that the Derry Provisionals received about twenty or thirty Armalite rifles, presumably from the US shipment.[20]

On 15 September 1970, during a quiet period between the riots of August just past and the riots of October to come, the first IRA bomb attack in Derry took place, marking the beginning of a limited IRA offensive in the city. By Christmas 1970, seven minor bomb attacks had been carried out in Derry, few enough that they could conceivably have been carried out by one or two small groups of people. No organisation claimed responsibility for any of these attacks. Given the commitment of the Provisionals to an offensive it seems likely most of these attacks were carried out by the small group of younger Provisionals. Farrell has written that the Provisionals were responsible for the vast majority of bomb attacks in Northern Ireland in these early months.[21]

The involvement in the IRA of a significant group of younger people had probably helped to move the Provisionals quickly towards a campaign. But the involvement of these younger members also determined that it would be a campaign quite unlike that of the 1950s.

The first IRA bomb attack in Derry was carried out on an electricity substation in William Street at the edge of the usual riot zone. It did little damage. Locals said they had seen four or five youths around the station just before the explosion in the early hours of the morning.[22] The age of the suspected bombers and the location of the attack characterises this bombing more as a further variation on rioting rather than as a distinct 'military' initiative. It can be seen as a move by rioting youths to take more extreme and violent action against the state and its symbols, as much as it can be seen as the start of a classic 'guerilla' campaign. This connection with riots was a common thread of almost all of the early IRA attacks in Derry. Either small bombs were placed against buildings in or around the areas where rioting took place, or small gelignite bombs were thrown at troops in the course of rioting, often by teenagers.[23] The new younger Provisionals learned some of their bomb-making skills in local libraries where their first step was simply to look up the entry for a common chemical in a standard encyclopaedia.[24] The first attack which strayed outside the usual riot areas took place in October 1970 when two gelignite bombs were thrown over a perimeter wall into an army base on the Strand Road in the city centre.[25] It was clearly intended to kill or injure soldiers, as the Provisional IRA would shortly begin to do in Belfast.

In the New Year, the bombings continued. Attacks on city centre premises began in which incendiaries were used for the first time.[26] Still, the attacks were sporadic and somewhat erratic. They ranged from bomb attacks on an electricity transformer near the city to fire-bomb attacks on shops and gelignite bombs thrown during riots. They included just one reported shooting incident, when two shots were fired at an army post during a riot in Waterloo Place.[27]

Throughout this time there were regular large-scale riots in Derry and in early February 1971, during a riot, a bus was hijacked by three masked men, one armed with a pistol.[28] It demonstrates the ever closer involvement of Republicans and IRA members in initiating and participating in rioting. By early 1971, the Provisional Republicans were very definitely on the offensive in Derry.

The extent to which the Republicans were still far from being a dominant force in the community is demonstrated by the fact that, as late as May 1971, the Bogside and Creggan were still 'in-bounds' to off-duty British soldiers.[29] That ended in May 1971 when an off-duty British soldier was shot and wounded when confronted by three men, one of them armed with a sub-machine gun, after leaving the house of his fiancée in the Bogside in the early hours of the morning.[30] After that, the Bogside and Creggan were placed out of bounds again, this time permanently.

Provisional politics

While the Derry Provisionals had gained new members since August 1969, the number of attacks they were carrying out does not suggest that they were swamped with recruits. It appears that the mass of those taking part in rioting were not interested in getting involved in such a campaign. According to Seán Mac Stiofáin, chief of staff of the Provisional IRA, the Provisionals were making 'slow progress' in Derry up until July 1971.[31] Clearly the Provisionals had advanced much further in their campaign in Belfast where they had killed several British soldiers by that time.

As was frequently noted, Derry was not a Republican city but rather had always given its allegiance to the cautious Nationalist party. The Republican tradition was far more marginal in Derry than it was in Belfast. Although Republican sentiment had grown in Derry recently, the Provisionals had not reaped the full benefit of this as the Officials were still strong in the city and were drawing in recruits too. During late 1970 and early 1971, the Provisional Republicans in Derry concentrated their energies on their military campaign, only making occasional public statements to, for example, condemn the British army's continuing but waning 'hearts and minds' campaign in Derry.[32]

When the Easter Commemorations of 1971 came round, the reported attendances at the two parades showed that the Officials had succeeded in retaining much of the support for Republicanism in the city. Once again, as in 1970, the Provisionals confined their parade to Catholic areas while the James Connolly Club, the Officials, marched to the city centre at Waterloo Place. It was estimated that 1,200 marched in the Provisional parade while 2,000 marched with the Officials. Thirty Republican Youth, presumably Fianna Éireann members, marched with the Officials, indicating that the Officials too were expanding the structures on which any military campaign would be based. The Provisionals had only six Fianna members marching, but this probably reflects the fact that the movement was going further underground as it took the offensive.[33]

The numbers present at both parades represent a further decrease on the previous years but they show that, if there was a decrease in Catholic identification with the Republican cause as the IRA began an offensive, there was also a significant increase in the hard-core support. Even though Republican parades seemed almost certain to end in riots (as these ones did), thousands marched in them. Still, this did not necessarily indicate a willingness to join either the IRA or Sinn Féin.

At the Provisional commemoration, Seán Keenan was less ambiguous about the Provisionals' principal aims and declared that people had a duty now 'to devote all our time and energies to the freedom and independence of our own country'.[34] It was a thinly disguised call for recruits for an IRA campaign and it is clear that such calls were not being answered to the satisfaction of the Derry Provisionals. The Patrick Pearse Sinn Féin Club in Derry held a public meeting a few weeks after the Easter marches (apparently the first such meeting they had held), presumably as part of an attempt to build political support. That meeting gives a clearer indication of the 'real' level of support for the Provisionals as a group (as opposed to vague support for a United Ireland or the Republican cause) than does the turn-out at the Easter commemoration.

At the meeting, the turnout was miserably low and although the harsh weather was partly responsible, Seán Keenan had no doubt that local apathy was also to blame. A speaker from Belfast, Seán Caughey, said that the low attendance showed 'a lack of guts'.[35] But perhaps it showed that, despite widespread hostility to the army, alienation from the state and aspiration to a united Ireland, few people in Derry supported an IRA offensive, and the Provisionals were still a relatively small and marginalised splinter group. Even by the spring of 1971, the Provisionals were by no means a major political force in Derry.

Although the Provisionals did not take much political action in Derry around this time, one of their initiatives did become quite active. At the end of May 1971, the Derry Provisionals set up the Women's Action Committee (hereafter WAC) of the Patrick Pearse Sinn Féin Club. Róisín Keenan, a daughter of Seán Keenan's, was prominent in this committee.[36] In their first public action, 300 women, followed by about 100 local youths, took part in a protest march from the Bogside to an army post in Derry city centre.[37] A key part of the army's 'honeymoon' in Derry had been the development of relationships between soldiers and local women. The WAC would be a chief agency of ending that aspect of the 'honeymoon'. Significantly, this march was not sparked off by any local grievances but was intended as a protest against British army brutality in Belfast. It shows that the Provisionals were trying to integrate Derry with their campaign in Northern Ireland as a whole, and were trying to raise awareness in Derry of the situation in Belfast.

The combination of apparently slow recruitment, and the virtual absence of shooting in Derry since August 1970, added to the clear way in which Provisional protests in spring 1971 aimed to link Derry in to the struggle in Belfast, added to Mac Stiofáin's assertion that Derry was a weak part of their organisation prior to July 1971, all tend to support the theory that in July 1971 the Provisional IRA in Derry deliberately and abruptly escalated their activities against the British army with the intention of advancing the Provisional Republican cause in Derry through the intensification of violence.

This is not to suggest, as the Widgery Report later did, that 'In the early summer of 1971 a good deal of progress had been made towards restoring normal life in Derry'[38] and that this normality was suddenly shattered by these actions. The IRA campaign had been proceeding since September 1970, large-scale riots had taken place on a regular basis since June 1970 and minor disturbances were taking place almost on a weekly basis throughout the first six months of 1971 in Derry. Nonetheless, in July 1971, there was a sudden deliberate escalation in the level of Provisional IRA activity in Derry which would mark the beginning of a new phase of the conflict in the city.

Official Republicans and Labour

Since the first riots of 1970, Labour party radicals had actively tried to prevent rioting in Derry and the Labour party Young Socialists who worked closely with the younger Official Republicans condemned the rioting as 'useless and pointless' and said it had taken on 'nationalist and sectarian overtones'.[39] In co-operation with the Official Republicans, they had tried to politicise the young rioters and direct their energies into pickets and protests.

Many of these young rioters moved into the Official Republican movement through this process and they began to apply pressure for an armed campaign,[40] effectively for a campaign which would supersede rioting and with the goal of a united socialist Ireland. It appears that it was on this basis that Martin McGuinness, for example, joined the Official

Republicans in October 1970. However, frustrated by the low level of military activity he left shortly afterwards to join the Provisionals.[41]

It is difficult to assess at exactly what point the Official IRA first took offensive action in Derry, since no group in the city was claiming attacks. However, towards the end of 1970 Cathal Goulding, chief of staff of the Official IRA, said 'a military campaign is being planned now by the IRA against the British army. We are going on the offensive.'[42] In reality, the Official IRA leadership were only reluctantly considering a campaign presumably under pressure from Republicans in the North in the wake of the Falls curfew and increased army repression. By early 1971, it seems the Official IRA were still only 'planning' a campaign.[43] When they did go on the offensive, they were poorly supplied with weapons and it seems the Dublin leadership deliberately held back from supplying them adequately.[44]

However, the fact that the Officials were now finally prepared to take military action might account for the fact that in late 1970, as Official Republican Brigid Makowski put it, there was a 'spirit of friendly co-operation' between those in both wings of the Republican movement in Derry and that 'Republicans on both sides sought to preserve communal ties.'[45] Prior to the Easter marches of 1971, the James Connolly Republican Club called on the Derry Provisionals to join the official commemoration. They emphasised too the wish to co-exist with the Provisionals when they said it would be 'a very sorry day for Derry Republicans if the internal strife prevailing in Belfast Republican circles takes root in Derry'.[46] This was in reference to a recent fatal feud between the two wings in Belfast which had started ironically *because* the Officials had now launched a military campaign.[47] As a former activist who moved between the two wings put it, 'In Derry you never had the Stickie Provo thing like in Belfast.'[48] It was almost as if the Derry Officials were still refusing to accept that the movement had split. Such an attitude clearly did not imply outright hostility to the small campaign now being waged in Derry by the Provisionals.

Over the months of rioting and the growing hostility to the British army, Labour radicals in Derry had moved ever closer to the Official Republicans and Eamonn McCann (the most influential of the radicals) had in spring 1970 finally come to the position that a united socialist republic should be the goal of socialists: that while the Protestant working class could not be won over by Irish nationalism, they could be won over by republicanism and the prospect of a socialist republic.[49]

Thus it seems the Republicans had succeeded in moving the Labour radicals significantly closer to their position and co-operation became even closer. Eamonn McCann records that in early 1971 Official Republicans and Labour party radicals again began joint arms-training sessions in Donegal.[50] However the Dublin leadership felt about it, the Derry Officials were now certainly preparing a campaign and they had managed to convince Labour radicals to join them in these preparations in a sort of military 'broad front' which seems to have developed in Derry more than anywhere else. The first definite indication of Official IRA military operations in Derry came in March 1971. In that month a UDR patrol on the outskirts of Derry stopped a car which had just crossed the nearby border with Donegal. When they did so, the driver of the car jumped out and ran away across the fields. Left behind in the car was a middle-aged passenger who said he was only getting a lift home from Buncrana. In the car were detonators, connectors and safety fuse; that is, bomb-making equipment.[51]

The RUC subsequently arrested Mickey Montgomery, an Official Republican and a veteran of the 1950s IRA campaign, claiming that he had been the driver of the car. Evidence was given in court that his thumb print had been found on the car mirror. Mickey Montgomery in his defence said that some time previously he had sat in that particular car and that perhaps it was then he had left his thumb print. He said the car was owned by a club of which he was a member. His story was supported by one of the owners of the car, Reginald Tester. Both Mickey Montgomery and Reginald Tester were members of the James Connolly Republican Club and of the Official IRA.[52] So, although Mickey Montgomery was found not guilty, a car apparently belonging to the James Connolly Republican Club had been found with bomb-making equipment. This suggests strongly that by March 1971, at the latest, the Derry Officials were engaged in a military campaign. Despite this, the Officials did not publicly announce a policy of 'defence and retaliation' until July 1971.

Perhaps the most curious feature of the development of the Official Republican movement in Derry through 1970 and 1971 was its increasingly strong links with Labour radicals. The two groups became so closely identified that when internment did come the army also tried to intern several of the Labour party radicals in Derry, although they failed.[53] After internment, many of these Labour members joined the Officials, and the Official Republican movement in Derry was composed in large part of people who had come to the IRA via the Northern Ireland Labour Party and a variety of minor marxist groups. It was a very different creature from the Provisionals and from Official IRA units elsewhere. This was partly due to the fact that in Derry, where sectarian conflict had been eclipsed, and virtually all conflict was between the British army and the Catholic working class and the young, Labour radicals could more easily view the conflict as an anti-imperialist and socialist struggle. The Official IRA in Derry after August 1971 engaged in what it saw as an anti-imperialist struggle, a 'revolution' inspired by left-wing ideas of destroying a sectarian and reactionary state in Northern Ireland and 'liberating' both Catholics and Protestants, rather than a traditional Irish nationalist campaign.

Forces for stability

While both wings of the IRA by early 1971 were committed in varying degrees to the intensification of conflict, there were powerful forces within the Catholic community in Derry strongly opposed to such a development and the consequent disruption of 'normal' daily life. An analysis which focuses simply on the conscious decision of Republicans to launch a campaign neglects the fact that, in most places, in most times, initiatives by such small, highly militant groups will not be successful to any great degree. The classic local example is the 1950s IRA campaign which was a spectacular failure in the absence of popular support. One factor which created the conditions for a successful campaign in 1970/71 was the disorder on the streets and the radicalisation of many young people.

However, probably even more important were developments within the most 'conservative' and cautious elements of the Catholic community which, although deeply traditional and often nationalistic, placed the maintenance of social order, stability and 'normal' life well ahead of dramatic political goals such as the achievement of a united Ireland. To this end they were prepared to accept the authority of the army and the RUC long after many moderate Catholics had become disillusioned with them. These forces were focused on the Catholic church and, though they did not dominate either party, were strong in both the SDLP and the Nationalist party. They were a major obstacle to any IRA campaign and were strongly rooted in the community. In many working-class areas throughout the North the Catholic church acted as a principal focus for opposition to both Official and Provisional Republicans.[54] For these forces to turn away from the established custodians of law and order would significantly alter the political balance within the Catholic community and remove many of the restraints, exercised by the community and community groups, on the militants. It was not a question of these forces in any way offering 'support' to the IRA. For them to withdraw 'support' from the army and the RUC and to lose the incentive to actively campaign against the militants would be enough to alter the situation fundamentally. They would resist this for a long time and as rioting began to intensify in late 1970, conservative Catholics in Derry launched an initiative to restore 'order' in the Creggan estate and rebuild the relationship of local youths to local authority in the form of the church and youth organisations. They confronted and condemned the forces which they believed were responsible for the worsening situation, the Official Republican and Labour radicals. In their own way, conservative forces in the Catholic community developed elaborate and unrealistic conspiracy theories about the disorder just as Unionists had done. In some cases, the rhetoric of 'communist conspiracy' employed by both Unionists and conservative Catholics was almost identical and reflected a shared confusion and wilful misinterpretation of events. In both cases, it stemmed from a sense of desperation that the established order and structures of authority seemed to be crumbling rapidly. However, the British army's solution to this breakdown would impact completely differently on these two groups. The similar rhetoric simply provided a brief illusion of common interest between Catholic conservatives and Unionists. Ultimately, conservative Catholics were still part of a 'disloyal' minority.

The political changes in Derry since 1968 had had major social effects on local youths. The experience of rioting and of constant conflict had created a 'hero' mentality among young males, a desire to prove themselves through confrontation with the army and the RUC.[55] It had also, in weakening the authority of the police and the state, weakened all other forms of authority. In other arenas of even greater civil disorder it has been noted that the concept of authority itself loses much of its meaning when state authority begins to be perceived as a hostile force.[56] In Derry, this was reflected among the young by the fact that local youth groups found them more difficult to work with, less inclined to accept the authority of adults and more connected to militant groups which were willing to work with the young and give them a measure of authority. In Derry, it was the Provisionals and the Official Republicans who were most welcoming to the radicalised youth.[57] In Derry, the rioters were regarded by the army, and by many conservative Catholics, as 'hooligans', that is, they were not seen to be politically motivated, but simply to have lost respect for authority, for 'law and order', and their actions were seen as 'criminal' rather than 'political'.[58]

The fact is that rioting was both political and criminal; it was part of a process of politicisation and also part of the rejection of law and order in general by many youths. For, at the same time as many of these youths were becoming involved with the Labour party, and the Official or Provisional Republicans, and youth participation in militant politics in Derry was increasing rapidly, the rate of ordinary crime and vandalism in the city was also soaring. Derry as a city, prior to 1968, had had a famously low rate of crime, commented on by judges, clergy, politicians and visiting academics.[59] In the course of 1970 there were increasingly frequent break-ins and burglaries and an increase in vandalism which reached epidemic proportions.[60] This rapid increase in crime and vandalism was seen by many conservative Catholics as linked with the rioting and civil disorder in the city.

A large section of the Catholic community, notably those strongly connected to the Catholic church, saw attacks on the army, not in the light of a 'fight for Irish freedom' but as a disruptive and destructive attack on social stability and established order which was on the same level and motivated by the same desires as were vandalism and burglary. Up to the beginning of 1971 these sections of the Catholic community looked to the restoration of control by the state forces, notably the RUC, as a solution to the crisis. To a great extent, their views accorded perfectly with those of the British government and even with the Unionist government which, after all, most Catholics had lived under with minimal resistance for half a century. When these forces finally came to reject the state, it was principally because the state was no longer seen as an agency for restoring stability and normality.

As rioting intensified in late 1970, these forces began to organise in order to restore a sense of stability. In November 1970, in response to the rising levels of crime and vandalism in Creggan estate, a Concern for Creggan committee was established. It brought together the local branches of the Nationalist party and the Independent Organisation (shortly to become the SDLP) with the two local tenants' associations, Creggan and Foyle Hill, and with local youth groups associated with the Catholic church, notably the local boys' club and the recently formed Creggan troop of the Catholic Boy Scouts of Ireland. It also involved local Catholic clergy and school-teachers.[61] The Catholic church, in the person of the local parish priest, Fr Rooney, was the focus for this initiative but this does not mean it was driven by the church. Rather it had the character of a lay Catholic initiative backed by the church. Its approach also clashed with other views within both the Nationalist party and the SDLP where the breakdown of social order was seen primarily as a political problem.

This initiative concentrated on the specific concerns about 'law and order' of the conservative wings of both the Nationalist party and the SDLP. The chief aims of the committee were to try and stop vandalism in the area, to prevent youths stoning buses serving the area and to halt the growing number of break-ins on the estate. The agencies the committee dealt with, such as the Londonderry Development Commission and the Community Relations Council,[62] were agencies which represented the reformed Northern Ireland which it sought to work with.

It was clear that the rapid increase in vandalism and crime in the area was part of a wider change, and many members of the Concern for Creggan committee felt they had identified the key factor in this broader change. There were hints of this at the first meeting when a speaker referred to 'a dangerous minority [which] seems bent on downgrading the estate and all who live in it',[63] implying a sense of purpose behind the vandalism. At a later public meeting in January 1971, the secretary of the committee, James R. Doherty (not to be confused with Nationalist party chairman James Doherty), was more explicit when he condemned 'fellow-travellers to whom church or state do not mean anything and who would influence young people. It would seem that they are working towards sheer anarchy.'[64]

This can only be understood as a reference to the local radicals; the Official Republicans (who had already been accused by the *Derry Journal* of promoting 'an alien cult'), and the Labour left. There was a strong belief that vandalism was being organised or encouraged by the radicals[65] and that therefore crime, rioting and attacks on the army were all part of a piece, of a plot to destroy society. When such conservative Catholics condemned those for whom church *and* state meant nothing, they were implicitly supporting the existing Northern Ireland state and characterising, as Unionists might have hoped, attacks on the Northern Ireland state as subversive of 'church and state'.

For this large section of the Catholic community religion was probably notably more important than nationality. These conservative Catholic forces were characterised in late 1970 and early 1971 by their strong links with the Catholic church, their willingness to co-operate with the state to see civil order restored and their insistent characterisation of disorder and crime as the product of a communist plot.

At a public meeting held by the Concern for Creggan committee in January 1971, the platform party included the local parish priest, Fr Rooney, and a local school principal, John Maultsaid, who was the chairman of the Derry Steering Committee on Community Relations and soon to become the chairman of the Derry RUC liaison committee. The meeting was chaired by William Smyth, the head of Creggan tenants' association and one of the sizeable number of Protestants still living on the estate at that stage and also soon to be a member of the

Derry RUC liaison committee.[66] Among those in the audience was John Hume but neither he nor most of the senior Derry SDLP members would be active in the committee itself.

One of the groups officially supporting the committee was the Creggan troop of the Catholic Boy Scouts of Ireland (hereafter CBSI).[67] It was the only CBSI troop in Derry and when it was established in early 1970 it was the first CBSI troop in the city in forty years.[68] It appears to have been established as a deliberate attempt to maintain social control and probably to provide a direct alternative to the Republican scouting movements. It was intimately connected to the Catholic church as demonstrated by the CBSI investiture in Creggan church in early 1971 which was attended not only by Fr Rooney but also by the conservative bishop, Neil Farren, whose pronouncements constantly referred to the need for stability. However, it is also notable that this investiture in Creggan in early 1971 was attended by an officer of the 1st Battalion the Royal Anglians who was the assistant cub leader for the Creggan CBSI troop.[69] The 'hearts and minds' campaign was still operating, but at a much reduced level, and its last connections were with these conservative Catholics. St Joseph's school in Creggan, run by John Maultsaid, was one of the last to be involved in a major 'hearts and minds' project in May 1970 when students from the school went on a ten-day adventure course with the Royal Anglians at Magilligan.[70]

Conspiracy theories were voiced again at the annual dinner of past pupils of St Columbs College, the Catholic boys' grammar school in Derry, in early 1971. At the dinner, John Maultsaid spoke, saying they wanted a return to 'normality'. Also present was Brian Morton, chairman of the Londonderry Development Commission. When toasting Bishop Farren, who was present, Mr Colm Duffy declared that 'Today in Ireland we are witnessing an all-out drive by misguided boys and girls to spread the scourge of Communism'.[71]

Above all, the efforts of conservative Catholics and of those involved in the Concern for Creggan committee were directed at local youths. After vandals wrecked a school in Creggan in May 1971, the committee organised an anti-vandalism 'covenant' which was signed by over 5,000 young people in Creggan and presented to the Development Commission.[72] Despite these efforts, vandalism in Derry was now 'reaching serious proportions' (as a Development Commission spokesman put it) and the Development Commission was forced to spend £3,600 on anti-vandalism measures in Creggan.[73]

Thus, even in early 1971, there were important sections of the Catholic community who had effectively accepted the limited reform package, who were willing to work with the RUC and still accepted the army as an essentially benevolent presence. They were organising within the community against crime but also against political forces which they saw as promoting destabilisation of society and the state. It is notable though that they did not focus on the more traditional Provisional Republicans and would not do so until the demise of the Official IRA in mid-1972. In a very real sense, they were committed to accepting the authority of the state. The reason they did not make more of an impact has a great deal to do with the decline of the authority of both church and state and with the fact that many people, young and old, including sections of the Nationalist party and the SDLP, were beginning to view the army as an aggressive force, not deserving of support.

The Nationalist party

Prior to the Westminster election of June 1970 in which John Hume supported Eddie McAteer as a unity candidate, the Derry Nationalist Party and the Independent Organisation, the predecessor of the Derry branch of the SDLP, had developed not only a joint programme but had agreed 'to take the necessary steps to set up a united party in Northern Ireland'.[74] The new party was to be based on 'a social and economic policy left of centre' and 'agreement that the National integrity of the country can only be restored with the agreement of the people of [or "in"] Northern Ireland'.[75] While the language was vaguely nationalist, the Derry Nationalist party which agreed to these principles before the election and re-affirmed them afterwards had moved very close to the Derry moderates and it seems it was objections from other sections of the Nationalist party in Northern Ireland which prevented a merger. After this, the two groups in Derry did move apart gradually as the Independent Organisation became involved in setting up the SDLP. Nonetheless they co-operated very closely in the DCCC which was established in late June 1970 and was very much a joint initiative.

It seems that after the failure of the planned merger with the Independent Organisation, the Derry Nationalists gradually began to return to 'basic principles' as they had done in August 1969 when Eddie McAteer had appealed for aid from the Republic. They renewed their focus on partition as the cause of the violence and its end as the only solution: a sort of conservative argument for the restoration of order through the abolition of the state. As we have noted, powerful elements in the Nationalist party and the Independent Organisation were diametrically opposed to this and were quite willing to accept the state. However, the concern for order was a constant theme.

This Nationalist party stance, which began with criticism of British army behaviour in quelling riots quickly developed into something more 'extreme'. In the process, the contradictions between the essential 'conservatism' of the Nationalist party (the fidelity to church, to authority and to law and order), and the party's stated aim of seeing Ireland re-united and thus the abolition of the state apparatus in the North, became clear and was one reason why the party went into further decline. It encompassed people who, adhering to the same conservative principles, 'understood' the IRA campaign now beginning and those who vehemently opposed it, depending on the respective importance they gave to the issues of 'stability' or to Irish re-unification. It was a clash between the party's actual historic role as a stolidly conservative Catholic institution within Northern Ireland and the ideal of a united Ireland to which it was pledged.

In October 1970, there was further widespread rioting in Derry. The *Derry Journal* focused on the rioting, calling it 'worse than senseless' and the throwing of a bomb during the riot, undoubtedly by a Republican group as 'a new and sinister departure'. The Nationalist party, on the other hand, preferred to focus on the 'baton-swinging troops' who had 'saturated' the Bogside with CS gas. They described them as 'an occupation army who use chemical warfare to preserve a corrupt state'.[76]

When the Derry Nationalist party was presented with a motion a few days later condemning the recent violence, the motion was rejected because, as Eddie McAteer put it, of 'the feeling by some members that there might be an equal need to condemn the authorities for failure to deal with the causes of violence'.[77] This marked a drastic shift in the attitude of the Nationalist party to rioting and moved them closer to the Provisional Republicans than any other group in the city. It was clearly not a unanimous feeling in the party and it provoked the resignation of three of the most senior members, including chairman Tom McDonnell; former chairman, former DCAC, serving DCCC and former corporation member James Doherty; and former corporator and serving DCCC member, Eugene O'Hare.[78] They were core members of the local party and apparently in an attempt to regain their support the Derry Nationalists issued a statement a few days later saying, that while they 'sympathised' with the 'frustrations' of the youth, they did 'not agree with their means of protest'. They also issued a formulaic condemnation of 'the hidden manipulators of these boys for their own evil ends'[79] which placed them back in line with conservative Catholic conspiracy theorists.

Nonetheless, the Nationalists continued to become more concerned with anti-partitionism and linked nationalism to the early civil rights demands when they demanded 'the basic right to assert our distinctive nationality, which is Irish',[80] a right which overtly referred to the Flags and Emblems Act which banned the display of the Irish flag but which also implied the 'national right' to a united Ireland.

As violence became endemic in Derry and the crisis in Northern Ireland deepened, the Derry Nationalists began to condemn the 'unwanted British political presence'[81] and to refer to the central issue of the 'failure' of partition.[82] By spring 1971, as the Provisional IRA was intensifying its campaign in Belfast, stressing, in contrast with the Official IRA, the traditional and essentially conservative aspirations to Irish unity which the Nationalists had long defined themselves by, there were calls from within the party for 'a more aggressive nationalism'.[83]

The essentially conservative Nationalist party could support a united Ireland on the grounds that violence was a result of partition. Suffering from the same delusions as the Provisionals and the Fianna Fáil elements who supported them, they believed a united Ireland could be achieved relatively quickly. This was easier to believe in Derry than it was in Belfast. But many in the Nationalist party had moved much further than this and by 1971 the Nationalist party had moved closer to the perspective of the Provisional Republicans than any other group had.

In March 1971, there was an illustration of this when a crowd of youths in the Bogside petrol-bombed an army jeep on patrol. Although the petrol bomb only damaged the bonnet, a soldier in the back of the jeep sprayed the interior with a fire extinguisher. The fire extinguisher contained a toxic gas and the concentration killed one of the soldiers in the jeep. Locals dragged two other soldiers out of the jeep and brought them to a nearby house to recover.[84] The soldier was the first person to die in the city in an incident related to the civil unrest since William King had died in October 1969, eighteen months before.

There was strong condemnation of the incident from John Hume and the Catholic bishop, Neil Farren, while the DCCC expressed its 'horror'. But Eddie McAteer was harsher. 'I am not taking part in this squalid game of selective condemnation. How can you distinguish between the links of this terrible chain?,' he said. The Derry Nationalist party condemned the 'senseless violence' but, as they put it themselves, 'in the same breath', they condemned Westminster and Stormont and said they were 'opposed to British military presence in Northern Ireland'.[85]

The crucial element in this political journey of the Nationalist party was the balance between the desire for stability and their ideological opposition to the British army. It was only when the army could be seen as contributing to instability, by brutality, 'invasions' of the Bogside and dubious convictions, all of which fuelled the anger of local youths, that the Nationalists were prepared to oppose them. In all of this the party was pushed or pulled along by events. It had no coherent policies and no political power and was not seen to be initiating anything. However, its drift towards hostility to the army reflects a wider trend as relatively conservative elements in the city found their traditional nationalism battling with their distaste for disorder.

The Unionist party

Since the Stormont election of February 1969, the City of Londonderry and Foyle Unionist Association had marched ever rightward, building strong links to right-wing Unionist MPs at Stormont such as William Craig and Harry West. The party in Derry built up a semi-formal allegiance not to the party leadership in Belfast but to the right-wing dissidents in the party. This allegiance was formalised in the West Ulster Unionist Council (hereafter, WUUC), established in April 1970 and headed by the Reverend Bertie Dickinson from Derry.[86] The WUUC united local right-wing Unionist associations in the west of Northern Ireland in a right-wing faction within the Unionist party. By late 1970, the Unionist party in Derry was split between three distinct factions: the supporters of the prime minister Sir James Chichester-Clark, the right-wing Craigites and an O'Neillite rump, each controlling different local associations around the city but with the 'Craigites' easily the strongest.[87] It was little wonder that the *Londonderry Sentinel* felt impelled to appeal for Unionist unity in early 1971.[88] The internal divisions came to a head in February 1971 when, amidst great acrimony, the Derry Unionist Council de-selected Albert Anderson as its candidate for the next Stormont elections (although he was the sitting MP) in favour of a young right-winger, Clifford Smyth, who had tenuous local connections. He would later leave the Unionist party to join the DUP.[89] Shortly after this, Chichester-Clark would resign as Stormont prime minister and be replaced by Brian Faulkner, who was more acceptable to the Unionist right wing.

In the midst of these disputes, there was a second burst of Unionist activism on social issues in the city. The competing wings of the party belatedly followed the lead of Leonard Hutchinson in Irish Street and in early 1971 began to get involved in housing issues, partly no doubt to strengthen the ground-level support for their factions in this uncertain situation.

In January 1971, residents in Aubery Street in the Fountain reinforced their demand for a derelict factory to be demolished, by placing a barricade across the street.[90] It was the first reported barricade in the Fountain since late 1969 and it had nothing to do with 'defence'. The experiences of civil disorder over the previous two years had raised the 'subversiveness' threshold and normalised tactics which would have seemed inherently disreputable and subversive before the troubles. Once the barricade was up, the case was taken up by the North Ward Unionist Association, a Craigite stronghold. The association organised a petition in the street for the demolition of the factory.[91] The case was taken up with the Development Commission by Albert McCartney, the head of the North Ward UA and a former Unionist councillor from a middle-class area some distance away. Shortly afterwards, McCartney took up the case of a footpath in bad condition near the (mostly Protestant) Northland estate.[92] It was the beginning of a sustained period of clientelist action by the North Ward UA which began to hold monthly (rather than annual) meetings and to deal regularly with tenants' issues.[93] Once again the novelty of such activity by a Unionist association should be noted. Some years earlier, as housing agitation developed in Creggan Estate, McCartney had invited people from the tenants' associations there to meet him and discuss their demands and complaints.[94] He was putting to good use whatever he had learned then. He and the young Jack Allen would be the only Unionist members of the old corporation to be elected to the new city council in 1973.[95]

Albert Anderson too turned his attention to housing, now that he had been de-selected as the Unionist candidate. He first addressed the need for housing for the elderly,[96] and then, when a tenants' association was established in the Fountain in May 1971, he spoke on the imminent redevelopment of the Fountain and the need for adequate compensation for those people losing businesses and houses.[97] Anderson also spoke of the need for the Fountain to be protected as it was redeveloped; that is, to be preserved as a Protestant area, defended from, rather than integrated with the Catholic areas around it.[98] Again we can see how, in circumstances of civil unrest, Protestant community activism was intimately bound up with sectarian issues of defence and neighbourhood integrity. Around the same time, senior local Provisional Republican, Seán Keenan, was suggesting that the Fountain be integrated with surrounding, mostly Catholic, areas as it was redeveloped.[99] Ultimately it was the tenants' association in the Fountain which would successfully pressurise statutory authorities to erect a peace wall around the district, a principal effect of which was to assure that the Protestant character of the area would be maintained.[100] This tenants' association was superseded in the early 1970s by a community association which had a security sub-committee. The head of this sub-committee maintained regular contact with the army and the RUC. He also maintained contact, through a Community Association in the Bogside, with organisations in Free Derry whose attitudes had important implications for the 'security' of the Fountain.[101]

In many places which were not as isolated as the Fountain, and where a more 'aggressive' approach was possible, loyalist paramilitary groups grew out of local tenants' associations.[102] They became a major new element in the conflict from late 1972 onwards. By mid-1971, two more tenants' associations had been established in Protestant estates in Derry, bringing the total number to four. These local groups would become ever more involved in issues of 'defence', setting up security committees, dealing with the army and paramilitaries and providing an organisational structure during events such as the Ulster Workers Council strike in 1974 when a loyalist workers' strike brought down a power-sharing government at Stormont.[103] Though the tenants' associations did not themselves become paramilitary organisations, their development was the first sign of a process of fearful, localised Protestant working-class organisation, which would later give rise to the phenomenon of mass-based loyalist paramilitarism.[104] They were the first organisations to emerge after the Unionist monolith had collapsed and they pointed the way to the future, in their increasingly equivocal attitudes to strict definitions of 'law and order' and their concern to maintain the integrity of 'Protestant' areas as well as in their willingness to make demands on the authorities.

Although some elements of the party were involved in social activism, the Unionist party was focused by mid-1971 more or less exclusively on the demand for greater repression of the Official and Provisional IRAs. Yet even this united call for repression should not be taken as evidence of any coherence in Unionist politics. The continuing confusion of Unionist responses is illustrated by the remarks in 1971 of R.M.H. Moore, the president of the Lower Liberties UA, a rural area between Derry and the Donegal border. While praising the long-since gone O'Neill and urging the need for good community relations, he called for rioters to be birched, for the size of the UDR to be doubled, and for internment to be considered by the government. In a curious blend of right-wing Unionist conspiracy theory and liberal O'Neillite nostalgia, he declared that the unrest in the North was 'part of the world Communist strategy of disruption and public disorder in any country that is prospering and progressing' and that 'specially trained Communist agents were very cleverly working up the old sectarian and political animosities in Northern Ireland to create anarchy and disruption'.[105]

By early 1971, the dominant reactions of Unionism were incoherent, unrealistic, obsessed with repression and still informed by ludicrous conspiracy theories. The only major developments in Unionism were happening at the level of community activism. What looked like 'developments' within the Unionist party were no more than different variations on the theme of disintegration.

The SDLP and the DCCC

In August 1970, opposition MPs at Stormont came together to form the SDLP after many months of difficult negotiations. In December 1970, the Independent Organisation became the Derry branch of the SDLP and the focus for SDLP organisation in the city and in north Co. Derry and north Tyrone. Ivan Cooper and John Hume joined the new party as did Claude Wilton who had become a senator at Stormont. Although there was Protestant participation in the party at a high level, these were Protestants who had been associated with the Catholic community in the civil rights campaign and who had depended on Catholic electoral support for the Liberal party and the Labour party. Thus, despite the involvement of such Protestants the party was identified with the Catholic community from the outset.

The Independent Organisation had operated for a year and a half before becoming a branch of the SDLP. The lack of a party affiliation had been a source of constant discontent[106] but it also meant that the party had developed strong independent structures and had a solid local base, based on advice centres and clientelist politics. This would prove extremely difficult for other parties to erode. The length of time it had taken to establish the SDLP had resulted in the Independent Organisation building strong links to the Derry Nationalist party and it was probably a factor in creating the space for a local non-parliamentary initiative such as the DCCC. On the other hand, with no organised political opposition at Stormont and no sense that anti-Unionist politicians were achieving anything, there had been a great opportunity for Republicans to promote their analysis and advance their position before the SDLP was established.

Although many of its senior members were also senior members of the Independent Organisation and then the SDLP, the DCCC operated independently of the party. This aroused divisions within the Derry SDLP as some members felt the DCCC was usurping the functions of the party, and was setting up its own political power base. It led to heated argument within the party.[107] Those involved with the DCCC and who had previously been involved with the DCDA were however very strong in the party. Of the five officers elected initially to the Derry SDLP, two were members of the DCCC and three had been on the DCDA in August 1969.[108] They had always been involved in dealing with the army through negotiation and bargaining and had also had strong links with Republicans. The DCCC's negotiating contacts with Republicans and the DCCC's ambiguous attitude to state authority which it had displaced on occasion, appears to have created unease among some SDLP members and the party in Derry was circumspect in its dealings with the DCCC,[109] despite the large overlapping membership.

In late June and early July 1970, directly after being formed, the DCCC briefly acted as a policing agent in Creggan and the Bogside. Even when this agreement with the army ended, the army continued to operate in Derry in negotiation with the DCCC. Michael Canavan, head of the DCCC, had regular meetings with the senior army officers in Derry in the months after the DCCC was set up and while rioting was going on.[110] He and the DCCC acted on occasion as go-betweens between Republicans – most likely the Provisionals – and the army.[111]

Many senior DCCC members who were also in the SDLP had worked in the DCDA with some of the people now leading the Provisional Republican movement in Derry. It seems they had some influence with them. It appears likely that at least part of the reason why the IRA offensive was so limited in Derry up to July 1971 was because of negotiation of some sort and certain political constraints on the Provisionals exerted by the DCCC.

In the riots of late June 1970, the army used CS gas for the first time in Derry and they used it again in the early August 1970 riots. In June, they had used vast amounts: over 1300 units in a couple of days.[112] During one or the other of these riots[113] a group of people, who could only have been Republicans, conveyed to DCCC members one night that if the army did not cease firing CS gas by 3 a.m. that morning they would use explosives. At that time explosives had not yet been used in Derry. Michael Canavan and other DCCC and SDLP members then went to the army and asked that they stop firing CS gas. The army, somehow aware of the 3 a.m. deadline, did so at the last moment.[114]

Thus, there was a process of negotiation to avoid an escalation of violence in which the DCCC and Catholic moderates were deeply involved. Although the Provisionals began a bombing campaign in September 1970, there are indications at different times of restraint on both sides for a variety of reasons, most frequently self-interest. However, there are also indications that the IRA was influenced by the political climate in the Catholic community, represented partly by the DCCC. The opposition to attempts to kill security force members for example is illustrated by the condemnation in Derry of a Provisional IRA attack in south Armagh in August 1970 in which two RUC men died. Strong condemnation came from Eddie McAteer, John Hume, Ivan Cooper and the *Derry Journal*, among others.[115] Eddie McAteer and Eamonn McCann both refused to believe it was an IRA action.

The SDLP felt that violence on the streets had allowed the Unionist government to fudge on reform and direct Britain towards a policy of repression. As the proceedings in parliament (which were their chosen focus) were over-shadowed by events in the streets, the SDLP became marginalised. The DCCC became in effect the main agency through which the moderates who had entered the sphere of politics could try to exercise influence on the streets in Derry.

However, the SDLP and the DCCC were not identical and because of its political nature the SDLP was more committed to working with the state, accepting, for example, the minor Unionist concession of offering party members places on parliamentary committees in June 1971. The decision to accept this provoked annoyance and dissent from some members in Derry.[116] Before this, the DCCC had called for a full power-sharing executive at Stormont.[117] There was co-operation between the DCCC and the SDLP but there were also clashes of interest. There were joint community initiatives involving local Derry branches of the SDLP, DCCC and a tenants' association, for example,[118] but there was also SDLP annoyance that the DCCC was taking on functions, such as organising a local meeting on redevelopment, which the SDLP saw as its function.[119]

On to another plane

The central political fact of late 1970 and early 1971 was the launching of a military campaign by the Provisional IRA and, to a lesser extent the Official IRA, in both Derry and Belfast. The conditions in which they began to thrive were created in large part by the failure to significantly change the state – by Unionists' reluctant implementation of reforms and the British government's decision to police Catholic areas with the British army rather than make the sort of dramatic changes which might (and admittedly might not) have secured Catholic acceptance of the police.

The IRA campaigns marginalised Catholic politicians, reducing their influence with the British who were now inclined to regard 'security' rather than 'reform' as the primary political 'problem' in Northern Ireland. But the IRA campaign also served to distance Catholic politicians and moderates from the state simply because moderates did not accept that a political solution had been implemented, as the British government claimed, and thus they could not support the sort of decisive repression of Republicans the government wished to implement.

The degree to which moderates and huge numbers of conservative Catholics were unwilling to accept such decisive repression of Republicans became clear on 9 August 1971, when the British army, on behalf of the Unionist government, swooped on houses across Northern Ireland and 'lifted' over 340 suspected Republicans and left-wing activists from their homes.

Notes and references

1 Cited in DJ, 18/8/70, p. 7.
2 DJ, editorial, 6/10/70, p. 4; Hume in DJ, 19/5/70; 'Onlooker' in DJ, 19/5/70, p. 4.
3 Cited in James Callaghan, *A House Divided* (Collins, London, 1973), p. 155.
4 Patrick Buckland, *A History of Northern Ireland* (Gill and Macmillan, Dublin, 1981), p. 140.
5 DJ, 18/8/70, p. 4.
6 DJ, 14/8/70, p. 2.
7 US Riot Commission Report, *Report of the National Advisory Commission on Civil Disorders* (Bantam Books, New York March 1968), p. 110.
8 Eamonn McCann, *War and an Irish Town* (Penguin, Harmondsworth, 1974), p. 80; DJ, 7/8/70, p. 1.
9 DJ, 7/8/70, p. 1.
10 DJ, 7/8/70, p. 1.
11 DJ, 7/8/70, p. 1.
12 DJ, 11/8/70, p. 1; 14/8/70, p. 2.
13 Shane O'Doherty, *The Volunteer. A Former IRA Man's True Story* (Fount, London, 1993), p. 83.
14 Interview with Anon. D, former member of the Republican movement in Derry.
15 DJ, 14/8/70, p. 1.
16 DJ, 9/7/68, p. 1; 26/7/68, p. 1; 9/8/68, p. 1.
17 Although Eamonn McCann says Carlin was still an Official Republican at this stage (interview 2 with Eamonn McCann), it was the Provisionals who

picketed the court (*An Phoblacht*, 1, no. 1, Sept. 1970) and other sources say he was by then a Provisional (interview with John Carlin, member of the Republican movement in Derry from the mid-1960s and of the Provisional Republicans after the split. Former Sinn Féin election agent, former internee).

18 DJ, 14/8/70, p. 1 and DJ, 27/10/70, p. 1.
19 Bishop and Mallie, *The Provisional IRA* (Corgi, London, 1988), p. 169.
20 Anon. D, interview.
21 Michael Farrell, *Northern Ireland: The Orange State* (Pluto, London, 1980), p. 275 and *This Week*, 12/3/71, p. 8.
22 DJ, 18/9/70, p. 2.
23 DJ, 2/10/70, p. 13; 13/10/70, pp. 6, 7, p. 18; 27/10/70, p. 2; 24/11/70; p. 1, 15/12/70, p. 1.
24 Anon. D, interview.
25 DJ, 27/10/70, p. 2.
26 LS, 10/2/71, p. 1, p. 13; 17/2/71, p. 11; 10/3/71, p. 2.
27 LS, 10/3/71, p. 30.
28 LS, 10/2/71, p. 1.
29 Michael Barthorp, *Crater to the Creggan. The History of the Royal Anglian Regiment. 1964–1974* (Leo Cooper, London, 1976), p. 98.
30 LS, 12/5/71, p. 14 and Barthorp, *Crater to the Creggan*, p. 100.
31 Seán Mac Stiofáin, *Memoirs of a Revolutionary* (R. and R. Clarke, Edinburgh, 1975), p. 157.
32 Barney McFadden in DJ, 12/1/71.
33 LS, 14/4/71, p. 7.
34 Ibid.
35 LS, 19/5/71, p. 21.
36 *An Phoblacht*, vol. 2, no. 9, September 1971.
37 LS, 2/6/71, p. 15.
38 Quoted in Eamonn McCann (with Bridie Harrigan and Maureen Shiels), *Bloody Sunday in Derry. What Really Happened* (Brandon, Kerry, 1992), p. 97.
39 DJ, 7/4/70, p. 5.
40 See McCann, *War*, p. 84.
41 Bishop and Mallie, *IRA*, pp. 144, 155; Kevin Toolis, *Rebel Hearts. Journeys within the IRA's Soul* (Picador, London, 1995), p. 302.
42 Cited in Simon Winchester, *In Holy Terror: Reporting the Ulster Troubles* (Faber, London, 1974), pp. 108–9.
43 Margie Bernard, *Daughter of Derry. The story of Brigid Sheils Makowski* (Pluto, London, 1989), p. 83.
44 McGuinness in Bishop and Mallie, *IRA*, p. 155, claims the Derry Officials, in late 1970 or early 1971 were trying to cause explosions with minimal quantities of explosives; J. Bowyer Bell, *The Irish Troubles. A Generation of Violence*, 1967–92 (Gill and Macmillan, Dublin, 1993), p. 282; interview with Anon. B, former member of the Republican movement in Derry.
45 Bernard, *Daughter of Derry*, p. 83.
46 LS, 31/3/71, p. 1.
47 Bishop and Mallie, *IRA*, pp. 161–3.
48 Anon. D, interview. 'Stickie' and 'Provo' were slang for the Official and Provisional Republicans respectively.

49 DJ, 1/5/70, p. 13.
50 McCann, *War*, p. 89.
51 LS, 24/3/71, p. 15.
52 DJ, 16/10/70, p. 3.
53 Interview with Terry Robson, chairman of Derry Labour Party Young Socialists in the early 1970s and member of the NILP executive. Member of the Official Republican movement from late 1971.
54 For a description of the political role of the Catholic church in the Catholic working-class neighbourhood of 'Anro' in Belfast see Frank Burton, *The Politics of Legitimacy: Struggles in a Belfast Community* (Routledge and Keegan Paul, London, 1978), pp. 93–4.
55 Interview with Dermie McClenaghan, Former Derry Labour party activist and member of the DHAC, the DCAC and (unbeknown to him) the DCDA. Former Youth Worker with Queen Street Youth Project 1971–2.
56 Sara M. Roy, 'Gaza: New Dynamics of Civic Disintegration. Economic dedevelopment in Gaza', *Journal of Palestine Studies*, vol. 22, no. 4, summer 1993.
57 See Roy, 'Gaza', for a discussion of close relationships in Gaza between Islamic militants and local youth.
58 Des Hamill, *Pig in the Middle. The Army in Northern Ireland 1969–1985* (Methuen, London, 1986), p. 71.
59 See DJ, 7/2/67; 9/5/67; 19/5/67 and LS, 8/11/67.
60 DJ, 7/4/70, p. 2; 28/4/70, p. 1; 22/5/70, p. 1; 31/7/70.
61 DJ, 27/11/70, p. 1.
62 DJ, 8/1/71, p. 1.
63 DJ, 27/11/70.
64 DJ, 12/1/71, p. 1.
65 Interview with Hugh Doherty, former president of St Mary's Boys Club, Creggan, and prominent member of the Independent Organisation and, later, the SDLP. Former SDLP mayor of Derry.
66 The rest of the eight members of the RUC committee included Alliance party members and old O'Neillites but no representatives from either the SDLP or the Unionist or Nationalist parties. LS, 27/1/71, p. 1 and DJ, 12/1/71, p. 1.
67 DJ, 27/11/70.
68 LS, 21/1/71. p. 29.
69 LS, 20/1/71, p. 29; DJ, 19/1/71, p. 1.
70 DJ, 1/5/70, p. 1.
71 LS, 17/2/71, p. 11.
72 LS, 19/5/71, p. 24; 26/5/71, p. 18.
73 LS, 23/6/71, p. 1.
74 PRONI, T3062/3.
75 Ibid.
76 DJ, 13/10/70, pp. 1, 4.
77 DJ, 16/10/71, p. 1.
78 Ibid.
79 DJ, 20/10/70, p. 2.
80 DJ, 10/11/70, p. 1.
81 DJ, 18/12/70.
82 LS, 24/3/71, p. 6.
83 LS, 5/5/71, p. 13.

84 LS, 3/3/71, p. 23.
85 Ibid.
86 LS, 28/4/70, p. 4.
87 LS, 3/2/71, 10/2/71, pp. 6, 19.
88 LS, 3/2/71, p. 6.
89 LS, 3/2/71, p. 25; 3/3/71, p. 6; 10/3/71, p. 1.
90 LS, 27/1/71, p. 1.
91 LS, 17/2/71, p. 1.
92 Ibid., p. 11.
93 LS, 19/5/71, p. 23.
94 Interview, with Mary Nelis, founder member and former chairperson, secretary, PRO of Foyle Hill Tenants' Association (Creggan). Former SDLP candidate for Derry City Council, currently a Sinn Féin member of Derry City Council.
95 S. Elliot and F.J. Smith, *Northern Ireland Local Government Elections, 1977* (Queen's University Belfast, 1977), pp. 125–30; DJ, 5/6/73.
96 LS, 5/5/71, p. 29.
97 LS, 26/5/71, p. 1; 23/6/71, p. 3.
98 LS, 14/7/71, p. 3.
99 LS, 9/6/71, p. 11.
100 Interview with Peter Simpson, former Secretary of the Wapping Lane Community Association (which included the Fountain estate) and head of its Security Sub-Committee in the early 1970s.
101 Ibid.
102 Steve Bruce, *The Red Hand. Protestant Paramilitaries in Northern Ireland* (Oxford University Press, 1992), p. 48.
103 Interview with Marlene Jefferson, former Ulster Unionist Party councillor and mayor of Derry. Worked closely with the Wapping Lane Community Association in the Fountain; Simpson, interview.
104 Mass-based by contrast with the UVF of the mid and late 1960s which was a much smaller, and more clandestine organisation than the UDA and even the UVF of the early 1970s.
105 LS, 10/2/71, p. 19.
106 Independent Organisation minutes, *passim*.
107 SDLP minutes, 9/3/71.
108 SDLP minutes, 8/12/70.
109 SDLP minutes, 16/3/71, 21/3/71.
110 DJ, 11/8/70, p. 4.
111 See Raymond McClean, *The Road to Bloody Sunday* (Ward River Press, Dublin, 1983), p. 98.
112 DJ, 30/6/70, p. 1.
113 McClean says it occurred before the first bomb attack in Derry – which was in September 1970. McClean, *Bloody Sunday*, p. 98.
114 McClean, *Bloody Sunday*, p. 98.
115 DJ, 14/8/70, p. 2.
116 SDLP minutes, 29/6/71.
117 LS, 24/3/71, p. 7.
118 SDLP minutes, 9/2/71.
119 SDLP minutes, 9/3/71.

7
On to a New Plane:
After July 1971

On to a new plane

On 22 June 1971, the Unionist government, headed since March by Brian Faulkner, offered places on Stormont parliamentary committees to the SDLP. It was the first Unionist offer of any form of participation in political decision-making to Catholic moderates. This offer was accepted by the SDLP with some misgivings. After making this minor concession, the Unionist government then embarked on a military 'solution' to the unrest, a 'solution' which would lead to the total alienation of Catholic moderates from the state.

In Derry, internment would be introduced after several weeks of ferocious conflict, at a time when Catholic alienation from the army had already reached an all-time high. It would be viewed by Catholics as the culminating act of a policy of uninhibited repression which had begun in early July 1971, and as a deliberate escalation of the conflict in an attempt to solve this conflict through massive repression.

After internment, the Unionist government at Stormont was utterly rejected by even the most conservative of Catholics. It was no longer even regarded as an appropriate agency to negotiate with. Stormont was rejected but so too were the British government and the British army. The very people in the Catholic community who had tried to work with the state to restore social order and prevent vandalism came to regard the army as a scourge. They condemned the soldiers in the same essentially conservative terms in which they had once condemned vandals and rioters.

The scale of this process of alienation locked much of the Catholic community, including moderates, into a basic rejection of the authority of the Northern Ireland state. In large part, this was also a rejection of the British state which was implementing repression on behalf of the Unionist government. By the time direct rule from London was introduced in March 1972, Britain had already become as much an object of hostility as Stormont had been. This rejection of the state was based, not primarily on nationalist 'instinct' (although there was a distinct increase in nationalist sentiment), but on the experience of British army and government actions since mid-1970. In the case of many conservative Catholics it was a long delayed and reluctant rejection.

Although large numbers of Catholics, even at the height of this alienation from the state, continued to reject the IRA, the army retained virtually no active allies within the Catholic community. This was a dramatic shift from the situation of only a few months before. In May 1971, off-duty British soldiers had still been able to walk into the Bogside to visit friends. By August 1971, the only way they could enter was in groups several hundred strong, at the dead of night.

After internment, the conflict moved on to a new plane and in many respects, despite British government initiatives and a continuing reform programme, it would remain on that plane for many years afterwards. The comprehensive alienation of huge sections of the Catholic community from the state had the effect of transforming the Republican movement from a small, marginal and conspiratorial group of individuals, linked by family and tradition, into a major force within the Catholic community. It also pushed Catholic moderates away from seeking an accommodation solely within the state. Internment made it clear that the British government was prepared to repress the Catholic population at large in order to preserve Unionist rule. It demolished the last vestiges of trust in the British government's intentions. It seemed to demonstrate that, without continuous concerted Catholic pressure, Britain would be content to see Unionist majority rule restored if it could be done without great difficulty. It was not that the Catholic community turned instinctively to the vision of a united Ireland. Rather they turned decisively away from Northern Ireland as a state and away from the idea of Britain as a benevolent external force.

Towards internment

Given the high levels of disorder, it is surprising that, as July 1971 began, neither the IRA nor the British army had yet killed anyone in Derry. Although there was continued severe rioting in the city in the first half of 1971, the situation had not escalated to a shooting war as it had in Belfast. The Provisional IRA seem to have deliberately refrained from shooting at the troops. We must assume there was pressure, perhaps from younger recruits, perhaps from the Provisionals in Belfast, to end this restraint.

According to the army, two shots were fired at soldiers in Derry on Sunday 4 July 1971 after a minor riot.[1] This in itself was an unusual occurrence, only the third reported shooting incident in the city in the previous eleven months, and the first in three months. The following night a dozen shots were fired at two army posts in Derry.[2] The next night, Tuesday, after minor rioting, six more shots and a burst of machine gunfire were fired at another army post. Later that night, at midnight, two cars drove up to an army post and shots were fired from both cars at the post; an hour later, more shots were fired. According to the British army, soldiers did not fire back in any of these cases.[3] These attacks were an abrupt and deliberate escalation of the Provisional IRA offensive in Derry. Eamonn McCann said it could be 'doubted whether initially there was mass support for this escalation'.[4] A number of sources have suggested that the Provisionals brought in, or sent in, two men to the city to deliberately intensify the campaign.[5]

In any case, it was not these gun attacks by the Provisionals but subsequent actions by the British army which boosted the standing of the Provisionals in Derry and produced a veritable flood of new recruits to the Provisional IRA. On the night of Wednesday 7 July there were no reported shooting incidents, although the army would later characterise Wednesday as the fourth day of shooting incidents.[6] There were, however, riots which did not begin to die out until the early morning of Thursday 8 July. Even by the army's account, there had been no shooting at troops that night when a twenty-eight-year-old welder, Séamus Cusack, stepped into the open in William Street shortly after midnight and apparently leaned over to pick something up. Civilian eyewitnesses, among them Willie Breslin, a senior Labour party activist, and Nell McCafferty, secretary of the Derry Labour party, were unanimous that Cusack was completely unarmed when a soldier fired and hit him in the thigh.[7]

Cusack was driven to a hospital over the border in Letterkenny, Co. Donegal, because of the fear that he would be arrested if brought to Altnagelvin hospital in Derry. He died of blood loss shortly after he arrived. A number of accounts since then have categorically stated that Cusack was not an IRA man and was not armed.[8] The suggestion that he was an IRA man was widely regarded among Derry Catholics as a simple lie to justify the murder of an unarmed man. It was not considered even as a serious attempt at an explanation. The shooting of Séamus

Cusack provoked what the *Londonderry Sentinel* described as 'rioting of unprecedented ferocity'.[9]

Rioting continued into the following day, and at one point two or three gelignite bombs were thrown from a rioting crowd at troops. None of the soldiers was seriously injured. A soldier then opened fire, killing Desmond Beattie, a nineteen-year-old youth.[10] The soldier later stated at the inquest that, directly after the explosions, he had seen Beattie in a group of men at a barricade, with a flame in one hand and a 'dark object' in the other (implying that he was about to light a gelignite bomb). He said that he had then shot and killed Beattie before he had managed to touch the flame to the bomb. This account suggests a remarkably rapid and accurate reaction on the part of the soldier, all the more remarkable when it is considered that bombs had just exploded near him, and the bomber he aimed at and killed was amongst a crowd of people. It was widely regarded by many Derry Catholics as a lie. Forensic tests showed that Beattie had not handled any explosives.[11]

Derry was small enough that a large proportion of Catholics in the city could trace a personal connection with the two men, neither of whom were known as Republicans.[12] It was perceived that the army was wilfully and blatantly covering up the shootings and that the British government was weighing in behind them. The commanding officer of the Royal Anglians asserted that 'there was no possibility that the soldiers could have made a mistake in shooting the men'.[13] This judgement was apparently based solely on the accounts of the soldiers at the scene. In response to comments criticising the troops' actions in these cases, one British academic suggested that, if the British commander 'had been St Michael and his soldiers angels or archangels, someone would have complained that Lucifer was ejected from heaven with more force than was necessary'.[14] Very few Derry Catholics would have found such a comparison appropriate. On the other hand, the resolution adopted after these shootings by the North Ward Unionist Association 'expressing concern at the wanton damage to property which ... has caused unnecessary increases in the rates and taxes' displayed a calculated contempt on the part of some local Unionists.[15] After the shooting of Séamus Cusack, black flags flew from houses in the Bogside. Protest marches to the city centre ended in massive riots. After Beattie was shot dead, barricades were erected in Creggan and the Bogside and large crowds attacked the army post at Blighs Lane, between Creggan and the Bogside. It was the beginning of a virtual siege of the post which lasted for several days as IRA gunmen began to fire at the base and at soldiers all over the city, massively restricting their mobility as had not been the case during earlier riots.[16]

In response to the increase in gun attacks, the army launched a massive search operation in Creggan, the first such search in Derry, flooding the estate with CS gas. During the operation, troops fired shots at a rioting crowd and claimed to have hit a 'ringleader' of the rioters. Now the troops no longer bothered to claim that they were firing at 'gunmen'. As attacks on the army at Blighs Lane, which was known as 'Fort Essex' increased, the army began to fire back from inside the base and full-scale gun battles took place. Rioting and shooting continued day after day.[17]

The initial ferocity of the rioting had eased a little after about two weeks when another incident, which seemed again to demonstrate army contempt for local people, sparked off further intense riots. On the afternoon of Saturday 24 July, two Saracen armoured cars and an army truck were travelling 'very fast'[18] through the Bogside when the truck skidded on to a footpath, crushing a nine-year-old boy against a wall, killing him. The two soldiers in the truck jumped out, and after a short time got into one of the armoured cars. The convoy then sped on. Over the following half-hour, a huge crowd gathered in the street. Five RUC men eventually arrived to examine the scene of the crash. As they were about to leave the scene afterwards, they were stoned and attacked. Members of the DCCC who were on the scene had to bring some of the RUC men to safety in a nearby house.[19]

When five armoured cars arrived on the scene to retrieve the lorry and the equipment inside it, they were met by a barrage of stones from the huge crowd. After an abortive attempt to salvage the lorry during which troops fired rubber bullets at the crowd, the armoured cars eventually left the scene of what had now become a massive riot. As they drove away, teenagers were still clinging to the sides of the armoured cars.[20] A week of renewed fierce rioting followed, including a night of burning buildings, bomb attacks, shooting, petrol-bombing and rioting in Creggan, the Bogside and Brandywell which was described as one of the worst nights of violence ever in the city. By the end of July, a 'quiet' night in Derry was one with a few minor local riots and one or two bombings.[21]

A few days after the shootings of Cusack and Beattie, the Provisional Republicans held a public meeting in the Bogside which became a recruiting rally for the IRA. The general secretary of Sinn Féin, Walter Lynch, said 'We are not going to wait another generation for freedom. The IRA is prepared and is in the field. The people are on the streets behind us and we are going forward to victory.'[22] An estimated 1,500 people attended the rally and after it, according to McCann, people 'formed a queue' to join the Provisional IRA.[23] The killings by the army had brought the Provisionals in Derry a long way from where they had been two months before when they couldn't attract a decent crowd to a public meeting, never mind recruit IRA volunteers in public. The Provisionals were benefiting from increased hostility to the troops and attracted support principally on the basis that they alone were prepared to attack the army at every opportunity.

At the same time as the Provisional Republican rally was taking place, SDLP MPs were meeting in John Hume's house nearby. After the meeting, fearful of the dramatic rise in militancy in Derry and probably impelled by the wing of the party in Derry which was involved in the DCCC and was closely in touch with the increasingly militant mood on the ground, the MPs called on the British government to set up a full public inquiry into the killings of Cusack and Beattie and said, that if it was not granted, they would withdraw from Stormont. The DCCC backed the SDLP position and Michael Canavan, representing the DCCC, said that without an inquiry 'there could be no further support for the present institutions here'.[24] Barry White has written that, 'viewed from anywhere but Derry, it seemed like over-reaction'.[25]

In Derry however, now the scene of endless chaotic rioting and gun-battles, threatening to withdraw from the Stormont parliament seemed the only way to assert the authority of Catholic moderates, the only way in which they could appear to be active and in some way effective. When the British government refused an inquiry, the SDLP withdrew from Stormont, began to give thought to an 'alternative assembly' and in effect ceased to co-operate with the Unionist government in any way. It is notable that this process took place before internment was introduced and was a direct response to the uniquely chaotic situation in Derry. However, this SDLP decision caused dissension within the party among elements who thought they should continue to work within Stormont. The chairman of the Derry branch took temporary 'leave of absence' from the SDLP in protest at the decision.[26]

It was in these circumstances, of Provisional Republican expansion, the decisive rejection of the Unionist government by Catholic moderates and continued massive rioting in Derry, that the Unionist and British governments considered the approaching Apprentice Boys parade in Derry on 12 August. They decided to ban the parade and also, partly to placate Protestants who would be enraged at the banning of the parade and partly because of the worsening rioting in Derry and Belfast, to introduce internment.

In the early hours of 9 August 1971, troops raided houses all over Northern Ireland, taking over 340 people into custody. In Derry city, sixteen men were 'lifted'. It was a very small number compared with elsewhere in the North. However, it included at least five senior

Provisionals, including Seán Keenan and three senior Officials, including Mickey Montgomery and the O/C of the Official IRA in Derry, who had been prominent in radical social activism in the city before the Troubles. Although a few of those 'lifted' in Derry were arrested by mistake or were uninvolved,[27] the great majority, while not necessarily IRA members, were active Official or Provisional Republicans. However, this does not demonstrate an impressive level of RUC intelligence information. Of the sixteen men arrested in Derry, the names of at least eight of them had appeared in the local papers in connection with Republican activities in recent months, usually as speakers at meetings, or even letter-writers to the local papers. The fact that two senior Official Republicans, including the O/C of the Derry IRA, were released a few days after their arrest and interrogation[28] suggests that the RUC and the army, while they could identify Republicans, might not have been aware of who was running the military operations. In particular, they appear to have had virtually no information on the large number of teenagers who had recently joined the Provisional IRA and would shortly be in leadership positions. The immediate effect of internment in Derry was to remove the older leadership of the Provisionals from the scene. Control of the movement began to pass to the young recent recruits.

Internment, coming as it did after several weeks of rioting in Derry, appeared to be a calculated escalation of the conflict by the army. Rather than being seen as a sort of 'surgical' removal of leading Republicans, it was regarded as a frontal assault on Catholic areas. As the troops entered Creggan and the Bogside in the early hours of the morning, car horns blared, bin lids banged and car-headlights lit up the streets as huge crowds of people came out on the streets. There were 'numerous allegations of army brutality' as internees were taken from their homes in Creggan and the Bogside.[29] By the following evening, the Bogside and Creggan were surrounded by over thirty barricades and a new Free Derry had been born. Armed IRA men, both Official and Provisional, were operating openly on the streets, and six soldiers were shot and injured in Derry on that first day after internment.[30] A few days after internment, a British soldier was shot dead at the Blighs Lane army post, the first person killed by either Official or Provisional IRAs in Derry.[31]

Catholics and the state

Central to the disastrous failure of internment was the response of Catholic moderates. Even after the killings of Cusack and Beattie, there had been pressure within the SDLP in Derry to continue to work with the

Unionist government. After internment 'grass-roots feeling ... had hardened to an amazing degree'. At SDLP meetings Dr Raymond McClean was 'amazed to hear the fiery statements made by prominent citizens, whom I had previously regarded as comfortable "Castle Catholics" '.[32]

The fierce opposition of moderates to internment was determined by a number of factors. The first was that moderates had ceased to regard the army as a benevolent force over the past year and, in Derry since July, had seen them as a malevolent and dangerous force. They no longer felt obliged to support or explain army actions as they had done up to mid-1970. The second factor was that the situation on the ground in Derry during July 1971, with killings by the army, army raids and the unrestrained use of CS gas, had radicalised huge numbers of people, including the moderates in the SDLP. There had already been a decisive break with the state. Catholic moderates no longer felt any obligation to support or in any way contribute to the continuation of Unionist rule from Stormont, that is, to the stability of the state. Repression was designed to secure the position of that government and Catholic moderates thus had no incentive whatsoever to support such repression.

Apart from all this, there was the fact that the relationship between moderate and 'extreme' forces in the Catholic community was a complex one and even if the army had interned the 'right' people, it would not have assured them of support from Catholic moderates. The Republicans, particularly the older and more traditional Provisionals, were not regarded by moderates as an alien or particularly sinister force. In Derry, where senior SDLP and senior Provisional Republicans had worked together on the DCDA in August 1969, there were strong personal links between many in both camps.

But moderates did not merely fail to support internment. They organised against it, actively campaigned for a rent and rates strike and announced their determination to see the Unionist government toppled. As Hugh Logue of the SDLP and NICRA put it, 'They fail to realise that they are not facing the IRA or terrorists but facing a risen people determined not to rest until the system is broken.'[33] Thirty prominent Derry Catholics, among them J. Maultsaid, chairman of the Derry RUC liaison committee (and formerly involved with the 'Concern for Creggan' committee) and Stephen McGonagle, a member of the Development Commission who had probably been the most moderate member of the DCAC, resigned from their posts in protest at internment.[34] SDLP members also worked on behalf of the internees.

Prior to internment, a senior Derry SDLP member who had been in the DCDA met two Provisional Republicans whom he knew, on the street. They told him that they feared that internment would be introduced and that they would be taken in. In that event they asked him, could he do everything to ensure that internment was ended as quickly as possible.[35] After internment was introduced, an Internees Dependants Fund (hereafter IDF) was set up in Derry. It was initiated and administered almost exclusively by senior SDLP members. It was inspired at least partly by the personal links which had developed during the civil rights campaign between senior SDLP members and some of the older Provisional Republicans, such as Seán Keenan, who had now been interned.[36]

Prior to internment, the army had dealt with and negotiated with Catholic moderates regularly through the DCCC. After internment, the SDLP was unable even to find out where the internees had been taken to or what would happen to them. Ivan Cooper complained that 'the only time the army has any use for us is when they think we can help them. This was not one of those occasions.'[37] When reports began to emerge from inside the internment camps that a number of prisoners, including two from Derry, had been subject to experimental forms of torture, it increased the sense of helplessness of Catholic moderates, who could do little but publicise the details.[38] The army was now engaged in full-scale military repression and would resume negotiation with moderates only if this repression was not proving effective.

The army, stretched by the massive upsurge in violence across Northern Ireland after internment, had been unable to prevent the establishment of this new Free Derry. But, nine days after internment was introduced and shortly after the first British soldier had been shot dead in the city, the army launched an operation to smash the no-go area. In an operation beginning at 6.30 a.m. on 18 August 1971, 1,300 troops, supported by helicopters and armoured cars, began to remove the barricades. According to the army, nineteen barricades had been removed by lunchtime. Only five remained. The next day, the army announced that it had now removed a total of forty barricades. Army helicopters hovered above throughout the day. The next day, the removal of a further sixteen barricades was announced. However, the area was still surrounded by barricades which were being erected as fast as the army was removing them.[39] It was on the first day of this operation that troops, who came under heavy fire, shot dead Eamonn Lafferty, a nineteen-year-old Provisional IRA officer. Later that day, a crowd staged a sit-down in a middle-class area near the Creggan estate to prevent troops demolishing the barricades and entering Creggan. One of the troops on the scene was Paddy Ashdown who later became leader of the Liberal Democrats in Britain. One group of troops agreed with John Hume not to proceed but other troops arrived on the scene, refused to accept Hume's authority and water-hosed the crowd, arresting John Hume, Michael Canavan, Ivan Cooper and Hugh Logue, among others.[40] They charged Hume and the others with 'failing to move on command of a member of Her Majesty's forces'. This would later result in a court case in which it emerged that the British army had been carrying out arrests in the North without any legal authority since their arrival in August 1969. The British government resolved the situation by quickly passing legislation which retrospectively legalised army actions over the previous two years.[41]

This army operation to smash the barricades, during which rubber bullets and CS gas were used with great abandon, drew forth a critical statement from the Foyle Hill and Creggan Estate tenants' associations. The tenants' associations claimed the army had fired CS gas indiscriminately into people's houses and over rooftops 'at unseen targets'. They suggested the army should have directed the gas and the rubber bullets 'against rioters only'. They 'deplored the over-reaction of the troops, which endangered the health of our community, and damaged in no small degree the walls, fences, gardens and property of the residents'. It was a classically 'conservative' rejection of the army as a source of disruption and destruction. It showed that the army could no longer rely on any local support, even from those elements who had been most prepared to see the state take charge of restoring 'law and order'.[42]

After the failure of this operation it became clear to the army that, short of conducting a massacre of rioting youths (which would have severe military implications in its own way) it could not take control of Free Derry; there were simply not enough troops in the city. In Belfast, dozens of people had been killed in the days after internment. The city was in complete chaos and there was a lobby in Belfast and Stormont which wanted to 'let Derry burn', and focus efforts on restoring some semblance of public order in Belfast and to ignore Derry for the moment. Extra army units which had been intended for use in an 'invasion' of Free Derry in October 1971 were directed to Belfast instead.[43]

It was in these circumstances that the army again began to negotiate with moderates in Derry. After the failed attempt to regain control of Free Derry in late August, the British army GOC, Lt Gen Sir Harry Tuzo, came to the city and met with the prominent Catholic moderates and conservatives who had resigned from public offices in protest against internment and also with members of the DCCC. According to Hamill, Tuzo offered 'to stop military operations for a whole month if they could deliver peace'.[44] Although Hamill's sources say the offer was made to the moderates in order to 'call their bluff and describes the moderates almost with contempt, a truce went into effect and from about 20 August onwards an 'almost eerie' calm descended in the city as the continuous rioting of the past seven weeks came to an end.[45] The army made no further attempts to remove the barricades and, according to the *Londonderry Sentinel*, there was no sign of army or RUC patrols in the entire city. When minor trouble broke out on one occasion in the city centre, troops waited for two hours before confronting the rioters.[46]

This demonstrated that the moderates still had the capacity to wield a great deal of influence on the streets and it suggests strongly that at least some Republicans were co-operating with them in this. But what the moderates and perhaps even the older Provisional IRA leadership in the city could not deliver now was a suspension of the IRA campaign and although it appears there was little shooting, bomb attacks continued in Derry even after the rioting had stopped.

The unspoken truce ended after a court case at which John Hume, Michael Canavan and Ivan Cooper among others were charged in connection with the recent sit-down at the edge of Creggan. After the court case a riot broke out. According to the army, gelignite bombs and three shots were directed at the army and the army fired three shots in reply. Local witnesses said no shots had been fired at the army. A fourteen-year-old girl in the crowd, Annette McGavigan, was shot dead. There were suggestions from the army that she had been killed in 'cross-fire'.[47] At the inquest it emerged that she had been shot in the back of the head by a soldier.[48] Black flags went up in the Bogside and 'the fiercest rioting seen since 9 August then engulfed the area'.[49] There was a renewal of large-scale rioting, bombing and shooting. When a crowd of about 200 assembled in Creggan at night to stage a protest march at the killing, they had to call it off because gun battles were raging around the estate and it was simply too dangerous to try to march.[50]

By now, the largest political gatherings in the Catholic community in Derry were at funerals. Over 10,000 people walked behind the coffin and lined the route of Annette McGavigan's funeral which was 'one of the largest ever seen in Derry'.[51] Rioting ceased while the funeral took place. After the funeral, many people proceeded to a protest meeting in the city centre at which rioting broke out.

In that same week, another incident heightened tension even further. As two British army armoured personnel carriers (hereafter APCs) drove down Bishop Street at what one local called 'a powerful speed', the first APC hit and killed a three-year-old boy at the edge of the road but kept on driving. The second APC stopped, two soldiers jumped out, looked at the boy, then got in and drove off again.[52] By the time an RUC man arrived on the scene some time later, a crowd of about 150 people had gathered. As the RUC man put it, 'the atmosphere was electric'.[53] When he asked if anyone had witnessed the accident, there was complete silence. Some time later, a crowd of about 100 people laid siege to a nearby army post and severe rioting continued in the area for three nights. Incidents such as these inclined many to the view that, as Ivan Cooper put it, 'They treat us like bloody savages. They run us down as if they could do so with impunity.'[54]

By this stage the IRA in Derry had killed only one British soldier. The British army, on the other hand, had now killed two armed men[55] and three civilians while two children had died after being hit by army vehicles. These were the circumstances in which huge numbers of Derry Catholics, conservatives, moderates and 'extremists', could see the British army as a dangerous and malevolent force. In these circumstances, statements such as that from the Waterside Young Unionists that they were getting tired of 'the tendency to pamper the non-Unionist minority in Northern Ireland'[56] served only to illustrate the extent of the gap which had opened up between Catholics and Protestants in Derry. When even Alliance party moderates made statements like, 'if a soldier pushes us about, the cry goes up that we have no civil rights, no way of protesting. What happens if our civil rights are taken away by a handful of agitators making a burnt-out barbecue of our town' it demonstrated a poor understanding of what being 'pushed about' by soldiers entailed in Creggan and the Bogside.[57]

In early September 1971, after these fresh outbreaks of large-scale rioting and the end of the short truce, the army began to conduct a series of large-scale raids into the barricaded area which provoked strong reactions from ever more of those who, a few months before, had been involved in the Concern for Creggan committee. During the first of these raids, locals complained of 'wild and indiscriminate firing by the army' which left bullet holes in many houses in two Creggan streets and provoked many people to move out of the area.[58] The parish priest in Creggan, Fr Rooney, sent a telegram to the British prime minister, Edward Heath, calling for the withdrawal of the British troops from Creggan and the evacuation of the Blighs Lane post, which was the scene of a more or less permanent riot. He wrote that with the huge amounts of CS gas used by the army, Creggan was like a 'vast gas-chamber'.[59] A joint statement by the Creggan, Foyle Hill and Lone Moor tenants' associations, the DCCC and John Hume made the same demand.

John Hume suggested that 'people should ignore the army's presence entirely'.[60]

Around this time, local schoolteachers began to make strong criticisms of the army's behaviour. When troops came out of the Blighs Lane base one day to repair the perimeter fence, at the same time as local schoolchildren were passing on their way to school, the principal of the nearby infants' school went to ask the officer in charge why he had chosen that time. According to the principal, 'He told me that they considered that with children about, the dangers of them being fired at by snipers were lessened. I asked him if that meant the army was using children for cover and he replied that I could interpret their action whatever way I wanted. I was amazed and very angry.'[61] The army later said the principal had misunderstood and claimed that the officer had only meant that nobody would fire while the children were passing and that therefore they were not endangered by the army action.[62]

This particular criticism of the army was repeated in December when a statement signed by almost 350 local teachers said that 'troop movements seemed to be timed to coincide with movements of schoolchildren' and that 'troops are continually overreacting to relatively minor incidents and the indiscriminate use of gas and rubber bullets against children is frequent'.[63]

Criticism of army conduct in their regular raids into the area became even harsher. The two tenants' associations in Creggan had been involved in negotiations to get Ulsterbus bus services restored and to get street lighting and building work resumed in the area. 'All organisations' in the area (i.e., including the two IRAs) had agreed that barricades should be removed to allow bus services to resume, according to the tenants' associations but, they said, 'it appears that this does not suit the army' who launched a massive 'search operation' at this sensitive time. The tenants' associations said they 'viewed this action as sheer provocation'.[64] During one of these raids in November, which the army described as a 'small arrest operation' by 200 troops (during which no-one was arrested), a middle-aged housewife, Kathleen Thompson, who had come out to raise the alarm, was shot dead in her garden by a single shot fired by a soldier. Creggan and Foyle Hill tenants' associations issued a joint statement saying that the army had 'replaced harassment with intimidation and murder'.[65] By December, the Creggan SDLP was also unrestrained in its condemnation of the army. In the first days of December, 500 troops made a 4 a.m. swoop on Creggan. They left the area two and a half hours later having found a number of weapons in a garden on the estate. During these two and a half hours, they were confronted by several hundred rioters throwing bottles, stones, nail bombs and gelignite bombs. According to Ivan Cooper, troops fired 370 canisters of CS gas and 240 rubber bullets (later collected by local people).[66] The army claimed that it had shot three gunmen and a petrol-bomber and that only two soldiers had been injured – hit by bottles. Local sources, ranging from the SDLP to the tenants' associations, said the army had shot only one youth and that many more than two soldiers had been injured. Pensioners in Beechwood Crescent claimed troops had fired CS gas directly into their houses, smashing the windows, and many of them had to be evacuated.[67] After this raid, the Creggan SDLP said the army was 'now ready to use the jackboot tactics on defenceless people in order to bolster up a rotten Unionist government' and said 'the truth of any statements from the security forces is now, as never before, open to question'.[68]

In early December, after several such early morning invasions, which seemed designed simply to exhaust people on the estate, Fr Rooney and local moderates requested a meeting with the local army commander. He refused to meet them, saying there was nothing to talk about.[69] This signalled the definitive end, for the time being, of army attempts to negotiate with local conservatives and moderates. It was in these circumstances that both the Provisional and Official IRA became major forces in the Catholic community, attracting more recruits than they could handle and operating openly in the no-go areas.[70]

By mid-December, however, the army had brought an end to these large-scale raids. The local RUC and army commanders in Derry believed that the raids were counter-productive, damaging relations with Catholic moderates. Others in the security forces continued to push for a much more aggressive policy in Derry and documents provided to the Bloody Sunday Inquiry reveal the depth and intensity of these divisions. These internal divisions came to a head on Bloody Sunday and provide a large part of the explanation for army behaviour on that day.

Free Derry was not controlled by either IRA. The simple fact that there were two IRAs meant that no single group could dominate the area. Rather, a variety of groups took on various functions within the area. While both Provisional and Official IRA units patrolled the area in stolen 'staff-cars', the barricades were guarded by unarmed 'auxiliary IRA members' who were not members of the IRA itself and also by many who weren't affiliated to any group.[71] The Free Derry 'police' which was independent of both IRAs was in charge of much of the policing in the area.[72] Also active was the Catholic Ex-Servicemen's Association (hereafter CESA), a group of former members of the British army which was particularly active in Belfast in mounting vigilante patrols to protect Catholic areas. In Derry, the CESA tried to set up street committees for defence and had contacts with the SDLP, but does not seem to have been as active as it was in Belfast.[73]

Nonetheless, both the Official and Provisional IRA were powerful forces in the area and they began to take on a variety of functions. The Official IRA was the first group to organise alternative public transport, bringing people to and from the city centre in trucks[74] which were later superseded by black taxis run by both the Officials and the Provisionals. The Provisionals in particular became deeply involved in local 'policing' activities, frequently tarring and feathering people accused of involvement in petty crime.[75] They would also occasionally try to enforce pub-closing times to great criticism from the Officials.[76]

In early November 1971, there were three incidents in which young women who were going out with or were engaged to soldiers were tarred and feathered by groups of women in the Bogside and Creggan. Both the Officials and Provisionals denied involvement in, and strongly condemned, these actions. The Provisional's Women's Action Committee on the other hand, while denying involvement, described the attacks as a 'spontaneous reaction' to the shooting dead of Kathleen Thompson in Creggan.[77] These attacks forcibly brought an end to virtually all public contacts between local Catholics and the army. They also brought fierce criticism from the British national media which gave them extensive coverage.

Within 'Free Derry', there was competition between the Officials, who were initially the more numerous and better-armed group,[78] and the Provisionals but never the sort of serious feuding which broke out in Belfast. Disputes did arise when, for example, a volunteer would defect from one wing to the other taking with him what he regarded as his personal issue firearm.[79] However, conflict was confined mostly to 'rows in bars, guns pulled in clubs'.[80] The position of the Derry internees, both Official and Provisional, provided a strong motivation for Republican unity in Derry. The Derry internees issued regular joint statements from Long Kesh until December 1971, when the Officials and Provisionals began to organise anti-internment marches in competition with each other.

Although the Officials were taking action against the British army and killing soldiers, they always defined their actions either as 'defensive' or in 'retaliation' for the killing of Catholic civilians. On occasion, they strongly condemned the Provisionals' offensive campaign.[81] However, at least one account suggests that the Provisional and Official IRA in Derry frequently co-operated[82] and they issued at least one joint statement.[83]

A remarkable feature of both Republican movements in Derry at this time was the youth of many of their members. When a Derry Provisional IRA member died in an accidental shooting just after internment it gave a glimpse of just who it was that was now bombing the centre of Derry and attacking the British army. The IRA member who was accidentally shot was sixteen-year-old James O'Hagan. His two companions were arrested and charged with possession of gelignite and a rifle. They were aged seventeen and sixteen years old.[84] Eamonn Lafferty, the Creggan-based OC of a Provisional IRA unit which included at least one sixteen-year-old,[85] was nineteen years old and said to be an adjutant on the Bogside staff of the IRA, when he was shot dead in August 1971.[86] The Derry Official IRA also had active members as young as sixteen, one of whom died in a training accident in early 1972.[87]

This was in absolute contrast with the middle-aged founders of the Provisional IRA in Derry in early 1970, several of whom were now either interned or dead. The youth of IRA members in both wings is startling. It represented the transformation of Republicanism from an ageing conspiratorial hereditary movement to a mass organisation which was now in large measure being run by teenagers and young men. The middle-aged OC of the Provisionals' Derry Brigade who was 'continually agonizing about a campaign over which he had only nominal control' found himself being talked back to by teenage recruits.[88] After Bloody Sunday Martin McGuinness became OC of the Derry Brigade at the age of twenty-one. Most of the volunteers he commanded ranged in age from sixteen to their early twenties. It was these younger members who were taking the lead in military action. The older Republicans were not directly involved and, according to one former activist, this fact 'divorced them altogether from the struggle. They weren't seen as part of it.'[89] This was in many ways the culmination of the politicisation of children and young teenagers which had begun with the civil rights movement and which now saw young teenagers who had been throwing stones and petrol bombs during the early riots joining the IRA.[90]

In 1973, Seán Keenan was asked in Dublin what he had to say to criticisms that 'your young men are screaming for blood'. IRA members in Belfast had carried out a series of sectarian murders and he replied, speaking as a national figure in the Republican movement, that

I appreciate that situation very much. There was a lot of people came into the Republican movement around 1969 for the simple reason that it was necessary to have fighting men there at the time and we didn't have the time to teach them the niceties of republicanism ... But until this time I suppose we had more principled, dedicated people than the present situation allows us to have today. But I believe that eventually those boys will realize what the fight is all about and that it's not against Protestants.[91]

Despite the growth in popular support for the IRA, there were still powerful forces in the Catholic community actively opposed to the IRA and they had regrouped a month after internment when several northern bishops issued a statement condemning both internment and the use of violence to achieve Irish unity.[92] These forces concentrated most of their attention in Derry on the Officials who were seen to have 'alien' ideas and were accused by one priest of being 'communists pretending to be the IRA'.[93]

However, the effectiveness of conservative Catholic opposition to the IRA was limited by the situation on the ground. By the end of 1971, the two IRAs in Derry had killed between them a total of eight British soldiers but no civilians.[94] The British army by then had killed two IRA men and five civilians and was held responsible for the deaths of the two children killed by army vehicles. The IRA did not seem the more aggressive or threatening force to many people in Derry. In early January 1972 the Provisionals shot dead two RUC men near the edge of the Free Derry area. This was a new development, the first time that either IRA in Derry had killed locally-recruited members of the security forces.

The influx of new members created tensions with some of the older Republicans. In mid-February 1972 the Provisional IRA in Creggan kidnapped Thomas Callaghan, a middle-aged bus driver who was an off-duty UDR member. They then killed him. It was the first killing in Derry of a local off-duty member of the security forces. There was widespread local condemnation and some of the older Derry Republicans conveyed their criticism of this action and of the 'arrogance' of the younger IRA members to the Dublin leadership.[95]

On 30 January 1972, a huge anti-internment march, organised by NICRA which was by now closely associated with the Official Republicans, left Creggan Estate in the Free Derry area to attempt to march into Guildhall Square in Derry city centre. It was the largest protest march seen in Derry since the civil rights campaign in 1969. The march grew from 5,000 to about 10,000 strong as it moved down to the Bogside. As the march reached army barricades preventing the marchers from entering the commercial town centre, rioting broke out. The bulk of the crowd, however, did not go up to the barricades but moved instead towards the platform in Rossville Street where speeches were being given.

The 1st Battalion of the British Parachute regiment, the 'Paras', had been brought into the city especially for the day of the march. The 'Paras' were 'élite' combat troops, and it was the first time they had been deployed in Derry. They were deployed against the rioters and as the huge crowd scattered, the Paras moved forward and opened fire in several areas around Rossville Street. In the space of minutes they had shot dead thirteen unarmed civilians. A fourteenth man died later. The Paras claimed to have come under a hail of fire but civilian witnesses unanimously rejected this claim and none of the dead was found to have been armed. The only soldier to be shot was one who shot himself in the foot. Only one of the dead was identified as a Republican; he was a seventeen-year-old member of Fianna Éireann. All of the dead were men; six of them were aged seventeen.[96]

On numerous occasions over the previous months, troops had battled huge crowds in Creggan against a backdrop of gunfire and bombs and had only occasionally killed people. On Bloody Sunday there was less violence from the crowd than there had been during many of these confrontations in Creggan and the Bogside. Thus, to many in Derry, the army appeared to have carried out a calculated massacre of unarmed rioters, deliberately escalating the conflict. As January 1972 ended, IRA units had killed nine soldiers and two RUC men in Derry, but no civilians. The British army had by now shot dead a total of two IRA men and nineteen unarmed Catholic civilians.

Thirteen of those civilians had been shot dead in mid-afternoon on the street in front of large crowds of people who could see that they were not armed. Many of those who witnessed the killings, and later testified that victims were unarmed, were respected local figures. It was in these circumstances that, as Ivan Cooper put it, 'moderate young men'[97] and women joined the IRA in large numbers. Among them would be the sons and daughters of senior members of the Creggan and Foyle Hill tenants' associations and of the DCAC and the DCDA. By March 1972, about twenty young women were active members of the Derry Official IRA, although usually restricted to secondary roles. According to one of them '[before Bloody Sunday] we thought the army [i.e., the IRA] was too risky, but then after Bloody Sunday you didn't care if it was risky or not, you were going to be shot anyway so you might as well be shot for something as for nothing'.[98] Apart from those who responded in this way, there were many other moderate people in Derry, both young and old, who, while supporting the SDLP, were now just as alienated from and hostile to the British government and army as Republicans were. Hostility to the state and a contempt for official definitions of law and order transcended the political divisions between Catholic moderates and militants. The IRA was extreme now only in the methods it was prepared to use, rather than in its rejection of the legitimacy of the state itself.

Although many would continue to reject the IRA, McCann suggests that the 'understanding' that 'turning to the gun was an understandable response ... was shared by many – quite likely the majority – who, nevertheless wished for a different, non-violent response'.[99] The methods of the IRA might be rejected, but those hundreds of young Derry Catholics who joined the IRA would not be rejected by the Catholic community. The distance which many of the cautious and conservative Nationalists had travelled over the previous two years is illustrated by an interview with Eddie McAteer in the highly emotional atmosphere which followed Bloody Sunday. Speaking of the IRA, McAteer said '... the lads who have been reviled as murderers, thugs, terrorists, etc. etc., will be seen for what they are, as genuine freedom fighters doing their best with the limited weapons at their disposal'. Of rioting youths, whom the Nationalists had strongly condemned until late 1970, he said 'They do their small part and a lot of their young lives have been wrecked and at least they deserve a word of thanks. At least they fought their own way for Ireland with whatever lay at hand.'[100]

Figures are not available for the number of people from Derry who were imprisoned for IRA activities but the suggestion by the Provisional IRA in 1986 that between 8,000 and 10,000 of their members have been imprisoned[101] suggests that anything up to 1,000 people from Derry have been interned or jailed for Provisional IRA activities alone.[102] The scale of participation in the IRA in this relatively small provincial town with a Catholic population of about 50,000 in the 1970s emphasises that the militant Republican tradition was no longer in any way marginal to the Catholic community in Derry.

While there are no detailed figures available for the total number from Derry, there are snapshots which give us an idea of the scale of involvement. In January 1975, over sixty people from Derry city were in the internment camp at Long Kesh.[103] In 1978, seventy-six people from Derry were serving prison sentences for Republican paramilitary activities.[104] No more than six of these were among those who had been in Long Kesh in January 1975. By the late 1980s, thirty-nine Provisional IRA members in the city had been 'killed in action'.[105]

As late as July 1971, the Provisional and Official IRAs in Derry had still been relatively minor and marginal organisations seeking urgently to expand their bases. After internment, and particularly after Bloody Sunday, they became mass organisations presenting a major challenge to the authority of Catholic moderates. Eventually, in the early 1980s as Provisional Sinn Féin began to contest elections, it became clear that it was a strong mainstream element in the Catholic community.

The development of a marginal conspiratorial movement into a mainstream part of Catholic politics was made possible only by the responses of the British government and army in July and August 1971, which signalled that Catholic dissent would be repressed, not addressed and that, to avoid antagonising the Protestant majority, major changes in the way the state was policed and governed would not be made. Prior to July 1971, the army still had a friendly relationship with some sections of the Catholic community in Derry. After July, that relationship ended. Moderates in the DCCC had always negotiated with the army on the basis of army recognition of Catholic moderates as an alternative source of authority and of army tolerance of a certain degree of autonomy in the Bogside and Creggan. After internment, the army began to operate a military solution which culminated in Operation Motorman in July 1972 when the barricades around Free Derry were finally dismantled. Although the British government had prorogued the Stormont parliament in March 1972 and instituted direct rule of Northern Ireland from London, by then the British government and army had become as much the objects of hostility as the Unionist government had been before.

In retaliation for Bloody Sunday, the Official IRA planted a bomb in the Officers' Mess at the Parachute Regiment's headquarters at Aldershot in England aiming to kill large numbers of soldiers. Instead, it killed five cleaning women, an army chaplain and a gardener. It was one of the first IRA attacks in Great Britain and over the following years, although the Officials called a halt to their military campaign, the Provisional IRA would plant innumerable bombs both in Britain and in Northern Ireland, many of which killed large numbers of civilians. Nonetheless, the IRA campaign would retain widespread support among Northern Catholics, in large part because of the experiences of the first few years of the conflict. One of the largest death tolls inflicted during the conflict was on Bloody Friday in Belfast in July 1972, when the Provisional IRA set off twenty-six bombs in the city centre killing nine civilians and two British soldiers. Bloody Friday increased pressure on the British army to take 'decisive action' against the IRA, and Operation Motorman in which the British army occupied the former no-go areas in Belfast and Derry, was launched shortly after this.[106] On the day of Operation Motorman, IRA members left three car bombs in the main street of the village of Claudy, nine miles from Derry. They failed to give a warning in time. The bomb explosion killed nine civilians, including a young girl.

In the course of 1972, sixty-two people were killed in the conflict in Derry and in a couple of nearby villages with strong links to the city. The two IRAs killed seventeen British soldiers, one of them a local youth on leave from the army. They also killed two RUC men and three UDR men, two of them off duty. Two IRA members were killed by their own bomb. The British army killed seventeen Catholic civilians – fourteen of them on Bloody Sunday. They killed six IRA members. Loyalists killed five civilians, four Catholics and a Protestant, in an attack on a bar. In addition, nine civilians, five Protestants and four Catholics, were killed in the IRA bomb attack in Claudy.[107]

By 1976, violence had declined considerably and the pattern had changed dramatically. In that year, eighteen people died in Derry city and nearby villages. Only one person, a Catholic civilian, was killed by the British army. Twelve people were killed by the IRA, four of them regular British soldiers. Four were local members of the security forces and one was a prison officer. In addition the IRA killed three civilians, one of them a Protestant. Four Catholic civilians were killed by loyalists, three of them in villages just outside the city. By this stage, many in the Catholic community had come to see the IRA as the principal aggressor in the conflict, while Loyalist killings had eclipsed killings by the security forces.[108] Despite this, hostility to the security forces and the state remained high even among Catholics who did not support the IRA.

After Operation Motorman in July 1972, the British army entered into a long-term military occupation of Creggan and the Bogside. After physically occupying these areas, the army began to operate through a system of population control and surveillance. Troops repeatedly carried out 'block searches' of entire streets, not making or intending to make arrests but gathering 'intelligence' about every household in the area and every member of those households.[109] Huge numbers of young men were regularly arrested and taken to army barracks for questioning – not in connection with any offence, but simply in order to gather information and build up a political profile of virtually every person living in the occupied areas.[110] The army patrols that constantly patrolled and searched these estates 'treated the population like dirt', as an SDLP councillor put it.[111] The army began to control Catholic areas simply by collecting information about and monitoring almost every single person in these areas.[112]

After Operation Motorman, Creggan Estate was flooded with troops who established a new base at 'Piggery Ridge' above Creggan and controlled the estate with house-searches, patrols, vehicle checkpoints, and overt and covert observation posts around the estate. One battalion operating in Creggan Estate in 1973 set up no fewer than nineteen covert observation posts hidden in the roofs of houses and flats. By the end of their tour, twelve of these posts were still 'un-compromised', that is, locals had never known they existed. This was done, as the chronicler of this regiment put it, 'to help dominate the estate'.[113] Despite the scale of the military presence, there was regular large-scale street rioting and gun and bomb attacks on the troops until the mid-1970s, and both Creggan and the Bogside continued to be ferocious battlegrounds for years after the barricades had been removed.[114]

A British army journalist reporting from Creggan in 1974 wrote that '... every man, woman and child seem to object to the presence of the army' and that 'friendly contact with the local people is virtually non-existent'.[115] That the same writer could then say the troops were 'helping to make a solution possible by doing their "bit" ', indicated what that solution was, that is, the successful 'domination' of Catholic areas. After four or five years of 'domination', through house-searches, screening arrests and covert observation posts, it was, in military terms, a considerable success. By 1978, Creggan and the Bogside had been to a great extent 'pacified' and brought back under the control of the state by sheer military effort, which had utterly exhausted the opposing 'army'.

By this time, it seemed to many in Creggan that 'the war was over' and an American journalist in Creggan described the Troubles almost as a thing of the past.[116] But incredibly, in 1978 there were more armed security force members operating in Northern Ireland than there had ever been before, more even than at the height of the conflict in 1972.[117] In the early 1970s, there were about 100,000 Catholic households in public housing in Northern Ireland, those most likely to have their houses searched. Between 1971 and 1979, the British army and the RUC carried out 308,000 recorded house-searches in the North.[118] The reality was not that 'the war was over' but that many areas of Northern Ireland were now under permanent military occupation and surveillance. It would require almost as many armed security forces in the 1990s to simply maintain the state as it had done in 1972 to smash the barricades and forcibly occupy 'no-go' areas like Free Derry.

The British army and the British government looked at the effects of 'domination' and 'control' in terms of the steady decrease in killings and bombings. By 1978, the idea of 'an acceptable level of violence' first mooted by Reginald Maudling, grew in popularity. Writers such as Barry White suggested that that level had effectively been reached with violence now contained in certain 'enclaves'. He suggested the British government take no further initiatives but continue to run things as they were now doing, 'based on the will of the majority'.[119] That is, the will of the majority would be implemented through the permanent coercion of the minority.

Such optimistic analyses of the situation were based on a wilful underestimation of the extent to which both 'extremist' and moderate Catholics, particularly in places such as Derry, had been comprehensively alienated from the Northern Ireland state.

Huge sections of the Catholic population regarded the state and its security forces as alien and hostile, as an enemy. The solution based on domination had served only to reinforce these views. Those Catholics who did not regard the state as alien or hostile nonetheless felt no allegiance to it. While many Catholics developed a strong loyalty to an alternative state – a united Irish Republic yet to be created – many others, who did not, rejected utterly the existing state. Into the 1980s and the 1990s, many commentators continued to misconstrue the division between Catholic moderates and 'extremists' on the issue of violence as an acceptance by Catholic moderates that the solution to the conflict rested with the ending of the IRA campaign, by repression, and the marginalisation of the Provisional Republicans and their supporters. It underestimated the extent to which moderates could not endorse repression by a state they felt no loyalty to, of a Republican movement which was supported by huge numbers of people in the community they belonged to. It also ignored the fact that such Catholic moderates had long ago ceased to accept that the British army was a peace-keeping force or the British government a neutral arbiter.

Protestants and the city

After the British army came onto the streets in Derry in August 1969, the Protestant community became to an extent disassociated from the conflict in the city. After the initial sectarian clashes in which William King, a Protestant from the Fountain, died, conflict in the city was almost exclusively between the British army and sections of the Catholic community. The army took over control of security from the RUC and relations between the two forces were not good.[120] Because the RUC was not involved in dealing with rioting in Catholic areas, no section of the Protestant community had much access to information about what was going on in Catholic areas. The fact that, in Derry, RUC and UDR men were initially seldom involved in conflict and were seldom the target of IRA attacks until late 1971 meant that Protestant loyalty focused on the 'Protestant' city centre which was being bombed, rather than on the 'local' Northern Irish security forces. While the army was seen to be taking 'tough' action and Protestants were not being killed, there was little impetus for loyalist paramilitary activity.

The first hints of loyalist paramilitary organisation in Derry surfaced in December 1971, by which time internment was clearly seen to have failed. In that month, the Association of Loyalist Workers (hereafter ALW or LAW as it soon became known) began to organise in local factories, some of which had mainly Protestant workforces.[121] This was partly a response to anti-internment strikes and was aimed to prevent or counter such strikes. It also reflected a strong desire among the Protestant working class to help maintain the state if the British lost the will to do so.

The LAW was a working-class initiative but it was intimately connected to the right wing of the Unionist party through the Vanguard organisation. Vanguard was set up at a meeting in the Apprentice Boys hall in Derry by William Craig on 27 January 1972.[122] It was a continuation of the moves by the autonomous right-wing local Unionist associations to move the party back to the right which had begun in response to the minor reforms in late 1968. Now, for the first time, these Unionists began to openly co-operate with groups that publicly defied the law.

Following a loyalist march in Derry organised by Vanguard and the DUP and backed by LAW in early June 1972,[123] barricades were set up in Protestant areas of Derry to put pressure on the British government to smash the Catholic no-go areas. It was a measure of the massively increased tolerance in Protestant areas for illegal action, justified on the grounds that the British government was not fulfilling its duties. However, it is notable that loyalist paramilitary activity in Derry began as a means to pressure the British government to take stronger military action against the Catholic community. Partly in response to this pressure, the British army smashed the no-go areas in Derry and Belfast in July 1972. However, it was some months after July 1972, when it became obvious that the massive 'Operation Motorman' had, like internment, signally failed to end the crisis and 'defeat' the IRA,[124] that loyalist paramilitaries in Derry began to take armed action.

Nelson has written that 'Protestants find extra-legal violence hard to justify. Belief in their respect for the law is a crucial means of distinguishing themselves morally and politically from Republicans.'[125] However, in recent years, Protestants in Derry, having experienced the loss of the Unionist corporation, had been forced to organise in their own interests. This organisation had strayed outside the law (in the building of protest barricades and the rejection of housing allocations made by statutory bodies). By 1972, there had been an erosion of Protestant allegiance to the law and order of the state. Barricades were erected, however, not in defiance of the state but to put pressure on the state to impose 'law and order' on Catholic areas. In December 1972, the UDA shot dead five people (four Catholics and one Protestant) in a random attack on a bar on the edge of a Catholic area of the Waterside. Such attacks were carried out in defence and support not necessarily of the existing state but of a more 'hard-line' state which loyalists were trying to create, through Vanguard and pressure within the Unionist party, which would decisively 'crush' Catholic resistance.

In recent years there has been debate as to whether loyalist violence is a 'response' to IRA violence. The fact that the first killing by loyalist paramilitaries in Derry did not take place until December 1972, over two years after the IRA campaign began, is significant. Extreme loyalists had harried and harassed civil rights marches from the first day of the civil rights campaign. Loyalists had planted bombs in early 1969 before any IRA bomb had been planted. They had opened fire during rioting in August and October 1969 and in August 1971. However, as late as November 1971, Neil Blaney could declare 'We are told that there will be a Unionist backlash. Where has it been in the past two years? Surely we must take things as we see them ... there will be no backlash now.'[126]

Bruce suggests that loyalist paramilitaries and Republicans were 'equally sectarian'.[127] The Provisional IRA killed hundreds of Protestant civilians in bomb attacks and sectarian assassinations. Nonetheless, most of the killings carried out by the IRA were of members of the security forces. In Derry, where loyalists carried out relatively few killings, and in Belfast where several hundred people were killed by loyalists, virtually all of these killings were deliberately aimed at uninvolved Catholic civilians.[128] Both in their actions and in their rhetoric, loyalist paramilitaries emphasised their hostility to Catholics as a group, often in racial terms, and regarded virtually all Catholic civilians as legitimate targets.

A writer in the Derry UDA paper *Ulster Defender* in 1973 condemned those who suggested that there were 'decent' Catholics and claimed that the vast majority of Catholics supported the Provisional IRA campaign. Another UDA writer, reflecting a popular racial stereotype, wrote that

'Ulster was built by Protestant industry. Ulster belongs to the people who made her prosper ... not to the parasites of Bogside, Creggan, Falls, Ballymurphy and other thieving criminals.'[129]

UDA writers also dealt happily in the currency of pure racism in a way which Republicans did not, complaining, for example, that 'slimy papist politicians slither across our TV screens' with their 'black bog-Irish faces'.[130] Burton noted a similar racist strain in loyalist attitudes in the early 1970s to 'Anro', a working-class Catholic neighbourhood in Belfast where the IRA was extremely active. Anro was 'variously referred to as "the septic boil", "the mau-mau jungle", "the cannibal village" and so on' in local loyalist broadsheets.[131]

Initially, the UDA had strong links through Vanguard with right-wing sections of the Unionist party and with the DUP, which in Derry in August 1972 was 'urging every able-bodied Loyalist ... to support the aims and objects of the Ulster Defence Association' and announcing that 'when the battle is over and done with, victory will be ours through the endeavours of the UDA'.[132] The DUP was particularly fond of bestial imagery, calling for the British government to 'authorise the mucking out of the Gobnascale byre'[133] and referring to IRA gunmen as 'vermin' in 'the sewers of the Bogside'.[134]

While the British government and army pointed to the existence of both Protestant and Catholic paramilitary groups as renewed evidence (after the débâcle of Bloody Sunday, which had called their neutrality into question) that they were acting as a neutral, peace-keeping force, the army and the state related to the two sets of paramilitaries in utterly different ways. As the first loyalist vigilante groups emerged, the Unionist government gave qualified approval to them.[135]

There was conflict between the troops and loyalists but it was a conflict which loyalists wanted to avoid and which arose, as they saw it, only because troops tried to suppress their activities, which, in loyalist terms, were carried out in support of the army. As the South Derry UDA put it in an open letter to a newly-arrived British regiment in 1973, asking them not to carry out searches in Protestant areas; 'Remember, we are your friends – unless you decide otherwise.'[136] Loyalist paramilitaries, however, were never a dominant factor in the conflict in Derry.

Paramilitary activity was only the most dramatic and visible sign of the changes in the Protestant community. The confused or often non-existent ideology of loyalist paramilitary groups[137] reflects the fact that groups such as LAW and the UDA were inspired by the fear induced by changes at local level rather than by any ideology. The Vanguard organisation, uniting right-wing Unionist party members and the UDA, demonstrates how the UDA did not seek to challenge the Unionist party but to work within it. Although LAW and the UDA were focuses for mass Protestant working-class action, they were essentially conservative responses to the collapse of the authority of the Stormont government. In many ways, they were impelled by the same factors which had seen tenants' associations set up in Protestant areas in Derry after the fall of the Unionist corporation – the need for the Protestant working class for the first time since the establishment of the state to look to new forms of organisation now that the Unionist party was failing in its primary goal of maintaining stability.

Prior to 1968, Derry was a city which symbolically and, to a great extent literally, belonged to Protestants.[138] In the city centre, the War Memorial, the Apprentice Boys hall, the Church of Ireland cathedral, the Protestant schools and halls, and of course the city walls encircling them, were all symbols associated with the Protestant community. Most Derry Protestants lived on the West Bank of the Foyle, the side on which the city centre was situated. Eight of the twelve Unionist councillors before 1969 were elected from the West Bank. There were Protestant public housing estates at the Glen, at Northland and at Belmont, north of the city boundary. Unionist councillors and Protestant professionals lived in middle-class estates along the Northland Road and north of the city along the Culmore Road. Protestants were in a majority in many parts of the West Bank.

In the years following the outbreak of conflict, there began a gradual drift of Protestants, first from Creggan and the Bogside, later from middle-class estates, which would drain virtually the entire Protestant population out of the West Bank and away from the city centre and the symbols of the Protestant city. This, combined with other developments, served to alienate Derry Protestants from the city itself in the same way that Catholics had once been alienated from the Unionist-controlled city and its symbols, and continued to be alienated from the state of Northern Ireland. In many ways, Derry Protestants felt that, in the course of the Troubles, 'their' city had been blown up, taken over and rebuilt as a different city, not a 'loyal' city, not even 'Londonderry' any more.

The way the Protestant community related to the city began to change in the first years of violence. Rioting in the city centre, in which Protestant business premises and buildings associated with the Protestant community such as churches or halls were damaged, marked the beginning of the physical assault on the 'Protestant' city centre. The establishment of the no-go areas shut off large areas of the city from the security forces and to a great extent from local Protestants. For many Protestants, it was 'terrible to think that there was a no-go area in our city'[139] particularly when those areas ran along the edge of the city centre.

When the IRA began to target city centre businesses, which were almost invariably Protestant, in early 1971, it seemed like an extension of, or a variation on, the riots which had brought destruction to the city centre. It was the city centre which both the RUC and the army had always sought to protect when they cordoned off the Bogside during the earlier riots. Protestants in Derry saw the IRA campaign of the very early 1970s, not in terms of seeking a united Ireland, nor even of sectarian warfare nor yet of attacking Britain, but above all in terms of destroying the city. Protestants felt that they were 'just watching' as Derry was 'burning to the ground',[140] and that the IRA were 'making a burnt out barbecue of our town'.[141] Many Protestants felt that the IRA and the rioters, and ultimately, the Catholic community as a whole, were seeking to 'destroy' the city. DUP activist Gregory Campbell, for example, felt that the civil rights protesters who marched on Bloody Sunday should not be permitted to march out of the 'no-go' area and into the city centre because 'they had no right to march in a city which they wanted to destroy'.[142]

To an extent, Unionism and Protestant political sentiment began to focus on the 'Protestant' city centre and the city centre traders became a strong political voice. After internment, right-wing Unionists suggested that loyalists should prepare, within the law, 'to assist actively the security forces in a war in which there could be no place for passive spectators', as Unionist MP James Molyneaux put it.[143] Protestant city centre traders in Derry said they might need a 'vigilante force' to protect their premises.[144] The Derry Unionists, asking why the army had not protected traders from 'intimidation' during the one-day anti-internment strike, said that if it were to happen again they would support a 'Defence Association' for city centre business owners.[145]

Prior to the Bloody Sunday march, the Commander Land Forces, Major General Ford, met with the Strand Road Traders' Association in Derry, and Hamill cites their complaints on security as evidence of a 'climate of opinion' which would support 'teaching a lesson' to local rioters.[146] To a great extent, these business owners were now core representatives of local Unionist opinion. In these early years, before IRA attacks on the RUC and UDR began in earnest, the 'Protestant' city centre became a focus for Protestant loyalty in Derry and attacks on these businesses were seen as sectarian and deliberately directed against

Protestants.[147] When the chairman of the Alliance party in Derry, Dr Joe Cosgrove, a Catholic, said Derry could be proud of its shops and called on all Derry people to do their Christmas shopping in Derry in December 1971, it was part of a debate with strong political implications.[148]

Catholics did not feel the same loyalty to the city centre as Protestants did, neither to the mostly Protestant-owned shops nor to the historic buildings or the city walls. Eamonn McCann recounts how 'a supporter of Mr Hume', looking at the city hall in Derry shortly after the Provisional IRA had blown up the inside of it, remarked, 'Of course I don't agree with this bombing at all but I must admit, the Guildhall's looking well.'[149] This illustrates the sense that the city itself, the buildings, were representative of Unionist power. As the Alliance party was urging people to shop in Derry city centre at Christmas 1971, the *Derry Journal* by contrast was printing a Co. Donegal Christmas shopping guide supplement for the first time.[150]

As the commercial centre of Derry was blown up systematically and the city became a dark bleak place, Catholics turned to the towns and villages just over the border in Donegal. In a direct reversal of the usual pattern, people from this provincial city began to travel in large numbers to outlying towns up to twenty-five miles away for a huge variety of reasons. Above all, the social life of huge sections of the Catholic community in Derry began to take place on the other side of the international border. There had been a longstanding pattern of both Catholics and Protestants from Derry crossing the border to go to the beach or play the slot machines, or belonging to golf clubs or having caravans in Donegal. However, with virtually every dance-hall or disco bombed in Derry, buses, taxis and cars began to ferry thousands of teenagers out to discos and bars in Moville, Buncrana and even twenty-five miles away to Letterkenny every Friday, Saturday and Sunday night. The social life of the vast majority of young Catholics was being conducted on the other side of the border, a situation which was reversed only in the late 1980s as new discos and nightclubs were opened in Derry.[151]

If the bombing campaign physically obliterated much of the city which Protestants had identified with, most famously Walkers Pillar, but equally importantly many old established Protestant businesses, it was the movement of population which really altered the way Protestants related to the city. In the twenty years after the Troubles began, the vast majority of Protestants living on the West Bank of Derry left it. This movement was utterly different from the drastic movement of population which occurred in Belfast. Although there were some cases of intimidation, the vast majority of those who moved had not experienced either threats or violence.

The first large-scale movement of Protestants out of Catholic areas of Derry took place after internment in August 1971 and resulted primarily from the chaotic violence and the absence of the forces of law and order rather than from intimidation. Prior to August 1971, cases of Protestant families intimidated out of Creggan or the Bogside had been few and far between.[152]

In the days after internment, Protestant families began to leave the 'no-go' areas. The largest single movement recorded in the local newspapers was that of thirteen Protestant families who moved out of streets in the Long Tower area. There had been shouts in the street at night for Protestants to 'get out or be burnt out' but there was no reported physical violence.[153] The DUA (forerunner of the DUP) was involved in providing transport for some of the families who left the no-go areas at this time.[154] These families then squatted in houses on the Waterside and at Academy Road on the West Bank – an area which was mostly Catholic but outside the 'no-go' area. In the months after this, the Democratic Unionist Association in Derry actively took up the cases of others who wanted to leave the no-go areas arguing '... no person can be expected to live in an area where the Queen's writ does not run'.[155]

By March 1972, there were still many Protestants living in the 'no-go' areas and the DUA had taken up the cases with the Northern Ireland Housing Trust of forty-three families who wanted to be housed in other areas. The DUA complained that Protestants in the 'no-go' areas had to stop work and show black flags after Bloody Sunday. They also complained that some Protestant men 'had been subject to interrogation by the lawless element'. Children wearing the uniform of a Protestant school had been attacked on the way to school and some now had to go to school in regular clothes.[156] There were no reports of sectarian petrol-bomb attacks or shooting incidents however.

Although it was from the no-go areas that Protestants fled initially, Protestants also began to leave areas on the West Bank where there was little or no violence and where Protestants were in a solid majority. There were a number of factors in this development, chief among them the beginning of Provisional IRA attacks in Derry in early 1972 on RUC and UDR members. Prior to internment, there had been little serious threat to the lives of RUC or UDR members in Derry. Up to then RUC men holidayed over the border in Co. Donegal with little fear.[157] There were UDR men living in Creggan and, as late as August 1971, in

Shantallow, which would become a strongly Republican area.[158] RUC men lived in all of the estates on the West Bank where Protestants lived and in the early 1970s the RUC made it known they could not guarantee their security in many parts of the West Bank of Derry.[159]

RUC members were not, however, ordered to move house and some were among the last to leave the West Bank. In 1982, there was still one RUC man living on the West Bank who was just about to move to the Waterside when he was shot dead by the Provisional IRA outside his local church while off duty. A significant factor in the movement of the Protestant population now was the slow exodus of RUC members (and, to a far lesser extent, UDR men, who tended to come from rural areas). Some RUC members were impelled to leave, having been threatened by receiving bullets in the post, and others by the killings of RUC or UDR men in areas on the West Bank such as Belmont. It is notable, however, that this was not a sudden dramatic movement but one which began in 1972 and ended in 1982. The fact that RUC members were leaving was only one factor in creating a 'crisis of confidence' among Protestants on the West Bank. The fact that secluded respectable middle-class estates along the Culmore and Northland Roads began to empty of Protestants had a great deal to do with the fear in the early 1970s that there would be a full-scale civil war. Protestants on the West Bank feared that 'there was going to be a takeover here',[160] that if any part of Northern Ireland became detached in the course of civil war, it would be the West Bank of Derry. For many Protestants who had not experienced intimidation or violence of any sort in their areas, 'the thing was to move'.[161]

There was a quite startling drift in population which was not a result of direct intimidation and violence. In one peaceful middle-class estate of about fifty houses, off the Culmore Road, only two Catholic families had lived there before the Troubles began. Although there was no significant intimidation, and the only violence in the area was occasional IRA attacks on a nearby army base, Protestant families gradually left the estate to live on the Waterside. By the early 1990s, there were only two Protestant families left on the estate.[162] The same process took place all over the West Bank as middle-class streets and estates far from the 'no-go' areas, some of which had been completely Protestant,[163] gradually became completely Catholic.

The public housing estates at the Glen and Northland, which had been overwhelmingly Protestant and strongly loyalist, gradually became more Catholic. As public housing became available, it was offered to Catholics, the vast majority of those on the housing waiting list. Catholics did not fear these estates as they did those on the Waterside, simply because they were effectively surrounded by Catholic areas, and loyalist paramilitary groups or youth gangs could not organise in such areas for very practical reasons.[164] Thus these estates were not 'protected' from Catholic 'infiltration' and in a city with a large Catholic majority which dominated the housing list, it was only a matter of time before they became notably less Protestant.

This process was accelerated in both working-class and middle-class areas by the fact that Protestants, looking for their first house, did not consider the West Bank. One Protestant solicitor with offices on the West Bank says that not once since the Troubles began has a young Protestant couple, buying their first house through him, decided to buy a house on the West Bank.[165] Many Derry Protestants abandoned the West Bank of the city as 'alien territory'[166] and with it, they also abandoned the city centre, the old walled city and some of the traditional Protestant institutions on the West Bank, including a number of churches.

In 1973, the first elections to the new Londonderry city council took place. The United Loyalist Group, a local alliance in Derry of the Unionist party, the DUP and Vanguard[167] took nine of the twenty-seven seats. Of these, three seats were on the West Bank. By 1993, Unionists of all varieties held only eight of the thirty seats and not one of these was on the West Bank.[168] In the Northland ward that covered most of those old middle-class areas which had been home to Unionist councillors, and included most of the old North ward (which had had a Protestant majority in 1967), the two Unionist candidates took only 8 per cent of the vote in 1993 (to the SDLP's 57 per cent and Sinn Féin's 23 per cent). Over two thirds of that Unionist vote went to an independent Unionist who had broken with the party because he had accepted the recent name-change of the city council to Derry City Council.[169]

The DUP suggested in the late 1980s that a separate Waterside council be set up covering all of the Derry City Council area except the West Bank of the city. It would have had a large Catholic minority. It represented a symbolic total abandonment of the West Bank of the city and 'lost' territory. The proposal would have symbolically abandoned the old city centre, the walls, the Cathedral and churches, the schools and halls, in perpetuity, to people on the West Bank. It showed how the city itself, even the historic loyalist centre, had ceased to be a focus for loyalty and that some Derry Protestants had come to totally reject the city itself and identified not with Derry as a whole, but only with the mostly (but by no means overwhelmingly) Protestant Waterside.

As new nightclubs and bars opened in the city centre and the social life of Derry city centre revived in the late 1980s and early 1990s, the Protestant community played little part in it. Many Protestant youths on the Waterside did not frequent the new clubs and bars on the city side.[170] The city centre, the civic life of the city, was alien to many of them and was dominated by the Catholic community.[171]

When Derry began to be rebuilt in the mid 1980s, those most heavily involved in it were Catholics like Paddy Doherty, head of the Inner-City Trust and one-time member of the DCAC and DCDA. Projects, such as the new Foyle Bridge, were associated with John Hume, now the Westminster MP for Foyle and an MEP. As Magee College expanded, promoted by, among others, Michael Canavan (formerly of the DCAC, the DCDA and the DCCC)[172] it drew ever more students from across the border, as did the technical college on the Strand Road. The new city identified solidly not with loyal Catholics reconciled to Northern Ireland, but with the very people who, in the early 1970s, had gradually turned against the state and rejected the possibility of a solution within its boundaries. The perception that the city had changed hands was confirmed when the taunt by Provisional Sinn Féin to 'Vote John Hume for a better Londonderry' was answered by the formal change of name from Londonderry City Council to Derry City Council in 1984.

Derry Protestants have regarded the killings of local UDR and RUC members as attacks on the Protestant community as a whole. In addition, the DUP has alleged that there was discrimination against Protestants in the city, primarily in the allocation of funds to the Waterside. However, it is not primarily because of atrocity or discrimination that Derry Protestants are alienated from the city and the city council. To a great extent, it is because of the sense that the Catholic community is in the ascendant, in public symbolism, in controlling the image and the development of the city, and in building ever-stronger links across the border, making Derry an Irish city in much the same way Unionists had long maintained it as a British city.[173] Their alienation is also based on the frustration of being in a permanent minority and mirrors the sense of alienation which Northern Catholics felt in Northern Ireland as a state.

One effect of this changed 'ownership' of the city was that the Provisional IRA in Derry virtually ceased bombing the commercial city centre from the mid-1980s onwards, mounting no more than a handful of symbolic attacks in the ten years before the August 1994 IRA cease-fire. What security remained in the city centre after the mid-1980s was designed to protect not the city but the troops and RUC members who patrolled it and a few buildings such as the courthouse, identified with the state security apparatus. In the late 1980s, all security fencing was removed from around the Guildhall, the headquarters of Derry City Council, while higher and stronger barriers were built around RUC stations and the courthouse. Although the Provisionals continued to carry out attacks, the city lost the grim sense of unresolved conflict that still existed in Belfast where the late 1980s saw a dramatic increase in sectarian killings by loyalist paramilitaries. A few years before the 1994 ceasefires, people were saying: 'the war is over [in Derry]'.[174]

Notes and references

1 LS, 21/7/71, p. 1.
2 LS, 7/7/71.
3 LS, 14/7/71, p. 1.
4 Eamonn McCann, *War and an Irish Town* (Penguin, Harmondsworth, 1974), p. 90.
5 Fr Denis Bradley in W. H. Van Voris, *Violence in Ulster. An Oral Documentary* (University of Massachusetts, 1975), p. 284, and *The Suppressed Report on the Derry Massacre*, article by *Sunday Times* journalists, Sayle and Humphrey, 3/2/72 (Organisation of Revolutionary Anarchists, London, November 1972) (pamphlet), p. 2. which suggests that two senior Belfast Provisionals came to Derry in June 1971 to 'organise the movement' in the city.
6 LS, 14/7/71, p. 1, p. 19, pp. 20–1.
7 DJ, 27/7/71, p. 1; LS, 28/7/71, p. 10. They gave testimony to an independent inquiry sponsored by the Socialist Research Council.
8 Patrick Bishop and Eamon Mallie, *The Provisional IRA* (Corgi, London, 1988), p. 183; McCann, *War*, pp. 89–90; Michael Farrell, *Northern Ireland: The Orange State* (Pluto, London, 1980), p. 280; Shane O Doherty, *The Volunteer. A Former IRA Man's True Story* (Fount, London, 1993), p. 94; Simon Winchester, *In Holy Terror: Reporting the Ulster Troubles* (Faber, London, 1974), p. 149.
9 LS, 14/7/71, p. 19.
10 LS, 21/7/71, p. 1; DJ 27/7/71, p. 1, reports of evidence at inquest.
11 Winchester, *In Holy Terror*, p. 149.
12 O'Doherty, *Volunteer*, p. 93; interview with Andy Barr, long-time resident of Derry.
13 LS, 14/7/71, p. 20.
14 Rupert Moss in I. Hamilton and R. Moss, *The Spreading Irish Conflict* (Conflict Studies, no. 17) (Institute for the Study of Conflict, London, 1971), p. 20, quoting British Labour party policician Roy Hattersley's remarks on another event.
15 LS, 21/7/71, p. 1.
16 LS, 14/7/71, p. 26.
17 LS, 14/7/71, pp. 20, 21, 26.
18 DJ, 27/7/71, p. 1. citing a named local witness.
19 DJ, 27/7/71, p. 1.
20 LS, 28/7/71, p. 20; DJ, 27/7/71, p. 1.
21 LS, 4/9/71, p. 15.

22 LS, 14/7/71, p. 21.
23 McCann, *War*, p. 90.
24 LS, 14/7/71, p. 21.
25 Barry White, *John Hume, Statesman of the Troubles* (Blackstaff Press, Belfast, 1984), p. 112.
26 SDLP Derry Branch minutes, 23/7/71.
27 McCann, *War*, p. 92; interview with John Carlin, member of the Republican movement in Derry from the mid-1960s and of the Provisional Republicans after the split. Former Sinn Féin election agent. Former internee.
28 DJ, 13/8/71, p. 11.
29 DJ, 10/8/71, p. 1.
30 LS, 11/8/71, p. 3.
31 IT, 11/8/71.
32 Raymond McClean, *The Road to Bloody Sunday* (Ward River Press, Dublin, 1983), p. 117.
33 DJ, 24/8/71, p. 1.
34 Farrell, *Orange State*, p. 283.
35 Interview with Willie O'Connell, formerly a senior member of the Independent Organisation, the DCDA and the DCCC. SDLP member of Derry City Council and former mayor of Derry.
36 McClean, *Bloody Sunday*, p. 120.
37 DJ, 10/8/71, p. 1.
38 See Compton Committee, *Report of the Enquiry into Allegations against the Security Forces of Physical Brutality in Northern Ireland arising out of Events on the 9th August, 1971*, Cmd. 4823 (HMSO, London, 1971).
39 LS, 25/8/71, p. 7.
40 Hume, interview, LS, 25/8/71.
41 White, *Statesman*, pp. 1–4.
42 DJ, 24/8/71, p. 1.
43 Des Hamill, *Pig in the Middle. The Army in Northern Ireland 1969–1985* (Methuen, London, 1986), p. 71.
44 Ibid., p. 70, citing an officer who was present; see also Winchester, *In Holy Terror*, p. 177 and LS, 1/9/71, p. 1.
45 LS, 1/9/71, p. 1.
46 LS, 1/9/71, p. 1.
47 DJ, 10/9/71, p. 11; DJ, 7/9/71, p. 1.
48 Eamonn McCann (with Bridie Harrigan and Maureen Shiels), *Bloody Sunday in Derry. What Really Happened* (Brandon, Kerry, 1992), p. 68.
49 Ibid., p. 59.
50 DJ, 7/9/71, p. 1.
51 DJ, 10/9/71, p. 5.
52 DJ, 10/9/71, p. 1.
53 DJ, 14/12/71, p. 14, evidence at the inquest.
54 DJ, 14/9/71, p. 6.
55 One of them was Hugh Herron, a former Republican active in the 1950s. He was not affiliated to any IRA faction. He was shot dead by British troops after opening fire on them with his own personal firearm (interview with Mitchel McLaughlin).
56 DJ, 10/9/71, p. 9.
57 DJ, 8/10/71, p. 6.

58 DJ, 14/9/71, p. 1.
59 DJ, 17/9/71, p. 1.
60 DJ, 14/9/71, p. 1.
61 DJ, 17/9/71, p. 5.
62 Ibid.
63 DJ, 10/12/71, p. 1.
64 DJ, 15/10/71, pp. 1, 9.
65 DJ, 9/11/71, pp. 1, 7.
66 DJ, 7/12/71, p. 1.
67 Ibid.
68 DJ, 7/12/71, p. 5.
69 DJ, 14/12/71, p. 6.
70 McCann, *War*, p. 97.
71 Interview with Terry Robson, chairman of Derry Labour Party Young Socialists in the early 1970s and member of the NILP executive. Member of the Official Republican movement from late 1971; McCann, *War*, p. 99.
72 McCann, *War*, p. 100.
73 DJ, 3/12/71, p. 1.
74 Robson, interview.
75 *Starry Plough*, no. 3, April 1972.
76 *Starry Plough*, no. 3, April 1972.
77 DJ, 12/11/71, p. 1 and 16/11/71, p. 5.
78 O'Doherty, *Volunteer*, p. 99.
79 Robson, interview.
80 Carlin, interview 2.
81 DJ, 10/12/71, p. 15.
82 Derek Dunne, 'MacGiolla's Guerillas', *In Dublin*, 1/10/87, p. 20.
83 As in DJ, 10/12/71, where they claim in a joint statement to have killed one British soldier and wounded others during an army incursion into Free Derry.
84 LS, 25/8/71, p. 21.
85 O'Doherty, *Volunteer*, p. 90.
86 *An Phoblacht*, vol. 3, no. 1, Jan, 1972.
87 *Starry Plough*, no. 2, March, 1972.
88 O'Doherty, *Volunteer*, p. 107.
89 Interview with Anon. D, former member of the Republican movement in Derry.
90 Paddy Doherty in Van Voris, *Violence*, p. 132.
91 Keenan in Van Voris, *Violence*, p. 294.
92 Paul Bew and Gordon Gillespie, *Northern Ireland. A chronology of the Troubles, 1968–1993* (Gill and Macmillan, Dublin, 1993), p. 39.
93 McCann, War, p. 109.
94 A ninth British soldier who was shot in 1971 died in early 1972.
95 Maria McGuire, *To Take Arms. A year in the Provisional IRA* (Macmillan, London, 1973), pp. 92–3.
96 See McCann, *Bloody Sunday*, for a detailed critique of the Widgery Report, the British government report which exonerated the soldiers who carried out these killings; McClean, *Bloody Sunday*, pp. 127–46; see also the Widgery Tribunal, *Report of the Tribunal Appointed to inquire into the Events of Sunday, 30th of January 1972, which led to Loss of Life in Connection with the Procession in Londonderry on that day*, HC 220 (HMSO, London, 1972).

97 Interview with Ivan Cooper, member of the Young Unionist party in Mid-Derry in the mid-1960s. Member of the Derry Labour party in the later-1960s. Former chairman of the DCAC. Former Independent and, later, SDLP MP at Stormont for Mid-Derry.

98 Women for Irish Freedom, *Irish Women Speak* (Women for Irish Freedom, Brooklyn, NY, 1973) (pamphlet), p. 25.

99 McCann, *Bloody Sunday*, p. 55.

100 McAteer in Van Voris, *Violence*, p. 15.

101 Bishop and Mallie, *IRA*, p. 112.

102 On the crude calculation that, as Derry has been the site of over 10 per cent of killings in Northern Ireland up to 1986 and the deaths of 10 per cent of IRA members who had died up to 1986, it is reasonable to assume that around 10 per cent of Provisional IRA prisoners came from Derry.

103 *Irish People*, 18/1/75.

104 H-Block Relatives, *The Heart of the Matter*, no place of publication (pamphlet), 1979.

105 DJ, 1/4/88.

106 Patrick Buckland, *A History of Northern Ireland* (Gill and Macmillan, Dublin, 1981), p. 160.

107 Malcolm Sutton, *Bear in Mind These Dead ... An Index of Deaths from the Conflict in Ireland* (Beyond the Pale Publications, Belfast, 1994).

108 Ibid.

109 Michael Barthorp, *Crater to the Creggan. The History of the Royal Anglian Regiment 1964–1974* (Leo Cooper, London, 1976), p. 117.

110 Robin Evelegh, *Peace Keeping in a Democratic Society. The Lessons of Northern Ireland* (C. Hurst and Co., London, 1978), p. 120.

111 Interview with Pat Devine, former DCAC steward, leader of the SDLP group on Derry City Council, former Mayor of Derry.

112 Paddy Hillyard, 'Law and Order', in John Darby (ed.), *Northern Ireland; the Background to the Conflict* (Appletree, Belfast, 1983), p. 37.

113 Barthorp, *Crater to the Creggan*, p. 118.

114 See Frank Burton, *The Politics of Legitimacy: Struggles in a Belfast Community* (Routledge and Kegan Paul, London, 1978) for a description of life in a Catholic working-class neighbourhood in Belfast in the months after Operation Motorman.

115 Unit Feature, 'On Top of the Creggan. 2nd Battalion the Queen's Regiment', in *Visor*, Serial no. 3, 14/3/1974.

116 Anthony Bailey, *Acts of Union. Reports on Ireland 1973–1979* (Faber and Faber, London, 1980), pp. 139–69.

117 Figures listed in Steve Bruce, *The Red Hand. Protestant Paramilitaries in Northern Ireland* (Oxford University Press, Oxford, 1992), p. 297.

118 Ronald Weitzer, *Policing Under Fire. Ethnic Conflict and Police-Community Relations in Northern Ireland* (SUNY Press, Albany, 1995), p. 131.

119 Barry White, 'From Conflict to Violence: the Re-emergence of the IRA and the Loyalist Response', in John Darby (ed.), *Northern Ireland; the Background to the Conflict* (Appletree, Belfast, 1983), p. 196.

120 Chris Ryder, *The RUC. A Force Under Fire* (Methuen, London, 1989), pp. 114, 120.

121 DJ, 17/12/71, p. 6.

122 Clifford Smyth, *Ian Paisley. Voice of Protestant Ulster* (Scottish Academic Press, Edinburgh, 1987), p. 34.

123 DJ, 1/6/72, p. 11.

124 David Barzilay, *The British Army in Ulster*, 4 volumes (Century Services, Belfast, 1973–81), vol. 1, 1973, p. 59.

125 Sarah Nelson, *Ulster's Uncertain Defenders. Protestant Political, Paramilitary and Community groups and the Northern Ireland Conflict* (Appletree, Belfast, 1984), p. 14.

126 DJ, 23/11/71, p. 5.

127 Bruce, *Red Hand*, pp. 56–8.

128 Sutton, *Index of Deaths*, pp. 195–206.

129 *Ulster Defender*, January 1973.

130 Ibid., February 1973.

131 Frank Burton, *Politics of Legitimacy*, p. 132.

132 *Londonderry Loyalist*, no. 12, August 1972, p. 6.

133 Ibid., no. 10, May 1972.

134 Ibid., no. 8, March 1972.

135 Bruce, *Red Hand*, pp. 47–8.

136 *The Ulster Defender*, May 1973.

137 See Bruce, *Red Hand*, pp. 226–8.

138 Seventy-five per cent of company votes in the city, based on business ownership, were held by Protestants – in a city which was only 33 per cent Protestant, DJ, 10/11/67. (Figures calculated by the Derry Catholic Registration Association.)

139 Interview with Jim Guy, Independent Unionist councillor, former mayor of Derry, former Ulster Unionist party councillor, former secretary and lieutenant-governor of the Apprentice Boys of Derry, former secretary and grand master of the City of Derry Grand Orange Lodge, former honorary secretary of Londonderry and Foyle Unionist Association.

140 Interview with Bertie Faulkner, former Alliance party member of Derry City Council, worked closely with tenants' associations on the Waterside.

141 Alliance party activist, Snoo Sinclair in DJ, 5/10/71, p. 6.

142 *Irish News*, 31/1/92, p. 9.

143 LS, 25/8/71, p. 3.

144 LS, 18/8/71, p. 1.

145 LS, 18/8/71, p. 4.

146 Hamill, *Pig in the Middle*, p. 88.

147 Cooper, interview; *Belfast Newsletter*, 2/3/93.

148 DJ, 17/12/71, p. 1.

149 McCann, *War*, p. 106.

150 DJ, 10/12/71.

151 In conversation with Carol-Ann Barr and Garbhan Downey.

152 DJ, and LS, October 1968–August 1971, *passim*.

153 LS, 25/8/71, p. 6.

154 Interview 2 with Gregory Campbell leader of DUP group on Derry City Council; DUP activist since the early 1970s, member of the Young Unionists in the early 1970s.

155 *Londonderry Loyalist*, no. 8, March 1972.

156 Ibid.

157 Interview with Anon. C, long-time resident of Derry.

158 DJ, 14/9/71, p. 2.

159 Interview with Anna Huey, long-time resident of the West Bank of Derry.

160 Ibid.

161 Ibid.

162 Ibid.

163 Such as Crawford Square, interview with Claude Wilton, Ulster Liberal party candidate for City of Londonderry seat in 1965 and 1969. Former Chairman of the DCAC and of the SDLP, former Northern Ireland Senator for the SDLP and Solicitor.

164 Interview with Peter Simpson, former Secretary of the Wapping Lane Community Association (which included the Fountain estate) and head of its security sub-committee in the early 1970s.

165 Wilton, interview.

166 Gregory Campbell in *Irish News*, 19/8/93.

167 Interview with Marlene Jefferson, former Ulster Unionist Party councillor and mayor of Derry; worked closely with the Wapping Lane Community Association in the Fountain; Campbell, interview 2.

168 LS, 6/6/73, DJ, 21/5/93, p. 6.

169 DJ, 21/5/93, p. 6.

170 Faulkner, interview.

171 See Desmond Bell, *Acts of Union. Youth Culture and Sectarianism in Northern Ireland* (Macmillan, London, 1990).

172 Interview with Michael Canavan, founder member of the Derry Credit Union, formerly a senior member of the DCAC, the DCDA, the DCCC and the Independent Organisation; former SDLP assembly member.

173 See interview with Gregory Campbell in DJ, 30/7/93.

174 A remark made by both an SDLP and a former Alliance party activist in Derry. A rich source of information relating to sectarianism and segregation in Derry are the publications produced by Templegrove Action Research Limited. They include; Dave Duggan, *A Report of a Public Hearing on The Experiences of Minorities in Derry Londonderry* (Templegrove Action Research Ltd, Derry Londonderry, 1996); Ruth Moore and Marie Smyth, *A Report of a Series of Public Discussions on Aspects of Sectarian Division in Derry Londonderry held in the period December 1994–June 1995*, Templegrove Action Research Ltd, Derry Londonderry, 1996); Marie Smyth, *Life in Two Enclave Areas in Northern Ireland: A Field Survey in Gobnascale and The Fountain, Derry Londonderry After the Ceasefires* (Templegrove Action Research Ltd, Derry Londonderry, 1996); Marie Smyth (in collaboration with Ruth Moore), *Three Conference Papers on Aspects of Sectarian Division: Researching Sectarianism, Borders within Borders, The Capacity for Citizenship* (Templegrove Action Research Ltd, Derry Londonderry, 1996); Marie Smyth and Ruth Moore, *Two Policy Papers: Policing and Sectarian Division in Derry Londonderry and Urban Regeneration and Sectarian Division* (Templegrove Action Research Ltd, Derry Londonderry, 1996).

...y Sunday in Context

The first edition of this book didn't deal with Bloody Sunday at length. The events of the day had been dealt with in detail elsewhere, most notably in Eamonn McCann's *Bloody Sunday in Derry: What Really Happened*, in which he made a devastating critique of the Widgery report.[1] It didn't seem necessary to add to that. But although Bloody Sunday was only dealt with briefly it was in a sense what the book was all about. How had violence gradually escalated to the point at which 13 unarmed civilians could be shot dead by British soldiers in Derry in the middle of a Sunday afternoon?

The Bloody Sunday Inquiry established in 1998 under Lord Saville has generated fresh debates about the context within which the events of that day should be understood. Those concerned to defend the actions of the army have emphasised the context of intense IRA activity in the months preceding Bloody Sunday and the danger that 'the IRA were likely to exploit the situation' as General Sir Robert Ford, architect of the army operation on the day, put it.[2] They argue that it is understandable if mistakes were made in the intensely dangerous and unpredictable situation in which the army was operating that day.

Context is vital to understanding the events of the day, but in a much more complex way than is suggested by these arguments. This chapter focuses on one aspect of the escalating conflict in Derry between 1968 and 1972, which is particularly useful in contextualising army actions on Bloody Sunday: the well-established and extensive networks of communication and negotiation which had developed in the city as violence became endemic from late 1968 onwards, and the way in which these networks functioned in the approach to Bloody Sunday and on the day itself.

269

Well-established patterns of communication and negotiation

One of the most striking features of the early stages of conflict in Derry was the high level of contact and negotiation between the security forces and a wide range of forces in the Catholic community, including Republicans, before people became locked into a 'long war' and the very act of communication came to be seen as an act of treachery.

The aims of these communications and negotiations tended to be quite limited, and the line between mutual signalling of intentions and fully-fledged negotiations was often blurred. Arrangements to keep the peace were generally short-term and temporary, always subject to disruption if one side or the other decided it no longer suited its longer-term aims, and always limited by the fact that it was difficult for any party to talks to provide absolute guarantees about behaviour on their 'side'.

Negotiation and the exchange of messages about respective intentions were regularly used to reduce or avert violent confrontation from the beginning of the civil rights campaign in late 1968. The first civil rights march in Derry, on 5 October 1968, ended in widespread violence. Several weeks later, on 16 November, a massive march proceeded across Craigavon Bridge in Derry towards the city centre. The march had been banned from entering the city centre and there were fears of severe violence as the marchers came up against the police cordon enforcing the ban. The day passed off reasonably peacefully however.

A key factor in this was a secret agreement between some of those leading the march and the local RUC authorities. In the interests of avoiding violence, some of the civil rights leaders agreed to prevent marchers from breaching the barricade *en masse*. In return, the police agreed to allow a token breach by several individuals. They left open other routes into the centre, thus allowing the marchers to enter the city without breaching the police line. Those taking part in the march were not aware of the agreement and some prominent participants only learnt of the agreement some two decades later.[3]

Some months later, in April 1969, another agreement was made. As hundreds of RUC men took up positions at the edge of the Bogside after a period of intense rioting in the city, large numbers of people were evacuated from the area up to Creggan estate. People only returned to their homes after clergy brokered agreement under which the RUC agreed to withdraw. Once again, a major crisis had been averted through compromise arrangements.[4]

When British troops were deployed on the streets of Derry after major rioting in August 1969, the army agreed not to enter the Free Derry area, and remained outside the area for several weeks. During this period there was regular open communication and negotiation between the army and a range of forces in the Catholic community, including some of those who would go on to establish the Provisional IRA in the city. The willingness of army authorities to compromise in order to avoid confrontation was illustrated most dramatically by the incident in which the army organised for the exchange of an old Ulsterbus to take the place in a Rosemount barricade of a brand new Ulsterbus that had been hijacked.[5]

Under intense political pressure from Unionist politicians the army in turn gradually applied increasing pressure on the Free Derry negotiators. Catholic moderates and conservatives played a central role in ensuring that the barricades came down peacefully and security force patrols resumed.

Once again, a situation with the potential for catastrophic violence had been dealt with through negotiation, but here for the first time we see the importance of political pressure in ending arrangements that reduced violence by limiting security force activity.

Relations between the army and local Catholic youths soured over the following months and a series of gradually escalating mini-riots culminated in persistent major rioting in Derry in June 1970. Local moderates, conservatives and Official Republicans, though not the Provisionals, took part in negotiations with local army and RUC commanders. As a result of these talks, a major initiative was taken to reduce violence by reducing security force activity. For a two-week period, the army and RUC stayed out of the Bogside and Creggan while policing of the area was carried out by a coalition of local moderates and conservatives.[6]

After two weeks, during which there were no reported incidents, the army brought the agreement to an end. When the *Derry Journal* asked an army spokesman at Lisburn why the arrangements had been ended he reportedly replied, 'the army is subordinate to the Stormont government. We will fall in with their plans.'[7] There was no public suggestion that the arrangements had failed to reduce violence or that this was the principal reason they were ended.

In July and August 1971 there was a dramatic upsurge in violence in Derry and a full-scale 'shooting war' began. In the wake of Internment in August 1971, the army once again negotiated an agreement with moderate and conservative forces in the Catholic community aimed at reducing violence.

This local agreement was negotiated at an extraordinarily high level. The GOC, General Sir Harry Tuzo, head of the British army in Northern Ireland, and Howard Smith, the British Government Representative in Northern Ireland, were both involved. They were brought together with local Catholic moderates and conservatives by the local RUC and army commanders in Derry. This local agreement involved a direct British government input at a time when the Unionist government in Stormont was still officially in charge of security. General Tuzo agreed to end routine military patrolling in the city and to avoid taking any new military initiatives in order to give moderates a chance to use their influence to prevent violence. The *Londonderry Sentinel* described how an 'almost eerie' calm descended on the city after the agreement went into place and the relentless rioting of the past seven weeks petered out. There was no sign of army or RUC patrols from one end of the city to another.[8] The agreement was followed by a dramatic reduction in levels of violence in the city, but it did not bring it to a complete end.

Senior army figures describe the end of the August 1971 arrangements in terms of failure. Desmond Hamill, for example, quotes a staff officer apparently present at the meeting who says of the Catholic moderates 'of course they didn't deliver',[9] while General Ford has stated that 'the "low" profile of the security forces resulted in increased violence and IRA activity'.[10] For defenders of the army, the August agreement presents proof that the army had given conciliation a chance, that they had gone to extraordinary lengths to restore order by peaceful means, and that such approaches had failed.

Given the wider political context at the time, it is arguable that these arrangements, for all of their flaws, were actually a limited success. The arrangements did not bring a complete end to violence but they led to a significant reduction. Although the original agreement on 20 August stipulated that the arrangements would last for a month, the policy of not carrying out routine patrols in Creggan and the Bogside and not taking major military initiatives actually persisted until mid-November. When the army broke with this policy and launched a series of major operations in Free Derry in December 1971, they reverted to a policy of relative restraint within a few weeks.[11]

The August 1971 agreement represented continuity with an important and established strand in security force policy in Derry, attempting to avoid or reduce violence through communication and negotiation with forces in the Catholic community.

While it had not always proved possible to prevent violence, the agreements had all delivered short-term reductions in violence. They involved difficult compromises and were difficult to maintain, and on the security force side there was constant political pressure to end such arrangements. When they were ended it was because of a mixture of failings and political pressure, not simply because they did not work. These agreements were driven by a political preference for maintaining the support of Catholic moderates and negotiating reductions or modifications in security force activities to allow moderates to exert their influence to reduce violence. These agreements involved key individuals who were relied on and were part of a well-developed and informal network of communication, some of it secret, which linked the security forces to a wide range of forces within the Catholic community in Derry. This is not to argue that these arrangements were the key to securing peace in the city, merely that this approach was a well-established strand in army and RUC policy in Derry, enjoying support at the highest political levels. While agreements were flawed the army nonetheless knew that they could deliver reductions in violence and that certain channels of communication were reliable.

Central to this established practice of negotiation and compromise in the interests of limiting violence was Chief Superintendent Frank Lagan, the RUC commander in Derry. The British army had regularly relied on these networks and had made agreements through them. In the approach to Bloody Sunday, Frank Lagan made desperate attempts to once again avert confrontation through those networks.

Frank Lagan's network

In late 1969, the RUC was subject to major reform and a large swathe of senior personnel were removed. As part of this process, Frank Lagan, a Catholic from Co. Derry, took over command of the RUC in Derry. Lagan's appointment seems to have been a central element in the reform of the RUC, aimed specifically at rebuilding relationships in Derry where the RUC had been comprehensively rejected by even the most moderate and conservative forces in the Catholic community. His deputy, Superintendent Patrick McCullagh, testified at the Bloody Sunday Inquiry that Lagan 'was trying to start a new sort of policing ... He was trying to bring in an inclusiveness in policing which other people clearly resented.'[12] According to Brendan Duddy, a key figure who became involved in intensive and secret contact with Lagan, Lagan had been 'placed to make it easy to develop ... contact'.[13]

To this end Lagan and McCullagh made themselves available to a wide range of forces within the Catholic community. As McCullagh put it,

'Mr. Lagan and I both, therefore, opened our doors to anyone that wanted to see us, at any time, and indeed they did come to see us.'[14] McCullagh's testimony gives a flavour of the kind of things people would contact them about: 'people complaining of rudeness, people complaining of being stopped unnecessarily, people complaining of being searched unnecessarily and it went through to people complaining of being assaulted and, at the other end, people being killed by the Army'.[15] They developed extensive contacts with a wide range of forces in the Catholic community in Derry, and built up strong relationships of trust in several cases.

We are provided with a glimpse of the nature of the relationships they developed in McCullagh's description of some of the phone calls he received in the immediate aftermath of Bloody Sunday. Shortly after the shootings by the Parachute Regiment, Dr Thomas McCabe phoned McCullagh asking for safe passage to the Rossville Flats to treat people there who had been injured. He provided the licence-plate number and other details about his car. In the space of ten minutes McCullagh had contacted the army, asked that relevant army units be notified of the car details and had phoned McCabe back to let him know this had been done. A short time later Father Anthony Mulvey phoned to say that the Paras should be removed from the Rossville Flats area and McCullagh phoned Lagan to pass the message on. It provides a glimpse of the kind of things people felt they could ask, and the way in which Lagan and McCullagh were used to responding to these kinds of requests.[16]

Further illustration of the way in which Lagan's network operated, and a hint of the extent of the internal struggles he faced, is provided in the account of an Official Republican about an incident in late 1975 or early 1976, shortly before Lagan retired. When the wife of an Official Republican who had been arrested was refused permission at Strand Road barracks to visit her husband, the senior Republican who was accompanying her phoned a Republican activist who gave him Brigid Bond's number. Bond was a prominent Civil Rights activist in Derry who had strong links to the Official Republicans. She played a central role in altering the route of the civil rights march on Bloody Sunday. He was told that Bond would be able to ensure that the arrested man's wife would get the visit she was entitled to because of Bond's contact with Frank Lagan. When he phoned Bond she said 'leave it with me' and when he phoned back 10 or 15 minutes later she said that they would now be allowed in. But when they returned to the gate, a Special Branch member overrode the instructions the RUC officer on the gate had received and they were refused entry again. When the Official

Republican phoned Bond to tell her this she phoned Lagan again. When they returned to the gates, the wife of the prisoner was finally allowed in to visit. The Official Republican understood that Lagan had threatened the officer on duty that he himself would come down to the gate to ensure that his order was followed if entry was refused again.[17]

Lagan's network was part of an approach to the conflict which fitted well with British support for reform in late 1969 and early 1970, but which was at odds with the Stormont government approach of increasing repression, increasingly supported by a newly-elected Conservative government in Britain from the summer of 1970. The conciliatory approach was also strongly opposed by senior figures in the British army. Lagan's deputy, McCullagh, has stated that both he and Lagan were 'disappointed' that Internment was brought in and that it 'substantially set back' their plans.[18] When the Unionist government re-armed the RUC, Lagan continued to send his officers on to the streets of Derry unarmed in the hope that this would be taken as a sign of good intent.[19] By late 1971, Lagan's approach was clearly at odds with the dominant thrust of security policy and throughout this period Lagan was 'fighting a serious internal battle'.[20] But Lagan was by no means on his own. He 'was being encouraged to do what he was doing' and he was 'utterly protected' for much of his tenure in Derry by senior British public servants who Brendan Duddy describes as 'the cutting edge of British diplomacy'.[21] As Duddy put it, 'Lagan's power didn't come from Derry.' It did not derive only from his formal position as head of the RUC in the city, but from a brief to rebuild relationships which was sanctioned by 'senior British personnel whose task was to report directly back to the British government'.[22] The policy of conciliation and negotiation which Lagan was following, was a persistent and powerful strand in British policy in the North.

Lagan, MacLellan and Ford

Much debate around the Bloody Sunday Inquiry has centred on shifting British army and government policy in the six months prior to Bloody Sunday. The central question for critics of the army is whether the evidence suggests that Bloody Sunday is consistent with a new aggressive policy in Derry, a break with the previous approach. To acknowledge differences about the appropriate approach on the day is to acknowledge, firstly, that there was another choice, another way to behave on the day that leadership was aware of and that they chose an appro⸱ more confrontational than necessary. It strengthens the case that in certain important senses, deliberately directed at the highest levels, even if no direct orders to kill civilians were given. For those central to the Bloody Sunday planning, in particular General Sir Robert Ford, it has been important to present army action on the day as consistent with established trends in army policy, not as a new and extraordinary initiative, and not a source of major policy differences within the army.

Since Frank Lagan made determined efforts to prevent a major confrontation from taking place on the day, it has been important for some of those defending army action on the day to present him as a figure that the military could reasonably be expected to marginalise and ignore.

Contemporary documents written by General Ford and the statement he made to the Inquiry suggest that Lagan was not the kind of figure the army could be expected to put its faith in. In a much-quoted 'personal and confidential' memo to the GOC, Sir Harry Tuzo, on 'The situation in Londonderry as at 7th January 1972', General Ford wrote that 'I was disturbed by the attitude of both the Brigade Commander [Brigadier Pat MacLellan] and the Battalion Commander, and also, of course, by Chief Superintendent Lagan.' In his statement to the Bloody Sunday Inquiry, General Ford explained his attitude to Lagan by saying that 'Insofar as Chief Superintendent Lagan was concerned I was aware that the GOC did not have confidence in him. My own impression ... was that the Chief Superintendent was depressed and pessimistic' and that 'there was a feeling that he was closely identified with the Bogside community'.[23]

Lagan's extensive connections were spread widely across the city and he was particularly well connected to Catholic conservative and moderate forces. It is a range of connections that does not seem well covered by the term 'Bogside community' until you realise that this is of course a euphemism for Derry Catholics and that Ford seems to have regarded this in itself as a problem.

One of the clearest statements of this negative view of Lagan is provided in a letter which Brigadier Pat MacLellan, the commander of British troops in Derry, sent to Ford after Lagan had testified to the Widgery Tribunal in 1972: 'His sympathies, not unnaturally, lie entirely with the Catholic Community and he makes no secret of his contempt for Stormont policies ... His attitudes have hardened during the last six months with that of the Catholic Community and this has led him to allow his emotions to influence his professional conduct.'[24]

Although Frank Lagan was the most senior police officer in the city and would therefore be expected to have a central role in planning for the civil rights march, the argument goes, the army did not have faith in him because he had allowed his professional judgement to be clouded by the fact that he was a Catholic and was unduly sympathetic to the concerns of the Catholic community. This provides much of the explanation as to why he should be so sidelined in these preparations and his advice rejected.

But the military leadership in Derry had relied heavily on Chief Superintendent Lagan in the approach to Bloody Sunday, and even on the day itself when he was a key source of intelligence about the march. Virtually all of MacLellan's statements about army policy in 1971 and 1972, including those in relation to the Bloody Sunday march, place him far closer to Lagan than to General Ford. MacLellan repeatedly emphasised the need for restraint and the need to avoid alienating moderate Catholics. In his statement, for example, he says 'It was imperative ... that the army acted honourably and, in our pursuit of the IRA, do everything we could to avoid alienating people.'[25]

In addition, there is ample evidence that MacLellan and Lagan had an excellent working relationship. MacLellan himself said in evidence to the Inquiry, 'My relationships with Mr. Lagan at this stage were good, I think. I trusted him and I understood he was in an extremely difficult position, but his advice he gave me was balanced and good, I thought.'[26] Brendan Duddy recalls that 'On numerous occasions that I made a request to Lagan, Lagan would say to me, "I'll talk to MacLellan." '[27] Colonel Roy Jackson, who from August 1970 until October 1971 chaired the Londonderry Security Committee which was central to the shaping of army policy in the city, stated that Lagan 'gave me unstinting support. He was ... a fountain of information, knowing whom to contact should a difficulty be foreseen ... His was an unenviable task, but his advice always demanded respect.'[28] It appears that this reliance on Lagan was at the heart of Ford's discontent with the army command in Derry. Ford stated in his evidence to the Bloody Sunday Inquiry that MacLellan 'had initially, understandably, accepted the situation as it was' in Derry when he took over command in October 1971.[29] This was a situation in which Lagan was a major source of information about the Catholic community and in which he actively promoted a policy of conciliation. Lagan attracted such disquiet not because he was marginal but because he was central to security policy in the city.

Criticism of Lagan has represented his professional position and strong connections to the Catholic community as in some sense contradictory, but this is a false contradiction. The army relied on Lagan not despite, but precisely because of, these strong connections to the Catholic community. When we consider together Lagan's central role in

shaping army policy in Derry, his key involvement in negotiated compromises, and his extensive network of contacts we get a picture of
Lagan not as a marginal individual but as a key driver of a policy
approach in Derry which powerful figures in Stormont and in the British
army wished to bring an end to.

Secret negotiations and communication around Bloody Sunday

Many of Frank Lagan's contacts were public but a number of them were
surrounded by intense secrecy. For example, even thirty years after
Bloody Sunday, and after she had died, Lagan did not publicly name
Brigid Bond as his key contact within NICRA in his statement to the
Bloody Sunday Inquiry.

Among the most intensive and secretive contacts Lagan was involved
in were those with Brendan Duddy, a local Catholic businessman and
political activist. More than thirty years later, Duddy spoke on the record
about these contacts for the first time. His evidence adds considerably to
our understanding of the way in which these networks worked in the
approach to Bloody Sunday, and of the way in which they were used in
desperate attempts to prevent a major confrontation on the day.

Duddy had been associated with the radical left in the early stages of
the civil rights campaign and was immersed in the intense political
debate and activity surrounding the campaign. He also had longstanding relationships with prominent Nationalist party politicians, such as
James Doherty, and was strongly connected to leading SDLP figures,
such as John Hume and Ivan Cooper, although he opposed Cooper and
Hume's decision to contest the Stormont elections in 1969 because he
felt it left the civil rights campaign on the streets leaderless. He had
grown up in a mixed street in the Glen Road area where some of his
closest relationships were with Protestant neighbours. He felt that he
understood Protestant and unionist attitudes to the escalating violence
in the city in a way that many other nationalists and republicans did
not. He was particularly appalled at the killing, a few days before Bloody
Sunday, of two RUC officers, Peter Gilgunn and David Montgomery,
having known Gilgunn well. He felt that the killing of local Protestants
serving in the RUC and the UDR was the worst aspect of the developing
IRA campaign. In addition to this broad range of strong contacts in Derry,
Duddy also had contact with two key Provisional Republican figures at
national leadership level, Ruairí Ó Brádaigh and Dave O'Connell (Daithí

Ó Conaill). As violence began to develop around the early civil rights marches Duddy began to deliberately lower his public profile and to focus on efforts behind the scenes aimed at reducing tensions.[30]

Duddy developed an intensive and long-term co-operative relationship with Frank Lagan, a relationship focused on finding ways to reduce tension and de-escalate violence. Initially they worked at a low level, dealing with individual cases. After Bloody Sunday these efforts moved onto a higher level and Duddy would play a crucial secret role in efforts to achieve a negotiated settlement to the conflict over the following decades.

In the months prior to Bloody Sunday Frank Lagan and Brendan Duddy were meeting on a regular basis. Their co-operation focused on ways to prevent the escalation of violence in the city. Lagan was open to ways of operating that would avoid unnecessarily alienating large numbers of people in the Catholic community. Duddy gives the example that if Special Branch became aware that explosives were being stored in a building they might be inclined to leave them in place until they were handled, in order to bring a more serious charge against the people involved. Lagan would be content for the explosives to come into the hands of the RUC 'at an equilibrium price', in a way that would avoid imprisoning people with the consequent radicalisation of a wide circle of relatives and friends.[31] What Lagan got in return was, as Duddy put it, 'pacification'.

Duddy recalls that Lagan 'was extremely worried' about the Bloody Sunday march. According to Duddy, Lagan contacted him about the march some time around 20 January. 'He told me that he needed agreements there'd be no IRA men on the march and no IRA [weapons].' Duddy argued that there was no need to seek such assurances because 'it was totally known ... there couldn't be shooting at a march'.[32] That is, it was patently obvious that the IRA could not politically afford to endanger marchers by starting a gun battle at a march. Lagan was absolutely insistent that he needed guarantees that there would be no weapons and eventually Duddy reluctantly agreed to seek assurances.

Several days before Bloody Sunday Duddy went to speak to Malachy McGurran, the representative of the national leadership of the Official Republican movement with responsibility for Derry. He told him he needed an assurance that there would be no Official IRA weapons on the march. Duddy was confident that McGurran had the authority to give such an assurance. Duddy recalls that McGurran argued that there was no need for any kind of formal assurance since it would not make any sense for the Official IRA to endanger marchers. McGurran said, 'I'm now telling you they will not be there' while resisting the request for a formal assurance. Duddy insisted that this was not enough. Pressed by Duddy, McGurran finally and reluctantly gave an assurance.

In the case of the Provisionals Duddy did not approach the local organisation in Derry as he felt this would unnecessarily expose him. Duddy approached a senior figure in the national leadership with Lagan's request. 'I impressed on them that this was being deeply requested by Lagan.' He didn't get a reply from the Provisionals until a few days before the march. 'The agreement came back that the weapons would be removed but they reserved the right to march on their own streets. I came back to Lagan and said "Right, both groups have agreed that there will be no weapons." '[33]

In his statement to the Bloody Sunday Inquiry, Frank Lagan stated 'I did not receive any intelligence, assurances, information or understandings about what to expect in the Bogside on Bloody Sunday from anyone in the IRA or from any politicians or the clergy.' This does not contradict Duddy's account as he was neither politician, clergyman nor in the IRA.[34]

However, Lagan also stated 'I cannot recall having any other intelligence, assurances, information or understandings from anyone else [apart from the sources he lists] about possible IRA activity in the Bogside on Bloody Sunday.'[35]

This seems to contradict Duddy's account, but is less categorical than the previous reference and doesn't rule out the possibility that Lagan might have forgotten. This sense of uncertainty is also present in a later paragraph in the statement. In introducing a catalogue of 'intelligence, assurances, information or understandings that I can remember receiving about what to expect on Bloody Sunday' Lagan qualifies the list by saying 'although there were probably more'.[36]

Lagan's statement emphasises RUC and army sources of intelligence around Bloody Sunday and there is little sense in the statement of the wide range of contacts and sources of information that Lagan could draw on and which have been mentioned by several military, RUC and civilian witnesses at the Inquiry.[37]

Although Frank Lagan's statement seems to contradict Duddy's account, Duddy's account fits well with the general picture of Lagan's extensive networks and efforts for peace which has emerged at the Inquiry.

Much of the evidence about IRA intentions on Bloody Sunday presented at the Inquiry has been problematic, some of it involving secondhand accounts, and some of it describing contacts which were quite vague. Duddy's account provides the clearest and most direct evidence that we have. The unique force of his account comes above all from the fact that his involvement in secret contact around Bloody Sunday was not an isolated event. In the following years and decades, Brendan Duddy was a key figure in secret communication and negotiation between the leadership of the Provisional IRA and the British cabinet via senior MI6 and later MI5 personnel. Peter Taylor has described Duddy's central role after 1972, without naming him.[38] Duddy's account is the strongest evidence we have that assurances of IRA intentions on Bloody Sunday had been given directly to the security forces. On the day itself, a number of IRA members carried weapons on the march and fired isolated shots. But these actions have the character of a failure of leadership control rather than an organised IRA action. It does not undermine the point that the general intention of the leadership of both the Provisional and Official IRA to avoid confrontation during the march had been communicated directly to the security forces.

In one sense, Duddy's account simply reinforces what we already know, that Frank Lagan believed there would be no IRA shooting on the day. This is stated plainly and unequivocally by Lagan in his statement. But in other ways it adds hugely to our understanding of the day. In Duddy's account it was Lagan who took the initiative to seek IRA assurances, and who insisted on the need for such assurances. It presents a picture of a situation where Lagan was involved in energetic and intensive efforts to ensure that the day did not become an occasion for major violence, and was applying pressure in any way he could to both the security forces and the IRA. Much of the debate at the Inquiry has focused on the question of what information was available to the security forces about the levels of threat to expect on the day. In the light of this evidence about the extent of Lagan's efforts to avert confrontation, it might be useful to put more weight on the question of why Lagan's stated belief that there would not be IRA shooting on the day did not inform army action to a greater extent.

Planning the army operation on Bloody Sunday

When considered in the context of the well-established networks in the city aimed at preventing confrontation and reducing violence, the sequence of events around planning for the march is very suggestive.

Frank Lagan requested a meeting with Brigadier MacLellan to discuss the march on the Monday beforehand.[39] It is notable that Lagan took the initiative and proposed his plan before the Brigadier or HQNI had finalised plans of their own. Lagan proposed that the march be allowed to proceed to its destination in the city centre in order to reduce the risks of violent confrontation. His deputy, Patrick McCullagh, explained the thinking behind Lagan's proposal in his statement to the Inquiry. 'At the time Frank Lagan and I were trying desperately to reduce the temperature of the general situation and we did not think we could do this by coming into conflict ...' with the marchers that day.[40]

Given that Lagan was in regular contact with one of the key march organisers, Brigid Bond, it is useful to think of Lagan's proposal as the first phase of a process of negotiation at one remove. None of those involved would have used the term 'negotiation', but Lagan was effectively conveying his assessment of the respective positions back and forth between MacLellan and Bond.

Although MacLellan argues that he did not agree with Lagan's stance at the meeting, Lagan and McCullagh state that he did, or at least that he did not oppose it. The message that MacLellan then sent to Ford is entirely compatible with their interpretation of the meeting. Certainly the sequence of events that followed, suggests that General Ford got the firm impression that MacLellan was advocating Lagan's approach.

In a message to General Ford that evening, MacLellan described Lagan's view that confrontation around the march would 'shatter such peace as is left in the city; create intense violence and remove last vestiges of moderate goodwill' and stated that 'I agree that consequences of stopping march will be very serious and reckon that my present permanent force levels almost certainly inadequate if we are to face situation Lagan envisages.'[41]

Given that Ford had recently said he was 'deeply disturbed' at the approach of MacLellan and Lagan, we can only imagine his initial reaction to receiving this particular proposal. Not only was Lagan suggesting that they not implement the ban on marches but, by all appearances, MacLellan was supporting Lagan's view. Ford's response was swift.

MacLellan sent his message to Ford on Monday evening. Ford phoned him on Tuesday evening.[42] MacLellan described Ford's call in his statement. 'As a result of the signal I had sent, on Tuesday 25th January I received a telephone call from CLF ... he wished to have my outline plan by 0830 hours Wednesday, 26th January 1972 together with a marked-up map ... He also told me that he had decided to use the occasion to scoop up as many hooligans as possible and spoke of arresting 300–400.'[43]

Within hours of receiving a suggestion to let the march through and do everything possible to avoid confrontation, Ford was announcing on the telephone not only that the march would be stopped, but that the day would be used as an opportunity for an arrest operation on a scale the city had never seen before. The seizing of 342 people across Northern Ireland in the Internment operation in August 1971 had led to an immediate and spectacular intensification of violence across Northern Ireland. Ford now wanted to arrest as many as, or more than, had been taken into custody on the night of Internment. It is useful to think of the sequence of events in these terms:

1. Lagan proposes a plan to avoid violent confrontation at all costs.
2. Ford counters with a plan to stage an unprecedented major confrontation.

This is best understood not as a disagreement on the most effective approach to the march, nor as a contest between an important senior army officer and a marginal policeman, but as a confrontation between two radically opposed policy approaches, both of which were well established within the security forces.

MacLellan was told that he should produce a plan based on Ford's ambitious offensive operation by 8.30 the next morning. That is, he was asked to draw up the plan that night; 'so we had eight hours to produce the plan', MacLellan told an interviewer some years later.[44]

After Ford had received the plan on Wednesday morning he phoned and ordered MacLellan to come to HQNI by helicopter that afternoon. 'When he had read my outline plan, General Ford instructed me to attend a meeting with him at his HQ on 26th January 1972', as MacLellan put it. The tone of the Brigade Major, Michael Steele's statement conveys that same sense of pressure being applied from above: 'Brigadier MacLellan and I were required at short notice to go to Headquarters Northern Ireland in a helicopter to meet the CLF.'[45]

MacLellan described this meeting in his statement to the inquiry. 'I was given a direct order by General Ford to launch an arrest operation if the soldiers were attacked by the hooligans and he specifically allotted 1 PARA for the task. This was not a matter for debate and there was no discretion as far as I was concerned.'[46] When presented with MacLellan's description of the meeting at the Inquiry Ford said, 'I would agree with every word.'[47]

MacLellan elaborated on his description of this meeting in evidence to the Inquiry. 'As far as I can recall ... he was really – this was not a sort of debating association, it was what the army would call an orders group, he would say "this is what you are going to do, boom, boom, boom." I think he made about eight or ten points.'[48]

The sequence and speed, the hints of the tone of the conversations and meetings strongly suggest that Ford's reaction to the Lagan proposal was not merely swift but furious. It seems sensible to interpret it as the application of major pressure to MacLellan to fall in line with a tougher stance ordered from above, and to break with Lagan's approach.

It is almost as though the evidence of just how conciliatory Derry commanders were prepared to be, of just how persistent the Lagan line was, had provoked Ford into taking direct personal control and into planning an operation that would be the opposite of the Lagan plan, an opportunity for confrontation.

It marked a dramatic break with, and a disruption of, a local policy which had strong elements of conciliation and compromise and restraint.

On the day: direct rejection of contact

One piece of evidence about events on Bloody Sunday itself provides stark illustration of the extent to which Operation Forecast, the army plan for the day, represented a calculated rejection of an approach based on communication and compromise.

The aspect of Lagan's original plan which was most criticised, was the suggestion that the march be allowed to proceed to the city centre. While an arrest operation was made part of the plan for the day by General Ford, even Ford held that the central purpose of the operation was to stop the civil rights march entering the city centre. An operational order prepared by General Ford's Aide De Camp stated that the protesters wanted to hold a rally in the city centre 'and thereby show the weaknesses of the security forces' and that 'CLF has decreed that the march must be stopped at all costs'.[49] Many other documents stress the central importance of this goal.

In the light of this emphasis on stopping the march, Lagan's most dramatic piece of evidence seems puzzling:

> When I arrived at Brigadier MacLellan's offices at about 2 pm on Bloody Sunday I ... saw Brigadier MacLellan and General Ford standing next to each other facing the door through which I had just come. I approached them and told them about the NICRA information [that the march organisers had agreed that the march would be

diverted away from the barriers and they would not attempt to enter the city centre]. Neither Brigadier MacLellan nor General Ford responded. General Ford immediately turned away from me and Brigadier MacLellan quickly followed ... I must say that I was very disappointed by the lack of response. I thought that they would be delighted to hear that the confrontation at the William Street barrier would be averted.[50]

If we take at face value the army's emphasis on stopping the march, Lagan's information should have come like a bolt from the blue. The central purpose of the army operation that day had been achieved through secret channels of communication which had produced a major concession by the marchers. Lagan had originally tried to use his influence to have the march allowed to proceed to the Guildhall, but he had subsequently tried to persuade Brigid Bond that the march should be diverted in order to avoid violence. Brendan Duddy says that when he spoke to Bond on the Friday before the march and urged her to change the route because it would give the army an excuse to take tough action, she was still undecided. She did not know if she could pull it off, if she could persuade the rest of the organisers to agree to this change. Though both Bond and Duddy were in contact with Frank Lagan, neither of them mentioned his name, such was the sensitivity surrounding these contacts.[51] Lagan had been working behind the scenes to have the march diverted, and on the morning of the march he finally heard that these efforts had paid off.

It is only in the light of Lagan's central role in the city in negotiating compromises which the army had regularly relied on in order to reduce violence, that we can appreciate the significance of Ford's abrupt rejection of this message from Lagan. He was not simply ignoring the message: he was rejecting the messenger and an established channel which had been used to avert confrontation before.

Putting the Lagan–Duddy connection in context

In the light of the descriptions of Frank Lagan by General Ford and Brigadier MacLellan in 1972, it is important to emphasise the extent to which Lagan enjoyed the confidence and backing of key public servants shaping British government policy.

In the autumn of 1971 Howard Smith, the UK Government Representative in Northern Ireland, asked Frank Steele to act as his deputy in Belfast. Smith had been involved in the August 1971 agreement to reduce army activity in Derry. He later went on to become the director of MI5. Steele was a senior member of MI6 and was subsequently at the heart of negotiations between the British government and the Provisional IRA leadership in June 1972, after the British government abolished Stormont and brought in Direct Rule from London.[52]

A document released by the Public Records Office in London in 2004 provides Steele's account to the Secretary of State for Northern Ireland of a visit to Derry in April 1973. He was accompanied by his newly appointed colleague, Michael Oatley. Steele reported discussion on a proposal that the Bogside and Creggan be policed by a locally recruited unit of the RUC reserve which would wear new uniforms that were to be introduced to the RUC as a whole at a later stage.

'There was much interest in the proposal ... that there should be local units of the RUC reserve manned by Cregganites and Bogsiders selected by the head of Londonderry police (Mr. Lagan who is much trusted and respected locally) from candidates put forward by local Creggan and Bogside associations.' Steele reported widespread agreement that this 'was well worth trying' and suggested that it might also be applied elsewhere in Northern Ireland.[53]

Barely a year after senior British army officers were suggesting that Lagan's position was untenable, a senior and central figure in the British administration in the North was recommending a radical conciliatory scheme for policing in Derry that would have relied heavily on Lagan's personal reputation in the Catholic community. Lagan continued to be central to an approach which enjoyed support at the highest levels of the British administration in Belfast.

After the collapse of the IRA ceasefire in July 1972, and the ending of public contact, an initiative was taken to establish a secret and closely guarded channel of communication between the Provisional IRA leadership and the British government. Frank Lagan played a key role in facilitating the practicalities of this situation in the early days.

Brendan Duddy was at the centre of the initiative, dealing with the Provisional IRA leadership on the one hand and with MI6 members Frank Steele and later Michael Oatley, on the other, in secret negotiations and contacts that would operate, on and off, at varying levels of intensity, for the following 20 years. The channel of communication was a political initiative based on the belief, held strongly by Duddy, that the conflict would ultimately be brought to an end, not by military victory by either side, but by dialogue between both parties culminating in a negotiated settlement.

Duddy worked to persuade both sides that dialogue was the only way forward. He commented that it was a very lonely path in the 1970s and throughout the 1980s, and that only his pacifist views and core Christian belief in non-violence sustained him. This dialogue culminated in secret negotiations between the Provisional Republican leadership and the British government leading up to the IRA ceasefires and the Good Friday Agreement.[54]

It is not possible to understand the significance of the role that Frank Lagan and Brendan Duddy played on Bloody Sunday without understanding that the genealogy of the dialogue which was a crucial component of the peace process can be traced directly back to the developing co-operative relationship between Lagan and Duddy in Derry in the months before Bloody Sunday.

Rejecting contact and accepting risks

Operation Forecast represented a direct and deliberate rejection of an established policy in Derry of restraining security force activity in order to avoid alienating Catholic moderates. It represented a rejection of the networks and channels through which compromises and tacit agreements were made. Such contact was rejected not only because it had failings and weaknesses but also because it necessarily involved difficult compromises on the part of the security forces and because it was based on a policy approach that was anathema to some senior army commanders.

The extent to which the practice of communication was rejected is illustrated most clearly by the fact that Frank Lagan's news on Bloody Sunday, that the march organisers had agreed not to attempt to march to the city centre, was ignored. There was a refusal to even acknowledge the clear signal that march organisers had abandoned their stated plan in order to avert confrontation. Nothing illustrates more clearly that it was a central purpose of the army operation on Bloody Sunday not only to stop the march but also to break with an established practice of conciliation and restraint in Derry.

This rejection of attempts to avert confrontation on Bloody Sunday is compounded by the fact that the compromises necessary to avoid large-scale confrontation on Bloody Sunday do not compare with those the army had made in the summer of 1970 and in August 1971. All they had to do on Bloody Sunday was to not launch a major offensive operation. The path to averting major confrontation had rarely been clearer and as simple.

In direct response to a plan driven by the central goal of avoiding escalation and confrontation through negotiation and compromise, General Ford ordered a major arrest operation on a scale never before seen in Derry on a day when thousands of civilians would be on the streets. The occasion chosen to make an abrupt break with the policies of negotiation and compromise in the city could hardly have involved greater risks to civilians.

Notes and references

1 Eamonn McCann (with Bridie Harrigan and Maureen Shiels), *Bloody Sunday in Derry: What Really Happened* (Brandon, Kerry, 1992).
2 As Ford wrote in a letter to Peter Taylor about a documentary Taylor had made about Bloody Sunday, 3/2/92 (attached to General Ford's statement to the Bloody Sunday Inquiry – hereafter BSI).
3 Eamonn McCann, *Socialist Worker*, no. 51, p. 6, Oct. 1988, and Ivan Cooper, interview.
4 John White, *John Hume: Statesman of the Troubles* (Blackstaff, Belfast, 1984), pp. 76–7, and John Hume, interview.
5 DJ, 22/8/69, p. 1; Michael Canavan, interview.
6 DJ, 10/7/70. p. 15.
7 DJ, 14/7/70, p. 1
8 LS, 1/9/71, p. 1.
9 Desmond Hamill, *Pig in the Middle: The Army in Northern Ireland, 1969–1985* (Methuen, London, 1986), p. 70.
10 General Sir Robert Ford, statement to the BSI, 23/3/00, 3.13.
11 Ford, statement, 3.31, citing a report by the Chief of the General Staff, G44.
12 Evidence of P.M. McCullagh to the BSI, 12/9/02, TS232, 89–90.
13 Interviews with Brendan Duddy, 2004.
14 Patrick Mary McCullagh, 'Notes of Discussion with Eversheds', 20/7/2000, 6. This is effectively P.M. McCullagh's statement to the Inquiry and is cited hereafter as McCullagh, statement.
15 McCullagh, evidence, 11/9/02, TS231, 100.
16 Supt. P.M. McCullagh, Statement to the Widgery Tribunal, 7/2/1972 (attached to his statement to the BSI).
17 Notes of conversation with former member of the Official Republican movement, April, 2004.
18 McCullagh, Statement, 9.
19 McCullagh, evidence, 12/9/02, TS232, 85.
20 Duddy, interviews.
21 Ibid.
22 Ibid.
23 Ford, statement, 4.5.
24 Letter from Brigadier Pat MacLellan to Major General Robert Ford, Derry, 15/3/72.
25 MacLellan, statement, 8.
26 MacLellan, evidence, 19/11/02, TS261, 23.

27 Duddy, interviews.
28 Colonel Roy Jackson, supplemental statement to the BSI, 10/1/03.
29 General Sir Robert Ford, evidence, 4/11/02, TS256, 13.
30 Duddy, interviews.
31 Duddy, interviews.
32 Duddy, interviews.
33 Duddy, interviews. See also Duddy, statement to the BSI, 15/6/04.
34 Frank Lagan, statement to the BSI, 13/12/98, 21.
35 Lagan, statement, 20.
36 Lagan, statement, 23.
37 Lagan, statement, 23–8.
38 Peter Taylor, *Provos: The IRA and Sinn Féin* (Bloomsbury, London, 1997) pp. 166–72, 319–23; and Peter Taylor, *Brits: The war against the IRA* (Bloomsbury, London, 2001), pp. 163–71, 233–5. Duddy was first named publicly in relation to contact between the IRA and the British government in Ed Moloney, *A Secret History of the IRA* (Penguin, London, 2003. Originally 2002), pp. 207, 257, 406. The contacts he was involved in have also been discussed, without naming Duddy, in Eamonn Mallie and David McKittrick, *Endgame in Ireland* (Coronet Lir, London, 2002), pp. 98–123.
39 MacLellan, evidence, 22/11/02, TS264, 42.
40 McCullagh, statement, 19.
41 Cited in MacLellan, evidence, 19/11/02, TS261, 37–8.
42 According to Ford's 1972 statement to the Widgery Tribunal, cited in Ford, statement, 7.13.
43 MacLellan, statement, 32–3.
44 'Major-General Pat MacLellan 9.12.83' (document attached to MacLellan, statement) PIN 15467, B1279.003.
45 Major-General Michael CM Steele, statement to the BSI, 6/10/00, 13.
46 MacLellan, statement, 36.
47 Ford, evidence, 4/11/02, TS256, 19.
48 MacLellan, evidence, 19/11/02, TS261, 49.
49 Operational order prepared by the ADC to the CLF, G82A.521.1, cited in McCullagh, evidence, 12/9/02, TS232, 79.
50 Frank Lagan, statement, 13/12/98. 87–8.
51 Duddy, interviews.
52 Taylor, *Provos*, pp. 137–45.
53 Frank Steele, 'Visit to Bogside and Creggan on 4/5 April 1973'. Confidential report. FCO 87/221, PRO, London. Available online at CAIN Web Service 'New Year Releases 2003 – Public Records of 1972', <http://cain.ulst.ac.uk/publicrecords/1972/>.
54 See Taylor, *Provos*, pp. 319–23 and 329–32.

Conclusion

The conflict as a cause of the conflict

It is a central argument of this book that occasions of violent confrontation play a crucial role in promoting the escalation and continuation of conflict. The development of a violent conflict is influenced and shaped by the contemporary events which make up that conflict to a much greater extent than the development of a non-violent political process is. This is because conflict is so much more intense and immediate than 'peacetime' politics.

Given that contemporary events of violence can have such a powerful influence on individuals and communities, a fuller description of those events can, of its own, explain much of the motivation for the subsequent actions of different parties to a conflict. The initial confrontations are crucial to understanding subsequent developments and can be accounted a principal 'cause' of the conflict. The process by which conflicts develop and escalate must be central to any understanding of these conflicts.

When large-scale riots broke out on 5 October 1968 after the first civil rights march in Derry it seemed to one of the march organisers that the '... effect seemed to be out of all proportion' to the housing and employment issues they had been protesting about,[1] particularly since those grievances had been borne so quietly for decades. However, there was one grievance that the riots were not so obviously out of proportion to. It was a grievance that the organisers of the march had not been protesting about, that had not even existed when they set out on their march. That grievance was the attack on the civil rights march by the RUC. From the very first day of the civil rights campaign in Derry the grievances addressed by the campaign were being superseded by grievances produced by violent confrontation surrounding the campaign. From the outset, the response of the state and its forces of law and order to Catholic mobilisation was an issue capable of arousing far more anger and activism than the issues around which mobilisation had begun. Police behaviour and their interaction with loyalist protesters probably did more to politically mobilise large sections of the Catholic community than did any of the other grievances. At the same time, the outbreak of violence in Catholic areas did much to reinforce right-wing Unionist resistance to reform, on the grounds that demands for reform masked an IRA conspiracy and concession of reforms fed that conspiracy. It made the security forces a principal focus for Protestant loyalties and reinforced the support of many Protestants for the RUC and their resistance to reform of the force.

Writers working in the area of conflict resolution have described situations '... in which the initial issues around which a conflict begins are vastly outweighed by new issues produced by the conflict'.[2] To a great extent such a situation developed in Northern Ireland from the earliest stages. Throughout the first months of the civil rights campaign each new confrontation produced new grievances, sowed the seeds for the next confrontation and shifted the 'battleground' further away from its previous location.

In this respect, the sequence of events in the early months is essential to an understanding of the escalation of conflict and of why the granting of the bulk of reforms originally demanded by the civil rights movement did not resolve the situation. At each stage of the crisis, the Unionist government held out until it had reached or gone over the brink of violence before making the minimal concessions possible and announcing that there would be no further concessions. Reform went hand in hand with riot and civil disorder in 1968 and 1969, granted to try to salvage a situation just after it had gone beyond salvaging, always granted just too late to really make a difference. One person one vote, for example, was granted shortly after the April 1969 riots in Derry during which Sammy Devenny, who later died, was severely beaten by the RUC, and large sections of the population of the Bogside had been evacuated to Creggan in response to the threat of an RUC 'invasion' of the area. To say that the grievance over one person one vote had been superseded by other grievances by then, would be to understate the case. The sequence in which reform was granted taught the cynical lesson that 'reform', and the British government interventions which prompted it, were dependent on the conflict and that the progress of reform was inseparable from the pace and progress of the conflict. Thus reform was in large part a product of the conflict. It was not something apart from the conflict which could help to resolve it.

From the first day of the civil rights campaign in Derry, violent confrontation had itself produced one central new grievance; the behaviour of state security forces. This was an issue that went to the heart of the relationship between the state and the newly mobilised Catholic community. By July 1969, at the latest, 'law and order', or more specifically 'policing', had completely displaced the other issues around which the civil rights campaign had begun.

Law and order

The question of how public order was maintained in Northern Ireland was identified as a civil rights issue by the Northern Ireland Civil Rights Association from the beginning.[3] From the foundation of the state, public order had been maintained by a militarised police force and large auxiliary police forces drawn almost exclusively from the Protestant community. The Special Powers Act gave virtually unlimited powers of repression to the Stormont government, powers exercised through the RUC and the B-Specials. Riots and clashes between Catholic crowds and the RUC were an infrequent but persistent occurrence in the North during the 1950s and 60s. Despite this, the authority of the RUC as a force for public order had by and large been accepted in Catholic areas of Derry. Public protest throughout the 1960s had focused primarily on housing and employment issues and not on 'law and order'. It was only as violence escalated after 5 October that the behaviour of the RUC and the B-Specials became a central concern of the civil rights movement. However, the abruptness and intensity of the rioting which followed the RUC baton charge of 5 October 1968 showed how thin had been the crust of legitimacy on which acceptance of the RUC's authority had been based. Given RUC conduct on the day, many people in Derry had few inhibitions about attacking the police force of a state which the mainstream of the Catholic community felt no loyalty to.

As early as January 1969 the issue of repression had almost completely displaced the other issues the civil rights campaign had been addressing. When a broadly-based civil rights campaign was revived in Derry in March 1969 universal suffrage had still to be granted but yet this campaign was focused solely on the new Public Order Bill which gave increased powers to the security forces to prevent public protests. 'Policing', the methods by which public order would be maintained, had become *the* civil rights issue.

Not alone was the problem of policing a political issue in the conflict, it also directly fuelled the conflict at a very practical level. The slide into violence in Derry was accelerated by the fact that there was no force for public order, no body that could quell trouble, that could 'police' the developing disturbances. The RUC could not maintain public order because they were a principal party to that disorder and a principal cause of it. From a very early stage the RUC was unable to 'police' civil rights demonstrations in Derry, and only the presence of hundreds of DCAC stewards ensured that marchers did not clash with the RUC. By mid-1969, at the latest, groups of Catholic youths in Derry were starting trouble with the specific aim of drawing the RUC out onto the streets so that they could attack them. In the circumstances, sending the RUC to the scene of public disorder was like pouring petrol on flames. If some way had been found to resolve the issue of public order, much of the fuel for further escalation would have been removed.

The failure to resolve the issue of policing played a major part in laying the ground for the Battle of the Bogside, which developed into a pitched battle between the mainstream of the Catholic community in Derry and the RUC, intermittently supported by groups of loyalists. The 'battle' very nearly destroyed Northern Ireland as a state. As the RUC lost control of the situation the British army was called in by the Stormont government as support for the RUC in enforcing state authority. The army chose initially to recognise temporarily the authority of alternative forces in the Catholic community in 'Free Derry'. However, within weeks the army was acting according to the imperative of restoring state authority in Catholic areas and they became hostile to these alternative forces.

In the search to restore public order and the authority of the state throughout its territory, the reform of the RUC and disbandment of the B-Specials after October 1969 provides a key moment. Immediately after the reform of the RUC it became clear that the 'new' RUC was incapable of enforcing law and order in the former 'Free Derry'. The first 'new' RUC men to appear in the area were jeered. At this crucial juncture the British army decided that it would take over the policing of the former 'Free Derry'. It was several months before the IRA had carried out any attacks in Derry. That is, the British army became the local 'police' force in large Catholic areas of Derry, and consequently became involved in confrontation on the streets, not in response to the threat posed by the IRA but because it had proved impossible to provide an acceptable police force, a force which could restore state authority without beginning a spiral of violence. The army brought its own special failings and the particular disaster of abrasive colonial 'policing' to the situation, but this should not obscure the fact that its presence was a product of the failure to provide acceptable forces for law and order. IRA campaign or not, it was only with extraordinary measures that the authority of the state could be exercised in these areas. As a policing agency, the army rapidly became as 'unacceptable' as the RUC had been and thus a source of further disorder. Once again, as in the early months of the civil rights campaign, the issue of how public order would be maintained in large Catholic areas was not simply a product of violent conflict, or an issue incidental to the conflict. The failure to resolve this issue was a prime cause of the conflict which ensued. It played a major part in creating the conditions in which the marginal militant Republican tradition could gather widespread support in the Catholic community.

At several times between 1968 and 1972, the Bogside and Creggan were 'policed' by groups drawn from the Catholic community – sometimes dominated by moderates, sometimes by Republicans. On a number of these occasions the decision of state forces to tolerate these forms of 'policing' for short periods led directly to a decrease in violent conflict. Clearly on each occasion there were major problems with these local forms of policing. Many in the areas concerned were unhappy with them, on occasion they meant that paramilitary organisations had relatively safe bases from which they could operate, and they were very much the product of crisis conditions. They suggested nonetheless that forms of policing originating in the Catholic community, and not deriving from the state, had the potential to resolve certain immediate problems of public order and to help de-escalate conflict. By providing policing agencies which were not a target for attack locally, it removed one major source of conflict. The fact that state authorities generally dismantled these alternative forms of authority as quickly as possible, even when they were dominated by moderates, demonstrated that the state could not afford to take this route to 'normal' policing. Because even the most moderate of forces in the Catholic community had little sense of loyalty or commitment to the state, any developments which allocated some responsibility for public order to forces emanating from the Catholic community eroded the authority of the state itself and had the potential to erode its territorial integrity. That the state was not averse to seeing public order maintained by auxiliary forces drawn almost entirely from the Protestant community was demonstrated by the existence of the B-Specials and later the UDR. That the state was tolerant to a degree of local vigilante groups drawn entirely from the Protestant community was demonstrated by its attitude to the emergence of such groups in Protestant areas in the early 1970s.[4] The rejection of similar groups drawn from the Catholic community had less to do with arguments over 'forms of policing' than with the relationship of the state to the 'disloyal' Catholic community.

The establishment of the first 'Free Derry' in January 1969, from which the RUC was excluded and which was patrolled by local vigilante groups, gave a concrete example of the direct progression from rejection of the police force to rejection of the authority of the state to the erosion of the territorial integrity and therefore the sovereignty of the state. From the appearance of the first 'no-go' area in Derry, Unionists identified this erosion of the state's sovereignty as a key issue. Unionists consistently demanded that such areas be brought fully back under state authority, however difficult that might prove.

A key factor in the state's instability was the fact that its control over large parts of its territory had always been implicitly coercive, maintained by a massive and heavily armed set of security forces. One geographer has suggested that Northern Ireland is 'territorially overbounded', including areas at the margins of the state which have 'never been fully integrated ... within the political structure and framework of Northern Ireland'.[5] But it is probably more accurate to say that 'overbounding' begins at the edges of Belfast city centre. From the core outward, Northern Ireland included 'alien' territory, compact areas with clear boundaries which were overwhelmingly Catholic and over which, in times of crisis, the state could only exert authority through the use of extraordinary methods.

From mid-1970 onwards, the British government joined the Stormont government in arguing that repressive security was determined solely by the scale of the paramilitary threat and that, however much they might affect the general public, the enemy at which they were directed was a small number of irreconcilable gunmen. The only obstacle to normal policing was therefore the paramilitary campaigns. It was on the basis of such arguments that many moderate Catholics gave tacit support to state security forces in their struggle against the IRA, particularly after the end of internment in 1975. While the paramilitary campaigns continued there was relatively little debate on the future of policing.

When the IRA and loyalist paramilitaries declared ceasefires in late 1994 a public debate on policing began. The Good Friday Agreement of 1998 placed policing reform at centre-stage, recognising it as one of the key issues to be resolved. Fundamental reforms have been made, but policing and the decommissioning of paramilitary weapons remain the two great obstacles to full implementation of the agreement. The fact that Sinn Féin had still not signed up to support the new Police Service of Northern Ireland six years after the Agreement emphasises the persistent difficulties around the issue. When and if they do, it will present a huge challenge to Republicans.

The crisis of policing has been at the heart of the conflict from the beginning. While many of the original civil rights demands had been met by an early stage, the conflict itself had moved the role of state security forces towards the top of the agenda from the outset. Issues of repression and the question of how public order would be maintained were not solely a product of conflict. They were a principal cause of conflict and the factor that made escalation and the descent into chaos so effortless.

Loyalty

From the foundation of the state Unionists argued that religious discrimination did not exist in Northern Ireland and that nobody suffered discrimination on the basis of their religious beliefs and practices. On the other hand, Unionists regularly justified discrimination against Catholics on the grounds that they were 'disloyal' to the state and wished to see the state dismantled. These arguments were part of the currency of mainstream Protestant opinion in Northern Ireland and were not confined to an extremist fringe.[6] As one 'unsurprised' academic writer has put it, 'Since a sizeable section of the Catholic community opposed the very existence of the Northern Irish state, it is hardly surprising ... that they were denied government employment.'[7] Even Protestant liberals such as Barritt and Carter writing about marches and parades in 1962 could argue that it would be 'unreasonable' to expect the Unionist government 'to treat expressions both of loyalty and disloyalty with that even-handed "justice" which is demanded by Nationalist opinion'.[8] The issue of 'loyalty' to the state is frequently an issue in conflict situations where ethnic minorities seek an independent state or seek to join another state. It has provided the principal justification for discrimination against entire ethnic groups in some of these situations.[9]

Townshend has written that 'the simple loyalist chain of perceptions – Catholic/disloyal/dangerous to state/excluded from power – was recognised by "enlightened" unionists as being circular'.[10] That is, 'enlightened' Unionists accepted that Catholics could not be expected to be 'loyal' if they were not treated equally. This argument implied that, granted equal treatment, Catholics would accept the state, except perhaps for a small minority of irreconcilables who could be isolated and relatively easily repressed. It was an argument which left entirely intact the principle that the disloyal should not be treated equally. It just assumed that there would be very few of them once reform had been implemented. It is the argument underlying the assumption that reform should have 'solved' the problem in 1969 by convincing Catholics to accept the state, to become 'loyal'.[11]

The fact that quite the opposite happened seemed to reveal that Catholic 'disloyalty' was a devious constant which could not be altered by reform, that the civil rights movement itself was a devious and disloyal ploy and that reform merely weakened the state rather than strengthened it. Reform failed to strengthen the state and thus serve Unionist goals. It also failed to deliver full equality and 'civil rights' to the Catholic community in the area which, from 1969, was at the core of Catholic discontent – policing and law and order. Events from 1968 onwards showed that, in situations of political crisis and conflict, the threshold at which loyalty was set was so high that virtually the entire Catholic community was 'disloyal'. That is, in times of crisis this 'enlightened' Unionist argument justified the repression of more or less the entire Catholic community.

Many elements in the Catholic community in Derry would co-operate enthusiastically with, and offer whatever support they could, to both the British army and the RUC well into 1971; elements such as the Catholic church and prominent lay Catholics in the schools, in local youth groups, in tenants' associations and even in political parties, such as the SDLP and the Nationalist party.

However, even conservative Catholics who accepted the *bona fides* of the army long after moderates had ceased to do so, would ultimately be forced to reject the legitimacy of the state. Conservative Catholics accorded legitimacy to and supported the army, not on the basis of 'loyalty' to the state as most Protestants did, but as an agency for keeping order in the absence of the RUC or a broadly acceptable police force. When the army began to implement policies which dealt with the Catholic community as a whole as a problematic community this support was eroded.

When no-go areas were set up in Derry after internment in August 1971, the army decided to deal with this 'secession' through massively disruptive periodic 'invasions' of the area. Conservative Catholics, represented in part by the alliance which had formed the 'Concern for Creggan Committee' (the Nationalist party and the SDLP, the tenants' associations and local priests and teachers), came to regard the army as a disruptive force, a source of chaos and destruction. Many conservative Catholics were committed to law and order and were fully prepared to accept the authority of the state as a force for public order. However, when the state itself became a source of disorder they did not regard that state as worth maintaining. In this sense, they were 'disloyal' and in this sense, virtually the entire Catholic population was 'disloyal'.

In the early 1970s, a large section of the Catholic community in Derry became actively hostile to the state and committed to its destruction through force of arms. The state was unequivocal in its assertion of its right to militarily repress and defeat this section of the Catholic community. In theory, in return for reform in some areas, other sections of the Catholic community should have been prepared to co-operate in this repression. Large sections of the Catholic community would never give even tacit support to the IRA, would campaign against and condemn them and oppose them wherever and whenever they could. It did not mean, however, that they could actively support a war being waged by the state. As the section of the Catholic community to be repressed expanded in size the dwindling number of 'loyal' Catholics found itself called upon to endorse ever greater repression directed against ever greater sections of its own community. 'Loyalty' ultimately meant supporting a war waged on the entire population of Catholic working-class areas such as the Bogside and Creggan.

It reached a stage in Derry in 1972 where even the most conservative and apolitical of Catholics in such areas found themselves numbered amongst the dangerously 'disloyal', a threat to the state, and subject to a rigorous military occupation, which necessarily treated the entire Catholic population of these areas as suspect individuals from a suspect community.

Support for repression is often framed by Unionists as the key test of the goodwill of Catholic moderates. They argue that if Catholic moderates genuinely oppose violence and the IRA, then they should not complain about efforts aimed at wiping out the IRA. As a DUP representative put it in 1992 'decent people want gunmen and bombers taken out of their midst'.[12] This implies that 'decent people', whether Protestant or Catholic, will support increased repression. In the circumstances where moderate and conservative Catholics cannot support such repression, it implies that there are virtually no 'decent' Catholics and, in turn, justifies massive and open-ended repression of this 'disloyal' community as a whole.

'Loyalty' to a state founded explicitly for Protestants who were loyal to Britain, is not something that Northern Catholics could ever effectively prove, particularly as assessing loyalty necessarily involves the prediction of future behaviour in times of crisis. Loyalty, in this case, was a matter of belonging. Catholics could hardly prove loyalty through joining the British army, when the ranks of the IRA in the 1970s, as much as in the 1920s, have always included former British soldiers. They could hardly prove it by joining the police except in times of crisis. The ranks of the RIC, the all-Ireland and mainly Catholic predecessor of the RUC had melted away as an IRA campaign began in the 1920s and some of the Catholic members had actively cooperated with the IRA.[13] The only way in which loyalty could really be proven by Catholics was by active participation in the battle against Irish nationalists and republicans. It was a loyalty test that few Catholics could ever pass.

The state of Northern Ireland was created for and by a clearly defined 'imagined community'.[14] That community was loyal to Britain and it was Protestant. Only belonging to the 'imagined community' of people the state was designed for could guarantee loyalty. If 'the ultimate long-term legitimation of a particular nation-state grouping … is wholly dependent upon the extent to which that state can claim to represent a specific national identity unique to it, meaning that it has people with characteristics it can call its own',[15] Northern Ireland had rested its long-term legitimation, its separation from the rest of Ireland, on being a state for loyal British Protestants. They were the people the state could 'call its own'. If redefined solely as a 'loyal' British community, according to the liberal Unionist formula which seeks to grant full civil rights to Catholics in return for full acceptance of the *status quo*, it still remains effectively a Protestant community.

The international system of sovereign states, each exercising sole jurisdiction over 'essentially' domestic affairs, what international relations scholars call the 'Westphalian' system, legitimises and elevates the cultures, languages, territories and collective identities of certain groups through statehood. In inverse proportion, it reduces the status of groups not elevated to statehood and ultimately can criminalise their very identity. It makes many ethnic or national groups, not identified with the state they find themselves in, guilty of the crime of disloyalty or, when not actively and visibly disloyal, under permanent suspicion of the crime, not primarily through their actions, but simply through their belonging to a particular group. Arguably, one of the most important benefits of statehood for an ethnic group is that it automatically gives members of the group or groups identified with the state the attribute of 'loyalty', and almost as automatically gives the burden of 'disloyalty' to groups not identified with the state. In the particular case where a minority has opposed the very creation of the state, it has demonstrated its disloyalty even before the state comes into existence, and it is hard to see how such a group can ever prove its loyalty to the satisfaction of the group or groups on whose behalf the state was created. This problem is compounded in a situation where a state is created at least partly in order to 'escape' the rule of a particular group and yet includes large numbers of that group within its boundaries. That group can hardly avoid being suspected as potential allies of the group whose rule has been 'escaped'. This 'escape' from the threat of being ruled by Irish Catholics, perceived as a threat for a variety of reasons, was a prime motivation behind the creation of the Northern Ireland state.

There is a certain logic in the arguments of many Unionists that the state cannot and should not treat equally both 'loyal' and 'disloyal' communities. The logic of these arguments is that full equality for Catholics cannot be granted within the Northern Ireland state. The key issue of law and order which was at the core of the escalating conflict in Derry from 1968 to 1972, bound up as it is with the issues of sovereignty and territorial integrity, can only be resolved in the context of a basic political settlement which can earn the loyalty (rather than the quiescence) of the mainstream of the Catholic community. The Good Friday Agreement guaranteed full participation at the highest levels of government to all political parties with significant electoral support. It reshaped Northern Ireland into a state which, for the first time, could make a reasonable claim to the loyalty of the bulk of the Catholic population, an achievement reflected in the fact that an estimated 95 per cent of Northern Catholics voted in favour of the Agreement.

Notes and references

1 Interview with Dermie McClenaghan, former Derry labour party activist and member of the DHAC, the DCAC and the DCDA.
2 Jeffrey Z. Rubin, Dean G. Pruitt and Sung Hee Kim, *Social Conflict: Escalation, Stalemate, and Settlement* (2nd edn.) (McGraw-Hill, New York, 1994), McGraw-Hill Series in Social Psychology, p. 70, n. 1, citing C.A. McEwen and T.W. Milburn, 'Explaining a Paradox of Mediation', *Negotiation Journal*, vol. 9, 1993, pp. 23–36. McEwen and Milburn have used the term *metaconflict* to describe such a situation. Stephen Ryan provides a brief summary of the literature dealing with the importance of violent conflict itself in the perpetuation of conflict; see Stephen Ryan, 'Transforming Violent Intercommunal Conflict', in Kumar Rupesinghe (ed.), *Conflict Transformation* (St Martin's Press, New York, 1995), pp. 225–6.
3 In fact NICRA's initial objectives suggested a much greater concern with law and order issues than with housing and employment discrimination; Bob

Purdie, *Politics in the Streets. The Origins of the Civil Rights Movement in Northern Ireland* (Blackstaff, Belfast, 1990), p. 133.

4 See, for example, Steve Bruce, *The Red Hand. Protestant Paramilitaries in Northern Ireland* (Oxford University Press, Oxford, 1992) pp. 47–8.

5 J. Neville H. Douglas, 'Northern Ireland: Spatial Frameworks and Community Relations' in Frederick W. Boal and J. Neville H. Douglas, *Integration and Division. Geographical Perspectives on the Northern Ireland Problem* (Academic Press, London, 1982), p. 113.

6 D. P. Barritt and C. F. Carter, *The Northern Ireland Problem: A Study in Community Relations* (Oxford University Press, London, 1962), pp. 67–8, p. 123.

7 Christopher Hewitt, 'Discrimination in Northern Ireland: a rejoinder', *British Journal of Sociology*, vol. 34, no. 3, 1983, pp. 450–1.

8 Barritt and Carter, *Northern Ireland*, p. 126.

9 Frank Wright, *Northern Ireland: A Comparative Analysis* (Gill and Macmillan, Dublin, 1987), p. 142, gives the example of the Croat minority in post 1920 Yugoslavia, a minority which solved the 'loyalty' problem in the 1990s by achieving Croatian statehood.

10 Charles Townshend, 'The supreme law: public safety and state security in Northern Ireland', in Dermot Keogh and Michael H. Haltzel, *Northern Ireland and the Politics of Reconciliation* (Woodrow Wilson Center Press and Cambridge University Press, 1993), Woodrow Wilson Center Series, p. 93.

11 For some recent discussions of Unionist conceptions of 'loyalty' see Thomas Hennessey, 'Ulster Unionism and Loyalty to the Crown of the United Kingdom, 1912–74', in Richard English and Graham Walker (eds.), *Unionism in Modern Ireland: New Perspectives on Politics and Culture* (Gill and Macmillan, Dublin, 1996), pp. 115–29 and Pamela Clayton, *Enemies and Passing Friends: Settler Ideologies in Twentieth Century Ulster* (Pluto, London, 1996), pp. 113–34.

12 Peter Robinson in *Belfast Newsletter*, 24/3/92, p. 3.

13 Michael Farrell, *Arming the Protestants: The Formation Of the Ulster Special Constabulary and the Royal Ulster Constabulary 1920–27* (Brandon, Co. Kerry, 1983), p. 14.

14 To use Benedict Anderson's term for nations, Benedict Anderson, *Imagined Communities* (Verso, London, 1983).

15 John Bornemann, *Belonging in the Two Berlins; Kin, State, Nation* (Cambridge University Press, 1992), Cambridge Studies in Social and Cultural Anthropology, p. 31. Bornemann is concerned with how each of the two German states engaged in nation-building after World War II through '[re]create[ing] a unique group which retells its history in categories and periods congruent with those used by the state in its own accounts', p. 32.

Maps

Ireland

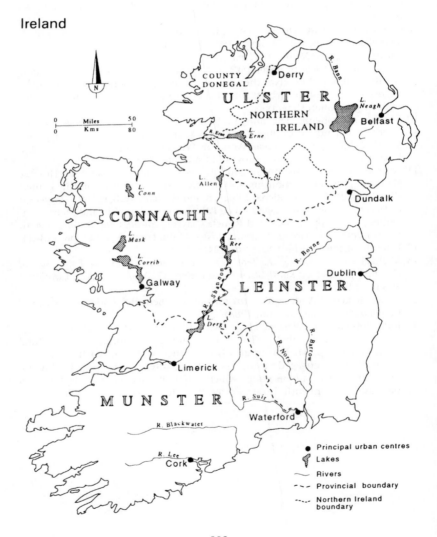

Derry in the Late 1960s: Religion and Class

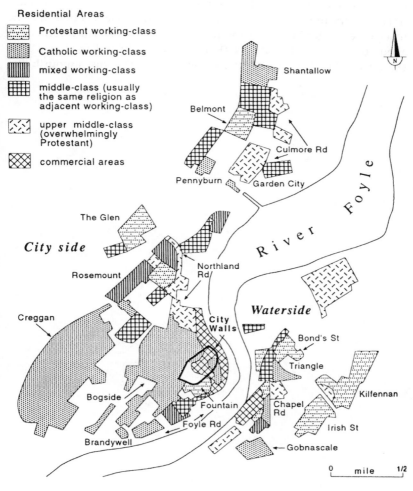

Residential Areas

Protestant working-class

Catholic working-class

mixed working-class

middle-class (usually
the same religion as
adjacent working-class)

upper middle-class
(overwhelmingly
Protestant)

commercial areas

Shantallow

Belmont

Culmore Rd

Pennyburn

Garden City

River Foyle

The Glen

City side

Rosemount

Northland
Rd

Waterside

Creggan

City
Walls

Bond's St

Triangle

Kilfennan

Bogside

Fountain

Chapel
Rd

Foyle Rd

Brandywell

Irish St

Gobnascale

0   mile   1/2

This map is not intended to be correct in every detail but rather to give
a necessarily crude picture of the complicated socio-religious geography
of Derry as conflict began in the late 1960s.

It distinguishes between areas on a class basis in order to emphasise
that prior to and throughout the Troubles, large areas of the city would
not be directly involved in protest or open conflict. It also distinguishes
between upper-middle-class areas and middle-class housing estates and

terraces. While the middle-class areas often had complex ties to the working-class communities nearby, upper-middle-class areas were almost completely isolated from such areas. At the same time, any arbitrary attempt to classify residential areas by social class is bound to be inaccurate. I only hope that the results will be useful. For information about the city in the late 1960s I am especially indebted to Claire Dobbins and to Andy and Terry Barr but all errors are my responsibility.

Derry and its Environs; Local Government Electoral Boundaries

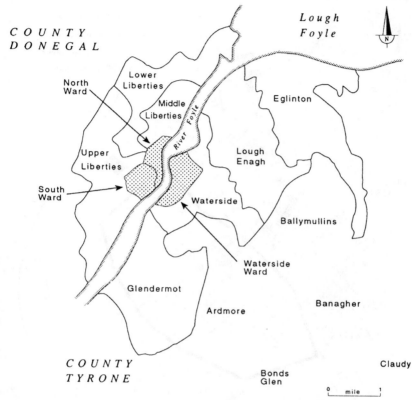

This map shows the relation of Derry County Borough (the area controlled by Londonderry Corporation) to the surrounding areas controlled by Derry Rural District Council until 1969. The Foyle
constituency which the Nationalist party leader Eddie McAteer represented at Stormont from 1953 to 1968, and which John Hume won in
1969, consisted of all areas west of the Foyle except for the North Ward
of the city while the City of Londonderry constituency, held by the
Unionist Party, was composed of the North Ward and all of the districts
outlined on the east bank of the Foyle in this map. All of the area shown
and the named wards to the east were included in the area run by the
Londonderry Development Commission from 1969 until 1973 and
since then by Derry City Council. This map is based on a map in
'Londonderry. One Man, No Vote', CSJ (Pamphlet) 1965.

Civil Disturbances in Derry following the Civil Rights March of
5 October 1968

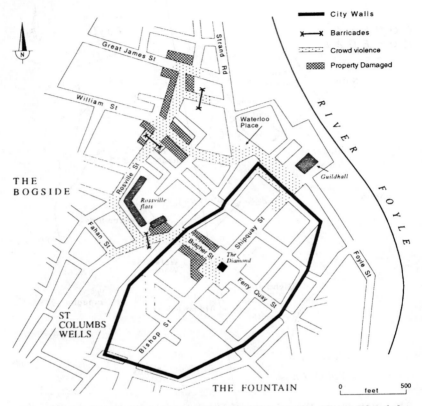

This map shows the pattern which rioting took in the aftermath of the
5 October 1968 march in Derry and the battleground for much of the
rioting of the following three years.

Bibliography

1. Primary sources

(a) Official publications

Cameron Report, *Disturbances in Northern Ireland. Report of the Commission Appointed by the Governor of Northern Ireland*, Northern Ireland Cmd. 532, HMSO, Belfast, Sept. 1969.

Census of Northern Ireland, 1951, 1961, 1991.

Compton Committee, *Report of the Enquiry into Allegations Against the Security Forces of Physical Brutality in Northern Ireland Arising out of Events on the 9th August, 1971*, Cmd. 4823, HMSO, London, 1971.

Dáil Éireann Debates.

Frameworks for the Future, HMSO, Northern Ireland, February 1995.

Hunt Committee, *Report of the Advisory Committee on Police in Northern Ireland*, Cmd. 535, HMSO, Belfast, 1969.

Macrory Report, *Reshaping of Local Government – Further Proposals*, Cmd. 530, HMSO, Belfast, 1970.

James Munce Partnership, *Londonderry Area Study*, 1968.

Northern Ireland Constabulary List and Directory (Annual), Belfast.

Northern Ireland Constitutional Proposals, Cmd. 5259, HMSO, London, March 1973.

Northern Ireland Hearings Before the Sub-committee on Europe of the Commission on Foreign Affairs, House of Representatives, 92nd Congress, 2nd session, 28 and 29 February and 1 March 1972. US Government Printing Office, Washington, 1972.

Northern Ireland Housing Executive, Annual Reports.

Report of the Irish Boundary Commission, 1925, Irish University Press, Shannon, 1969.

RUC Chief Constables Reports (Annual).

Scarman Report, *Report of Tribunal of Inquiry into Violence and Civil Disturbances in Northern Ireland*, 1969. vols. 1 and 2, Cmd. 566, HMSO, Belfast, 1972.

Statistical Abstract of Ireland (compiled by Central Statistics Office), the Stationery Office, Dublin.

Stormont House of Commons Debates.

Ulster Year Book, HMSO, Belfast (Annual).

US Riot Commission Report, *Report of the National Advisory Commission on Civil Disorders*, Bantam Books, New York, March 1968.

Who's Who (London).

Widgery Tribunal, *Report of the Tribunal Appointed to Inquire into the Events of Sunday, 30th of January 1972, Which Led to Loss of Life in Connection with the Procession in Londonderry on that Day*, HC 220, HMSO, London, 1972.

(b) Newspapers and periodicals

Barricade Bulletin (Derry, members of the Derry Labour party, 1969)
Belfast Newsletter

Belfast Telegraph
Boston Globe (Boston)
Comhar (Dublin)
Connacht Tribune (Galway)
Derry Citizens Defence Association Newsletter (DCDA, Derry, 1969)
Derry Emigrant Bulletin
Derry Journal
The Derryman (Bogside Community Association, Derry)
Fingerpost (Derry)
Fortnight (Belfast)
Free Citizen (Belfast, People's Democracy)
Hibernia (Dublin)
The Independent (London)
The Independent on Sunday (London)
Indfo (Independent Organisation, Derry)
In Dublin
Irish News (Belfast)
Irish People (New York, Irish Northern Aid Committee)
Irish Press (Dublin)
Irish Times (Dublin)
Londonderry Loyalist (DUP)
Londonderry Sentinel
Loyalist News (Shankill Defence Association, later UDA, Belfast)
Magill (Dublin)
New Society (London)
New York (New York)
Nuacht Náisiúnta (Official Sinn Féin, weekly internal bulletin, Dublin)
Nusight (Dublin)
An Phoblacht (Provisional Sinn Féin, Dublin)
Ramparts (Derry Labour party)
An Réabhlóid (People's Democracy)
Reality (Derry Housing Action Committee)
The Rising of the Moon (Committee for Justice in Northern Ireland, Boston, MA)
The Round Table
Starry Plough (Official Republican Movement, Derry)
Socialist Worker (Socialist Workers Movement, Dublin)
Sunday Press (Dublin)
Sunday Tribune (Dublin)
This Week (Dublin)
Times (London)
Ulster Defender (UDA, Derry)
Ulster Independent (ULDP, Derry)
United Irishman (Official Sinn Féin, Dublin)
Visor (Weekly Report for British Soldiers in Northern Ireland)
Voice of the North (Monaghan)
The Voice of Labour (Derry Labour and Trade Union party, Derry, 1975)

(c) Oral evidence

Glen Barr, senior member of LAW and the UDA in the early 1970s. Derry, April 1988.

Teresa and Andy Barr, long-time Catholic residents of Derry. Derry, April 1988.

Gregory Campbell, leader of DUP group on Derry City Council; DUP activist since the early 1970s; member of the Young Unionists in the early 1970s. Interview 1, Derry, April 1988; Interview 2, Derry, August 1993.

Michael Canavan, founder member of the Derry Credit Union; formerly a senior member of the DCAC, the DCDA, the DCCC and the Independent Organisation; former SDLP assembly member. Derry, June 1993.

John Carlin, member of the Republican movement in Derry from the mid-1960s and of the Provisional Republicans after the split; former Sinn Féin election agent; former internee. Interview 1, Derry, June 1993. Interview 2, Derry, August 1993.

Ivan Cooper, member of the Young Unionist party in Mid-Derry in the mid-1960s; member of the Derry Labour party in the later 1960s; former chairman of the DCAC; former Independent and, later, SDLP MP at Stormont for Mid-Derry. Derry, July 1993.

Seán Cronin, former Washington correspondent of the *Irish Times*; former O/C of the IRA during the 1950s campaign and former officer in the Irish army. Washington DC, April 1993.

Tony Crowe, chairman of the Diamond Trust for the regeneration of the Fountain area. Derry, July 1993.

Liam Deeney, former member of CJNI, Boston and spokesman for the Boston unit of Noraid; formerly an active Republican in Derry in the 1950s. Boston, September 1992.

Pat Devine, former DCAC steward; leader of the SDLP group on Derry City Council; former mayor of Derry. Derry, June 1993.

Hugh Doherty, former President of St Mary's Boys Club, Creggan, and prominent member of the Independent Organisation and, later, the SDLP; former SDLP mayor of Derry. Derry, March 1988.

Patrick L. Doherty ('Paddy Bogside'), head of the Innercity Trust; formerly a member of the DCDA, DCAC and founder member of the Credit Union in Derry. Derry, July 1993.

Mike Flannery, founder member of the Irish Action Committee and former president of the Irish Northern Aid Committee (Noraid) in the United States. New York, May 1993.

Bertie Faulkner, former Alliance party member of Derry City Council; worked closely with tenants' associations on the Waterside. Derry, July 1993.

Jim Guy, Independent Unionist councillor; former mayor of Derry; former Ulster Unionist party councillor; former secretary and lieutenant-governor of the Apprentice Boys of Derry; former secretary and grand master of the City of Derry Grand Orange Lodge; former honorary secretary of Londonderry and Foyle Unionist Association. Derry, June 1993.

William Hay, DUP member of Derry City Council; former mayor of Derry; DUP activist since the early 1970s; former member of the Young Unionists in the late 1960s. Derry, November 1992.

Anna Huey, long-time Protestant resident of the West Bank of Derry. Derry, November 1992.

John Hume, MEP, MP, former Stormont MP for the Foyle constituency; former member of DCAC; former member of the DCCC; chairman of the University for Derry Committee (1965) and founder member of the Credit Union in Derry. Derry, August 1993.

John Hurley, president of the Boston unit of the Friends of Irish Freedom; formerly president of the Boston unit of Noraid. Boston, May 1993.

Marlene Jefferson, former Ulster Unionist Party councillor and mayor of Derry; worked closely with the Wapping Lane Community Association in the Fountain. Derry, July 1993.

Eamonn McCann, active in the Derry Labour party in the late 1960s and early 1970s; formerly a member of the DHAC and the DCDA; editor of the *Starry Plough*, the Official Republican paper in Derry in 1972. Interview 1. Derry, March 1988, Interview 2. Derry, November 1992.

Dermie McClenaghan, former Derry Labour party activist and member of the DHAC, the DCAC and (unbeknownst to him) the DCDA; former youth worker with Queen Street Youth Project 1971–72. Derry, July 1993.

Berna McIvor, chairperson of the Foyle Constituency branch of the SDLP; former SDLP election agent; member of WELB; member of WHSSB and of the probation board for Northern Ireland. Derry, July 1993.

Mitchel McLaughlin, Sinn Féin member of Derry City Council; joined the Republican movement in 1966; stayed with the Officials after the split in 1970 but later joined the Provisionals. Derry, October 1988.

Eamon Melaugh, member of the Republican movement in Derry from the early 1960s until *c.* 1967; prominent in the Derry Unemployed Action Committee in the mid-1960s and the Derry Housing Action Committee in the late 1960s; member of the DCAC and prominent civil rights activist; later active in the Workers Party. Derry, March 1988.

Mary Nelis, Founder member and former chairperson, secretary, PRO of Foyle Hill Tenants' Association (Creggan); former SDLP candidate for Derry City Council; currently a Sinn Féin member of Derry City Council. Two interviews. Derry, July 1993.

Billy and Dolores Ó Caomhanaigh, both active in the Derry Labour party in the late 1960s and early 1970s. Derry, November 1992.

Willie O'Connell, formerly a senior member of the Independent Organisation, the DCDA and the DCCC; SDLP member of Derry City Council and former mayor of Derry. Derry, July 1993.

Fionnbarra Ó Dochartaigh (Finbar Doherty), member of the Republican movement in Derry from the early 1960s; formerly a member of the DHAC and the DCAC; member of the Official Republican movement after the 1970 split; founder member of the IRSP. Derry, July 1993.

Terry Robson, chairman of Derry Labour Party Young Socialists in the early 1970s and member of the NILP executive; member of the Official Republican movement from late 1971. Derry, July 1993.

Peter Simpson, former secretary of the Wapping Lane Community Association (which included the Fountain estate) and head of its security sub-committee in the early 1970s. Derry, July 1993.

Claude Wilton, Ulster Liberal party candidate for City of Londonderry seat in 1965 and 1969; former chairman of the DCAC and of the SDLP; former Northern Ireland senator for the SDLP and solicitor. Derry, November 1992.

Unattributable interviews

Anon. A, former senior member of the DCDA. July 1993.

Anon. B, former member of the Republican movement in Derry. July 1993.

Anon. C, long-time resident of Derry. July 1993.

Anon. D, former member of the Republican movement in Derry. 1995.

This book also draws on interviews in September 1992 and spring 1993 with Kevin Cullen of the *Boston Globe*, Eamonn McKee at the Irish embassy in Washington DC, Fr Seán McManus of the Irish National Caucus, Niall O'Dowd of the *Irish Voice* in New York, New York lawyer Paul O'Dwyer, John Ridge of the Ancient Order of Hibernians, New York, Pádraig O'Malley at University of Massachusetts Boston, Bill O'Donnell, director of Boston Ireland Ventures, Michael Donlan of the Committee for a New Ireland in Boston, Frank Costello, co-chair of Boston–Ireland Ventures and Kevin O'Neill at Boston College.

It draws too on a telephone conversation with Fergus McAteer, former member of the Young Nationalist Party in Derry and of the Irish Independence Party, and on conversations with Garbhan Downey of the *Irish News and Derry Journal*, Elaine Huey and Carol-Ann Barr in Derry.

Interviews carried out in 1992 and 1993 were recorded by shorthand notes. Interviews lasted between thirty minutes and three hours. A number of the interviews which I carried out during my MA research in 1988 and which I drew on for this thesis are included. With the exception of the interview with Glen Barr, the 1988 interviews were all tape-recorded.

(d) Documents relating to the Bloody Sunday Inquiry

Available online at <http://www.bloody-sunday-inquiry.org/>

Duddy, Brendan, statement to the BSI, 15/6/04.

Ford, General Sir Robert, statement to the BSI, 23/3/00.

Ford, General Sir Robert, evidence to the BSI, 4/11/02.

Jackson, Colonel Roy, supplemental statement to the BSI, 10/1/03.

Lagan, Frank, statement to the BSI, 13/12/98.

McCullagh, Supt. P.M., statement to the Widgery Tribunal, 7/2/72.

McCullagh, Patrick Mary, 'Notes of discussion with Eversheds', 20/7/00.

McCullagh, Patrick Mary, evidence to the BSI, 11/9/02, 12/9/02.

MacLellan, Brigadier Pat, letter to Major-General Robert Ford, Derry, 15/3/72.

'Major-General Pat MacLellan 9.12.83', PIN 15467, B1279.003.

MacLellan, Major-General Andrew Patrick Withy, statement to the BSI, 22/3/00.

MacLellan, Major-General Andrew Patrick Withy, evidence to the BSI, 19/11/02, 22/11/02.

Steele, Major-General Michael CM, statement to the BSI, 6/10/00.

(e) Other primary sources

Apprentice Boys of Derry, *Members Ticket*, 1971.

Derry Republican Movement (Official), *Co-operation on What, and for What?*, Internal document, for discussion only, Derry, 4/2/70.

The Faithful, photograph, with names, of the final meeting of the Derry Citizens Defence Association, October 1969.

Independent Organisation in Foyle constituency, *Minutes of Executive Committee Meetings*, March 1969–May 1970.

Londonderry Development Commission, Municipal Functions minutes, 1969–1970.

PRONI T 3062/3, *Memo to Nationalist Party Executive Committee (From the Derry Nationalist party, on negotiations between the Derry Nationalist party and the Independent Organisation in Foyle constituency) c.* summer 1970.

Scarman Tribunal Evidence, *Transcripts of Evidence Submitted to the Scarman Tribunal during Sittings in Derry,* September 1969.

SDLP Derry and Foyle branch, *Minutes of Executive Committee Meetings.* December 1970–October 1971.

Steele, Frank, 'Visit to Bogside and Creggan on 4/5 April 1973'. Confidential report. FCO 87/221, PRO, London. Available online at CAIN Web Service 'New Year Releases 2003 – Public Records of 1972' <http://cain.ulst.ac.uk/publicrecords/1972/>.

Ulster Unionist Council Yearbooks, 1960–74.

Ulster Unionist Party, Directory (Annual).

2. Secondary sources

(a) Books

Allen, Charles, *The Savage Wars of Peace. Soldiers' Voices 1945–1989,* Futura, London, 1990.

Anderson, Benedict, *Imagined Communities,* Verso, London, 1983.

Arthur, Paul, *The People's Democracy,* Blackstaff, Belfast, 1974.

Asher, Michael, *Shoot to Kill, A Soldier's Journey Through Violence,* Viking, London, 1990.

Aughey, Arthur, *Under Siege. Ulster Unionism and the Anglo-Irish Agreement,* Blackstaff, Belfast, 1989.

Bailey, Anthony, *Acts of Union. Reports on Ireland 1973–1979,* Faber and Faber, London, 1980.

Bardon, Jonathan, *A History of Ulster,* Blackstaff, Belfast, 1992.

Barritt, D.P. and Carter, C.F., *The Northern Ireland Problem: A Study in Community Relations,* Oxford University Press, London, 1962.

Barthorp, Michael, *Crater to the Creggan. The History of the Royal Anglian Regiment. 1964–1974,* Leo Cooper, London, 1976.

Barzilay, David, *The British Army in Ulster* (4 volumes), Century Services, Belfast, 1973–81.

Bayor, Ronald H., *Neighbours in Conflict. The Irish, Germans, Jews and Italians of New York City, 1929–1941,* Johns Hopkins University Press, Baltimore, 1978.

Bell, Desmond, *Acts of Union. Youth Culture and Sectarianism in Northern Ireland,* Macmillan, London, 1990.

Bell, Geoffrey, *The Protestants of Ulster,* Pluto Press, London, 1976.

Bell, J. Bowyer, *The Secret Army. A History of the IRA,* MIT Press, Cambridge, MA, 1974.

Bell, J. Bowyer, *The Irish Troubles. A Generation of Violence, 1967–1992,* Gill and Macmillan, Dublin, 1993.

Bernard, Margie, *Daughter of Derry. The Story of Brigid Sheils Makowski,* Pluto, London, 1989.

Bew, Paul, Gibbon, Peter, and Patterson, Henry, *The State in Northern Ireland,* Manchester University Press, Manchester, 1979.

Bew, Paul, Gibbon, Peter, and Patterson, Henry, *Northern Ireland, 1921–1994: Political Forces and Social Classes,* Serif, London, 1995.

Bew, Paul and Gillespie, Gordon, *Northern Ireland. A Chronology of the Troubles, 1968–1993*, Gill and Macmillan, Dublin, 1993.

Bew, Paul and Patterson, Henry, *The British State and the Ulster Crisis. From Wilson to Thatcher*, Verso, London, 1985.

Bishop, Patrick and Mallie, Eamon, *The Provisional IRA*, Corgi, London, 1988.

Boal, Frederick W., Douglas, J. and Neville H., *Integration and Division. Geographical Perspectives on the Northern Ireland Problem*, Academic Press, London, 1982.

Boal, F.W., Murray, R.C. and Poole, M.A., 'Belfast: the urban encapsulation of a national conflict', in Clarke, S.E. and Obler, J.L., *Urban Ethnic Conflict: A Comparative Perspective*, Institute for Research in Social Science, University of North Carolina, Chapel Hill, 1976, pp. 77–131.

Bornemann, John, *Belonging in the Two Berlins; Kin, State, Nation*, Cambridge University Press, Cambridge, 1992 (Cambridge Studies in Social and Cultural Anthropology).

Boulton, David, *The UVF, 1966–73. An Anatomy of Loyalist Rebellion*, Torc Books, Dublin, 1973.

Boyd, Andrew, *Holy War in Belfast*, Anvil Books, Kerry, 1969.

Boyd, Andrew, *Brian Faulkner and the Crisis of Ulster Unionism*, Anvil Books, Kerry, 1972.

Bruce, Steve, *God Save Ulster. The Religion and Politics of Paisleyism*, Clarendon Press, Oxford, 1986.

Bruce, Steve, *The Red Hand. Protestant Paramilitaries in Northern Ireland*, Oxford University Press, Oxford, 1992.

Buckland, Patrick, *A History of Northern Ireland*, Gill and Macmillan, Dublin, 1981.

Burton, Frank, *The Politics of Legitimacy: Struggles in a Belfast Community*, Routledge and Keegan Paul, London, 1978.

Cairns, Ed, *Children and Political Violence*, Blackwell, Oxford, 1996.

Callaghan, James, *A House Divided*, Collins, London, 1973.

Carson, Willie, *Derry Through the Lens*, Donegal Democrat, Donegal, September 1976.

Carson, Willie, *A Decade and a Half*, Donegal Democrat, Donegal, 1985.

Clark, Dennis J., *Irish Blood, Northern Ireland and the American Conscience*, Kennikat Press, Port Washington, New York, 1977.

Clark, Dennis J., *Hibernia America. The Irish and Regional Cultures*, Greenwood Press, Westport, Conn., 1986.

Clarke, Liam, *Broadening the Battlefield. The H-Blocks and the Rise of Sinn Féin*, Gill and Macmillan, Dublin, 1987.

Clayton, Pamela, *Enemies and Passing Friends: Settler Ideologies in Twentieth Century Ulster*, Pluto, London, 1996.

Collins, Tom, *The Irish Hunger Strike*, White Island, Dublin, 1986.

Committee on the Administration of Justice, *The Misrule of Law: A Report on the Policing of Events During the Summer of 1996 in Northern Ireland*, CAJ, Belfast, October 1996.

Connor, Walker, *Ethnonationalism: The Quest for Understanding*, Princeton University Press, Princeton, 1994.

Coogan, Tim Pat, *The IRA*, Pall Mall, London, 1970.

Crawford, Robert, *Loyal to King Billy*, G. Hurst, London, 1987.

Cronin, Seán, *Washington's Irish Policy, 1916–1986, Independence, Partition, Neutrality*, Anvil Books, Kerry, 1987.

Curran, Frank, *Derry. Countdown to Disaster*, Gill and Macmillan, Dublin, 1986.
Curtis, Liz, *Ireland: The Propaganda War. The British Media and the Battle for Hearts and Minds*, Pluto Press, London, 1984.
Darby, John, *Conflict in Northern Ireland: The Development of a Polarised Community*, Gill and Macmillan, Dublin, 1976.
Darby, John (ed.), *Northern Ireland. The Background to the Conflict*, Appletree, Belfast, 1983.
Darby, John, *Intimidation and the Control of Conflict in Northern Ireland*, Gill and Macmillan, Dublin, 1986.
De Baróid, Ciarán, *Ballymurphy and the Irish War*, Pluto, London, 1990.
Deery, Leo and O'Kane, Danny, *Doire. A History of the GAA in Derry*, Derry Co. Board GAA, 1984.
De Paor, Liam, *Divided Ulster*, Penguin, Harmondsworth, 1970.
Deutsch, Richard and Magowan, Vivien, *Northern Ireland: Chronology of Events* (3 volumes), Blackstaff, Belfast, 1973–75.
Devlin, Bernadette, *The Price of my Soul*, Pan, London, 1969.
Dewar, Lt Col. Michael, *The British Army in Northern Ireland*, Arms and Armour Press, London, 1985.
Dillon, Martin, and Lehane, Denis, *Political Murder in Northern Ireland*, Penguin, Middlesex, 1973.
Dillon, Martin, *The Shankill Butchers. A Case Study of Mass Murder*, Arrow Books, London, 1990.
Dillon, Martin, *The Dirty War*, Arrow Books, London, 1991.
Doherty, Paddy, *Paddy Bogside*, Mercier, Cork, 2001.
Douglas, J. Neville H., 'Northern Ireland: Spatial Frameworks and Community Relations' in Boal, Frederick, W. and Douglas, J. Neville H., *Integration and Division. Geographical Perspectives on the Northern Ireland Problem*, Academic Press, London, 1982, pp. 105–35.
Duggan, Dave, *A Report of a Public Hearing on The Experiences of Minorities in Derry Londonderry*, Templegrove Action Research Ltd., Derry Londonderry, 1996.
Dunne, Derek, and Kerrigan, Gene, *Round Up the Usual Suspects. Nicky Kelly and the Cosgrave Coalition*, Magill, Dublin, 1984.
Dunstan, Simon, *The British Army in Northern Ireland* (Uniforms Illustrated, no. 4), Arms and Armour Press, London, 1984.
Egan, Bowes and McCormack, Vincent, *Burntollet*, LRS Publishers, London, 1969.
Elliot, Sydney, *Northern Ireland Parliamentary Election Results, 1921–1972*, Political Reference Publications, Chichester, 1973.
Elliot, S. and Smith, F.J., *Northern Ireland Local Government Elections, 1977*, Queen's University Belfast, Belfast, 1977.
English, Richard and Walker, Graham (eds.), *Unionism in Modern Ireland; New Perspectives on Politics and Culture*, Gill and Macmillan, Dublin, 1996.
English, Richard, 'The Same People with Different Relatives? Modern Scholarship, Unionists and the Irish Nation', in English, Richard and Walker, Graham (eds.), *Unionism in Modern Ireland: New Perspectives on Politics and Culture*, Gill and Macmillan, Dublin, 1996, pp. 220–35.
Evelegh, Robin, *Peace Keeping in a Democratic Society. The Lessons of Northern Ireland*, C. Hurst and Co., London, 1978.
Farrell, Michael, *Arming the Protestants: The Formation Of the Ulster Special Constabulary and the Royal Ulster Constabulary 1920–27*, Brandon, Co. Kerry, 1983.

Farrell, Michael, *Northern Ireland: The Orange State*, Pluto, London, 1980 (2nd edn).

Farrell, Michael (ed.), *Twenty Years On*, Brandon, Kerry, 1988.

Faulkner, Brian (ed. John Houston), *Memoirs of a Statesman*, Weidenfeld and Nicholson, London, 1978.

Fields, Rona, *Society Under Siege. A Psychology of Northern Ireland*, Temple University Press, Philadelphia, 1977.

Flackes, W.F, *Northern Ireland: A Political Directory*, Gill and Macmillan, Dublin, 1980.

Foot, Paul, *Who Framed Colin Wallace?*, Pan Books, London, 1990.

Foster, R.F., *Modern Ireland 1600–1972*, Penguin, Harmondsworth, 1989.

Fraser, Morris, *Children in Conflict*, Secker and Warburg, London, 1975.

Garrow, David J., *Bearing the Cross. Martin Luther King, Jr and the Southern Christian Leadership Conference*, Jonathan Cape Ltd, London, 1986.

Geldard, Ian, and Craig, Keith, *Irish Terrorism*, Institute for the Study of Terrorism, London, 1988.

Guelke, Adrian, *Northern Ireland, The International Perspective*, Gill and Macmillan, Dublin, 1988.

Hall, Michael, *20 Years, a Concise Chronology of Events in Northern Ireland from 1968–1988*, Island Press, Newtownabbey, 1988.

Hamill, Des, *Pig in the Middle. The Army in Northern Ireland 1969–1985*, Methuen, London, 1986 (revised paperback edn).

Hamilton, Andrew, Moore, Linda and Trimble, Tim, *Policing a Divided Society: Issues and Perceptions in Northern Ireland*, Centre for the Study of Conflict, University of Ulster, 1995.

Hamilton, I. and Moss, R., *The Spreading Irish Conflict* (Conflict Studies, no. 17), Institute for the Study of Conflict, London, 1971.

Harbinson, John F., *The Ulster Unionist Party, 1882–1972*, Blackstaff, Belfast, 1973.

Harris, Rosemary, *Prejudice and Tolerance in Ulster: A Study of Neighbours and 'Strangers' in a Border Community*, Manchester University Press, Manchester, 1972.

Hastings, Max, *Ulster 1969. The Fight for Civil Rights in Northern Ireland*, Victor Gollancz, London, 1970.

Hennessey, Thomas, 'Ulster Unionism and Loyalty to the Crown of the United Kingdom, 1912–74', in English, Richard and Walker, Graham (eds), *Unionism in Modern Ireland; New Perspectives on Politics and Culture*, Gill and Macmillan, Dublin, 1996, pp. 115–29.

Hillyard, Paddy, 'Law and Order', in John Darby (ed), *Northern Ireland; the Background to the Conflict*, Appletree, Belfast, 1983, pp. 32–60.

Holland, Jack, *The American Connection. US Guns, Money and Influence in Northern Ireland*, Poolbeg, Swords, Co. Dublin, 1989 (Irish edn).

Holroyd, Fred, *War Without Honour*, F. H. and Nick Burbidge, Medium Publishing, Hull, 1989.

Horowitz, Don L., *Ethnic Groups in Conflict*, University of California, California, 1985.

Horowitz, Don L., *Community Conflict: Policy and Possibilities*, Centre for the Study of Conflict, University of Ulster, Coleraine, 1990. Occasional paper no. 1.

Jackson, H., *The Two Irelands: A Dual Study of Inter-Group Tensions*, Minority Rights Group, London, London, 1971.

Keith, Michael, *Race, Riots and Policing. Lore and Disorder in a Multi-Racist Society*, UCL Press, London, 1993.

Kelley, Kevin, *The Longest War. Northern Ireland and the IRA*, Brandon, Kerry, 1982.

Kelly, James, *Orders for the Captain*, Published by James Kelly, Dublin, 1971.

Keogh, Dermot and Haltzel, Michael H., *Northern Ireland and the Politics of Reconciliation*, Woodrow Wilson Center Press and Cambridge University Press, 1993 (Woodrow Wilson Center Series).

Kerr, Adrian (compiled by), *Perceptions; Cultures in Conflict*, Guildhall Press, Derry, 1996.

Kinghan, Nancy, *United We Stood. The Story of the Ulster Women's Unionist Council, 1911–74*, Appletree, Belfast, 1975.

Kingsley, Paul, *Londonderry Revisited. A Loyalist Analysis of the Civil Rights Controversy*, Belfast Publications, Belfast, 1989.

Kitson, Frank, *Low Intensity Operations: Subversion, Insurgency and Peacekeeping*, Faber and Faber, London, 1971.

Lacey, Brian, *Siege City: The Story of Derry and Londonderry*, Blackstaff, Belfast, 1991.

Lee, Joseph, *Ireland, 1912–1985. Politics and Society*, Cambridge University Press, Cambridge, 1989.

Lijphart, Arend, *Democracy in Plural Societies: A Comparative Exploration*, Yale University Press, New Haven and London, 1977.

Limpkin, Clive, *The Battle of Bogside*, Penguin, Harmondsworth, 1972.

Lupo, Alan, *Liberty's Chosen Home: The Politics of Violence in Boston*, Little, Brown and Co., Boston, 1977.

McAllister, Ian, *The Northern Ireland Social Democratic and Labour Party*, Macmillan, London, 1977.

McCafferty, Nell, *The Best of Nell*, Attic Press, Dublin, 1985.

McCafferty, Nell, *Peggy Derry. A Derry Family at War*, Attic Press, Dublin, 1988.

McCann, Eamonn, *The British Press and Northern Ireland*, Northern Ireland Socialist Research Centre, London, 1971.

McCann, Eamonn, *War and an Irish Town*, Penguin, Harmondsworth, 1974.

McCann, Eamonn (with Harrigan, Bridie and Shiels, Maureen), *Bloody Sunday in Derry. What Really Happened*, Brandon, Kerry, 1992.

McClean, Raymond, *The Road to Bloody Sunday*, Ward River Press, Dublin, 1983.

McCluskey, Conn, *Up Off Their Knees. A Commentary on the Civil Rights Movement in Northern Ireland*, Conn McCluskey and Associates, Republic of Ireland, 1989.

McCorkell, Aileen, *A Red Cross in My Pocket. Derry/Londonderry 1968–1974*, Workers' Educational Association, Belfast, 1992.

McElroy, Gerald, *The Catholic Church and the Northern Ireland Crisis, 1968–1986*, Gill and Macmillan, Dublin, 1991.

McGarry, John and O'Leary, Brendan, *Explaining Northern Ireland. Broken Images*, Blackwell, Oxford, 1995.

McGuffin, John, *Internment*, Anvil Press, Kerry, 1973.

McGuire, Maria, *To Take Arms. A Year in the Provisional IRA*, Macmillan, London, 1973.

McKeown, Michael, *The Greening of a Nationalist*, Murlough Press, Dublin, 1986.

McLarnon, J. and Corkey, P., *A Survey of Facts, Figures and Opinions Relating to the Economic Situation in Derry*, Northern Ireland Community Relations Commission, Belfast, 1971.

MacStiofáin, Seán, *Memoirs of a Revolutionary*, R. and R. Clarke, Edinburgh, 1975.

Mallie, Eamonn and McKittrick, David, *The Fight for Peace: The Secret Story behind the Irish Peace Process*, Heinemann. London, 1996.

Mallie, Eamonn and McKittrick, David, *Endgame in Ireland*, Coronet Lir, London, 2002.

Masotti, Louis and Bowen, Don (eds), *Riots and Rebellion*, Sage, Beverly Hills, 1968.

Meenan, Hugo, *No Time For Love* (fiction), Brandon, Kerry, 1987.

Menendez, Albert, *The Bitter Harvest. Church and State in Northern Ireland*, Robert B. Luce, Washington, DC, 1973.

Miller, David W., *Queen's Rebels*, Gill and Macmillan, Dublin, 1978.

Moloney, Ed, *A Secret History of the IRA*, Penguin, Harmondsworth, 2003 (originally 2002).

Moloney, Ed and Pollak, Andy, *Paisley*, Poolbeg, Swords Co. Dublin, 1986.

Moody, T.W., *The Londonderry Plantation, 1609–41, The City of London and the Plantation in Ulster*, William Mullan and Sons, Belfast, 1939.

Moore, Ruth and Smyth, Marie, *A Report of a Series of Public Discussions on Aspects of Sectarian Division in Derry Londonderry Held in the Period December 1994–June 1995*, Templegrove Action Research Ltd, Derry Londonderry, 1996.

Morgan, Austen and Purdie, Bob (eds), *Ireland: Divided Nation, Divided Class*, Ink Links, London, 1980.

Mullin, the Reverend T.H., *Ulster's Historic City. Derry/Londonderry*, Coleraine Bookshop, Coleraine, 1986.

Murphy, D., *Derry, Donegal and Modern Ulster, 1790–1921*, Derry, Aileach Press, 1981.

Nelson, Sarah, *Ulster's Uncertain Defenders. Protestant Political, Paramilitary and Community Groups and the Northern Ireland Conflict*, Appletree, Belfast, 1984.

O'Brien, Conor Cruise, *States of Ireland*, Panther Books, St Albans, 1974.

O'Brien, Conor Cruise, *Passion and Cunning and Other Essays*, Paladin Grafton, London, 1990.

Ó Dochartaigh, Niall, 'The Politics of Housing: Social Change and Collective Action in Derry in the 1960s', *in Derry and Londonderry: History and Society*, Geography Publications, Dublin, 1997.

O'Doherty, Shane, *The Volunteer. A Former IRA Man's True Story*, Fount, London, 1993.

O'Dowd, Liam, Rolston, Bill, and Tomlinson, Mike, *Northern Ireland. Between Civil Rights and Civil War*, CSE Books, London, 1980.

O'Halloran, Clare, *Partition and the Limits of Irish Nationalism*, Gill and Macmillan, Dublin, 1987.

O'Leary, Brendan and McGarry, John, *The Politics of Antagonism, Understanding Northern Ireland*, Athlone Press, London, 1996.

Oliver, J., *Working at Stormont*, Institute of Public Administration, Dublin, 1978.

O'Malley, Padraig, *The Uncivil Wars, Ireland Today*, Blackstaff, Belfast, 1983.

O'Neill, Terence, *Ulster at the Crossroads*, Faber, London, 1969.

O'Neill, Terence, *Autobiography*, Hart-Davis, London, 1972.

O'Sullivan, Michael P., *Patriot Graves. Resistance in Ireland*, Follett Publishing Co., Chicago, 1972.

Patterson, Henry, *The Politics of Illusion. Republicanism and Socialism in Modern Ireland*, Hutchinson Radius, London, 1989.

Peck, John, *Dublin from Downing Street*, Gill and Macmillan, Dublin, 1978.

Polenberg, Richard, *One Nation Divisible. Class, Race and Ethnicity in the United States since 1938*, Viking, New York, 1980.

Probert, Belinda, *The Political Economy of the Northern Ireland Crisis*, The Academy Press, London, 1978.

Purdie, Bob, *Politics in the Streets. The Origins of the Civil Rights Movement in Northern Ireland*, Blackstaff, Belfast, 1990.

Purdy, Ann, *Molyneaux: The Long View*, Greystone Books, Antrim, 1989.

Rapoport, David. C. (ed.), *Inside Terrorist Organisations*, Columbia University Press, New York, 1988.

Rose, Richard, *Governing Without Consensus*, Faber, London, 1971.

Royle, Trevor, *Anatomy of a Regiment. Ceremony and Soldiering in the Welsh Guards*, Michael Joseph, London, 1990.

Rubin, Jeffrey Z., Pruitt, Dean G. and Kim, Sung Hee, *Social Conflict: Escalation, Stalemate, and Settlement* (2nd edn.), McGraw-Hill, New York, 1994 (McGraw-Hill Series in Social Psychology).

Rupesinghe, Kumar (ed.), *Conflict Transformation*, St Martin's Press, New York, 1995.

Ryan, Stephen, 'Transforming Violent Intercommunal Conflict', in Rupesinghe, Kumar (ed.), *Conflict Transformation*, St Martin's Press, New York, 1995, pp. 223–65.

Ryder, Chris, *The RUC. A Force Under Fire*, Methuen, London, 1989.

Ryder, Chris, *The Ulster Defence Regiment, an Instrument of Peace?*, Methuen, London, 1991.

Ryle Dywer, T., *Charlie. The Political Biography of Charles J. Haughey*, Gill and Macmillan, Dublin, 1987.

Sacks, Paul, *The Donegal Mafia*, Yale University Press, New Haven, Conn., 1977.

Shannon, Elizabeth, *I Am of Ireland, Women of the North Speak Out*, Little, Brown and Co., Boston, 1989.

Shea, Patrick, *Voices and the Sound of Drums*, Blackstaff, Belfast, 1981.

Smyth, Clifford, *Ian Paisley. Voice of Protestant Ulster*, Scottish Academic Press, Edinburgh, 1987.

Smyth, Marie, *Life in Two Enclave Areas in Northern Ireland: A Field Survey in Gobnascale and The Fountain, Derry Londonderry after the Ceasefires*, Templegrove Action Research Ltd, Derry Londonderry, 1996.

Smyth, Marie (in collaboration with Ruth Moore), *Three Conference Papers on Aspects of Sectarian Division: Researching Sectarianism, Borders within Borders, The Capacity for Citizenship*, Templegrove Action Research Ltd, Derry Londonderry, 1996.

Smyth, Marie and Moore, Ruth, *Two Policy Papers; Policing and Sectarian Division in Derry Londonderry and Urban Regeneration and Sectarian Division*, Templegrove Action Research Ltd, Derry Londonderry, 1996.

Soja, Edward W., *Postmodern Geographies. The Reassertion of Space in Critical Social Theory*, Verso, London and New York, 1989.

Stetler, Russell, *The Battle of the Bogside. The Politics of Violence in Northern Ireland*, Sheed and Ward, London, 1970.

Stewart, A.T.Q., *The Narrow Ground: Aspects of Ulster, 1609–1969*, Faber and Faber, London, 1977.

Sunday Times Insight Team, *Ulster*, Penguin, London, 1972.

Suttles, Gerald, *The Social Order of the Slum. Ethnicity and Territory in the Inner City*, University of Chicago Press, Chicago, 1968.

Sutton, Malcolm, *Bear in Mind these Dead … An Index of Deaths from the Conflict in Ireland*, Beyond the Pale Publications, Belfast, 1994.

Sweetman, Rosita, *'On Our Knees'. Ireland 1972*, Pan Books, London, 1972.

Target, G.W, *Bernadette, The Story of Bernadette Devlin*, Hodder and Stoughton, London, 1975.

Taylor, Peter, *Families at War*, BBC Books, London, 1989.

Taylor, Peter, *Provos: The IRA and Sinn Féin*, Bloomsbury, London, 1997.

Taylor, Peter, *Brits: The War Against the IRA*, Bloomsbury, London, 2001.

Tilly, Charles, Tilly, Louise and Tilly, Richard, *The Rebellious Century, 1830–1930*. Dent, London, 1975.

Tilly, Charles and Tilly, Louise (eds.), *Class Conflict and Collective Action*, Sage, Beverly Hills and London, 1981.

Toolis, Kevin, *Rebel Hearts: Journeys within the IRA's Soul*, Picador, London, 1995.

Townshend, Charles, 'The supreme law: public safety and state security in Northern Ireland', in Keogh, Dermot and Haltzel, Michael H., *Northern Ireland and the Politics of Reconciliation*, Woodrow Wilson Center Press and Cambridge University Press, 1993 (Woodrow Wilson Center Series), pp. 84–9.

Van Voris, W.H., *Violence in Ulster. An Oral Documentary*, University of Massachusetts, MA, 1975.

Watt, David (ed.), *The Constitution of Northern Ireland. Problems and Prospects*, National Institute of Economic and Social Research, Policy Studies Institute, Royal Institute of International Affairs (Joint Studies in Public Policy 4), Heinemann, London, 1981.

White, Barry, 'From Conflict to Violence: The Re-emergence of the IRA and the Loyalist Response', in John Darby (ed.), *Northern Ireland; the Background to the Conflict*, Appletree, Belfast, 1983, pp. 181–96.

White, Barry, *John Hume, Statesman of the Troubles*, Blackstaff Press, Belfast, 1984.

Whyte, J.H., 'How Much Discrimination was there under the Unionist Regime, 1921–1968?' in Gallagher, T. and O'Connell, J. (eds.), *Contemporary Irish Studies*, Manchester University Press, Manchester, 1983.

Whyte, John H., *Interpreting Northern Ireland*, Clarendon Press, Oxford, 1991 (paperback edn).

Wichert, Sabine, *Northern Ireland Since 1945*, Longman, London, 1991.

Weitzer, Ronald, *Policing Under Fire. Ethnic Conflict and Police–Community Relations in Northern Ireland*, SUNY Press, Albany, 1995.

Wilson, Tom, *Ulster, Conflict and Consent*, Basil Blackwell, Oxford, 1989.

Winchester, Simon, *In Holy Terror: Reporting the Ulster Troubles*, Faber, London, 1974.

Wright, Frank, *Northern Ireland: A Comparative Analysis*, Gill and Macmillan, Dublin, 1987.

(b) Articles

Bayley, John and Loizos, Peter, 'Bogside Off its Knees', *New Society*, 21/8/69.

Boal, F.W. and Buchanan, R.H, 'The 1969 Northern Ireland Election', *Irish Geography*, vol. 6, no. 1, 1969, pp. 22–9.

Boal, F.W., 'Territoriality on the Shankill-Falls Divide, Belfast', *Irish Geography*, vol. 6, no. 1, 1969, pp. 30–50.

Busteed, M.A. and Mason, Hugh, 'Local Government Reform in Northern Ireland', *Irish Geography*, vol. 6, no. 3, 1971.

Compton, P.A. and Boal, F.W., 'Aspects of the Inter-Community Population Balance in Northern Ireland', *Economic and Social Review*, vol. 1, no. 4, July 1970.

Douglas, W.A. and Zulaika, J., 'On the Interpretation of Terrorist Violence: ETA and the Basque Political Process', *Comparative Studies in Society and History*, vol. 32, 1990.

Dunne, Derek, 'MacGiolla's Guerillas', *In Dublin*, 1/10/87, pp. 18–23.

Feeney, V.E., 'The Civil Rights Movement in Northern Ireland', *Éire/Ireland*, vol. 9, no. 2, 1974, pp. 30–40.

Guelke, Adrian, 'American Connections to the Northern Ireland Conflict', *Irish Studies in International Affairs*, vol. 1, no. 4, 1984, pp. 27–39.

Harrison, P., 'Derry: From Conflict to Co-existence', *New Society*, vol. 31, 1975, p. 642.

Hewitt, Christopher, 'Catholic grievances, Catholic nationalism and violence in Northern Ireland during the Civil Rights Period: a reconsideration', *British Journal of Sociology*, vol. 32, no. 3, 1981, pp. 362–80.

Hewitt, Christopher, 'Discrimination in Northern Ireland: a rejoinder', *British Journal of Sociology*, vol. 34, no. 3, 1983, pp. 446–51.

Hume, John, 'John Hume's Derry', *Everyman*, no. 3, Benburb, 1970, pp. 117–28.

Kettle, M, 'Tale of Two Cities: People of Divided Derry', *New Society*, vol. 49, 1979, p. 875.

Lijphart, Arend, 'The Northern Ireland Problem: Cases, Theories and Solutions', *British Journal of Political Science*, vol. 5, no. 3, 1975, pp. 83–106.

McEwen, C.A. and Milburn, T.W., 'Explaining a Paradox of Mediation', *Negotiation Journal*, vol. 9, 1993, pp. 23–36.

O'Callaghan, J, 'Inside the Derry Ghetto', *New Statesman*, 21/1/72.

O'Hearn, Denis, 'Catholic grievances, Catholic nationalism: a comment', *British Journal of Sociology*, vol. 34, no. 3, 1983, pp. 438–45.

Purdie, Bob, 'Was the Civil Rights Movement a Republican/Communist Conspiracy?', *Irish Political Studies*, vol. 3, 1988, pp. 33–41.

Roy, Sara M., 'Gaza: New Dynamics of Civic Disintegration. Economic dedevelopment in Gaza', *Journal of Palestine Studies*, vol. 22, no. 4, summer 1993.

Todd, Jennifer, 'Two Traditions in Unionist Political Culture', *Irish Political Studies*, vol. 2, 1987.

Todd, Jennifer, 'Northern Ireland Nationalist Political Culture', *Irish Political Studies*, vol. 5, 1990, pp. 31–44.

Unit Feature, 'On Top of the Creggan. 2nd Battalion the Queen's Regiment', in *Visor*, Serial no. 3, 14/3/1974.

Whyte, J. H., 'Interpretations of the Northern Ireland Problem: An Appraisal', *Economic and Social Review*, vol. 9, no. 4, July 1978.

Wright, Frank, 'Northern Ireland and the British–Irish Relationship', *Studies*, no. 78, pp. 151–62.

(c) Unpublished dissertations

McLaughlin, Eithne, *Maiden city blues: Employment and unemployment in Derry city*, Ph.D, QUB, 1986.

Ó Dochartaigh, Niall, *Before the Troubles; Derry in the 1960s. An examination of the origins of a violent conflict*, MA, UCG, 1989.

Robinson, Alan, *A social geography of the city of Londonderry*, MA, QUB, 1967.

(d) Pamphlets

Bloody Sunday Initiative, *Political Guide To Derry*, Bloody Sunday Initiative, Derry, *c.* 1992.

Campaign for Social Justice in Northern Ireland, *Northern Ireland: The Plain Truth*, CSJ, Dungannon, 1964.

Campaign for Social Justice in Northern Ireland, *Londonderry: One Man, No Vote*, CSJ, Dungannon, 1965.

Campaign for Social Justice in Northern Ireland, *Northern Ireland: The Plain Truth*, (2nd edn.) CSJ, Dungannon, 1969.

Curran, Frank, *Ireland's Fascist City*, Derry, *Derry Journal*, 1946.

Derry City Council, *Derry City Council Working for You, A Citizens Guide*, Derry, *c.* 1992.

Foley, Gerry, *Ireland in Rebellion*, (no place of publication) October 1971.

Foley, Gerry, *Problems of the Irish Revolution: Can the IRA Meet the Challenge?*, New York, August 1972.

Foley, Gerry, *Draft Thesis on the Irish Revolution*, Revolutionary Marxist Group, undated (*c.* 1972) (A Policy for the Fourth International).

Government of Ireland Information Bureau, *The Story in Pictures of the North's Distress*, Dublin, August 1969.

Government of Northern Ireland, *Ulster the Facts* (series of pamphlets 1969–71).

H-Block Relatives, *The Heart of the Matter* (no place of publication), 1979.

Irish Republican Publishing Bureau, *Freedom Struggle by the Provisional IRA*, Irish Republican Publishing Bureau, Dublin, June 1973.

National Graves Association, *The Last Post. The Details and Stories of Republican Dead 1913/1975*, National Graves Association, Dublin, April 1976 (2nd edn).

Northern Ireland Civil Rights Association, *Massacre at Derry*, Northern Ireland Civil Rights Association, Belfast, *c.* 1972.

Northern Ireland Civil Rights Association, *'We Shall Overcome' ... The History of the Struggle for Civil Rights in Northern Ireland, 1968–1978*, Northern Ireland Civil Rights Association, Belfast, 1978.

The Suppressed Report on the Derry Massacre. Article by *Sunday Times* journalists, Sayle and Humphrey, 3/2/72. Printed by the Organisation of Revolutionary Anarchists, London, November 1972 (2nd printing).

Women for Irish Freedom, *Irish Women Speak*, Women for Irish Freedom, Brooklyn, NY, 1973.

Index